PORTRAYING THE SELF:
SEAN O'CASEY AND
THE ART OF AUTOBIOGRAPHY

PORTRAYING THE SELF:
SEAN O'CASEY
&
THE ART OF AUTOBIOGRAPHY

Michael Kenneally

Irish Literary Studies 26

COLIN SMYTHE
Gerrards Cross, Bucks

BARNES AND NOBLE BOOKS
Totowa, New Jersey

First published in 1988 by Colin Smythe Limited
Gerrards Cross, Buckinghamshire

British Library Cataloguing in Publication Data

Kenneally, Michael
Portraying the self: Sean O'Casey & the art of
autobiography. — (Irish literary studies,
ISSN 0140-895X ; 26)
1. O'Casey, Sean — Criticism and interpretation
2. O'Casey, Sean — Biography   3. Authors, Irish
— 20th century — Biography
I. Title   II. Series
828'.91208   PR6029.C33Z/

ISBN 0-86140-250-2

First published in the United States of America
by Barnes & Noble Books, Totowa, New Jersey 07512

Library of Congress Cataloging in Publication Data

Kenneally, Michael
Portraying the self.
(Irish literary studies; 26)
Bibliography: p.
1. O'Casey, Sean, 1880–1964 — Technique.
2. O'Casey, Sean, 1880–1964 — Biography.
3. Dramatists, Irish — 20th century — Biography
— History and criticism.
4. Autobiography.
I. Title   II. Series
PR6029.C33Z658 1987   822'.912[B]   86–28894

ISBN 0–389–20714–4

Produced in Great Britain
Set by Grove Graphics, Tring, Hertfordshire,
and printed and bound by Billing & Sons Ltd.
Worcester

TABLE OF CONTENTS

For Rhona:

ACKNOWLEDGEMENTS

Grateful acknowledgement is made to Macmillan, London and Basingstoke; Macmillan Publishing Co., Inc., New York; and the Macmillan Company of Canada for permission to quote from O'Casey's autobiography: *I Knock at the Door*, *Pictures in the Hallway*, *Drums Under the Windows*, *Inishfallen, Fare Thee Well*, *Rose and Crown*, and *Sunset and Evening Star*.

For permission to quote from the holographs and typescripts of the six autobiographical volumes in the Henry W. and Albert A. Berg Collection, I would like to thank the New York Public Library (Astor, Lenox and Tilden Foundations) and, in particular, Eileen O'Casey.

Several pages of Chapter II appeared in *O'Casey Annual No. 3* as 'Joyce, O'Casey and the Genre of Autobiography;' brief sections of Chapters III and IV appeared in *O'Casey Annual No. 2* as 'Models and Mediators in the Autobiography of Sean O'Casey;' and another portion of Chapter III appeared in a somewhat different form in *O'Casey Annual No. 1* as 'The Changing Contents of O'Casey's Autobiography.' I am grateful to the editor of the *Annual*, Robert G. Lowery, for permission to republish these materials. Part of Chapter III and a brief sequence from Chapter VI appeared in *The Canadian Journal of Irish Studies*, Vol. 6 (Fall 1980) and Vol. 7 (Fall 1981) as 'Principles of Organization in *Drums Under the Windows*,' and 'Autobiographical Revelation in O'Casey's *I Knock at the Door*.' I thank Dr Andrew Parkin, editor of *CJIS*, for permission to use this material.

I would like to acknowledge assistance from the Professional Development Committee of Marianopolis College for granting me sabbatical leave during which part of this book was completed.

I wish to express my appreciation to Professor Eric Domville (New College, University of Toronto), under whose genial direction the original but quite different version of this study was written as a doctoral dissertation. I am also grateful to Professor W. David Shaw (Victoria College, University of Toronto), in whose graduate seminar I first studied autobiographical literature, and who later very kindly read the manuscript of this book and offered valuable suggestions.

Gratitude is also due to several others who, in ways that each will know, sustained and encouraged me during the writing of this book: my mother, Maureen Kenneally, Grace and Tom Brett, Father Jerome Lantry, Pauline and Reuben Richman, Jim Morrison and, especially, Annette and Odd Rost.

It is a particular pleasure for me to thank four other individuals whose practical assistance and sensible advice greatly facilitated the writing of this study and enhanced its value: Professor Ronald Ayling (University of Alberta, Edmonton) who, from the beginning, encouraged my work on O'Casey's autobiography, and offered useful comments at various stages of the manuscript's evolution; Professor Finn Gallagher (Master, Otonabee College, Trent University, Peterborough, Ontario) for taking the time for a rigorous reading of parts of the manuscript, for making many recommendations which improved it, and for doing so with a sensitivity and charm typical of his *grámhar* nature; Robert G. Lowery (Editor, *Irish Literary Supplement*) for his helpful comments on parts of the manuscripts, for his practical support of my work on O'Casey, and especially for his warm friendship; and, in particular, Professor Joseph Ronsley (McGill University, Montreal) and his wife, Joanne, for their continual encouragement, wise counsel and unfailing kindness.

Finally, I would like to express my deep gratitude to my wife, Rhona, for her abiding love and sound critical judgement; the former sustained me in the writing of this book, while the latter prompted me to improve it.

INTRODUCTION

Sean O'Casey's autobiography has not received critical attention commensurate with either its large presence in his literary canon or its accomplishments as autobiographical literature. Until quite recently, few serious attempts were made to understand his purposes or evaluate his procedures in this extraordinarily rich, highly experimental and complex effort at self-portrayal.

Initial readers of the work tended to be sharply divided in their estimation of its merits. The critic, David Greene, and the playwright, Denis Johnston, along with Brooks Atkinson, the *New York Times* reviewer who was a lifelong advocate of the plays, all believed that O'Casey's reputation will rest, ultimately, not on his stature as a dramatist — however great it may be — but on his achievements as autobiographer. Other critics, most notably Irish ones such as Oliver St. John Gogarty, Sean O'Faolain and Ulick O'Connor, have taken the opposite view, claiming that the work has dubious value as personal revelation and less as literature. Such a strong dichotomy of response points to the need for a thorough examination and evaluation of O'Casey's autobiography.

From the beginning, readers have been confronted with the questions of factual reliability and artistic worth, for O'Casey frequently chooses to disregard specific historical reference points and is indifferent to the kind of chronological sequences that would facilitate an understanding of the story's unfolding as a replica of the life lived. Furthermore, it has always been difficult for critics and reviewers to assess the work separately from the partisan and emotional reactions to O'Casey the man and the playwright. Consequently, early readers of the autobiography have usually been extremely selective and subjective in responding to this inordinately long and occasionally uneven work. Those who commended it have pointed to the many passages in which O'Casey establishes the authenticity of his account of his past by means of his lyrical and dramatic writing, his ability to create an authoritative mood and atmosphere, while those who reacted negatively have seen in it his penchant for overblown and self-indulgent prose, for melodramatic and outrageous situations, and for overly-bitter parody and satire. Frequently, the self-portrait was praised or rejected depending on whether or not its account of the author's life and times coincided with the reader's own experiences or knowledge of the events described. As often as not, then, O'Casey's autobiography has been read and evaluated in accordance with the literary sensibilities or historical awareness of its readers, rather than on its own terms.

To complicate matters still further, earlier responses to the work were based on vague, if any, perceptions of, and only partially formulated assumptions about, the autobiographical genre. Long neglected as a branch of imaginative literature, autobiography has only in the last decade or two begun to receive the kind of critical scrutiny and ingenuity of response traditionally accorded more recognised and clearly acceptable forms of literature. Consequently, the lack of established and widely accepted critical principles has compounded the difficulties inherent in exploring and making sense of this unusual example of the form. Latterly, however, critics of O'Casey's autobiography have readily accepted the imaginative dimensions and literary qualities which the genre is capable of embodying, and have proceeded to examine, with illuminating results, particular facets of the work. Indeed, in the only collection of essays devoted to the autobiography, the range of insights provided by critics willing to accept the autobiographical legitimacy of O'Casey's experiments in self-portrayal emphasizes the richness and complexity of the work, and indicates the difficulties involved in any coherent reading of it. Yet, despite the increased attention of those willing to see it as a work dealing in imaginative rather than factual truth, and employing literary devices to do so, no reading has yet outlined an overall critical framework to facilitate its comprehensive evaluation as autobiographical literature.

Chapter II of this study will attempt to outline some of the theoretical and critical issues inevitably raised in any discussion of the autobiographical genre. In turn, these principles will be related to O'Casey's enthusiastic and often unique response to the challenges and possibilities of literary self-portrayal. However, before such a discussion takes place, Chapter I will trace O'Casey's perception of his increasingly comprehensive and complex self-portrait. As this first chapter should make clear, O'Casey himself perceived his autobiography as an undertaking which, in its conception, scope and methods, was distinct from his other writing. Although he was to discover additional purposes and possibilities as the work grew and evolved, his ultimate plan was to provide an account of his life from his beginnings down to the present. Once the process of autobiographical definition was underway, his impulse, despite the work's ever-growing length and the periodic temptations to conclude it at an apparently logical point (such as his departure from Ireland for London), was to persevere until he had brought the story line down to his own temporal plane. The desire to merge the objective self being recorded with the subjectivity of the recording self dictated the nature of his perspective on his past; for readers of the auto-biography this is the key to an understanding of the identity it embodies and to an appreciation of its unique literary qualities.

O'Casey's particular perspective also explains why his work must be understood not as a series of autobiographies, as some critics would assume, but rather as a single and unified self-portrait comprising six partial sketches. Such an understanding is essential to a recognition of the author's purposes, and to a full appreciation of the nature of his creation. Nor are the six volumes to be viewed as a coherent whole merely because of O'Casey's statement that his goal was to complete his self-portrait until it merged with his contemporary existence. As this study will attempt to demonstrate, O'Casey devised many strategies to structure the work so that it possesses an organic unity, so that the personae of Johnny/Sean are perceived as vital precursors of the man sitting at his desk writing the autobiography. Each of the six books is a contribution towards that end, not an end in itself. In constructing the autobiography, O'Casey carefully builds on experiences presented in previous volumes, expands on their significance, and evaluates them in terms of subsequent phases of his life. Thus, while individual volumes may provide fragmented perceptions of O'Casey at given points in time, none can give a complete picture of the author. The six volumes — including, especially, the final two, whose auto-biographical validity has been questioned — constitute the cumulative self-portrait.

To illustrate the unity of O'Casey's self-portrait, to indicate his innovations in autobiographical form, and to suggest some of his achievements as an autobiographer, the second chapter of this study will set forth the work's defining features as autobiographical literature. As will become evident, an autobiography, particularly one written by a creative writer, is never simply a biography which happens to be written by its own subject but is a literary text with its own integrity and inviolability. Consequently, one should not look to autobiography for objectivity, factual reliability, chronological order and attempted completeness, although a portrait may possess, in various degrees, some or all of these characteristics. Nor should one approach the work anticipating a presentation of historical events and figures in a manner which duplicates one's own understanding and perception of the past, whether derived from personal experience or other accounts of history. All autobiographies are self-serving, and self-portraits of literary artists are usually concerned more with the truth embodied by experiences and made accessible by an imaginative replication of them than with the truth of biography or history. Furthermore, although its essential purpose remains that of self-definition, a literary autobiography may employ a variety of narrative strategies and representational techniques which, in creating images of the self developing in the past, will frequently sacrifice and transform the specific details of personal history.

The very presence of such overt literary dimensions underlines the tenuous and often misunderstood territory inhabited by autobiography, closely bounded as it is on the one side by memoirs and on the other by the autobiographical novel. As we shall see, while all three forms share the initial impulse to reflect on and describe selected aspects of past selves, an autobiography transforms the biographical experiences of personal history for purposes different from those of either the memoir or the autobiographical novel. In doing so, it reveals itself as a literary genre in its own right, capable of affording access to a particular kind of truth, and providing it in a form which lends itself to much structural and stylistic innovation. In defining some of the artistic and literary perspectives from which O'Casey's work can be read with profitable results, this study will be concerned, then, with clarifying some of the parameters of literary autobiography and suggesting some of the crucial areas where it is distinguishable from related forms which also examine and transform elements of one's past.

What may become evident from this discussion is that all autobiographers are constantly confronted with decisions on three fronts: they must select representative episodes from their past so that the materials of the work approximate the life lived, or at least that part of it which the author wishes to consider; they must order and shape those experiences in accordance with their perception of their known or emergent purposes; and they must continually devise ways of narrating their story, of recreating, through the medium of words, amorphous and intangible events and remembered feelings. An examination of O'Casey's autobiography in terms of these three principles of selection, organization and representation will constitute the core of this study. If the consequences of decisions pertaining to these factors are acknowledged and interpreted, it should become clear that O'Casey's readers are provided with an evolving series of images of his former selves.

But if O'Casey's success in establishing these images is to be appreciated and their function to be understood, the autobiography must also be viewed in the context of a long tradition of autobiographical writing. Thus, the principles behind his approach to autobiographical form can be explored in more detail and with more insight by reference to a generic background which stretches, in varying forms and modes, back to St Augustine and beyond. Examined with this tradition in mind, the materials of O'Casey's autobiography will be seen to possess certain patterns and to evince technical and literary features endemic to the genre. When these traditional elements of autobiography are combined with O'Casey's idiosyncratic treatment of the past and his unique narrative methods, the result is an autobiography which offers numerous and diverse self-images. It is in the variety and nature of such images, the daring with which they are created, that both the authenticity and complexity of O'Casey's self-portrait reside.

However, as will be stressed throughout this study, an autobiographer's attempted act of self-replication, the process of choosing, arranging and presenting past experiences, produces images of the self which are a more legitimate reflection of present identity than they are an accurate account of the historical individual. It is by responding to the images created of earlier selves, by attempting to understand the rationale for their presence and to perceive their function in suggesting an overall perspective on the life, that a reader gains insight into the identity of the autobiographer. For this reason, autobiography may offer but selective and circumspect biographical and historical information on its author. This is particularly true of a self-portrait such as O'Casey's, which is so much an individualistic exploration of autobiographical form and which so readily attempts to discover new ways of providing access to identity. While the work may indeed embody concrete historical facts and encompass specific information on personal history, it is finally controlled by the desire to get at the truth of the life through imaginative means, to give the life-story artistic shape and cohesion. O'Casey's autobiography, then, offers authentic indices of revelation about the author rather than about its subject; it is this identity — the complexity of his personal consciousness — that lies at the heart of the literary self-portrait and should be explored by readers of the work.

Because this study proceeds from the premise that the identity being sought is ultimately suggested by the sum of O'Casey's structural devices and literary methods, by the series of indicators to the self which constitutes the work, the autobiography will be considered as a self-contained text which can be approached and understood in its own right, without external knowledge of its author and without the assistance of information derived from other sources. A literary autobiography is a unified and self-sufficient creation which provides for its own explication. And yet, most readers are likely to bring to the work some familiarity with the facts of O'Casey's life. Such knowledge is potentially as detrimental as it can be useful. Prior assumptions about O'Casey the dramatist can limit a full appreciation of O'Casey the autobiographer, just as possessing information on O'Casey's life may possibly obscure the validity of the self-images created in the autobiography. Similarly, possessing data on historical figures and events can impede an understanding of O'Casey's purposes, preventing the perception of a man who, in many respects, is quite distinct from the individual suggested by other sources. Consequently, outside information on O'Casey himself, as well as on other people and events, must be used in a circumspect and particular fashion — to discover how he has shaped and interpreted such materials, whether he has been faithful to them, deviated from them, or transformed them. Having established the degree of manipulation and rearrangement to which experiences and events are subjected, the reader must then attempt to assess the autobiographical implications of such treatment. Therefore, extra-textual knowledge may legitimately be applied to a reading of the autobiographical text not to see if it coincides with one's own perception of objective facts but only to discern the author's autobiographical purposes. For this reason, every effort will be made throughout this study to use external information, whether derived from O'Casey's letters or from independent biographical and historical sources, to substantiate that which has been established or confirm that which has been suggested by the text itself. Likewise, in an attempt to remain faithful to the self-sufficiency of the text, this study tries as much as possible to maintain the distinction between creator and subject which O'Casey has established through his use of evolving personae. Although this entails the somewhat awkward procedure of

referring to Johnny and Sean as protagonist and hero, of continually trying to separate the historical and contemporary selves
of O'Casey, it is a fundamental distinction which is necessary if his
purposes and accomplishments are to be recognized fully.

A reading of Sean O'Casey's autobiography based on the
preceding premises should suggest that the work possesses merit
and deserves attention far beyond that of a mere sourcebook of
biographical and historical information. When relevant critical
approaches are applied to it, the self-portrait reveals that its
structural and stylistic elements simultaneously embody and
enhance the process of autobiographical revelation; it emerges as
a compelling work of literary creation, a testimony to O'Casey's
imaginative and artistic powers; and, finally, it establishes itself not
only as belonging to a long tradition of autobiographical writing
but as an innovative and exciting response to the possibilities
offered by the autobiographical form. When the many components
of O'Casey's challenging work are examined, it will be seen to
provide a comprehensive portrait of its author and, in doing so, to
establish itself as a major accomplishment in modern autobiographical literature.

1. CONSTRUCTING THE HOUSE OF LIFE

Sean O'Casey's six-volume autobiography is an extraordinary self-portrait composed over an extended period of his literary career. The first four instalments — *I Knock at the Door* (1939), *Pictures in the Hallway* (1942), *Drums Under the Windows* (1945), and *Inishfallen, Fare Thee Well* (1949) — deal with the years from his birth in 1880 to his emigration from Ireland in 1926. The last two books — *Rose and Crown* (1952) and *Sunset and Evening Star* (1954) — cover his life from his arrival in England until approximately 1953. In 1956, the six books were published as a two-volume set entitled *Mirror in My House*.

The regularity with which the succeeding volumes appeared belies the autobiography's tentative beginnings and its long, often hesitant evolution.[1] It is clear from his correspondence that, at the outset, O'Casey was not working with a master plan and had only a vague notion of the scope of his undertaking; indeed, it was only after some initial experiments that he actually set out to write the work as we know it. Moreover, even after he had embarked on the narrative of his past life, he did not anticipate the kind of extended creation it would become. Only during the actual process of recording his personal history did he recognize that, if all of the significant nuances in the relationship between former selves and present identity were to be rendered, he could satisfactorily complete his autobiography only by continuing its story down to his own temporal present. And yet, despite the growing length of the work, the moment which he saw as the logical culmination of the life-story — himself sitting at his desk writing it — continued to recede. Nevertheless, O'Casey pressed on with the account of his life until he finally brought the narrative down to the present. His efforts to achieve that goal are central to an appreciation of his self-portrait and help to explain many of the characteristics which make it a unique autobiographical experiment.

Although *I Knock at the Door* was not published until 1939, its origins can be traced as far back as August 1926 when O'Casey, newly-arrived in London, wrote to his publisher, 'I have thought of writing a book reminiscent of my experiences.'[2] At this stage, however, it appears that O'Casey's attitude to this proposal was somewhat ambiguous. In an interview with the *Observer* in October 1929 he said, 'I have also written part of an auto-biography,' a statement which he reiterated in a February 1930 interview with *Theatre Guild Magazine*. Yet, years later, in a letter to William J. Maroldo in August 1962, he wrote: 'As for my own "Auto-biography," it was not first-conceived as such, but just as incidents I had experienced. Indeed, three of them appeared in print before the idea of a biography came into my head.'[3] From the perspective of the man who had completed the comprehensive and highly unusual autobiography, O'Casey obviously felt — his statements in the earlier interviews to the contrary — that his initial efforts at self-reflection were far different from the final shape they acquired in the finished work. In any event, writing in a 1956 *New York Times* article, 'Sidelighting on Some Pictures,' O'Casey reiterated that the earliest autobiographical sketches were begun without any governing pattern in mind. In the intervals between composing plays, he had started writing about 'past experiences — the moulds in which myself was made.'[4] Although he was clearly drawing on personal experiences, O'Casey was not yet convinced that he had embarked on a work of autobiographical portrayal. His ambiguous perspective is evident from the presence in two notebooks of seemingly different material. In an October 1930 entry in the holograph notebooks, he outlined a plan for a volume of seventeen short stories, the ideas for only some of which were obviously autobiographical. These stories — he preferred to call them sketches or pictures — were written in the first as well as third person, and appear as one continuous narrative without the later divisions of chapters and titles. In another notebook of this period, O'Casey wrote a narrative comprising selected personal incidents up to about the age of eight. During the early thirties, then, he continued to write what he called 'biographical sketches' with no apparent comprehensive perception of their ultimate form. He was still somewhat circumspect at the thought of writing a fully-fledged autobiography, for, as he later acknowledged in his December 3, 1948 letter to Ralph Thompson,

I was a bit shy about the idea [of writing an extended self-portrait] at first, and took a long time to think it over. I thought that no man liveth and dieth to himself, so I put behind what I thought and what I did the panorama of the world I lived in — the things that made me.[5]

In addition to being uncomfortable with the inherently self-centred nature of the genre, O'Casey may have been hesitant because of the peculiar autobiographical style and form he had already attempted in some of his sketches. Even later, when he had obviously perceived his autobiographical purposes, his letters show a continuing awareness of the experimental nature of his 'fantastic pages of biography.'[6]

In 1934, the publication of 'The Protestant Kid Thinks of the Reformation' in the *American Spectator* helped crystallize O'Casey's perception of his purposes; that childhood vignette met with such success that 'the biography started in earnest.'[7] Assured that his individualistic approach to autobiographical writing was readily accessible, O'Casey proceeded to select and assemble his various materials on the basis of new-found principles. Having once perceived his autobiographical goals, he progressed rapidly with the writing of the work.

By October 7, 1938, with *I Knock at the Door* completed, O'Casey acknowledged that the logical culmination of his autobiography would have to be at the point when the narrative story would catch up to him in the autobiographical present. In an outline of subsequent volumes to Harold Macmillan, O'Casey explained:

The Book [*Knock*] — the 23 chapters or sections is an organic whole — at least I hope it is—; and the whole book is autobiographical, from Alpha to Omega, of the first twelve years of my life. I have thought of two more volumes: 'Come On In'; and the third 'The Lighted Room.' The second to consist of what happened till I joined the Irish Movement, & the last to deal with all or most of what happened afterwards.

No longer merely a series of childhood sketches, the work had blossomed in his mind as a comprehensive account of his development through his past world.

With his autobiographical goal clarified, O'Casey quickly began work on the next volume. As early as November 28, 1939, he wrote to George Jean Nathan, 'I do an odd chapter of 2 vol. of "I Knock at the Door"; to be called, I think, "Rough House".' On March 30, 1940 he wrote to Peter Newmark: 'I am busy on my autobiography, (now isn't lifestory a better word than that?) & hope to have most of another volume done by the end of the year'. Significantly, in a letter to Daniel Macmillan discussing the completion of *Pictures*, O'Casey now envisaged a still larger work: 'I had thought of four [books] altogether, with the last one to be

called, "The Clock Strikes Twelve." What the intervening one may
be called, God only knows; if indeed any other thing can be
written.'[8] This note of hesitancy appears at various points in the
compositional history of the autobiography. On March 10, 1942,
O'Casey admitted to Nathan, 'I dread looking forward to writing
the next volume.' However, the writing proceeded apace, so that
by February 8, 1944 he could tell Nathan he hoped to see the third
volume published before the end of the year. On June 9, 1944 he
wrote to Daniel Macmillan,

I have almost chosen the title of DRUMS UNDER THE WINDOWS for
this number. I will send on the other chapter as soon as it is done. I was
thinking of writing a short FLASH FORWARD to describe my thoughts at
the present (some of them anyway), and so give an unusual end to it. I
think I shall finish it off with a fourth volume to be called THE CLOCK
STRIKES TWELVE.

It is not surprising that O'Casey was acutely aware of, indeed
somewhat daunted by, the huge amount of material to be dealt
with to bring the narrative from the end of *Drums* (which closes
with his account of the 1916 Rebellion) up to his own present. In
the face of the work's growing length as well as difficulties in
bringing it to a satisfactory conclusion, the idea of a 'flash forward'
was appealing. As he worked on the fourth volume, O'Casey's
uncertainty over its proposed conclusion increased. In a June 1945
letter he referred to it as 'the 4th vol (the last, I think), to be called
"The Clock Strikes Twelve",' and a year later he saw it as 'the "last"
vol. of Biography. It will end at the time when I leave Ireland for
England.'[9] Yet, by February 4, 1947, he was again less sure that
the autobiography would be completed. He wrote to Brooks
Atkinson,

As for the rest of the 'biography,' I am ending it (for the present) on the
morning of my departure from Ireland for England. That episode meant,
not only another day, but a new life; so I put the fife in my pocket for
awhile, till I learn a new tune or two in the new places I visit, & the new
life I live. I haven't yet decided on the title for this vol., but I think it will
be 'The Long Day Over.'

On March 14, 1947, he told Nathan of the difficulties he had in
finding a suitable title, and informed him that it would be called
'Goodbye At the Door.'
    In deciding on a title for this fourth volume, O'Casey confronted
a problem which stemmed from the titles he had given the previous

volumes. In 1938, even as the writing of *Knock* had been going smoothly, he had struggled to find a suitable title for this first autobiographical volume. He wrote to Harold Macmillan on June 21 of that year:

I'm not satisfied with the title 'The Green Blade'; and I am trying to think of another — 'Father of the Man', or 'Of Such is the Kingdom of Heaven' — too long? 'Studies' in Autobiography seems to have too much of a scholastic touch about it for me. I'll have to try to make the sub-title simpler.

Years later, in the letter to Maroldo referred to above, he explained his change of mind:

I first intended to take titles for the work from 'First the Green Blade, then the Corn, then the Full Corn in my Ear'; but the rapid development of what I was conceiving in my mind, additional ideas crowding in after the conception of previous ideas, made me alter the titles to the present ones which top the various volumes.

Having selected former titles under the spontaneous intensity of the creative moment, O'Casey was now presented with a unique dilemma as he searched for an appropriate name for the fourth volume. The three previous titles had drawn on the metaphor associating life with a house, a symbolic building which is presented as being entered fully at manhood. Thus, *Knock* suggests the years of preparation in which the boy grows towards adolescence, while *Pictures* encompasses the series of images capturing the youth's first tentative steps into the world of adult life. With *Drums*, the individual is fully ensconced in the symbolic building of his life which is the exciting period of Ireland's national revival; the lines from Yeats's *Purgatory* — 'Study that house,/I think about its jokes and stories' — which serve as epigraph, simultaneously evoke this era and strengthen the architectural metaphor. When O'Casey completed each of these individual volumes he had always anticipated writing a further volume; consequently, it was not necessary to contemplate in specific terms the implications of the title for the concluding book. Now, however, with his uncertainty about continuing the work, the issue of the title for the fourth volume became a pressing concern. On the one hand, as the letters make clear, he sensed that the work was only temporarily stopped and he would eventually carry the story up to the present. Yet, on the other hand, using the title 'Goodbye at the Door' would suggest the completion of the series begun with

I Knock at the Door. This use of the house metaphor would give
the fourth volume an implication with which O'Casey was clearly
uncomfortable, since, in terms of this metaphor, many rooms of his
house of life had not yet been described. To name a few, there was
marriage and fatherhood, the acrimonious break with the Abbey,
the writing and critical reception of the majority of his plays, his
trip to the United States, and his wartime years in England. If
significant experiences such as these were omitted, both proposed
titles, 'The Clock Strikes Twelve' and 'Goodbye at the Door,'
would be misleading.

O'Casey's difficulty also resulted from his use of the house
metaphor in a dual fashion, to indicate his life in general as well
as his years in Ireland. In the first three books, he did not have to
discriminate between using the metaphor to describe his personal
life or his years spent in Ireland since they were, of course,
synonymous.[10] In particular, while his own activities in the
struggle to liberate Ireland could be viewed as coinciding with the
larger national effort, distinctions in the use of the metaphor were
not necessary. But one of the purposes of the fourth volume was
to trace the divergence between his vision of Ireland and the
emergent reality of the Free State. Thus, for example, in suggesting
some of the features of the new society — which he saw as being
inconsonant with earlier Irish patriotic ideals — O'Casey equates
Ireland with a building, the windows of which have been changed:

Almost as long as Sean could remember, the life of Ireland was lived in
a hall whose walls were roof-high stained-glass windows, nationally
designed; but these were giving place now to glass that gave back the
colours of pietistic twist and glossied tantrum. The window where Wolfe
Tone had shone in his sky-blue coat and bright epaulettes of a brigadier,
now showed the wan figure of Bernadette raptly listening to the Bells of
St Mary's; in the one which had Robert Emmet in his gay green coat,
carrying a plumed hat in his hand, stood now the black-clad, smiling-faced
Father Malone in his new Sunday hat. (IV, 272–273)[11]

This growing disillusionment with the new social order in Ireland,
as well as his departure for England, put pressure on O'Casey to
clarify his metaphors. For example, while he still had the tentative
title of 'Goodbye at the Door' for the fourth volume, in his
notebooks (holograph number 19) he had given the title 'A House
Abandoned' to the opening chapter of the fifth volume. But the
titles of the earlier volumes had not explicitly equated the house
metaphor with his Irish years, although, of course, the books dealt
with nothing else. His acknowledgement of the distinction is

implicit in his choice of *Inishfallen, Fare Thee Well* (the opening line of Thomas Moore's poem of farewell to Ireland) as the title for the fourth book. The switch from an architectural to a spatial metaphor allowed O'Casey to suggest the end of his Irish years, without implying the conclusion of the autobiography; in short, the title left open the possibility of another volume.

While the April 1947 letter to Daniel Macmillan which announced the title choice indicated that the series had ended, within a few months O'Casey was again writing to Macmillan with a proposal for 'writing a further vol. dealing with my arrival in England, and carrying it on, maybe, to the day that now is.'[12] In the light of past experience, his caution about the possibility of carrying the story down to the present is not surprising. As well, the thorny issue raised with the title of the fourth volume may very well have heightened O'Casey's recognition of the different nature of the task of writing about his life in exile. In any case, he sensed correctly that to deal with his years in England would require a change in emphasis and tone, both of which factors gave pause to the actual process of making a start on the next volume. On October 31, 1947, he wrote to Daniel Macmillan: 'The vol. on my impressions since I came to England will take a lot of thinking about; but I may try to start it soon in a rough way. It would be, I think, a more thoughtful one, and less exciting, which may be a good or bad thing. I'm not sure.' O'Casey's wariness in beginning the next book is understandable; indeed, the obvious temptation to end the narrative at the seemingly logical point of his departure from Ireland must have been great. Not only was there the matter of the necessary adjustments in handling the new material but, perhaps even more daunting, was the awareness of the creative energies required to complete the book — he was, after all, sixty-eight and had still not covered the last third of his life.

Notwithstanding these obstacles, O'Casey's desire for comprehensiveness carried the day. As is evident from the letters already quoted, once he had decided that the work would indeed be one of self-portrayal, his assumption was that the life-story would continue down to his own temporal vantage point. He makes this clear in his December 3, 1948 letter to Ralph Thompson, a book reviewer for the *New York Times* who had written and apparently asked O'Casey about his initial perceptions of the autobiography's scope. O'Casey replied: 'Oh, yes, I had an extended work in mind when I definitely started out on I KNOCK AT THE DOOR. How far, I wasn't sure, but I imagine till Death opened the door softly for me. . . .' To conclude the work after the fourth volume would mean not only that the experiences of twenty years would be missing but that those already recorded would suffer by not being seen in the context of the whole life. Incidents and episodes already analysed might rely for their ultimate meaning on the juxtaposition of events belonging to later years. For example, if the source of much of O'Casey's bitterness with the Abbey Theatre in the fourth volume is to be understood fully, it would have to be considered in the context of his account, in the fifth volume, of the Abbey's treatment of *The Silver Tassie*. Thus, despite the attractiveness of quitting after the fourth volume, O'Casey's instincts told him to press on for the sake of experiences already presented as much as for those still to be recounted.

If O'Casey's switch in metaphors is suggested by the title of *Inishfallen, Fare Thee Well*, it is confirmed by his naming the fifth volume *Rose and Crown*, a common designation not only for an English pub but for the country as a whole. This understanding of the title is confirmed in the chapter which bears the same name as the fifth volume, in which O'Casey describes the 1926 General Strike as the death knell for the established social order in England: 'The Crown is crushed, the Rose is withering. England's golden day is going, England's golden day is going, England's golden day is gone.' (V, 96) The implication of his choice of title for the fifth volume is that, for the moment at least, he viewed his life as being lived in two distinct symbolic houses: one representing his life in Ireland; and the other, his new life in England.

When the writing of *Rose* was well underway, O'Casey saw once again that it would be insufficient to complete his story. In January 1951, he wrote to Daniel Macmillan: 'I've written a lot of a 5th vol. of biography, & now fear I shan't be able to end it without another one'.[13] *Rose* covers the period 1926–1935, from his arrival in England until he returned there after his visit to the United States. With the publication of the sixth volume, *Sunset and Evening Star*, the story line was carried from 1935 up to O'Casey's present in 1953; for the first time since the work was begun years earlier, the autobiographical hero and the author occupied the same temporal plane and had become one.

However, choosing a title for *Sunset* presented O'Casey with further difficulties. A letter to Nathan shows that as late as May 7, 1951, he planned to call it 'Goodbye at the Door.' But, once again, he rejected this title as unsuitable, even for this the concluding volume. At this juncture, O'Casey was confronted by a fundamental feature of the autobiographical process, particularly pronounced in those works which attempt to suggest a

comprehensive picture of the author's life. When an autobiographer has completed his self-portrait, the work becomes a
static definition of the self, a product of a specific temporal
perspective. Because one's identity can be modified by subsequent
events and experiences, the ideal conclusion of an autobiography,
as O'Casey himself indicated in the letter to Ralph Thompson, lies
in the author's own death: when the autobiographer continues to
live for a significant period, the future can bring further experiences
which will not have been recounted. Thus, not only will subsequent adjustments to the self, be they incidental or dramatic, go
unrecorded but their influence on how previous assessments may
be viewed, and perhaps modified, will not be registered. In
O'Casey's situation the ten years from the completion of the
autobiography until his death in 1964 wrought significant changes
in his life. On the artistic level, for instance, he had yet another
confrontation with Irish public officials over his writing. In 1958,
his play *The Drums of Father Ned* — along with works by Joyce
and Beckett — was criticized by the Archbishop of Dublin and
subsequently censored by the Tostal Theatre Festival. (In protest,
the works of all three writers were withdrawn; O'Casey himself
prohibited all professional productions of his plays in Ireland, a
ban which he maintained until 1964.) This incident would almost
certainly have qualified the somewhat tender and benign attitude
toward Ireland found as the autobiography draws to a close. On
a more personal level, the seventy-six-year-old O'Casey under-
went the anguish of watching his twenty-one-year-old son die of
leukaemia. As part of the catharsis of his grief, he gave an
intimately personal response to this tragedy in the beautifully-
controlled and deeply-evocative autobiographical essay, 'Under the
Greenwood Tree He Died.' The publication of this elegiac piece in
1961, along with two other autobiographical essays, attests to the
adjustments that would almost certainly have been made were it
possible to reflect such sentiments in the completed autobiography.

Looking at the autobiography prospectively rather than from the
later temporal distance, O'Casey could therefore not have been
cognizant that his use of house metaphors in his titles would
accentuate the critical dilemma which is posed for all autobiographers as the work moves to a conclusion. If *I Knock At the
Door* was perfectly suited to suggest the hero's arrival at the house
of adult life, 'Goodbye at the Door' was inappropriate for a man
who, though old and prepared for departure, was still intensely
involved in life. His commitment to the future is made clear on the
closing pages of the final volume where, having reflected on the

failures and accomplishments which echoed through his personal history, he continues:

he couldn't linger long among a crowd of echoes, however charming they might be; there were too many things to think of, too many things to do: things to think about, things to do in the home, in the wider community of the nation, in the widest community of the world. (VI, 232)

Given this involvement with life, O'Casey's choice of the title *Sunset and Evening Star* is a compromise suggesting the completion of the author's account of his life while in no way signalling the end of his life. Or, to use O'Casey's own imagery, although the sun was setting and the evening star was out, the blackness of the midnight hour had not yet enveloped his world. He admits at the end of the chapter 'Sunset' that 'Sean was now near to the door again, about to go out of life's house by the same door as in he went,' but he expresses the hope a few sentences later that he may linger a while yet. (VI, 205)

Although Sean was not yet ready to exit through the doorway of life, O'Casey paradoxically evokes this image visually on the dust jacket of *Sunset*, the design for which, along with that for other volumes, he closely supervised.[14] The cover of *Knock* shows a boy knocking on a door against a background of a Celtic cross, while that of *Sunset* depicts an old man drinking a parting toast to life outside a half-open door, with the same cross in the background. As well as hinting at the unity from first to last, the visual similarity underlines the narrative pattern whereby the story comes full circle to catch up with the contemporary autobiographer. The reappearance of the Celtic cross on *Sunset* also confirms the dual association of the house metaphor with his Irish years as well as his life in general. Within the volume itself, O'Casey interchangeably uses the metaphor in both these ways. For instance, the perception of Ireland as a separate building can be seen in the penultimate chapter, 'Outside an Irish Window,' which focuses specifically on Ireland. On the other hand, in the last chapter he salutes and commends the younger generation in the following terms:

The young were busy in the house of life that the old were leaving; throwing out some of the musty stuff, bringing the fresh and the new; changing the very shape of the house itself . . . placing new pictures on the walls; knocking out walls separating one family from another; polishing everything with a newer glow; opening the windows wider. (VI, 223–224)

However, even though O'Casey employs this metaphor in an alternating fashion, his choice of *Mirror in My House* as the title for the two-volume edition of the autobiography is evidence that he saw his primary use of the house metaphor in association with his personal life.[15]

What is perhaps more important about the choice of the architectural metaphor, rather than the more traditional auto-biographical one of clothes (Thomas Carlyle's *Sartor Resartus* is the prime example that comes to mind), is that it provides a significant indicator of O'Casey's intentions in the work. Clothes and costumes are convenient metaphoric guises which can reflect the inner person, the versions of the subjective self which were forerunners of present consciousness. O'Casey, however, in addition to charting the evolution of the private self, wished to lend his narrative wider dimensions by encompassing key historical events he had witnessed. While the primary thrust of the autobiography is to hold a mirror up to the house of his personal life, the use of the metaphor to suggest important developments in the Ireland and England of his time facilitates a modulation back and forth between individual and national identities, between the self and its world. Begun as an effort to provide 'Swift Glances Back at Things That Made Me,' the work gradually acquired a wider focus as O'Casey experienced 'the rapid development of what I was conceiving in my mind, additional ideas crowding in after the conception of previous ideas. . . .'[16] This broader focus, with its attendant consequences for content and structure, becomes particularly pronounced when the growing man actively participates in the social, cultural and political spheres of his world. As he changes and grows in the dynamic interplay with his reality, the autobiography adjusts to reveal that wider canvas. Thus, in *Drums* the work begins to take on the proportions of a national epic as O'Casey views his own story in representative terms, as he sees parallels between his own and the national struggle. In his July 8, 1945 letter to Lovat Dickson, O'Casey, writing of *Drums*, shows his awareness of this dimension of his autobiographical under-taking:

Prefatorily, let me say that in DRUMS UNDER THE WINDOWS, I primarily aim at doing something that Yeats might call 'unique'; that the whole work will be a curious biography, entirely, or almost so, different from anything else of its kind; and, in its way, a kaleidoscopic picture of the poorer masses as they surged around one who was bone of their bone and flesh of their flesh.

Couching his own story in this larger, representative mould, O'Casey gives an epic account of an individual's odyssey through his life and times. In the volumes subsequent to *Drums*, this wider dimension is manifested through additional adjustments in focus. *Inishfallen* casts the hero in the role of alienated artist struggling to assert his vision of reality in the face of social taboos, religious prohibitions and political restrictions. In the final two volumes, the protagonist is depicted as an archetypal figure of exile and isolation, the artist whose work is continually being rejected, the socialist whose beliefs are not readily accepted, and the Irishman whose country has achieved dubious independence. What began, then, as a series of childhood sketches grew into a multi-dimensional gesture of autobiographical definition, a work which must be approached as a unique and experimental exemplification of an already complex and nebulous genre.

2. O'CASEY AND THE GENRE OF AUTOBIOGRAPHY

A sensitive and comprehensive response to O'Casey's auto-biography is made difficult by the ill-defined nature of the genre and the lack of established critical principles. Autobiography is bordered on one side of the literary landscape by that somewhat similar chronicle of one's past, the memoir, and on the other by an even more problematical neighbour, the autobiographical novel. Occupying a tenuous and frequently trespassed ground between such related genres, autobiography has until very recently tended to hold more interest for the historian or the seeker of biographical facts than the literary critic. As a consequence, vague and unfor-mulated assumptions about its precise nature have often impaired critical reaction to and assessment of specific works, leading to statements either too limited to be useful or too conventional to deal with change and innovation. Hardly surprising, an inordinately long and multifaceted work of autobiographical definition such as O'Casey's, with its wide-ranging materials, its large cast of characters, its historical sweep, and — most pertinently — its highly experimental narrative strategies, poses unique problems for those wishing to make sense of the work. Over the past several years, however, an increasing number of critics have turned their attention to autobiography, producing a wealth of essays and full-length studies of both the genre itself and its individual practitioners. As will become evident throughout this study, much of this theoretical and analytical material is of immense value in facilitating an appreciation of O'Casey's experiments and accomplishments in the genre.

Although O'Casey's autobiography has not altogether escaped this recent critical attention, it has not been the subject of a sustained and rigorous analysis from a well-defined critical perspective. When its broad epic canvas and innovative means of realising the self are viewed from a coherent vantage-point, the autobiography not only takes a central place in the O'Casey canon but emerges as one of the foremost works of autobiographical exploration in the twentieth century. However, if O'Casey's purposes are to be understood fully, if his accomplishments are to

13

be appreciated in all their dimensions, the work must be seen as a unique manifestation of the possibilities inherent in the genre, a work which makes specific demands on its readers and establishes its own criteria for failure and success. What, then, are the perspectives from which O'Casey's autobiography must be approached? In light of its obvious inaccuracies in information, omissions of significant details, and blatant misrepresentations of fact, can it be considered a work of self-portrayal at all? Or has it moved beyond the limits of autobiography to inhabit some strange new literary territory? Such questions raise crucial issues about O'Casey's autobiography and lead to an inevitable discussion of the autobiographical process itself.

A workable and straightforward definition of autobiography is that it is an individual's written account of chosen experiences from his life. The most important implication of this definition — relevant to all works of self-portrayal — is that the finished creation is ultimately a product of present consciousness. One's past is irrevocably lost; all attempts to duplicate it in the present are but approximations of those vanished experiences. An autobiography is much more an accurate picture of the self which records personal history than it is a true account of the various selves being recorded; it reveals the man as he is, not as he was. This crucial facet of the autobiographical process governs the contents and forms of all works of self-portrayal. As will become evident in the ensuing discussion, this is also a key to the essential difference between autobiography and those related genres — memoirs, the autobiographical novel — which impinge on it so closely and, at times, so troublesomely. Only when all the implications of this particular characteristic of autobiography are understood can O'Casey's six-volume work be fully analysed and appreciated.

The preceding definition of autobiography — an individual's written account of chosen experiences from his life — underlines the selective process at the heart of the act of self-portrayal. Faced with a myriad of past experiences, all autobiographers recognize that they cannot hope to duplicate the totality of life. Of necessity, they must economize and foreshorten, depicting stages in personal evolution by selecting representative events from the amorphous past.

The definition includes another factor influencing choice of contents. Frequently in autobiographical works, whole episodes, even years, may be ignored or deemed unworthy of consideration, not necessarily for reasons of compression but because they are perceived as incompatible with the autobiographer's purposes. Thus, implicit in the definition as well is that an autobiographer initiates the process of recollection and self-portrayal with specific intentions in mind. And the genre of autobiography is capable of encompassing as wide a variety of intentions as there are autobiographers. An autobiographer may see as the object of his self-scrutiny a variety of purposes which, simultaneously or interchangeably, can be realized: self-formation, self-justification self-exaltation and self-discovery are among the most predictable motives behind the desire for self-portrayal. Self-explanation, perhaps the most common of autobiographical purposes, may stem from the individual's need to have his say, to confirm the validity of his life as he has lived it, but it may also be traced to the more deep-rooted desire to reassure himself and perhaps others, that his life adds up to something greater than the sum of its parts. Self-portrayal can thus become testimony to the individual's sense of inherent progression in his life, as well as being his contemporary perception of its ultimate meaning. The autobiographical act, in the words of Georges Gusdorf, 'appeases the more or less anguished uneasiness of an ageing man who wonders if his life has not been lived in vain, frittered away haphazardly, ending now in simple failure.'[1] In that sense, all autobiography is, finally, a gesture toward immortality, an effort to derive enduring significance from the fleeting years. Autobiography, then, is not a mere recounting by an individual of the history of his journey through life; it is a process likely to incorporate a variety of highly subjective, complex, and even contradictory, impulses.

However, because several characteristics conventionally perceived as those of autobiography would belong more accurately to the memoir, a recognition of the distinguishing feature of each genre is necessary for a fuller appreciation of autobiographical content. As has been suggested, the focus of autobiography is, ultimately, on the shaping of an inner identity; its centre of interest is subjective experience. The materials of a memoir, however, are primarily the external occurrences in which the writer has participated — things done, events witnessed, people encountered. A memoir presents the personal, social and historical events in the author's life which have marked his journey to the present. In contrast to this, external happenings are of importance to an autobiography only when they point to a better understanding of the developing self, or provide a clearer rationale for the unique

evolution of the author's current sense of identity. Unlike that of
the memoir, the emphasis in an autobiography is not so much on
what happened as on its personal significance.

A further distinction between the genres can be traced to their
different approaches to temporal sequence. Whereas a memoir is
usually concerned with time in a mechanical sense — events follow
one another because the calendar says they do — an autobiography
is more likely to present experiences following one another with a
more inward inevitability. In O'Casey's autobiography, episodes
are not necessarily placed in the context of linear time, since he
usually neglects to specify dates and temporal order. He himself
acknowledged that a sequential arrangement of experience was not
his goal. In 1952, writing to John Gassner after the publication of
Rose, he stated: 'I haven't tried to write a chronicle . . . all I've done
is to picture (as I saw it) the world of life as it flooded around me,
& as it welled up within myself.'[2] Although highlights of
development are often carefully orchestrated and prepared for in
his narrative, the information on intervening, quotidian life that
usually invests a memoir with cohesion and unity is noticeably
absent. For example, in the earlier volumes it is often impossible to
tell the age of the hero; in the middle volumes, it is not always
evident if, or where, he works; and, in the later volumes, it is never
clear what the precise details in his family situation are. Instead of
using the chronological sequences of factual occurrences that
would be the mode of the memoirist, O'Casey transforms events
into images designed to approximate the influences moulding the
inner man.

Even when they try to be so, autobiographers are never
completely objective about the shaping experiences of their past.
Frequently, an autobiographer will begin his work, in the tradition
of Rousseau, by stating that he intends to record his experiences
accurately and will resist the temptation to embellish or give false
emphasis. Yet, the very presence of such statements is an indication of the profound suspicion that autobiographers have about
the distortive powers of recollection. Most such writers, again
following Rousseau, proceed to compose highly prejudiced and
distinctly interpretative versions of personal history, quite different
from what objective accounts of the contours of their lives might
be. A writer who does adhere to his opening dictum usually
produces a work which fails to provide a sense of the individual's
growing as a result of successive encounters with his past reality:
the episodic recounting of incidents and events never captures the
feeling of creative discovery attendant upon the full exploration of

the emergence of a unique consciousness. A work focussing on personal history in this manner is more memoir than autobiography.

A classic example of close adherence to a simple narration of the demonstrable facts of life is Anthony Trollope's *An Autobiography*. Trollope begins with the following statement of purpose:

... it will not be so much my intention to speak of the little details of my private life, as of what I, and perhaps others around me, have done in literature. . . . That I, or any man, should tell everything of himself, I hold to be impossible. Who could endure to own the doing of a mean thing? Who is there that has done more? But this I protest; that nothing that I shall say shall be untrue. I will set down nought in malice; nor will I give to myself, or others, honour which I do not believe to have been fairly won.[3]

Because he scrupulously follows this course throughout the work, Trollope never provides any real insight into his subjective identity, any sense of subtlety or nuance which might explain his character. He sums up his marriage, for example, with the dismissive comment that 'My marriage was like the marriage of other people, and of no special interest to anyone except my wife and me.'[4] Of some interest, however, in a work that stringently pursues the path of factual accuracy, is the observation that 'A man does, in truth, remember that which it interests him to remember; and when we hear that memory has gone as age has come on, we should understand that the capacity for interest in the matter has perished.'[5] Trollope does not pursue the implications of this insight but continues his narration of dates, trips taken, and celebrities met. Perhaps as a result of some uneasiness with the mere factual data comprising the work, Trollope concludes:

It will not, I trust, be supposed by any reader that I have intended in this so-called autobiography to give a record of my inner life. No man ever did so truly and no man ever will. Rousseau probably atttempted it, but who doubts but that Rousseau has confessed in much [sic] the thoughts and convictions rather than the facts of his life.[6]

While it is patently clear that he has not attempted it, Trollope recognizes that any effort to capture the felt experiences of the subjective self is a movement away from 'the facts of life.' Because he has not tried to do so himself, we can appreciate Trollope's hesitancy in calling the work an autobiography; as an account of the external events of his life it would be much more accurately described as a memoir.[7]

The contents of autobiography are also vitally affected by the consistency with which an autobiographer pursues his initial intentions. Those autobiographers who do begin with the clearly perceived purpose of rendering subjective growth, and who consequently have an initial understanding of the premises on which the selection of contents is to be based, may soon recognize, however, that the autobiographical undertaking stems from a desire not so much to portray an identity already known and understood as to discover the significance of, or give meaning to, a life. Many autobiographies are written to bolster or verify the self-image when circumstances threaten to undermine it. The need for autobiographical definition often coincides with, or follows closely upon, a crisis or a series of experiences which threatens an individual's perception of identity. At such moments of doubt and uncertainty, his hold on the self is undermined as both the context and meaning of past experiences (previously believed to be understood) become blurred or obscured. Feeling that identity has broken its moorings from the secure ties of the past and now floats free and isolated in a turbulent and confusing present, he attempts to trace who he has been. He turns to his past to begin the process of shoring up the self, of defining a current identity. A dramatic instance of this phenomenon is found in the autobiography of H. G. Wells, which begins: 'I have a sense of crisis; that the time has come to reorganize my peace, if the ten or fifteen years ahead, which at the utmost I may hope to work in now, are to be saved from being altogether overgrown.'[8] By the time he has completed his long autobiography, Wells has regained his composure:

I began this autobiography to reassure myself during a phase of fatigue, restlessness and vexation, and it has achieved its purpose of reassurance. I wrote myself out of this mood of discontent and forgot myself and a mosquito swarm of bothers in writing about my sustaining ideas. My ruffled *persona* has been restored and the statement of the idea of the modern world state has reduced my personal and passing irritations and distractions to their proper insignificance.[9]

In the process of explaining the nature and characteristics of a personality, the autobiographical act can, then, assuage doubts about identity and counter threats to self-image.

If such works are initially as much acts of discovery and reassurance as of assertion and explanation, their materials are chosen on the basis of changing, even contradictory, purposes. An autobiography which originates in moments of doubt and uncertainty, and whose actual composition is part of the restorative process, operates on shifting principles of selection of materials. As a result of self-reflection and self-analysis, connections between past selves and present identity are re-established, and others previously hidden will often emerge from the palimpsest of the past to reinforce, modify, or even challenge. When autobiographical expression turns out to be as much an exploration as an authentication of identity, the principles on which materials are selected reflect an autobiographer's response to encounters with personal history.

In those autobiographies which were undertaken, even partially, to resolve doubts about identity, to assess the meaning of past experiences, or to discover the relationship between what the author was and what he had become, there is a point in the work — it can be arrived at gradually or dramatically — when the search is completed. Once the moment of self-understanding or self-assurance is reached, then the premises on which contents are chosen are changed. After achieving a keener understanding and awareness of himself, the autobiographer approaches remaining experiences with a new sense of insight and purpose: exploration has given way to knowledge. From that well-defined perspective, the autobiographer now evaluates and chooses materials in a manner similar to those autobiographies which have been composed *after* the crisis of identity has been resolved. Self-portraits initiated and written from an integrated perspective of recovery do, in fact, constitute the classic tradition of autobiographical literature. Augustine's *Confessions*, Gibbon's *Autobiography*, Rousseau's *Confessions* and Newman's *Apologia Pro Vita Sua* were all written subsequent to what is viewed as an experience of 'conversion', a moment when the individual suddenly recovers from despondency by seeing his life in a new context, possessing previously obscured purpose and direction. In those works of this type which deal only with a specific aspect of identity — Newman's spiritual quest, for example — the autobiographer does not feel the necessity of recounting experiences which, occurring after the moment of conversion, would serve to confirm its authenticity. When such writers perceive that no changes have occurred to alter the vision of life previously arrived at, they feel no need to carry the narrative down to the present. Believing that the historical self at the moment of conversion and the present identity are, in fact, similar, they not only validate the earlier self-awareness by presenting it as a contemporary belief but, in the

process, implicitly attest to the continuity of the life in the intervening years.

As we will see in subsequent chapters of this study, O'Casey's
autobiography partakes, in varying degrees, of both the 'crisis' and
the 'conversion' autobiographical paradigms. Much of the impulse
to turn to self-reflection and self-portrayal stemmed from the
period of artistic and personal uncertainty which characterized his
life for several years after his arrival in England. The series of 'Swift
Glances Back at Things That Made Me' was as much an act of
confirmation for himself as of assertion to others; the autobiographical initiative was a means of testing and authenticating
the validity of present identity. It was not a fully-fledged process
of self-exploration — his sense of self was too strong for that — but
it was an attempt to trace a consistency between former selves and
current self-perception, to confirm his present awareness in the
context of past experiences. For example, when O'Casey began the
autobiography, the most obvious feature of his life was that he was
a social, political and artistic exile from Ireland. When he had left
Ireland in 1926, he had no plans to remain in England permanently.
Although the decision to leave was a conscious one which he could
readily explain, it was only in the autobiographical process of
recounting his response to the shaping experiences of his past life
that his exile could be fully perceived — by him as well as by his
readers — as being a consistent outgrowth of his past. In tracing
the development of his social, political and artistic views during his
forty-six years in Ireland, he could confirm that his leaving, far
from being a spontaneous or casual event, was inevitable given the
widening disparity between the direction of Irish affairs and his
own views. In the autobiography, O'Casey could therefore confirm
the authenticity of the relationship between himself in the exiled
present and what he had been in the past, and he could do so with
a comprehensive understanding not available to him in the past.
Writing the work to clarify for himself and demonstrate to others
the forces that had moulded his unique character, O'Casey could
confirm the correctness of his former behaviour even though — or,
perhaps, because — it led to his present artistic and political exile.
Thus, the desire to search out those experiences which marked his
earlier indirect journey in self-development is a primary factor
governing his choice of materials for those volumes dealing with his
years in Ireland.

But once O'Casey, through the act of self-scrutiny and self-
portrayal, confirmed the features that define his identity — on
personal, social, political and artistic levels — the rationale for

choosing materials changes. Occasions are created in the fourth volume showing his former self articulating the tenets essential to his newly understood sense of identity. Concomitant with this awareness is the realization that this self, increasingly estranged from almost all aspects of Irish life, cannot live in such an inhibitive and conservative society. The moments of articulation which crystallize the protagonist's sense of self mark an important change in the work, since subsequent materials are chosen to reflect that new identity; the emphasis has now shifted from the desire to trace the evolution of the self, toward an assertion of the validity of his current self-perception.

The process of selecting incidents and events from one's past life is further complicated by the act of narration itself. All attempted duplication of the past in the present can be achieved only at the cost of much distortion. Indeed, the past itself was always merely a series of moments when the historical future was turning into the past; it never existed in the objective, static way that an autobiographer is, of necessity, forced to view it. Not only does the autobiographer presume to transform subjective states into an empirical realm but, more significantly, he further sacrifices the fluid, ever-changing nature of the past to the imperatives of narrative — the demands for order and plotline inherent in the act of self-writing. An autobiographer invariably makes a story of his life, shapes its structureless experiences into a patterned whole, sets up causes and effects, beginnings and endings. This attempt to give logical coherence, to impose rationalization, is what Georges Gusdorf calls 'the original sin of autobiography.' He explains:

The narrative is conscious, and since the narrator's consciousness directs the narrative, it seems to him incontestable that it has also directed his life. In other words, the act of reflecting that is essential to conscious awareness is transferred, by a kind of unavoidable optical illusion, back to the stage of the event itself.[10]

All autobiographers, then, transform *process* into achievement, impose on subjective experiences demonstrable shapes and describable contours, few of which are accurate reflections of what transpired as an individual viewed and responded to the passing events of life. The pressures of conceding life to a narrative design — no matter how loose its structure or amorphous its shape — result in the omission of certain incidents, an ordering of those which have been chosen, and, most distortive, the attempted

capturing of fleeting and modulating states of former consciousness. Thus, in selecting, arranging and presenting past events
in accordance with the teleological demands of narrative (a process
one critic has described as turning 'empirical facts into *art*ifacts')[11]
an autobiographer moves further away from what might be seen as
the ideal premise of the genre — an account of an individual's
conciousness moving through historical time. In autobiography,
then, the act of narration necessarily takes precedence over fidelity
to historical truth. Consequently, even 'conventional'
autobiographies which evince little formal or technical
experimentation are only a general approximation of the
individual's registering of reality; they are, 'stylized' self-portraits,
products of contemporary narrative imperatives rather than
personal history.

Further complications arise when it is understood that attempted
self-portrayal results in an identity which is neither the same
as the historical self nor in itself a completed new self. The act
of autobiographical revelation is not so much a vehicle for
resurrecting past selves but rather a means of pursuing an essential
and ideal self which, ultimately, escapes final definition. Each
practitioner of the autobiographical process aspires toward an
absolute self; but whether an individual can know that self or,
having once understood it, can render it as an entity which another
person can perceive, remains unanswerable. Consequently, in the
final analysis, autobiography remains more an indication of how
the self might be known than a successful depiction of the self. As
William Spengemann has observed, all autobiographers set up a
dynamic relationship between the two series of personae, the
supposed historical selves depicted in the text and the evolving
selves of present consciousness which simultaneously creates, and
reacts to, them.[12] Yet this tension remains but an indicator of the
author's absolute self; the attempt to render that self is a gesture,
an effort which is never fully completed. Even a highly
experimental autobiography such as O'Casey's, which devises
numerous narrative strategies to provide access to the self,
ultimately directs attention to the process itself rather than the
ostensible subject of the work. It is one of the inherent paradoxes
of the genre that the focus of autobiography is finally directed
away from the life as it was lived and toward the means by which
the life can be known and rendered on the page. And yet, it is in
the very attempt to present such insights, the effort to create
images which approximate an author's sense of an absolute self,
that a work achieves its true autobiographical voice, that it

becomes an authentic reflection of contemporary consciousness.

There are other factors influencing the materials of auto-biography. Trapped as he is within his present perspective on his past, an autobiographer wil be predisposed to trace a pattern in the evolution of former selves which finds culmination in contemporary tenets of identity. But access to the past world is possible only through the prism of memory, which in both its conscious and unconscious modes can be faulty and irrational, placing great importance on some experiences while censoring or even repressing others. Inadequacies in recollection are frequently compensated for by the assistance of interpretation and imagination. Indeed, it might be claimed, as Edwin Muir does in his autobiography, that imagination provides the only avenue of access to one's past:

Time wakens a longing more poignant than all the longings caused by the divisions of lovers in space, for there is no road back into its country. Our bodies were not made for that journey; only the imagination can venture upon it; and the setting out, the road, and the arrival: all is imagination.[13]

Thus, autobiographical memory — the ostensible means of resur-recting the past — produces a distorted account of experiences; this false emphasis is further compounded when events are given a retrospective coherence compatible with narrative imperatives. Exploration and evocation of former selves is, therefore, more a creative than a recollective act. Though seeming to provide access to earlier moments, the act of remembering and narrating the past is, in practice, a function of present consciousness. As James Olney puts it,

the autobiographer imagines into existence another person, another world, and surely it is *not* the same, in any real sense, as that past world that does not, under any circumstances, nor however much we may wish it, now exist.[14]

It is evident, then, that autobiographical memory must be under-stood to possess a scope and method of manifestation beyond its conventional, denotative function. It needs to be viewed in the broad comprehensive terms that Giambattista Vico saw it:

Memory has thus three aspects: memory when it remembers things, imagination when it alters or imitates them and invention when it gives them a new turn or puts them into proper arrangement and relationship.[15]

Only with such a non-restrictive understanding of memory can the
transformation of personal history by autobiographers such as
O'Casey be fully appreciated.

Because the issue of biographical accuracy in O'Casey's
autobiography has given rise to much misunderstanding and
controversy, it needs to be discussed in some detail. To begin with,
in his treatment of the events of his past, O'Casey was far from
being unique. Indeed, he need only have looked to the examples of
his fellow Irish writers, George Moore and W. B. Yeats, both
of whose autobiographies raise similar questions of factual
reliability.[16] The most striking feature of Moore's three-volume
Hail and Farewell! is his disregard for the truth of a given situation,
a fact all the more unusual in the light of his stated commitment
to the honesty of his story: 'if I were to introduce a thread of fiction
into this narrative, the weft would be torn asunder.'[17] Yet, as
different readers have pointed out, Moore is guilty on several
occasions of obvious falsehoods. Some of the more blatant of
these: he ascribes to himself a visit which a friend had made to
Chinon; he recounts in detail a meeting with Verlaine which never
took place; and the volumes are rife with conversations premised
on fabricated episodes. Yet, Moore would not consider these patent
fictions in the same light as would an objective witness. For him,
they embodied the spirit of a particular period, the essential mood
of a specific event, the remembered impression of a conversation.
If challenged, Moore would claim that he was attempting to
capture the essence of an experience rather than its prosaic details.
As John Freeman points out in his study of Moore,

Fact is to be distinguished from fiction, and yet fiction is not to be rejected;
for in Moore's case it often serves him as images serve a poet. That is to
say, it is false, and yet more illuminating than a narrow truth.[18]

Moore asserts likewise in *Vale* when he claims that 'the eyes of the
imagination [are] clearer than the physical eyes.'[19]

Yeats, too, was acutely aware of the inherent ambiguity of the
recollective process, as he reveals in the often quoted sentence from
the preface to *Reveries Over Childhood and Youth*: 'I have changed
nothing to my knowledge; and yet it must be that I have changed
many things without my knowledge'[20] Even this disclaimer of
conscious distortion is not quite accurate, as Yeats himself admits
in a letter to his father, in which, writing of the portrait of Edward
Dowden contained in the work, he says,

he was helpful and friendly when I began to write and I give him credit
for it. But in my account of Dublin I had to picture him as a little unreal,
set up for contrast beside the real image of O'Leary.[21]

Yeats and Moore both recognize, as most great literary autobiographers do, that beyond the details of historical truth lies the
more essential truth of the imagination, that autobiography — to
borrow Cleanth Brooks's statement about poetry — presents the
truth of coherence, not the truth of correspondence.

A dramatic example of imagination's overriding historical truth
can be seen in O'Casey's account of his first earnings as a writer.
In the autobiography, he says that, having written *The Story of the
Irish Citizen Army*, Sean 'was to get fifteen pounds on its day of
publication.' (IV, 19–20) He tries to cash the cheque to buy some
necessities for his sickly mother, who is near death, but no one will
honour it. He is, consequently, unable to provide her with a few
comforts in her last moments. Readers looking here for historical
accuracy may raise their eyebrows at O'Casey's conflation of
events. Mrs Casside died in November 1918, whereas the book on
the Citizen Army was not published until July 1919. Although it is
possible that O'Casey was promised payment on delivery of the
manuscript, *Lady Gregory's Journals* makes it clear that his
memory had insistently fused the two experiences.[22] In her entry
for June 8, 1924, she recounts how O'Casey, visiting her at Coole
Park, still grieved for his mother; Lady Gregory then goes on to
quote his statements about Mrs Casside's death and the £15 cheque:

I had written a little story. The publishers promised me £15 for it, and after
it was published I wanted the money and went three times for it but could
never get it. Then when my mother was so ill I had to go again to press
for it, and I did get it, but when I came back she was gone.[23]

The reliability of both accounts of these events is further undermined by his telling Lady Gregory that his mother's funeral 'had to
be put off until I could get change for the cheque. I thought I should
have to go to the bank, but I went to the Rector and he cashed it.'
In the autobiography, on the other hand, he says that a grocer
named Murphy cashed the cheque, but only after a delay of a few
days while he had established that there were funds for it.

The research of Martin Margulies has brought to light other
anomalies in the autobiographical account of Mrs Casside's death.
According to Margulies, Sean was not alone, since his brother
Michael, who had returned from the army two months previously,
was now living at home. It was Michael, not Sean, who registered
the death. And the dazed grief which the autobiography ascribes to
Sean hardly reflects his reported behaviour on that intensely
dramatic night.[24]

It is clear that in recollecting this experience, O'Casey gives an imaginative reconstruction rather than a factually reliable account. Yet, clothed in the narrative is O'Casey's remembrance of what remained for him the more enduring truth of the situation. Through a long, arduous life, Mrs Casside had had few moments to alleviate her struggle: her husband had died early, she had buried several children, and those who survived had not provided much material help to her. Earlier in this chapter recounting her death, O'Casey emphasizes that, although Sean's three brothers and sister 'were clever, each in his own way,' they had accomplished nothing with their lives: 'But they were all four failures: no one was there to point a way further on from where they found themselves when they entered into personal and responsible life'. (IV, 23) For many years, much of Mrs Casside's love, attention and hopes had been focussed on her youngest child, Johnny. But as she faces death, this son is in his late thirties, unemployed, with little prospect either of establishing a home and family life or of getting on in the world. She would die unaware that her son would indeed manage to transcend the limitations of his environment, would break the cycle of deprivation and unfulfilled aspirations by becoming a famous literary figure. She would never know that her life of sacrifice would be vindicated by her son's achievements as a great playwright. To O'Casey's retrospective eyes, the irony of his belated success is the governing framework in his narration of the events surrounding his debut as a paid writer. To reinforce the pathos of the situation as well as to strengthen the confluence of these two major events of Sean's life, O'Casey contrives to juxtapose them dramatically in the account of Mrs Casside's passing:

He'd disturb her no more: he'd let her come out of it her own way, or quietly go her own way out of the world.
   He went over to the fire, and set the kettle on it for a cup of tea. He pulled over the little table, set pen, ink, and paper on it, stiffening himself to go on writing his *Three Shouts on a Hill* — a shout at the Gaelic League, a shout at Sinn Fein, and a shout at Labour . . . He wouldn't part with this new work for less than twenty-five pounds. With cunning, that would keep him going for a year, and give him time to think of something else to do. (IV, 30)

Sitting at the table, he soon becomes aware of a pervading silence: he goes to the bed and discovers that his mother has died quietly in her sleep. Of significance in this account (aside from the unlikelihood of his attempting to write as his mother lay dying) is that O'Casey's imaginative reconstruction contains what is for him as autobiographer the essential truth: his mother died before his success might comfort her last days, and he was denied the pleasure of sharing with her the achievement of his long-held ambition. By dovetailing these experiences, O'Casey not only lends a bitter-sweet flavour to both of them but also signals the end of a significant period in Sean's life and the beginning of a more promising future.

This imaginative dimension of autobiography poses obvious difficulties for those seeking historical accuracy and factual reliability, particularly for those assuming it to be a characteristic of the genre to speak truthfully about the events selected. Although capable of encompassing factual truth, autobiographies are not necessarily, and never consistently, factually true. It is this understanding of the genre that led André Maurois to commend Goethe's choice of title for his autobiography: 'Goethe was wise enough to give his autobiography the title *Poetry and Truth*; and it is in fact almost impossible that a record of a life should not be a mixture of poetry and truths'.[25]

O'Casey himself claims that he is not unduly concerned with the truth of facts. In *Sunset*, he raises the issue of the nature of truth:

What is Truth? Man in his individual nature was still asking the question, and man in the mass was answering it. Facts, though true, were not Truth; they were but minor facets of it. Parts, but not the whole. (VI, 97–98)[26]

Even more revealing of O'Casey's ambivalence towards historical accuracy is a passage from a letter written in 1945, as the third volume of the autobiography was about to be published. Worried that some passages of the manuscript might be libellous, his publisher had his solicitor read them over. One of the sections he questioned was the chapter, 'House of the Dead', in which Sean is depicted visiting his brother-in-law, Benson, in a mental asylum. Organized around Sean's conversation with one of the doctors, the chapter gives a chilling, surreal picture of the institution. The solicitor's legal estimate of this material was forwarded to O'Casey: 'The Doctor in charge of the asylum, although not mentioned by name, is described in some detail and would presumably be easily identifiable. If alive, he might claim to be injured by this account of an interview with him.'[27] O'Casey responded to this legal opinion: 'The "doctor" here described never existed. He is purely a phantom of my imagination, as is most of the chapter. He couldn't be "identifiable" since he never lived. And anyway, the incidents, fantastic, took place forty years ago. The whole thing, bar the account of Benson's madness, is, of course, pure sardonic fantasy.' Not only is O'Casey's admission that the doctor was an imaginary figure revealing, of even greater significance is his indifference to the distinction between facts and fantasy: although 'the incidents, fantastic' — what he calls 'the whole thing' — are a product of his imagination, he still maintains that they 'took place forty years ago.' Here, O'Casey demonstrates a common attitude of autobiographers who hold that the truth of feelings, the remembered sense of the final meaning of events, is of more importance than an accurate account of them. It is his impressionistic and emotional associations of an experience that guide his attempt to define its present meaning for him. Indeed, from the very outset of the autobiography, O'Casey's use of the objectively distanced 'Johnny', his eschewing of the more immediate and traditionally responsible 'I' with the expectations of honesty and immediacy that it connotes, suggests that strict adherence to fact is not a priority for him.

Lapses in historical accuracy or biographical veracity, however, are by no means conscious efforts to deceive, or even to mislead. Distortions of truth, even blatant fabrications, though false, can be reliable indicators of identity. The truth of autobiography is not to be found by our testing a work against the actual facts as others might know them, but rather in our gradual assessment and eventual understanding of the autobiographer's attitude to the cumulative events of his history. As George Misch puts it, even an autobiographer who lies cannot 'deceive us as to character' for 'the spirit brooding over the recollected material is the truest and most real element in an autobiography.'[28] This is most evident in Rousseau's *Confessions*, a work considered by many to have initiated the tradition of modern autobiographical expression. While on one level it is full of falsehoods and apparent deceptions, on another it is a resoundingly honest and forthright self-portrait. The opening page of the *Confessions* sounds the note which established the work as a radical departure in autobiographical writing:

I have resolved on an enterprise which has no precedent, and which, once complete, will have no imitator. My purpose is to display to my kind a portrait in every way true to nature, and the man I shall portray will be myself.[29]

What marks the distinctly modern sensibility of Rousseau's autobiography is his awareness of the nature of the self and his recognition of the difficulties in being truthful when writing about it. For Rousseau, understanding and defining the self was an elusive proposition, not only in the moment-by-moment experience of living but particularly in the process of recollection. The truth about one's self, the true meaning of one's life, could not be summed up and presented as a known, finite entity; it would have to be embodied in the context of one's life. Selfhood cannot be explored analytically, but only through the presentation of experiences accumulated through the years. And the truth that ultimately can be known is a particular kind of truth, based on the feelings connected with an event rather than the accuracy of the factual details surrounding it. For Rousseau, this truth is absolute: 'I may omit or transpose facts, or make mistakes in dates; but I cannot go wrong about what I have felt.' (O'Casey himself uses strikingly similar words in a letter to Daniel Macmillan in which he says of the autobiography, 'Of course, some of my conceptions may be wrong — nay, all of them may be so — but they are all honest; though that isn't saying that they are true or proper'.)[30] Rousseau recognizes that the best means of providing access to the truth of his inner self is the presentation of remembered feelings. On the premise that he has no doubts about the truth of his feelings, he is not concerned with locating precisely the original experience that produced them. Nor, as Georges Poulet has noted, is it important to him 'that the emotion of the past and the emotion of the present overlap and mingle so intimately that one never knows whether the Rousseau who is speaking to us is the one who is narrating the story or the one whose life is being narrated.'[31] In the process of recollecting past experiences, Rousseau and all autobiographers lend a subjective quality to them which they did not possess as they initially occurred. In autobiography, the subjectivity of the recording self distorts the objectivity of the recorded self. In fact, in the very process of doing so, autobiography attains the level of truth which it is most capable of achieving.

An example of the supremacy in this dynamic relationship is seen in *Drums* when O'Casey wishes to reveal Sean's attitude toward religion at the time of his brother's death:

The hold of the faith had weakened well on Sean himself. Though he hadn't said farewell, the anchor was getting weighed, and his ship of life was almost about to leave the harbour. He no longer thought that God's right hand, or His left one either, had handed the Bible out of Heaven, all made up with chapter and verse and bound in a golden calfskin. Darwin's flame of thought had burned away a lot of the sacred straw and stubble, and following men had cleanly shown how incredible much of the Bible was, contradicting itself so often and so early that no one could argue with it, rearing up an imposition of fancy, myth, and miracle coloured by neither fact nor figure. (III, 27)

Here, O'Casey is seen attempting to balance the dual perspective inherent in the autobiographical process, to avoid describing unfolding events from the knowledgeable perspective of what they have become. However, in the very act of trying to suggest Sean's gradual loss of religious convictions, O'Casey's statements, and in particular their incredulous tone, belie the supposedly tentative, still-questioning remnants of earlier faith. The disbelief of the autobiographer takes precedence over former religious doubts.

The procedure of turning to one's past for purposes of self-scrutiny and self-exploration is, therefore, inextricably tied to contemporary consciousness. While an autobiographer may employ the conventional mode of distinguishing between the work's protagonist and his creator, neatly exchanging the mask of hero for that of narrator (third-person narration is but an elaboration of the mask), the reader is never quite fooled. Convention expects that we acquiesce to the ruse of role playing, but we seldom forget that although the unfolding drama contains a series of apparently historical characters — including, of course, the various metamorphoses of the protagonist — the director of proceedings remains the contemporary autobiographer. Despite limitations in the script inherited from his past, which will require that the earlier self play certain roles, the autobiographer-as-director has ultimate control over the performance. Because the role of contemporary orchestrator of ceremonies has been moulded by intervening events, the story recounted is more an indication of present identity than an explication of past selves. The reconstruction of former experiences, the demonstrable shape that narration imposes on them, is the true embodiment of autobiographical identity.

If, then, in contemplating past selves the autobiographical act is in fact a reflection of present consciousness, it can hardly be a reliable source of historical and biographical information. The term 'autobiography' can never be considered simply as a biography of an individual written by himself; certainly not if the denotations of objectivity and honesty usually associated with 'biography' are automatically transferred. This is particularly true of an autobiography such as O'Casey's, given the many experimental techniques and literary devices that he draws on to render his self-image on the page. Yet, until very recently, and still in some quarters, critical assessment of his autobiography has inevitably become entangled in the question of factual reliability. Reviews of succeeding volumes as they appeared became clear instances of a work being judged (and not surprising, often found wanting) by the wrong criteria.[32] For example, Padraic Colum, otherwise a sensitive reader of the work, encounters difficulties when he insists on looking for precise biographical data. Attempting to account for the extremely partisan images of, among others, Douglas Hyde, Arthur Griffith, George Russell and Constance Markievicz, Colum explains them away with the waggish maxim: 'One must hope that readers will take certain noted personages in the autobiography as interesting characters who have somehow got misnamed'.[33] On the basis of his own knowledge, Colum may certainly disagree with O'Casey's portrayal of these figures. But that awareness cannot be applied to an autobiography as it might to a historical or biographical work. Though O'Casey has given a highly distorted picture of these people, even treated some of them unfairly, what is of prime importance is that these are the terms in which he remembers and evaluates them. He does, of course, attempt to win us over to his perception of them since all autobiography involves special pleading and a distinctly subjective view of the world. But those who would seek an impartial account of events and people must look beyond autobiography. It is the image of O'Casey — whether favourable or not — which his opinions reveal that is of autobiographical importance. It may be salutary to compare objective facts with his use of them, as long as such a searching out of discrepancies is confined to establishing O'Casey's editorial stamp on experiences. Otherwise, the exercise of examining his materials for correlations to biographical and historical events can soon lead to troublesome and, ultimately, unanswerable questions. For example, in 'A Coffin Comes to Ireland', the opening chapter of *Pictures*, the attention of the biographical or historical critic would presumably be on whether these were, in fact, the actual circumstances in which the young Johnny learned of the death of Parnell: was the news made public in Ireland at this late hour of night? Did it appear in the early papers? Were these the actual weather conditions? Did Mrs Casside make those statements and Archie respond in this way? But this line of questioning becomes futile, indeed irrelevant, a few pages later when the awakened Johnny, sitting by the fire with a comic book, dozes into a reverie providing a summary of the various forces in Ireland which contributed to the destruction of Parnell, an account replete with vivid scenes in which St Patrick, 'calling over the banisters of the

top storey of heaven', encourages Irish Catholics to turn their backs
on Parnell and support Tim Healy. Later in the autobiography,
even more fantastical and surrealistic passages are to be found,
thereby confirming the unreliability of the text as a source of
factual information.

An example of the difficulties that can arise if the work is used
as source material is the controversy about O'Casey's origins
between David Krause, the editor of his letters, and the Irish
journalist, Anthony Butler. Butler strenuously criticizes Krause for
accepting O'Casey's claims, particularly in the autobiography, that
his was an impoverished upbringing in the tenements of Dublin.
To support his argument, Butler believes he has found factual
inaccuracies in the autobiography, citing the opinion of an O'Casey
niece who denied that the playwright was 'at any time reduced to
the condition he describes in his allegedly factual autobiography.'[34] It is hardly accurate, to say the least, to refer to a
work where St Patrick addresses Dubliners from the top of Nelson's
Pillar, Brian Boru plays chess with Mailmurra, and Eve convinces
Adam to leave paradise, as 'allegedly factual.' One has to
acknowledge that O'Casey's purposes have little to do with precise
facts, actual dates, real events — all the stock-in-trade of the
reference shelf — but rather that he uses the outlines of his personal
history as the framework through which he can explore his
consciousness and arrive at the essential truths which have shaped
and given meaning to his life.

The definition of autobiography as an individual's written
account of chosen life experiences embraces the question of form in
autobiography, at least to the extent that it is possible to do so. The
term autobiography, unlike those of the novel, the lyric poem, or
the sonnet (all of which indicate the form in which various possible
subjects are treated) in no way suggests the manner of dealing with
materials, or even the author's angle of perception on them.
Indeed, the term does not even specify prose as the proper means
of autobiographical expression; poetry, or a combination of poetry
and prose, is not necessarily excluded.[35] And the term gives only
a very general idea of the shaping principle that would order the
materials of the work: the progression of the hero from whatever
is the starting point — his birth or earliest moments — to the time
which the autobiographer sees as the culmination of that
development. We are left, then, with only the vaguest sense of
autobiographical form; it is ultimately determined by an author's
willingness to avail of the possibilities inherent in the genre. For just

as contents can be chosen on shifting and fluctuating principles, autobiographical form can likewise be a changing and dynamic phenomenon: it may be influenced by the inherent shape of experiences, by the author's perception of their cumulative significance, by the discovery of layers of meaning hidden in the past, even by the process of recovery itself. As the autobiographer recognizes, sees interrelationships, and attempts to trace connections with former selves, new formal options will present themselves. As autobiographical purposes shift and change, principles of form will grow and modulate. Indeed, this close dependency between intention and form is often such that the pursuit and exploration of formal options can modify an autobiographer's purposes. Consequently, just as readers should not necessarily look for consistency of intention, so also must they avoid seeking only a static and predictable form. As Francis R. Hart has suggested, 'the interpretative reader of autobiography is in search of an evolving mixture of pattern and situation'; he must seek to identify what is formative and distinctive by examining 'the total emergent reciprocity of situation and activity and pattern.'[36] In matters relating to form, then, an autobiographer's choice is much more open than in most other literary genres.[37] He is free to draw on a wide range of compositional techniques or representational devices to bring his self-image to the page; he can write a successful autobiography without being restricted to a single ordering principle or a static rhetorical posture.

O'Casey's enthusiastic and exuberant response to the technical and formal freedoms offered by the genre of autobiography has, more often than not, been reduced by reviewers and critics to a discussion of his virtuosity as a prose stylist. The autobiography has been as warmly commended for its evocative power as it has been coldly condemned for being derivative ('a poor imitator of Joyce' is a characteristic response) and uncontrolled. Most commentators who have transcended the issue of biographical and historical reliability tend to deal with the question of language, concentrating on O'Casey's prose modulations from passages of lyric beauty to sardonic humour, from outrageous farce to insistent polemics, from street dialogue to surreal images. Although a discussion of his stylistic variations is, as I hope to show in a later chapter, central to any assessment of O'Casey's achievements as an autobiographer, it should be placed in an overall critical framework if it is to be fully enlightening. Indeed, insistent concern with factual or stylistic aspects of the work can lead to a failure to acknowledge and explain more fundamental considerations of form. If an autobiographer has wide options in choosing contents, and great flexibility in narrating and presenting them, what, finally, are the restrictions and limitations which establish the boundaries of the autobiographical genre? If materials can be selected and arranged to reflect a variety of fluctuating purposes, what legitimate expectations can one have with regard to the form of an autobiography? Do not O'Casey's use of third-person narration and his creation of succeeding personae set up a contradition between the identity embodied in the work and the thrust of the autobiographer's life? In short, how can a work which often rearranges events, ignores chronological progression, incorporates blatant fantasies, and employs many of the literary devices associated with the novel, still claim our attention as autobiography? O'Casey's unique response to the genre, his experiments with all aspects of autobiographical form, have, in fact, frequently led to the conclusion that the finished work is an autobiographical novel. Although often unstated, such questions are at the heart of much of the tentative and ambiguous reaction to O'Casey's six-volume creation, and they need to be dealt with if the multifaceted qualities of the work are to emerge.

Despite O'Casey's use of fictional devices to give the work an overall design and unity characteristic of a literary creation, it does not become an autobiographical novel for a variety of reasons, all of which spring from the nature of the relationship between his former personae and himself as author. This is not to imply that a distinction between the genres can be made on the basis either of fidelity to biographical experiences or of literary treatment of them. Resorting to a scale that would place 'facts' or 'truth' at one end, and 'fiction' or 'invention' at the other is of little avail, since, as we have seen, all autobiographers select and transform experiences. In practice, then, the genres exist not at the extremities of some ideal scale but sufficiently close to raise crucial questions about both. What the genres often share — and, indeed, is the source of much of the confusion between them — is the presence, in various degrees and guises, of parallels in the lives of the protagonists and those of their creators. But each author chooses episodes from personal history for very different purposes. How this material functions — the contextual nuances in which it appears, the resonances it creates, the cumulative effects it achieves — constitutes the crucial differences between the genres.

To appreciate this essential distinction it is worthwhile to look briefly at James Joyce's use and transformation of biographical experiences in both *Stephen Hero* and *A Portrait of the Artist as a Young Man*. Pertinent to discussion of O'Casey is that in an autobiographical novel such as *Portrait*, selection and use of biographical data is governed solely by an author's aesthetic considerations and artistic goals; parallels with the author's personal life are incorporated into the narrative texture because of their suitability to his known or emergent literary purposes. In his treatment of these experiences, the complete scope of the novelist's inventiveness is, of course, available to him: the plot will unfold, the character will develop, the thematic thread will be rendered not in accord with the biographical contours of his life but under the dictates of his artistic criteria. For the autobiographical novelist, personal episodes can be touchstones of lived reality which act as points of imaginative departure but, under the exigencies of aesthetic goals, are soon left behind or radically transformed. While an autobiographical novel may have its origins in former versions of the self, its movement is centrifugal, away from a focus on its author and out to aesthetic goals.

As has been observed by many critics, Joyce's difficulties with *Stephen Hero* stemmed from both his proximity to the events being described and his artistic immaturity at the time of the work's composition. In 1906, the author of *Stephen Hero* existed on practically the same temporal plane as Stephen at the end of the fragment; this would have heightened the difficult in discerning what data might be artistically relevant or was merely historical true. The result was inclusion of many experiences which, to use Joyce's own terms, were 'personalized lumps of matter' whose 'individuating rhythm' had not been liberated.[38] Insufficiently transformed biographical events tended to blur the line dividing hero and author, and to work against the achievement of artistic goals.

More significantly, however, Joyce's editorial intrusions — the movement, back and forth between his own views and those of his hero, which Joseph Prescott and others have pointed out — also strengthened the identification of the hero with his creator.[39] Such intrusions are more blatant than those of the 'implied author' or 'fictional narrator' which Wayne Booth found in *Portrait*. These factors, together with Joyce's unclear perception of how the novel would conclude (Richard Ellmann notes that Joyce had not yet seen the climactic end of the work in his departure for the Continent in 1902, and before long had carried it beyond that date[40]) contributed to his frustration with the work. If he had no clear understanding where an unmistakable divergence could be made between hero and author, and if the significance of the hero's experiences had to be repeatedly interpreted by authorial intrusions, then the autonomy of the hero was continually being undermined. At the heart of Joyce's problem, then, was to establish the precise nature of the relationship between himself and his literary character, between biographical events and their potential as literary subject matter.

When writing *Portrait*, Joyce was removed in time by about eight years from the closest episodes being described. With this widening of the gulf to the past, and with the maturity of the intervening years (not the least of which was derived from the experience of writing *Stephen Hero*) Joyce found a perspective that freed him from an over reliance on the details of personal history. The new objectivity and control resulted in the striking differences noted by many critics: the concentration of material, the disciplined focus on Stephen's growing consciousness, the symbolic patterning, the irony, and the authorial distance. While Stephen in *Portrait* becomes a character similar to a former version of the author, the net result of these changes was to diminish the perception of Stephen as a precursor of the author. The various stages of Stephen's growing awareness of his artistic calling are presented as being remembered by, and sifted through the consciousness of, the mature Stephen. By employing this fictional narrator Joyce establishes a buffer between himself and the events of his personal history, thereby widening the distance between them. All experiences of Stephen at significant turning-points in his maturation lead into the self-perceived artist figure who is ready to leave Ireland at the end of the novel. By having the novel build toward this climactic moment in Stephen's life, the thrust of the work is centrifugal, out to Joyce's fictional narrator and away from Joyce the author.

A dramatic example of Joyce's use of personal data for artistic ends occurs when Stephen encounters the seabird girl and dedicates himself to his artistic vocation. In this scene, Stephen is shown to be mesmerized momentarily by the girl's beauty, before he responds with an outburst from his soul as he turns and goes. But the significance of the encounter for him is immediately apparent from its contextual shadings. Acting as a catalyst for Stephen, the girl helps to crystallize his vision of life's artistic potential. In a moment of transcendent insight he becomes aware of, and commits himself to, the values of a higher reality: 'To live, to err, to fall, to triumph, to recreate life out of life!' Because this incident is the climactic embodiment of Stephen's perception of himself as an artistic figure, it is an essential contributing factor in Joyce's achieving his aesthetic goals. That Joyce himself had some such encounter with a girl on Sandymount Strand is only of marginal relevance; it remains no more than a footnote to the main text.

To appreciate how O'Casey's self-portrait is different from Joyce's novel, it is salutary to look at a passage from *Inishfallen* dealing with an incident during a train trip Sean and Lady Gregory take from Coole Park to Dublin. While waiting for a connecting train at Athenry, Sean wanders alone through the old, desolate and windswept town. He is keenly aware of the sterility and decay which pervade the place, the former glory of which gave it the name 'Ford of the King.' Suddenly, out of a grey, half-sunken house a girl emerges, whose beauty, youth, and vitality hypnotize the surprised Sean:

A mass of brown hair gave a golden hue to a pale and trimly-chiselled face, with delicate ears, a straight and slender nose, dignifying a saucy-looking red mouth; while a pair of blue, softly luminous eyes met Sean's admiring stare. She was dressed in a brown coat, open, showing a thin white blouse against which her young breasts pushed, forming a pattern that told Sean they were finely turned and tempting. When she came to the top step, Sean saw that her legs flowed finely into the delightful curving of her body. (IV, 193)

Although he sees this girl as an image of beauty, he is unable to bring himself to address her, for 'His mind had been too full of the loneliness and the ruin to be so suddenly called upon to reflect with words the wonder in his mind.' Up to this point, there is little in O'Casey's description to indicate the autobiographical relevance of the passage; it is presented as a fleeting experience of the kind common in daily life, and seems to have no bearing on the development of Sean. The wistful, evocative power of the language, together with the cumulative impact of the details, might suggest that its significance has been lost sight of in the process of imaginative recollection. Indeed, in its essentials — the hero's beholding the girl whose beauty momentarily intrigues him — the passage is not dissimilar to Joyce's account of Stephen's encounter with the seabird girl. The key to the differences between the genres lies in the role which each incident plays, the overall function each is made to perform. It is significant that immediately after the initial description of the girl, O'Casey shifts the narrative focus to a more obviously autobiographical level:

He looked at his watch: it was time to go back to Lady Gregory, back towards Dublin. He went slowly back to the grimy station, imagining what he would have said to the lass while she walked by his side, or stood where she had been, to listen. He would have told her he knew all the big men of Dublin, all the poets, and was a friend of Lady Gregory's, and of the great poet, Yeats. He would tell her that he himself was a dramatist, and even something of a poet. (IV, 193)

The immediate development here is that he goes back to Lady Gregory, catches his train to Dublin, and muses about the girl. The evocation of Lady Gregory and Yeats, and the indication that Sean himself is a dramatist, strengthens his identification with the Dublin literary world of the time. But beyond this, for the exiled O'Casey, the girl, 'framed in the muddy-yellow decay of the house behind her, like a lone cherry blossom thrusting itself shyly and impertinently forward through the ragged, withering foliage of an ageing tree', is an archetypal Irish figure of youth and vitality being smothered before she can achieve fulfilment. The fourth volume has been tracing the various forces in Ireland which, at precisely the moment the dramatist was realizing his full potential, made his exile inevitable. To the retrospective autobiographer this vibrant girl doomed by her environment is emblematic of what might have befallen himself had he remained in Ireland. He makes this evident in the sentence which concludes this vignette:

Whenever his mind wandered again to the lonely wretchedness of Athenry, he would see this lovely figure, this bud of womanhood, longing for life, standing, alone and radiant, in the midst of the houses, quietly resolute in sinking to their own decay. (IV, 194)

By integrating the heightened description of the girl into the pattern of the house metaphor which, as remarked in Chapter I, is operative throughout the autobiography, O'Casey lends weight to his reasons for leaving Ireland, and confirms the wisdom of his doing so. He suggests his current view that had he stayed longer in Ireland, in his Irish house, he too could have found himself sinking into a sterile existence. But what is significant here is that the literary handling of the incident enhances rather than undermines the process of autobiographical revelation. Edwin Muir, in his lyrical and evocative autobiography, speaks of the temptation of pursuing the literary treatment of biographical material too far: 'I could follow these images freely if I were writing an autobiographical novel. As it is, I have to stick to the facts and try to fit [the images] in where they will fit in.'[41] Despite O'Casey's even bolder and more innovative means of rendering material, there can always be found a return to the 'facts', to the series of historical events which he perceives as having moulded his character.

What emerges from this comparison is that the relationship between author and former experiences is quite distinct for Joyce and O'Casey. Notwithstanding his exceptionally different means of presenting material, O'Casey's self-portrait evinces the defining characteristic of autobiography — his plot traces the process by which the protagonist becomes his own creator. This convergent or centripetal narrative pattern of autobiography may be likened, as Paul Ricoeur has observed, to a quest which is completed when the historical self becomes the present self. Ricoeur sees Augustine's *Confessions* as paradigmatic in this regard, for there

the form of the travel is interiorized to such a degree that there is no longer any privileged place in space to which to return. . . . The quest has been absorbed into the movement by which the hero — if we may still call him by that name — becomes *who he is*.[42]

Usually, as this process occurs, as the protagonist, increasingly resembles the author, the narrative pace slackens and the atmosphere becomes less highly charged. The autobiographical novel, on the other hand, usually builds to some decisive climax in the hero's development. The very meaning of an autobiographical novel coalesces in the events of the closing pages, not beyond them in the person of the author.

Because a developing thread in plot which finally extends out to the autobiographer is a crucial factor distinguishing an autobiography from an autobiographical novel, the presence of material which establishes just such a forward movement in the story should be readily apparent in O'Casey's self-portrait. And indeed, throughout the autobiography, despite its six-volume length and a compositional time span of over twenty years, O'Casey draws particular attention to the ultimate pattern of convergence between himself and his former selves. He emphasizes that the basic function of his contents — even those which are patently fictional — is to chart the inexorable development of the protagonist until he becomes the autobiographer.

The plot of the autobiography begins with the hero's birth announced in the ambitious, two-page sentence which opens the work. Following this is an imaginative reconstruction of the hierarchical world of late Victorian Dublin where the various social classes are epitomized by the different horse-drawn vehicles on the streets — landau, brougham, tramcar, laden lorry or jaunting car. Despite the cruelties and inequities which the newborn child must face in this world, he doggedly makes his way through the first eleven or so years of his life. At the end of the volume, with the discovery of a poem by Tennyson, the boy's introduction to the realities of his world reaches its first stage of completion: 'Well, he'd learned poethry and had kissed a girl. If he hadn' gone to school, he'd met the scholars; if he hadn' gone into the house, he had knocked at the door.' (I, 191)

The narrative plotline becomes a more pronounced feature of *Pictures* since the book is organized around a series of discoveries and initiations: the growing youth responds enthusiastically to Irish history; he learns about religion; he performs in theatrical events; he has his first sexual experience; and he continues to mature as a result of reading an eclectic selection of books.

In comparison to his growth in the first two volumes, the hero's progression in *Drums* is more diffuse and imperceptible, since the context in which it occurs becomes increasingly varied and complex. There is a series of tragic occurrences in his family which, along with his reading, leads to his loss of religious beliefs. His enthusiasm for nationalist ideals gives way to his growing commitment to socialism. Most revealing is the presentation of his first awareness of his desire to write. This occurs when, on visiting the body of a union member who has been killed by police batons, he reflects: 'A warning to Sean. Keep well away from them. That he'd do, for he wanted to live, feeling an urge of some hidden thing in him waiting its chance for an epiphany of creation.' (III, 222) The Joycean echo is significant in foreshadowing the nature of his future development. When *Drums* ends with the outbreak of the Easter Rebellion, he sees no particular reason for rejoicing; he has already decided 'that the workers wouldn't get much from this crowd if ever they came into power.' (III, 231)

Inishfallen carries forward the personal, political and literary stories of Sean's life, showing how developments on all three fronts made departure from Ireland inevitable. With the death of his mother and the end of a serious involvement with a girlfriend, significant emotional ties with Irish life are severed. The bitterness and destructiveness of the Civil War, the growing influence of the Catholic clergy, and the conservative leadership of de Valera make Ireland a social and political reality from which he feels increasingly alienated. When his extraordinary success as an Abbey playwright soon provokes controversy and resentment, his last remaining reasons for staying in Ireland are removed. At the end of *Inishfallen*, while acknowledging the people and events which 'had had a part in making his life as it was now, and in streaking it with many colours,' he believes that 'he would soon be crossing the border of his own life. To London!' (IV, 282)

With Sean's arrival in England at the beginning of the fifth volume, the materials of the autobiography become more specifically focused. Because his identity is now primarily defined as a dramatist, information is provided about his experiences in the London theatre and about the direction of his dramatic development, including the controversies over both *The Silver Tassie* and *Within The Gates*. The most significant personal event in this period is his meeting with the beautiful actress, Eileen Carey. With their marriage and the birth of a first child, his domestic life blossoms, despite financial insecurity and continued artistic frustration.

In *Sunset*, the story of Sean's evolution becomes much more gradual; there are now fewer major changes to be recorded. Instead, the materials tend to confirm and consolidate facets of identity defined earlier. While the period sees the writing of several new plays and continuing books of the autobiography, it is also a time of assessment and reflection on both his past world and his own accomplishments. When the black-outs, air raids and gas masks of the war finally give way to peace, O'Casey completes his epic self-portrait with Sean's farewell and benediction to the world. In this final volume (the title of which is taken from Tennyson's last collection of poetry), the focus, after much adjusting and re-adjusting of the lens, is on the respected but isolated author as he nears the end of his journey through life. The last chapter of the book, echoing the opening of the first volume, again equates the image of the house of life with his world:

Soon it will be time to kiss the world goodbye. An old man now, who, in the nature of things, might be called out of the house any minute. Little left now but a minute to take a drink at the door — deoch an doruis; a drink at the door to life as it had been with him and another to whatever life remained before him. Down it goes! Slainte! (VI, 218)

To reinforce the radical transformation of the Tennysonian world of his childhood, O'Casey again evokes the street vehicles of Victorian Dublin:

It was a long look-back to the time when he remembered wearing the black-and-red plaid petticoat — a little rob-roy; and he sitting on the doorstep of a Lower Dorset Street house, watching the antics of the older and braver kids let loose on the more dangerous roadside; in his ears the sound of lorry, dray, and side-car, with their iron-rimmed wheels, clattering over the stony setts of the street; in his nose the itching smell of dusty horse-dung. (VI, 218)

It is evident, then, that having begun with the birth of its hero, the work moves toward that moment when, on the final pages, he merges with his creator. Rather than present a tight chronological sequence, O'Casey approximates the biographical thrust of his past history and highlights the defining contours of his journey to the present. Yet, although he avoids many details of his personal evolution, pays scant attention to historical context and frequently interrupts the forward movement of the narrative, he establishes obvious bonds which show the integral relationship between protagonist and author and thereby confirm the generic nature of the work.

Another important facet of the relationship between an autobiographer and his former personae, one which also reinforces the disinction from an autobiographical novel, is the periodic validation of former experiences, especially at key moments of change and growth. This phenomenon goes beyond the obvious relationship between protagonist and author established on every page of the autobiography by all the strategies of composition. Nor is it the conventional and anticipated procedure of depicting the hero as a former version of the writer's self. It is a more direct intervention in the narrative, an expressed manifestation of the autobiographer's voice in the thread of historical materials; as such, it is a contemporary acknowledgement of responsibility for, if not identification with, the many precursory roles which emerge on the autobiographical page. (It is these obvious authorial intrusions that characterize the *Stephen Hero* manuscript, limiting the effect of transforming autobiographical experiences for literary ends.) In an autobiography, this intervention may function to underline the divergence between the usually naive and misguided hero and (not surprising) the more astute author; or, on the other hand, it may serve to confirm the validity of the hero's responses in a given situation, now that they are assessed from the more removed vantage-point of the author. Sometimes, though not as frequently, it may be the open admission that former actions were, on reflection, simply wrong. Manifestation of the author's voice may be seen as especially appropriate in a work employing third-person narration, where authorial presence has the appearance of being at a further remove from the more immediately and insistently present 'I' of conventional autobiographical narration. Notwithstanding its ostensible purpose, however, the author's intervention is a dramatic reminder, despite all the conventions of distance and historicity, of the ongoing bond between him and his former personae.

An example of explicit interjection in the historical context occurs in O'Casey's work when he describes Sean's response to having his first play performed on the Abbey stage:

Odd, he felt no great elation . . . He felt, though, as he stood quiet in the vestibule, that he had crossed the border of a little, but a great, new kingdom of life, and so another illusion was born in his poor susceptible soul. He didn't know enough then that it was no great thing to be an Abbey playwright; and afterwards, when he knew a lot more, he was glad he had suffered himself to feel no jubilation to mar his future by thinking too much of a tiny success. . . . (IV, 123)

Here, as contemporary autobiographer, O'Casey shows how his early naive self was a precursor to the wiser man who later emerged; and the confirmation in the present of that previous maturation reinforces the identity of the author with his protagonist. A less explicit but equally revealing instance of this feature of the work follows upon the long, opening sentence of the first volume. Having provided a detailed and vivid description of Mrs Casside's appearance three years after Johnny's birth, when she was aged forty, O'Casey continues:

And all this was seen, not then, but after many years when the dancing charm and pulsing vigour of youthful life had passed her by, and left her moving a little stiffly, but still with charm and still with vigour, among those whose view of the light of life had dimmed and was mingling more and more with a spreading darkness; and vividly again, and with an agonized power, when she was calmly listening to the last few age-worn beats of her own dying heart. (I, 11–12)

Obviously, the boy could not have so fully apprehended what his mother looked like when he was three; the adult's perception of his mother at forty is an imaginative projection into a past which he could hardly have even remembered. Later still, the youthful mother is conjured up again when the adult man observes the frail woman in her declining years. And, finally, her vigorous appearance is recalled yet again by the autobiographer writing twenty or so years after her death. The shared remembrances of all three personae affirm the lineage between the author and his precursory selves and, thus, attest to the work's generic nature. Among some of the more obvious prefigurations which O'Casey acknowledges, the stories of the sickly Johnny Casside, the enthusiastic nationalist Sean O'Cathasaigh, the ardent socialist Jack Casside, and the controversial dramatist Sean O'Casey all contribute to, and finally merge into, the identity of the auto-biographer.

A third and final distinction between an autobiographical novel such as Joyce's *Portrait* and O'Casey's autobiography lies in the role of literary devices. Frequently enhancing, indeed even creating the images which constitute the plot and structure of O'Casey's autobiography, are many fictional techniques which lend the work a cohesion and unity characteristic of a literary creation. In fact, his inordinate reliance on such devices serves to accentuate the basic tension at the heart of the autobiographical impulse: it is the conflict between what Roy Pascal, in his pioneering study of the genre, identifies as 'truth' and 'design.'[43] The precise terms of this relationship cannot be determined, however, by perceiving design as synonymous with ornamentation, a mere rhetorical flourish which, while pleasing, must not abrogate the claims of truth. Instead, as O'Casey repeatedly makes evident, an autobiographer's materials may often be the product of imaginative interpretation, creative arrangement or literary treatment: such strategies of design are employed to cast light on his protagonist's evolution. Whereas he may be as much concerned with the form and style of the work — its shape, language, and structural unity — as autobiographical novelists, such attention supplements, and indeed often embodies, his autobiographical truth. For example, O'Casey's orchestration of the incident of the girl at Athenry so that it is integrated into the metaphoric pattern of the house found throughout the work, is the key to his retrospective perception of the significance of that event. Similarly, on other occasions, obvious fictions are used to underline the autobiographer's present understanding of the meaning of earlier experiences. But his use of formal options and technical innovations occurs in the circumscribed context of rendering a life-story that has a defined destiny. Thus, while the account of his former selves may be presented through fabricated conversations, contrived events, unlikely scenes, even fantasies and reveries, those passages reinforce the forward movement of the plot. Despite the unusual nature of such techniques, they never obscure the fact that O'Casey's protagonist lives a preordained existence which denies him the kind of open-ended growth available to the hero of an autobiographical novel. In *Portrait*, because Joyce frees Stephen from the inevitability of auto-biographical destiny, and disallows whatever *a priori* assumptions a reader may have about Stephen's ongoing relationship with his environment, he can depict him charged with a potentiality which is not available to the predetermined role which O'Casey's protagonist must play. Seeing Stephen of the *Portrait* as a dramatic character who can respond freely to the forces of his world lends him an ambiguity and an openness toward life which is in contrast to the ultimate determinism which governs O'Casey's protagonist. Thus, notwithstanding O'Casey's many innovations in rendering former selves, his primary concern remains the presentation of those experiences he views as contributing factors to the shaping of his present identity; consequently, the work never does cross into the territory of the autobiographical novel. Since the final effect of the six-volume work has been to hold a mirror up to O'Casey's past life, refracting the imaginative reality of his hero's interaction with his world until he becomes the narrator, its autobiographical nature is confirmed.

The foregoing discussion posits that in selecting and patterning their materials to reflect the process by which earlier selves lead into contemporary identity, all autobiographies — and not just unusual examples of the genre such as O'Casey's — distort and transform personal history. As a written text masquerading as life experiences, a literary self-portrait is an unfaithful reflection of what occurred in the consciousness of the individual. Because an autobiographical narrative is a linguistic creation and therefore a metaphoric means of apprehending and rendering identity, the autobiographical truth it embodies is suggested not stated, approximated not defined. William Spengemann believes that autobiographical language is ultimately allegorical because 'whatever the explicit, sensible referent of any linguistic figure may be, its ultimate and principal referent is always the otherwise ungraspable self.'[44] Although this ideal self will remain elusive as a definable entity, the autobiographical process of pursuing it can itself become an indicator of its unique properties. Thus, the outlines of this perfect self — the truth about identity — can be forthcoming from a careful and comprehensive analysis of the work as literary creation. As Roger Rosenblatt has observed,

it is an ideal which must be read in interstices between subject and object within the autobiography, in the particular selections of the artist-self, and, just as often, in the guesswork that we apply to all books that move us.[45]

Consequently, a literary self-portrait such as O'Casey's which has expanded the imperatives of narrative by drawing extensively on the devices of fiction, which attempts to capture changing modulations of consciousness through innovative technical procedures, must be attended to with sensitivity and imagination. Indeed, O'Casey's eschewing of the more conventional autobiographical approaches, his use of unorthodox techniques of representation, can be viewed as more appropriate for indicating how an intangible self found expression in the amorphous past. A flexible and organic form can be readily acknowledged as being a better means of capturing the fluidity and unpredictability of life than the more rigid, formal structure of conventional auto-biography. As described in a later chapter, O'Casey is continually devising new technical procedures in an ongoing attempt to provide multiple avenues of access to the truth to which he believes his life has been witness. For example, in the closing autobiographical volume, he presents one of the criteria governing his selection and arrangement of material. Describing how he had begun the autobiography, he says that while writing plays he had thought about

setting down some of the things that had happened to himself . . . the things that had woven his life into strange patterns; with the words of a song weaving a way through a ragged coat, or a shroud, maybe, that had missed him and covered another. . . . First weave in a sable tapestry would be the colourful form of her whose name was Susan, ragged dame of dames, so quietly, so desperately courageous. (VI, 70–71)

Here O'Casey claims for himself the freedom to select and order the components of his autobiography in a pattern of his own devising: it is to be a series of images, scenes, characters and events woven into a narrative texture which would be a reflection of his perception of his journey through life. And what becomes evident from an examination of O'Casey's unique approach to auto-biographical form — the constant refocusing of materials, the casual treatment of time and reality, the alternating styles and rhetorical devices — is that his innovations, rather than obscuring the progression of biographical development or undermining the felt sense of individual identity, are the primary means of access to personal consciousness, to his autobiographical truth. In O'Casey's autobiography as in all successful works of self-portrayal — indeed, as with all great works of imaginative literature — form does not remain a mere key to purpose but becomes an expression of it.

A common response to O'Casey's autobiography has been to see it as a source of biographical information on the dramatist's life, and, in particular, as offering insights into his plays. Based, at best, on a somewhat generalized understanding of the genre, these approaches underestimate the value of studying the autobiography as a literary creation in its own right, and consequently overlook the self-images and personal vision it embodies. Certainly, there can be found accurate historical facts and precise personal details, but, at times, biographical episodes are conflated or transformed to achieve images of the self which, although derived from original experiences, are ultimately divergent from them. Like all great autobiographies, the work transcends the mere historical data of the life and, instead, displays the dynamic interplay that characterizes a current assessment of past reality. Rather than viewing the work from a literal or investigative position, readers should be prepared to submit to the more persuasive power of an imaginative interpretation of experience. Only then can an autobiographical identity emerge that will be truer to the author than any factual account of life could hope to be.

Unquestionably, important insights to O'Casey the dramatist can result from a comparison of how personal and historical incidents are manipulated and transformed for different purposes in the autobiography and in the plays. The tendency of such a critical exercise, however, is to remain one-sided, whereby a study of O'Casey's use of materials in the autobiography can provide added insights into his accomplishments in the plays. This may be salutary for an appreciation of the dramatist but, for an understanding of O'Casey's achievements as an autobiographer, critics must also acknowledge the presence and examine the role of 'dramatic' elements in the autobiography. During the long period in which the autobiography was written, O'Casey continued to explore new and experimental dramatic options in the plays. Many of these newly-devised approaches — the disregard for logic and consistency in temporal and physical settings, the movement away from reality, the rapid shifts in focus, the composite features of style — are in evidence throughout the autobiography. This is not at all to imply that an understanding of O'Casey the dramatist is a prerequisite to an appreciation of the self-portrait; it is to claim, however, that if his accomplishments as an autobiographer are to be understood, attention must be paid to all the means he employs as a literary artist in his effort to provide access to the auto-biographical self.

If O'Casey's autobiographical purposes are to be appreciated and his experiments with the genre to be recognized fully, focus must be directed on the complex interdependency of the autobiography's various elements: notwithstanding the work's extraordinary length, we must attempt to discover what, in the face of multiple options, is the rationale behind the materials chosen; we must explore the shifting principles of organization determining the shape of specific paragraphs, chapters and volumes; and, finally, we must assess the role of diverse representational techniques in the portrayal of the protagonist. Since these essential principles of the genre are vital indicators of autobiographical identity, the next three chapters of this study will examine them.

3. PRINCIPLES OF SELECTION

The sheer length of O'Casey's autobiography poses one of the major obstacles to a ready perception of the principles which have determined its content. Difficulties in acquiring a sufficiently wide perspective on the work, in achieving an overview that would facilitate seeing it in its totality, compound the problem of understanding the relevance and function of much of the information presented. Yet, because selection of materials is a basic key to an autobiographer's purposes, attempting to see the rationale behind the choice of contents and determining their role are primary responsibilities for the reader of autobiography. As was pointed out in the previous chapter, the essential factor governing an autobiographer's selection of materials is his desire to depict his protagonist evolving inexorably from his birth or early years to whatever is the perceived culmination of the life-story. It was also claimed that O'Casey's primary criterion in his choice of contents was to establish a plotline showing the ultimate connection between himself and the changing Johnny/Sean.

However, since the relationship between intention and autobiographical form is a dynamic, changing one, a unified and consistent purpose is hardly to be expected throughout the work. As Francis Hart has observed,

formal principles in autobiography evolve and fluctuate as autobiographical intentions interact and shift; a formal problem or option often refocuses the autobiographer's intention or even redefines the nature of his truth.

Such intentions, he continues,

complement or succeed or conflict with each other. Every autobiography can appropriately and usefully be viewed as in some degree a drama of intention, and its dramatic intentionality is another component of the autobiographical situation for the interpreter to attend to.[1]

An autobiography, then, may contain a variety of purposes which overlap and change, creating an organic rather than a strictly

logical unity. As we saw in the opening chapter, O'Casey acknowledged this spontaneous element in autobiographical writing
when he spoke, in the letter to Maroldo, of 'additional ideas
crowding in after the conception of previous ones.' To be aware of
this dynamic feature of the autobiography is not only to recognize
the shifting facets of identity it embodies, but to perceive the
function of many of its seemingly irrelevant passages. Some of
these purposes may emerge only briefly in the ongoing narrative,
while others may be orchestrated within a group of chapters or
throughout several volumes. In achieving their immediate goal,
such intentions also contribute to the autobiography's primary
purpose for they reveal the autobiographer's biases and prejudices,
show his judgement in operation and, in general, reflect the values
and qualities he both admires and dislikes. Although the contents
embodying secondary intentions may initially appear to obscure
the story of the protagonist's development — and even raise doubts
about the work's autobiographical character — ultimately, because
they reveal his personality manifesting itself by responding to
disparate forces, they can add significant dimensions to his
portrait.

The disproportionate amount of information O'Casey provides
on certain people may seem to have but tenuous reference to the
story of the developing protagonist. Yet, such apparently
disgressive material casts some of the secondary characters as
significant indicators of the hero's progress. Such characters are, in
fact, a common feature of autobiographical literature; because of
the influential role they play in the way a person comes to perceive
himself or conducts his life, they may emerge as models for the
protagonist. They allow him to crystallize and define a sense of
self, providing a matrix in which random events and experiences
can be seen to have an overall shape and purpose. Indeed, whether
or not certain figures were so perceived in the past, to the retrospective autobiographer models can be a useful means of
authenticating and structuring the episodes of daily life. As Stephen
Shapiro contends, 'by identifying with models, consciously or
unconsciously, selecting and rejecting, we synthesize the self that
best conforms to our ruling pattern, without ceasing to be
recognizable and typical.'[2] Through this process of identification,
information on models can suggest stages of the hero's evolution,
clarify his attitudes and beliefs, and establish his moral reference
points. O'Casey himself could have been defining the role of a
model when, in *Pictures*, he describes a moment of religious ecstasy

for Johnny as he views Dublin through transformed eyes. At this important point of awareness, the adolescent Johnny articulates the code of behaviour which is to be his guiding principle:

He resolved to be strong; to stand out among many; to quit himself like a man; he wouldn't give even a backward look at the withering things that lived by currying favour with stronger things; no busy moving hand to the hat for him. (II, 218)

His values and code of ethics would be modelled on St MacCua, who placed importance not on the world's wealth but on the simple things of life, particularly on the beautiful creations of the human imagination:

So, something like MacCua, he would seek the things that endured; his treasures would be books, bought by the careful gathering of widely, scattered pence. From life he had learned much; and from books he would learn more of the wisdom thought out, and the loveliness imagined, by the wiser and greater brethren of the human family. (II, 218)

The first model to appear in the autobiography is O'Casey's father, who died when the boy was only six. However, the memory of his father is complemented by the abiding influence he had in the Casside family, so that the father plays a significant role in the awareness of the growing youth. O'Casey traces the special affinity his hero feels for his father to Michael Casside's blunt, outspoken personality and his deep love of books. Indeed, it is the father's interest in learning that gives symbolic significance to one of the few specific memories Johnny has of him. Michael Casside's continual worry was 'the thought that, because of his eyes, Johnny would grow up to be a dunce, a thing that was an abomination in the sight of the lord.' (I, 36) Once, when he had sent Johnny out to buy some tobacco, the father had said, 'The dunce will forget what he's been sent for before he's halfway there.' (I, 36) When Johnny has successfully completed his errand, he receives his father's commendation: 'Then the wasted sensitive hand left the arm of the chair, and Johnny felt it resting on his head, as his father said softly and sadly, No, he is a brave little fellow, and his father's son'. (I, 36–37) By proving that he is not a dunce, by successfully passing this test of intelligence set by the learned Michael Casside, the boy presages his ability to earn his place in the world of books and learning.

Despite Michael Casside's faith in the value of books and his desire that his children be provided with proper schooling, his death and the continuing affliction of his son's eyes greatly reduce the chances of young Johnny's getting any education. But the image of the scholarly father, together with his expressed concern that the boy might be a dunce, are presented as persistent inducements to learning. In fact, this dunce motif is used in association with the various attempts to give the boy a formal education. For example, when, under pressure from the minister, Johnny is brought to school, his mother says:

You might as well be here . . . as to be at home, boring your eyes out looking at the pictures in the books your poor father left behind him. Besides your father would be unhappy in heaven, thinking of his little boy growing up to be nothing but a dunce. (I, 98–99)

Because of continuing problems with his sight Johnny attends school infrequently, so much so his ignorance becomes a source of worry both to his mother and his school-teacher sister, Ella. Finally, under Ella's tutelage, he begins studying a variety of books including a grammar book and, thus, his first serious effort at education is underway. Consequently, at the end of the first volume, he has progressed to the point where he can make sense of a poem by Tennyson. To the retrospective eyes of the autobiographer, the boy's interest in learning is the most significant development of his first eleven years; O'Casey gives much of the credit for that achievement to the influence of his father.

Although the image of the father recedes somewhat in succeeding volumes, he surfaces as a model of learning whenever the grown youth is depicted in the struggle to educate himself. In *Pictures*, O'Casey gives a vivid description of the inspirational role of Michael Casside in the intellectual growth of the teenage protagonist who is alive with curiosity about all facets of his world — geography, history, the function of the stars, the nature of the moon. Frequently, he finds that his father's books are, as yet, too difficult to provide answers to his questions but, undaunted, the boy vows 'he would learn, he would learn. . . . If his father had made himself into a scholar by boring into books, his son could do the same.' (II, 87) The image of his scholarly father, reinforced by the presence of his books in the home, is thus presented as the most significant factor in directing Johnny's introduction to the world of letters. It is hardly surprising that, more than forty years after his father's death, when Sean the successful literary figure set sail for England, he counts among his most valuable possessions 'the moral courage and critical faculties of his father, and his love of good books.' (IV, 286) The peresistence of the father's influence on the son's behaviour is seen when O'Casey, writing in his late sixties and describing Sean's former weakness of character, evokes the image of Michael Casside. At a social gathering of Dublin's *literati* Yeats discussed the *Plough* with Sean, praising it as 'the finest thing you have done. In an Irish way, you have depicted the brutality, the tenderness, the kindling humanity of the Russian writer, Dostoievsky.' (IV, 190) Sean happened to know from Lady Gregory that Yeats had read his first Dostoievsky novel only a few days before, and so he felt that Yeats was trying to impress him with a limited knowledge of Dostoievsky. Rather than having 'the courage to tell Yeats that he knew damn all about the Russian writer,' he

had put a smile of appreciation on his heat-stained face when Yeats had said it. Christ Almighty, what a world of deceits! Sean's father would have said how he felt and what he thought without a hesitation. He had let his father's memory down. He'd try to be braver the next time.'(IV, 191)

Michael Casside's role as a model also functions, in a more indirect way, by establishing other figures for the growing boy to admire. One of these is Charles Stewart Parnell, who emerges as one of the most significant models in the autobiography. During Johnny's formative years the name of Parnell occurs again and again, and although the boy is too young to understand what the politician represents, O'Casey has carefully shown the youth beginning to sympathize emotionally with him. Much of this attraction to Parnell is traceable to the pervasive influence of the dead Michael Casside. Just as the boy's father serves as a model in the world of books and learning, so does his approval of Parnell establish the latter as a model in the political arena. The first suggestion to the impressionable boy that Parnell is a positive figure comes from his mother's repetition of her dead husband's political views. When the Protestant Johnny plays with neighbouring Catholic children, they always conclude their games of imaginary battles and wars by singing the praises of Parnell, even though Johnny is uneasy about being associated with the Fenians. He reassures himself by remembering that 'his mother had told him his father had said that Parnell was a great Protestant, a great Irishman, and a grand man; and it was a good thing there was someone, anyway, fit to hinder the English from walking over the Irish people.' (I, 87) Later in the volume, Johnny listens to his mother, who considers herself a good and faithful subject of the Queen, defend Parnell when a fellow tram-passenger describes him as a ruffian destroying the country: 'Oh, said Mrs Casside reprovingly, whatever Parnell may be, he's far from bein' a ruffian. I'd say he's a son of a grand stock, an' a thorough genteman.' (I, 179)

The passenger retorts that Parnell is seeking to become the uncrowned king of Ireland, and Johnny observes his mother's measured reaction:

Mrs Casside stiffened. . . . If the thruth must be told, said she, after a pause, an' things allowed it, the counthry couldn't have a better king! Hear, hear, said several people in different parts of the tram. (I, 179)

In subsequent years, Mrs Casside continues to commend Parnell to the impressionable Johnny, always echoing the opinions of her husband.

The process of Johnny's sympathetic response to Parnell, under the guiding influence of his dead father, is highlighted during Johnny's visit to Kilmainham jail with his uncle. As they make their way through the streets, they become involved in a discussion of the religious and political affiliations of Irish martyrs. Although his uncle gives vague and evasive answers to Johnny's questions, the boy persists, for he fails to understand his uncle's claim that an Irishman, when he fights for England, is fighting for his country: 'Me Ma say me Da said it isn't, but that Ireland's our counthry; an' he was a scholar, an' knew nearly, nearly everything, almost; so it isn't, you see.' (II, 28) As the conversation proceeds, Johnny has to contradict his uncle's statements several times because they do not coincide with his father's opinion of Parnell. When, under further questioning, the uncle acknowledges that any Irishman who does not fight for England is a wicked man, the boy, with ingenuous logic, returns to the example of Parnell:

Why didn't Parnell fight for England an' not go again' the Queen?
I wouldn't say that Parnell went again' her.
Oh yes, he did, said Johnny deliberately; for me Ma heard me Da sayin' once that Parnell paid no regard to the Queen; and would sooner rot in jail than obey any law made by her, an' that he worked, night an' day, to circumvent them because, he said, English law was robbery. (II, 30)

Two chapters later, when Johnny and his brothers are involved in a pub-fight generated by a discussion about Parnell, the young boy is the hero of the day when, to make good their escape, he drives the horse and car amid shouts of approval for both himself and the dead politician. The young Johnny Casside feels sympathy and admiration for Parnell long he before can rationally appreciate either the man or his politics.

In later years, when Sean has matured intellectually, this early sympathy is confirmed by his analysis of Irish history. Parnell's political vision, his courage in the face of enormous opposition, and his betrayal by Catholic Ireland, all complete Sean's conception of him as a man of outstanding character and unique qualities. In the rest of the autobiography, Parnell is portrayed as the archetypal Irish martyr-hero eventually destroyed by the very people he tried to help. And O'Casey presents Sean as being very much in the tradition of those singled out for criticism and betrayal; he too is shown to be one of a long line of Irish figures driven into exile from the country they had sought to serve. At the moment of departure, Sean stresses that, although he is leaving Parnell's country, 'Parnell would be for ever very near to him.' (IV, 183) Of the railway station in Dublin on his way to England, he writes, 'It was from this sad site that the coffin holding Parnell came slowly out, borne by strenuous, tearful men, hesitating to part even with the dead body of their persecuted Chieftain.'(IV, 285) The suggestion here is that to avoid persecution himself, to escape the treatment meted out to people like Parnell, he had no option but to leave Ireland. Just as it was only in death that Parnell could find peace in Ireland, so must Sean leave the country if he is to live the life he envisions.

Parnell is also used as a yardstick for both historical and contemporary figures. Having established Parnell's positive qualities, O'Casey can associate his name with other figures in a symbolic language of approbation to suggest that they also embody the ideas and principles Sean believes in. For example, to express Sean's indignation over Ireland's treatment of Dr Michael O'Hickey, O'Casey describes him as 'a Parnell with a Roman white choker round his neck, fighting the battle of Banba's language.' (III, 32) And when O'Casey introduces Jim Larkin, he stresses Parnell's similarities with the union leader:

Here, too, had Parnell stood, defiant, speaking from the building's wide steps, like a flame-pointed spear on the people's altar, endurance and patient might in his beautiful wine-coloured eyes. The rascals, cleric and lay, out-talked thee, hissed thee, tore at Ireland to get at thee, and God remembered for many a long year, silencing their voice till He grew sorry for the work-worn people, and sent another man into their midst whose name was Larkin. (III, 187)

An historical figure who not only gains symbolic importance by being associated with the name of Parnell, but whose own name attains a similar stature, is Wolfe Tone, the Irish leader whose rebellion in 1798 led to his death in an English jail. Once again, it is in the conversation with the uncle that Tone's image first registers with Johnny; the boy is fascinated that Tone and other heroes in

Ireland's struggle against English domination (Emmet, Grattan, and Parnell) were, like himself, Protestant. Gradually, as he learns more about Tone and as his intellectual development continues, he recognizes him as a true hero of the Irish people. When the maturing Sean's support for nationalism has begun to fade because of his growing commitment to socialism, Tone is presented as the historical model who most appeals to him. Because Tone was not merely a nationalist but an internationalist who, as a follower of Thomas Paine, was a passionate believer in the rights of man, and who 'stood against control by monarch and prelate,' (III, 229) he occupies a central position in Sean's pantheon of heroes.

Having established Tone in this exemplary role, O'Casey can subsequently, as with Parnell, use his name in a symbolic language of approval for other figures. In praising Patrick Pearse's close understanding of Ireland's history, O'Casey writes: 'holier to him the lonely grave of Bodenstown, where Wolfe Tone's valour has changed to dust, than the place where St Patrick is said to be pinned down to an everlasting slumber.' (III, 242) Tone is also mentioned in O'Casey's discussion of Walter McDonald's attempts to have Catholics permitted to enter Trinity College. Four hundred and sixty-seven Catholic laymen drafted proposals supporting McDonald's position and submitted them to the Standing Committee of the Roman Catholic Bishops which was to decide the matter. Recounting how these proposals were summarily dismissed, he compares the supporters of McDonald both with ' "The Boys of Ormond Quay" whom Wolfe Tone longed to have at his side when he headed rebellion in Ireland' and with 'the dockers, carters, and coal-heavers' (IV, 256) who stood behind Jim Larkin in the 1913 Strike. The association with Wolfe Tone and Larkin establishes McDonald's place in Sean's list of great Irishmen. Thus evolves a network of models whose names can be used interchangeably as epithets of the highest commendation. In setting up this kind of interrelationship O'Casey introduces those people whose actions Sean supports, whose characteristics he admires, and whose example he would like to emulate. They represent the standards by which he judges himself, embody the courage he believes he possesses, and display the moral qualities he sees as integral to his own nature. Once the identifying features of these models have been established, O'Casey can evoke their names to chart stages in Sean's evolution. For example, in Chapter IX of *Drums*, when Sean has misgivings about the nationalists and is trying to decide where his true sympathies lie, he recollects instances in Irish public life of people running afoul of narrow-minded and suspicious Catholic patriots. The now highly resonant name of Parnell is evoked at the outset of the chapter — 'Look at what had happened to Parnell when he was breathless with extreme toil, and leaning on his sword before having another bout with the wily foe' — thereby indicating Sean's perspective on each of these incidents. (III, 143) Because his attitude toward the treatment of Parnell applies equally to the events recounted here, his assessment of their cumulative significance is an important factor in his decision, in the following chapter, to devote all his energies to his real brethren, the workers.

O'Casey's use of models goes beyond merely establishing his values and beliefs; he does share their ideals, admires their courage, approves of their behaviour, but his identification with them becomes more intense than that. Because he recognizes that the forces which opposed them stand as obstacles to his own development, he sees himself as part of this lineage of victims and martyrs. This strong affinity accounts largely for the seemingly non-autobiographical passages giving details of the various issues which engulfed these figures. Indeed, so close is the perceived bond between the protagonist and his models that the discussions of their victories and defeats, the analyses of their supporters and antagonists, assume the level of allegorical autobiographical language. In describing the forces that destroyed a Parnell or silenced a McDonald, O'Casey is not only providing auto-biographical insight by revealing where his sympathies lie, but is also outlining his perception of the opponents that would obstruct his own intellectual evolution and deny his vision of the world. It is possible, then, by attending both to the references to such models and the connotative overtones they acquire, to see further nuances of his personality, to understand his attitudes and beliefs, to perceive his scale of moral values, and to discover some of the shaping forces of his world.

Because Parnell and Tone occupy prominent positions in the pantheon of Irish heroic martyrs, they are readily accessible models who possess many of the emotional and political associations necessary to O'Casey's purposes. But there are lesser figures who must be rescued from oblivion, whose lives and activities must be explained, whose images must be recreated in the work, if their shaping influence on the hero is to be understood. These range from public personalities who are now forgotten to friends and family members. The most important individuals in the first category are Dr Michael O'Hickey and the Reverend Walter

McDonald, to each of whom a volume of the autobiography is dedicated. The very necessity of having to recount their achievements is evidence to O'Casey of their neglect. Consequently, he provides sufficient information on their lives to resurrect and preserve their memories, and to accord them recognition commensurate with their accomplishments. In *Drums*, at the end of the chapter recounting O'Hickey's fight to have Irish taught at the New National University, O'Casey writes:

Here is one who remembers you, O'Hickey . . . . here is one left to say you were a ray in Ireland's Sword of Light — a ray then, and a ray still, and no episcopal pall can hide its flaming. Though there be none to speak out your name, here is one to utter it in the same breath, with the same pride as those who speak out the names of Ireland's fair and finest sons; for you are one with her they call Cathleen, the daughter of Houlihan, though you have not been remembered for ever; one with her as is yellow-haired Donough who's dead; who had a hempen rope for a neckcloth, and a white cloth on his head. (III, 142–143)

Irish people often appear preoccupied with remembering the past, particularly the achievements of political leaders and public figures. Recalling the heroic deeds of Irish martyrs and enshrining their memories in a hallowed roll-call is a theme of many ballads and patriotic songs, and, in particular, of the *Dinnshenchas* tradition of Gaelic narratives which exalt the topography and heroes of ancient Ireland. And, as we will see in a later chapter of this study, O'Casey's style is marked by a wide range of correspondences to Irish characters, events and places, whether contemporary or historical, real or legendary, literary or mythological.

Part of the impulse of this remembrance stems from the concept of a recurring past, the idea by which succeeding generations are willing to become part of an ongoing tradition of sacrifice leading to Ireland's spiritual renewal and political freedom. As Richard Kearney has observed about the leaders of the Easter Rebellion, 'This extended genealogical invocation would have linked the 1916 heroes not only with their founding Fenian forebears of the preceding century, but also with former Irish patriots such as Emmet and O'Neill, and ultimately with the legendary heroes and deities of mythological Erin i.e. Oisin, Cuchulain, Manannan, Caitlin ni Houlihan and most importantly Fionn MacCuhall and his warrior band, the Fianna'.[3] The leaders in 1916 perceived their deaths as martyrdoms likely to be far more influential in achieving their goals than the actual rebellion itself, which they anticipated would probably fail. At his trial, Thomas Mac Donagh, a leader of the Rebellion and a proponent of the myth of sacrificial renewal, defended the Proclamation of Independence:

You think it already a dead and buried letter, but it lives, it lives. From minds alight with Ireland's vivid intellect it sprang, in hearts aflame with Ireland's mighty love it was conceived. Such documents do not die.[4]

O'Casey's eulogy for O'Hickey (quoted above), by evoking images of the Sword of Light and by conjuring up the memory of Cathleen Ni Houlihan's devoted sons, including the sacrificial death of 'yellow-haired Donough,' clearly associates the clergyman with this heroic lineage. In this tradition, to neglect or forget a person who has made sacrifices for Ireland's cause is the ultimate shame on his country. Governing O'Casey's selection of material on O'Hickey and others is the recurring desire to redress such shameful neglect; this same impulse is evident in one of his earliest publications, *The Sacrifice of Thomas Ashe*, which recounts the circumstances of that patriot's death and celebrates his legacy. (In *Juno and the Paycock* this desire to remember is parodied in Captain Boyle's proud — and highly ironic — boast that, though left with little else, he somehow retains the integrity of his claim to be an Irishman through the act of remembering: 'We don't forget, we don't forget them things, Joxer. If they've taken everything else from us, Joxer, they've left us our memory.')

In the chapter, 'Silence' at the end of *Inishfallen*, which parallels the 'Lost Leader' chapter of *Drums*, O'Casey recounts the disputes between Walter McDonald and the Irish Catholic hierarchy.[5] Again, what is stressed is that this man's name 'is never mentioned either in the religious or the secular Press. . . . There is a sombre and a secret and a sinister silence about this man who so modestly and so reverently questioned God.' (IV, 267) Associating the name of McDonald with that of O'Hickey, O'Casey resurrects the memory of these forgotten people 'subdued into silence by the vanity of the bishops and the dodgery of a pope.' (IV, 260) Both names recur with varying frequency in the autobiography until these men emerge as representatives of the human spirit triumphing over adversity. In the conduct of their lives — their honesty, moral vision, and fighting courage — and in the ignominy of their deaths, they have attained the status of heroes in the O'Casey canon. He shows that, in his twenties and thirties, he was influenced by the actions of these men and sympathized with their causes; this individualistic response to these issues in Irish public life reveals the protagonist as already outside the mainstream of nationalist sentiment. As autobiographer, with subsequent personal

experiences to reinforce his reading of such events in recent Irish
history, he can point to the similarities between the fights of
O'Hickey and McDonald against their adversaries and his own
struggles with the reactionary forces of Church and State. Thus, in
the processs of describing these men's exemplary behaviour and of
enshrining their memory, O'Casey reveals his perception of the
causes contributing to his present position as social and intellectual
exile from his country.

Unlike the detailed expression of admiration for a McDonald or an
O'Hickey, O'Casey's commendation for other, less important,
figures surfaces spontaneously in the process of autobiographical
recollection; such people make brief appearances, momentarily
changing the focus of several paragraphs or a chapter, before
disappearing offstage. For instance, in *Drums* O'Casey gives a short
account of the valiant efforts of a W. P. O'Ryan, whose Boyne Valley
Enterprises had done much to revive interest in Ireland's culture and
traditional crafts. However, statements O'Ryan made in *The Irish
Nation* aroused criticism from Cardinal Michael Logue; as a
consequence, O'Casey contends, O'Ryan was driven from the Boyne
Valley and, ultimately, from Ireland itself. In the autobiography,
O'Casey provides information which will help set the record straight
and salvage the memory of this defeated man: 'Over the grave of this
brave man, this cultured man, a silent hurrah'. (III, 23–24)

Other characters, more closely involved in Sean's life in Dublin,
are also singled out for expressions of praise, gratitude and honour.
Two of these are the Reverend Harry Fletcher, rector of Sean's local
church, and his successor the Reverend E. M. Griffin. For several
years, Harry Fletcher's enlightened religious views have a strong
appeal to the adolescent Johnny, culminating in his Confirmation
in the Church of Ireland at the age of eighteen. Fletcher also gives
much practical help to Johnny and his family, including arranging
to find a hospital bed for the seriously-ill Tom and paying for the
cab to take him there. *Pictures* is dedicated

To the memory of the Rev E. M. Griffin, BD, MA, one-time Rector of St
Barnabas, Dublin. A fine scholar; a man of many-branched kindness,
whose sensitive hand was the first to give the clasp of friendship to the
author.

Griffin's most memorable gesture is his attentive visits to the
Casside household when Tom is dying and, after Tom's death, his
paying of the funeral expenses. The friendship between Sean and
the rector is strengthened by their frank discussion of religious
issues, as well as by their agreement on the issue of teaching Irish

at the New National University. Later, under the influence of his reading of Darwin, Frazer and others, Sean is unable to subscribe to the religious beliefs represented by Griffin, who himself admits

the Higher Criticism has disturbed us sadly. The robe of truth has been pulled awry, and badly torn, John; but the truth is untouched. Here we see as in a glass, darkly, but one day we shall know all, and I am content to wait. (III, 84)

For Sean, who no longer possesses such faith or patience, 'life was to begin all over again, if he decided to think on, and who wouldn't do that?' (III, 83–84) Notwithstanding this divergence of views on religious questions, Sean's opinion of Griffin's kindness, integrity and courage remains unaltered. Consequently, the greatest tribute that he can give to this friend is the act of remembrance: 'However he might change, wherever he might be, whatever he might do, he could never forget the man, the Reverend E. M. Griffin'. (III, 97)

Yet another passing intention is accomplished later in this same volume, when Sean is presented at home, sick and bedridden, exhausted from long hours working for Jim Larkin's union without sufficient nourishment to restore his energy. A doctor sent by Seamus Deakin, a friend of Sean's, recommends that he build up his strength by eating substantial food such as porridge. Several days later, Deakin himself visits Sean, bringing him several magazines and books, 'a rich load of joy, for which Sean thanks him still.' (III, 207–208) After Deakin has gone, Mrs Casside discovers two gold sovereigns on the mantleshelf, and comments: 'He knew better than to offer them, so he left them quiet on the mantleshelf so's they wouldn't conflict with our pride. You'll have porridge for a few weeks now'. (III, 208) Even in the autobiographical present, O'Casey's pride allows him only the indirect expression of gratitude implicit in his recounting the incident.

O'Casey's desire to pay tribute to family members, to acknowledge the warm bond of affection and love reaching across the barrier of death, also surfaces periodically. In this category, by far the most moving and eloquent words are those extolling the many sterling qualities of his mother. In *Inishfallen*, Sean admits that after his mother's death, 'with all his feeling, he had never put as much as one green sprig on her grave; never paid it a visit after having helped to lay her there; and never would. The dead, worthy of remembrance, are worth more than a decorated grave.' (IV, 46) Instead, believing that only 'Thoughts in the memories of the living alone ruffle the dead into living again: the muffled drums of the

dead beating a faint roll of remembrance,' O'Casey now gives his
mother life once more. (VI, 72–73) This is accomplished in brief
glances, in sustained dramatic vignettes and, most notably, in 'Mrs
Casside Takes a Holiday,' the second chapter of *Inishfallen*, which
is a heartfelt and powerful tribute to the person who had been
Sean's 'comforter, his rod and his staff, his ever-present help in time
of trouble' for almost the first four decades of his life. (IV, 21) He
acknowledges the sense of inadequacy he felt at her death by not
being able to commemorate her virtues: 'None, save he, could
recognize her for what she was; and he was powerless to yield her
any words of praise, for if he spoke them, there were none to hear.
She would die alone — unhonoured and unsung.' (IV, 29) Now, by
creating images of her in the autobiography, O'Casey suitably
expresses his praise and preserves her memory.[6]

Another obvious and comprehensive purpose determining content
is O'Casey's desire to portray some of the public figures in the Ireland
of his time who, in varying degrees, helped to shape his reality. Sean
says in *Drums* that he wished 'he had his paint-box of ten colours
handy . . . that he might set down in colour the figures that passed
him by here.' (III, 211) The most important category of such people
is contemporary Irish writers, for many of whom O'Casey expresses
praise and respect. In the role of autobiographer, he had the
opportunity of giving his final assessment of the accomplishments
and personal qualities of these writers, regardless of his previous
attitudes. For example, despite the bitter and intense dispute with
Yeats over the Abbey's rejection of *The Silver Tassie*, O'Casey finally
forgives the man whose actions had caused him so much personal
anxiety and artistic frustration. In *Rose*, his description of Sean's
final meeting with Yeats, now sick and near death, concludes with
a moving expression of admiration:

Sean longed to cross to the coughing Yeats, and lay a warm, sympathetic
hand on his heaving shoulders; to say silently so that Yeats could hear,
God knows, if power were mine, you would be for ever young; no cough
would ever come to warn you that the body withers. (V, 111)

Sean's feelings stem from his conviction that 'there was no braver
man among the men of Eireann than W. B. Yeats. In every fray of
politics, in every fight for freedom in literature and art, in every
effort to tempt Dublin's city into the lure of finer things, the voice
of Yeats belled out a battle cry.' (V, 113) The account of Sean's
farewell to Yeats underlines the contrast between the poet's broken
physical state and the immortal stature of his writing:

Sean left him staring at the gas-fire, crouching in the big armchair. His greatness is such, thought Sean, that the Ireland which tormented him will be forced to remember him for ever; and as Sean gently closed the door behind him, he heard the poet coughing again: broken by the passing feet of his own black oxen. (V, 116–117)

George Bernard Shaw is another whose stature O'Casey wishes to extol and enhance, feeling certain that, as Sean says, this 'Kind man, brave man, wise soul, indomitable spirit of the indomitable Irishry' (VI, 187–188) will, like Yeats, long be remembered:

He will live in the life following his own for his jewelled courage, his grand plays, his penetrating wisdom, his social sense, his delightful, effective criticism of the theatre of his day, his fight for Ibsen, Wagner, Brahms, his uncanny knowledge of children, his battles for womanhood, and for his brilliant leadership in the thought of man. (VI, 177)

To the names of Yeats and Shaw is added that of Joyce, 'a lad born with a song on one side of him, a dance on the other — two gay guardian angels every human ought to have.' (VI, 173) Although O'Casey never met his fellow Dubliner, he greatly admired Joyce's genius and his courage in laying bare the social hypocrisies and religious prejudices of Irish life; consequently, positive references to both the man and his writing occur with varying frequency in the narrative. In a fanciful passage O'Casey establishes the prominence of Joyce, Yeats and Shaw by describing the consternation and havoc that would result if they were created bishops in Ireland:

What a grand bunch they'd be on the bench — Shaw, Joyce, and Yeats! . . . Was there ever such a one as the Bull from Shaw; was there ever such a one as the Pastoral from Yeats; was there ever such another as the Encyclical from Joyce! . . . What are the three boyo bishops doing now? Blessing the people. Blessing them — what with? Shaw's blessing them with him plays and Yeats is blessing them with his poems, and Joyce is blessing them with the comic laughter of a brooding mind. (VI, 177–178)

To this glorious triumvirate, O'Casey adds the name of Lady Gregory, whose many kindnesses to himself he appreciates and whose literary abilities he admires. His tribute to her in the autobiography is all the more poignant because it is tinged by a strong feeling of regret and self-recrimination when he remembers his treatment of her. Prior to the Abbey's rejection of the *Tassie*, he had had high esteem and warm affection for Lady Gregory; she had encouraged him when he was finding his way as a dramatist, and showed him every hospitality at her home in Coole Park. On the eve of the *Tassie* row, O'Casey had written her a touching letter

of encouragement and praise, in which he paid her what is for him
a tribute of the highest order by comparing her to his mother.[7]
Yet, a year later, when she had written expressing the desire to meet
him in London, his bitterness against Yeats and Lennox Robinson
was so intense that he refused on the grounds that he might offend
her with his comments on them. Later, he regretted that decision,
as is indicated in Sean's admission: 'This refusal was one of his silly
sins. He still thinks angrily of himself when he thinks of her, or
hears the name of the gracious gallant woman.' (V, 105) Meditating
on her death, he asks wistfully: 'Had she a place in the Universe
now? In the memory of some, she had. A fleeting immortality; the
leaves falling one by one from the tree of remembrance till the tree
is bare, and the tree is dead.' (VI, 29) He may be thinking here of
the tree at Coole Park on which are inscribed, among others, the
initials of Lady Gregory, Shaw, Yeats and himself, giving them a
form of recognition. He acknowledges that she is remembered and
honoured by Yeats, particularly in the poem, 'Coole Park, 1929,'
from which he quotes. In turn, he himself gives her a similar
immortality by praising her character and listing her virtues in the
passages which become both an elegy for Lady Gregory and an
appeasement of his guilt at his own high-handedness in his dealings
with her. And in eulogizing her literary gifts O'Casey adds her to
the ranks of Sean's Irish literary heroes:

W. B. Yeats of the lovely lyrics, Augusta Gregory of the little, the larger,
laughing plays and the wisdom of guidance, Shaw of the drama and the
prophecies, and Joyce of the sad heart and the divine comic mind,
touselling and destroying our mean conceits and our meaner vanities. (VI,
43)

By providing a portrait gallery of these writers, O'Casey not only
venerates their memories but, in the process, establishes significant
barometers which can clarify the protagonist's own literary and
personal standards.

Similarly, certain figures from the political arena appear in the
narrative so that their defining characteristics can be explained,
their accomplishments recorded, and their relationship with the
protagonist set forth. For example, there is praise and admiration
in the account of Jim Larkin's courageous commitment in rousing
Irish workers out of their lethargy,

not for an assignation with peace, dark obedience, or placid resignation;
but trumpet-tongued of resistance to wrong, discontent with leering
poverty, and defiance of any power strutting out to stand in the way of
their march onward. (III, 188)

Larkin's exemplary efforts on behalf of the working class make him a figure worthy of honour, particulary so since his vision of the worker's future so closely parallels that of Sean.

One of the most striking approbations of a political hero is accorded Patrick Pearse, the leader of the 1916 Rising. In 1914, O'Casey had expressed bitter condemnation of Pearse's action during the 1913 Dublin Lockout. In a letter to *The Irish Worker*, O'Casey wrote:

Pearse is worse than all. When the workers of Dublin were waging a life and death struggle to preserve some of the 'liberties' which ought to be common to all Irishmen, this leader of democratic opinion consistently used the trams on every possible occasion, though the controller of the Dublin tramway system was the man who declared the workers could submit or starve.[8]

Although such disagreements were obviously rooted in ideologically different perceptions of the conflict and its place in the struggle for Ireland's freedom, both men shared a love of Ireland and her culture. In fact, elsewhere in the autobiography, O'Casey, in praising Pearse's interest in ancient Irish folklore and myth and his efforts to make them accessible and known in contemporary Ireland, recounts how Sean himself had helped Pearse stage a pageant based on the mythological story of the Cattle Raid of Cooley. Predictably, the greatest commendation of Pearse is for his courage in leading the 1916 Rebellion and for his noble and honourable death:

Ah! Patrick Pearse, you were a man, a poet, with a mind simple as a daisy, brilliant as a daffodil; and like these, you came before the swallow dared, and took the Irish minds of March with beauty. . . .

Ah! Patrick Pearse, when over the hard, cold flags of a barrack square you took your last stroll and wandered to where the rifles pointed to your breast, you never even paused, for that was what you guessed you'd come to; you came close to them; the stupid bullets tore a way through your quiet breast, and your fall forward to death was but a bow to your enemies. Peace be with you, and with you comrades too. (III, 242)

As might be expected, not all of O'Casey's descriptions and portraits of contemporaries are complimentary. Judgements and criticisms of those who, notwithstanding the passage of time, still remain outside his circle of worthy people, are found throughout the autobiography. This list includes members of the Catholic hierarchy (Cardinal Michael Logue, Archbishop McQuaid), political leaders (de Valera, Cosgrave, Griffith), labour supporters (William O'Brien, Countess Markievicz), and writers (Lennox Robinson, Brinsley

MacNamara). His unflattering perception of these people might have originated from an ideological disagreement on political, literary or religious matters, or from their specific criticism of his own activities or writing. Whatever the issue and whoever the object of his attention, O'Casey always vigorously defended his beliefs and bluntly stated his opinion of adversaries.

One of the strongest condemnations in the autobiography is reserved for George Russell, Irish poet, mystic, painter, and editor of *The Irish Statesman*. When he met Russell in Dublin Sean considered him a sham who had little talent either in painting or literature. Later, Russell in his paper had criticized certain aspects of the *Tassie*; when O'Casey responded, a lively debate on modern art ensued between the two men.[9] The chapter in *Inishfallen* called 'Dublin's Glittering Guy' is a full-blown denunciation of Russell's life and work. He questions Russell's various theories of land reform, ridicules his painting, dismisses his writing, and cites instances of his pretentiousness and pomposity. He cannot understand

how Dunsany could overlook Yeats to hand the palm for poetry to A. E. What a mass of glittering monotony his poems are! All paralysed with a purple glow. Swing-exultation in them all. They make a mind dizzy. (IV, 196)[10]

O'Casey's conclusion is that Russell 'Wrote neverendingly, he talked incessantly, he painted persistently, he travelled immoderately, and, finally, he left behind him a handful of pebbles, sanctified with a little gilt, that he took to be jewels.' (IV, 216)

O'Casey's desire to depict a variety of figures from his past, and to present his perception of them, comprises one of the more important intentions which compete with his primary purpose of recounting the progression of the protagonist. Consequently, these fluctuating intentions exert considerable influence on the choice of contents. His accounts of all these people — whether they be models like Tone and Parnell, unsung heroes like McDonald and O'Hickey, public figures like Pearse and Yeats, or immediate family members — reveal the autobiographical hero assessing and judging individuals who have shaped him and his world. People met briefly, or those with whom meaningful relationships have been formed, people read about or those with whom he lived, all play varying roles, influencing the growth of the protagonist. Because of his position at the centre of his world, an auto-biographical hero's intellectual and emotional development can be better perceived and understood when both his dynamic involvement with, and evaluation of, secondary characters are clarified. Since autobiography is characterized by an unrelenting preoccupation with the protagonist's consciousness, with the influence of pivotal experiences on his changing levels of awareness, it remains an unreliable source of information on other people. Even autobiographies, such as O'Casey's, which aspire to place the hero in a dimension larger than his sole self rarely do so by portraying secondary characters accurately. Such people tend to become static embodiments of specific traits and values which the autobiographer responds to; they remain one-dimensional figures, products of the autobiographer's interpretative memory, and as such, not surprisingly, they bear but general resemblance to their real-life counterparts. They are never the subject of the book, which remains the autobiographer's life-story, shaped and structured from one angle of perception, his own.

Yet, however bereft of historical authenticity, secondary characters can reveal added nuances about, and subtle qualifications to, the emerging portrait; in the autobiographer's estimation of them, in his assessment of their virtues and faults, important insights and further aspects of his own personality are unfolded or confirmed. O'Casey's changed feelings toward Yeats, notwithstanding the deep resentment and the actual artistic consequences of the *Tassie* controversy, show his ability to transcend personal considerations and acknowledge Yeats's commendable qualities as an individual, as well as his high stature as a poet. O'Casey's self-recrimination about his behaviour towards Lady Gregory illustrates a readiness to accept his faults and admit his guilt — no small accomplishment for the proud and often stubborn playwright. And his immoderate criticism of Russell reveals his determined refusal to let the passage of time alter his firm conviction of the hollowness of the man and the superficiality of his work. From the perspective of autobiographical revelation, it is beside the point whether O'Casey is fair, balanced or even correct in his portrayal of secondary characters; ultimately, it is his perception of them, his description of their behaviour, his positioning of them in a scale of values he himself has defined that are of primary autobiographical significance. In fact, Yeats does much the same thing in his autobiography, presenting individual men and women as types: Synge is cast as the archetypal artist; Lady Gregory, as the ideal aristocrat. So, too, George Moore and Yeats are each recreated as characters in the other's autobiography, in an effort by each to authenticate his own version of the past. In displacing the ongoing account of the protagonist's development, materials focusing on such people, rather than being autobiographically irrelevant, can reinforce the veracity of the self, lending it all the ambiguous, even contradictory, components of a complex identity. Indeed, this mode of autobiographical revelation can often be more accurate and complete — precisely because it is less self-conscious — than conventional expressions of awareness. In praising figures such as McDonald or O'Hickey, or denouncing George Russell or de Valera, O'Casey provides revealing indices to his own character. For example, predominant in all his exalted portraits, the qualities stressed repeatedly, are their fighting spirit in the cause of personal freedom and their unwavering principles of honesty and justice. Likewise, Sean's criticism of real or perceived adversaries illustrates O'Casey's abhorrence of hypocrisy, weakness and pretentiousness. Complementing these impressions are the negative inferences to be drawn. O'Casey's squabbling over long-ago and sometimes quite insignificant incidents, his unwillingness to acknowledge the motivations of others' behaviour, his often self-righteous proletarian beliefs, all betray the vindictive, petty and uncharitable side of his personality. By attending to the manner in which secondary characters are depicted, we may appreciate the value of such seemingly extraneous material in its providing a more detailed, and perhaps more comprehensive, autobiographical portrait.

Since an autobiographer's perception of the truth of his past life is closely tied to the self-image he holds, the materials of the work can be prime indicators of the identity it embodies. This is especially true of those materials focusing on the circumstances originally contributing to the desire for autobiographical definition. The impulse or necessity to become involved in self-scrutiny at a particular moment in life can often be traced to a unique confluence of events public, private or both. Such experiences may be of sufficient import or intensity to sharpen or challenge a person's self-image, so that he responds by engaging in a work of autobiographical exploration designed to reveal and assert his contemporary understanding of the significance of his life. Events precipatating the process of self-portrayal may be spelled out in a preface (as Yeats does in *Autobiographies*) or on the opening pages of the work (as Wells does in *Experiment in Autobiography*). Apart from the rather generalised subtitle of his first volume, 'Swift Glances Back at Things That Made Me,' O'Casey offers no such statement at the outset of his autobiography. Consequently, if the dynamic relationship between content and purpose is to be fully appreciated, it is necessary to discover if the materials of the text reflect the circumstances of its origins.

Notwithstanding the work's extraordinary length and the diversity of its contents, even a cursory reading suggests that O'Casey gives singular attention to the Abbey's rejection of *The Silver Tassie*. No other event is returned to more frequently or analysed in such detail; repeatedly, the narrative draws attention to the paramount influence that the *Tassie* controversy had on the life of the protagonist. But to understand the implications of the play's rejection, it is necessary to view that event in the context of O'Casey's career up to 1928. The well-known highlights of this period need only be summarised. In the early 1920s O'Casey submitted several plays to the Abbey Theatre, the first three of which were rejected, but, responding to encouragement from Yeats and Lady Gregory, he tried again. In 1923 *The Shadow of a Gunman* was accepted by the Abbey and had a moderately successful initial production; in October of the same year *Cathleen Listens In* opened at the Abbey, and, in the following year, O'Casey had a more impressive production with *Juno and the Paycock*, which brought him wider recognition and some money. Early in 1926 his next play, *The Plough and the Stars*, while provoking demonstrations at the Abbey, was praised by many reviewers and staunchly defended by Yeats in his famous address to the Abbey audience. In the wake of this tempestuous success, O'Casey, a few weeks later, left Dublin on an open-ended visit to London. His reception there was in keeping with the colourful reputation that had preceded him. He was hailed as a strange genius who had emerged from the Dublin tenements, and whose play, *Juno*, won the Hawthornden Prize for the best work of the year by a new writer. It was obviously an exhilarating time for O'Casey: he was interviewed and photographed; he saw many of the plays being produced in London; he met famous people, such as Shaw and Augustus John; and, as the latest celebrity, he was invited to the homes of the wealthy.

Throughout this time, he was also busy preparing his next play for submission to the Abbey, for, though he had no plans to return to Dublin, he had not abandoned the Abbey Theatre. The subject matter of the new play would move beyond the concern shown in the earlier plays for the victims of Ireland's violence, to a wider sympathy for the victims of the First World War: 'He would show a wide expanse of war in the midst of timorous hope and overweening fear; amidst a galaxy of guns; silently show the garlanded horror of war'. (V, 31) In his approach to this material, he would continue the search, begun in the earlier plays, for new and experimental techniques since

There was no importance in trying to do the same thing again, letting the second play imitate the first, and the third the second. He wanted a change from what the Irish critics had called burlesque, photographic realism, or slices of life, though the manner and method of two of the plays were as realistic as the scents stealing from a gaudy bunch of blossoms. (V, 31)

In 1928, *Tassie* was completed and submitted to the Abbey directorate; the rejection of the play and, even more important perhaps, the condescending tone of Yeats's criticism began the celebrated *Tassie* row which was to have such a profound and lasting impact on O'Casey.

It must be remembered that the five years from the production of *Shadow* in 1923 to the submission of *Tassie* in 1928 had been an exciting and fruitful period in O'Casey's life. He had fulfilled his goal of seeing a play of his produced at the Abbey, he had received move money than he had ever seen at one time in his life before, and, despite the stormy reception of the *Plough*, he had won a respectable measure of literary recognition in both Dublin and London. As well, the emotional vacuum in his personal life caused by the death of his mother in 1918 had been filled by his recent marriage. The bold new material and experimental techniques of *Tassie* were conceived against the background of personal confidence that emanated from all these developments. O'Casey himself considered it 'the best play I've written' and he was so confident that it would be accepted and produced by the Abbey that he sent Lennox Robinson a recommended cast list.[11] Within the context of this self-assurance, the Abbey's rejection of the play was a serious challenge to his conception of himself as a writer of more than provincial interest. He had turned from the milieu of the Dublin slums, had focused his attention on broader themes, and the result was that Yeats, whose reputation as an influential man of letters O'Casey readily conceded, believed the play had no subject. In *Rose*, he stresses that Sean's long struggle to establish himself as a dramatist now seemed to have gone for nought. If his past successes at the Abbey could not guarantee the production of his next play, of what value was his reputation elsewhere? Once again he must overcome obstacles to establish his credentials as a serious writer: 'Sean's flying start had been rudely curtailed of its fair proportions, and he would have to start over again, and fight the battle anew.' (V, 66) Not surprising, then, that O'Casey vigorously countered Yeats's criticism, rejected his suggested revisions, and, while conceding that 'the play might not be what Sean thought it,' still maintained that 'it was far above three-fourths of the plays appearing on the Abbey stage, and it stood up, fearless and steady, to the higher standard of the theatre.' (V, 38) Despite this defence of the play, and notwithstanding the fact that Macmillan was going to publish it and C. B. Cochran was continuing with his plans for its London production, O'Casey still believed that the Abbey's decision would have far-reaching effects on several aspects of his life.

Of immediate importance was the impact on his domestic situation. Because of his newfound obligations as husband and father, Sean felt that 'life pressed more heavily on him than ever, for his anxiety was threefold now — for himself, for his wife, newly fledged with motherhood, and the babe, newly fledged with life. The play was very important to him.' (V, 40) In addition to such tangible consequences, the rejection of the *Tassie* struck a deeper and more sensitive chord in him. Because he was convinced of its worth and because he felt the Abbey (whose financial survival was in large part due to the success of O'Casey's earlier plays) owed him a production of the play, he was all the more shocked by its rejection. O'Casey's letters in the ensuing months attest to the obsessive vigour with which, again and again, he both explained the circumstances surrounding its rejection and reaffirmed its worth. His character was hardened in ways which had significant consequences for himself and his work: his warm friendship with Lady Gregory was noticeably tempered; for several years he took every opportunity to express his bitterness toward Yeats; and, ever after, he was suspicious of the Abbey's motives in its dealings with him. In fact, for many years his attitude toward several people was decidedly influenced by their response to the *Tassie*.[12] But, most importantly, O'Casey, who had initially been a little awed by the literary world he had so recently entered, recognized that from now on he would have to fight to defend the integrity of his artistic principles. He saw that if he were to preserve intact his conception of himself as a playwright free not only to choose his own subject matter but to treat it in whatever manner he saw fit, he would have to be prepared to defend his work; even, apparently, against the most ardent of his admirers. The years in which his plays were readily produced by the Abbey, and won general approval from critics, were over; with a few notable exceptions, O'Casey, the man and the artist, was alone.

As observed in the previous chapter, works of autobiographical definition are frequently undertaken soon after a series of taxing experiences or a moment of crisis, when the subject's sense of self is jolted. Jean-Paul Sartre, speaking of his own autobiography, argues that although one's conception of one's life changes in the autobiographical process of defining it,

there are moments at which it can be done. Either when one has reached a crisis, a point of arrival — which is rather rare — or a starting point, when a changing situation suddenly uncovers one's life in a new perspective.[13]

While the circumstances of the crisis can vary from a clear and dramatic disruption in one's life to a more gradual erosion of confidence and self-assurance, the consequences are similar. The individual's sense of self — 'Who I am' — is obscured, and the tendency is to ask the fundamental question, 'Who am I?' To answer this, he turns to self-analysis; he attempts to explain his personality and to examine why he thinks and behaves as he does. To begin such a process of self-scrutiny, the individual seeks in his past the evolution of his identity; he turns to autobiographical expression for self-understanding and self-definition. A. M. Clark has pointed to this characteristic of autobiographical writing:

Every autobiography is, in some way, the result, to return to Browning's metaphor, of the collapse of a frontage. Every autobiographer, I fancy, has passed through a kind of crisis, short and intense or protracted and cumulative in its effects, affecting mind, body, or estate, private or shared with others though on them it made no comparable impression. This experience is, in biological terms, the releasing stimulus.[14]

The autobiographer, then, begins the process of autobiographical definition, for, in the act of exploring and presenting the characteristics of his personality, he can assuage doubts about his identity and deflect threats to his self-image. Perhaps the classic example of the restorative value of autobiographical self-assessment is Wordsworth's *The Prelude*. Before he began work on 'The Recluse', which was intended to be his major poetic accomplishment, Wordsworth wished to reassure himself that he was qualified for such an undertaking; so he turned to an examination of the experiences of his past to trace the origin and development of his poetic nature. *The Prelude* itself, then, becomes the confirmation of his qualities as a poet.

If there ever was a period in O'Casey's life when he felt victimized and besieged by hostile forces, the aftermath of the *Tassie* rejection was it. On the one hand, he had no intention of compromising his artistic principles to have his work produced; on the other, if he did not, he would suffer continual financial anxiety and emotional stress. As he says in *Rose*:

Sean knew that the more he tried to put into a play, the less chance he'd have of a production in England, so he had to decide whether he would model a play so as to squeeze it towards triviality, or persist in experimental imagination, and suffer for it. (V, 130–131)

Here, in this dilemma threatening his identity as an artist or his responsibilities as a husband, was a crisis of sufficient magnitude to challenge his image of himself. In *Rose*, at the end of the chapter recounting the *Tassie* row, there is a passage which reveals much about his own perception of the predicament:

He would fight alone; one alone and not a second. He would fence in his own sour way, thrust, parry, and cut with his own blade of argument, in his own way, not according to rules perfumed with the stale musk of custom; but according to the measure of his own heart, the rhythm of his own mind, logical now, savage and sudden a moment after: in this fight, he would face any opponent, and thrust straight at the side where the heart lay. (V, 42)

In the immediate aftermath of the *Tassie* controversy his relationship with the Abbey continued to be stormy. The theatre periodically withheld royalty cheques, forcing the proud O'Casey to demand money he should have received automatically. In addition, the theatre issued a lawsuit against him for giving permission to Arthur Sinclair and his Irish Players to perform *Juno* and *Plough* in Cork and Belfast. The Abbey claimed that it had the production rights of these plays anywhere in Ireland, while O'Casey believed it held them only for Dublin. By hiring a solicitor and writing a series of strong letters, O'Casey convinced the directors that the Abbey's rights were limited to Dublin. The suit was dropped but the bad feelings and mistrust persisted.[15] Meanwhile, in the English press, Yeats was quoted as having made derogatory statements about O'Casey and the *Tassie*. Yeats denied having made the statements, but not before the now highly sensitive O'Casey had written to demand an apology. In 1929 also, Sinclair's production of *Juno* had a hostile reception from the citizens of Limerick, who successfully managed to prevent a production of the *Plough*. In the following year the same citizens burned the film version of *Juno* during a street demonstration against O'Casey. Later in the year, an Irish priest launched such a vicious attack on *Tassie* that the proposed Dublin premiere of the play had to be cancelled.

O'Casey's troubles did not end with the *Tassie*. In 1934 his next play, *Within the Gates*, opened in New York. It was planned that the play would go on tour in the United States and, from this, O'Casey hoped to make enough money to live on for a year. However, the play ran into strong and effective attacks from the clergy: its production was banned in Boston and the proposed tour of thirteen cities was cancelled. Once again O'Casey the playwright was under fire. He says despondently in *Rose*: 'Sean was being tossed about once more in the old sturm [*sic*] of style. Oh, God, here it is again!' (V, 202) He realizes sadly that 'Sean's additional reliable year went vanishing into the stuff that dreams are made on.' (V, 206) In 1935, when the Abbey finally produced *Tassie*, the play was again bitterly denounced in the Irish press by the clerics.[16] For almost ten years his work had been subjected to intense attacks which caused O'Casey artistic frustration and financial insecurity. It is hardly surprising that as late as two years after this he had not yet begun work on another play. He said, rather wearily, in a 1937 letter to George Jean Nathan,

I haven't started a new play yet. I am a little tired of all the rows that my plays caused. I haven't written one yet that didn't create a blaze . . . and I really hate quarreling although I like an argument as well as the next one. I am thinking about a play to be called 'The Star Turns Red' — the Star of Bethlehem, that is — but amn't sure that I'll go on with it, for it would sure cause another bloody big row![17]

What he did return to at this time is work on the autobiographical material he had begun in the late 1920s. As was pointed out in Chapter I, O'Casey seems to have been planning a volume of stories based on personal experiences while simultaneously viewing some of these sketches as potential autobiography. While the positive response to the appearance of 'The Protestant Kid Thinks of the Reformation' in the *American Spectator* did help to sharpen his sense of purpose, there can be little doubt that the years of artistic frustration as playwright were a contributing factor to the resumption of his autobiography. Certainly, the writing of it would serve the dual purpose of offering him an artistic freedom denied on the stage and, if he were lucky, of providing him with a source of income. Yet, while these were undoubtedly influential factors in his decision to turn to autobiography, they do not appear to have constituted its driving impulse. The change in his overall conception and approach seems to have stemmed from more deep-rooted causes. Because of the adverse critical response to his previous two plays, he was being denied the forum required for the full development of his dramatic potential and the free expression of his literary vision. More to the point, his newly acquired and long sought-after self-image as a recognized playwright and his status as Sean O'Casey the acclaimed Abbey dramatist were being seriously undermined by the series of setbacks begun with the *Tassie* rejection. His goal of artistically transforming material related to the First World War as he had the characters of the Dublin tenements reflected his ideal self-image as a major literary figure. This was the absolute self which O'Casey posited; as was pointed out in the last chapter, most autobiographers strain toward such a self which, though never realized to its fullest, is what they measure achievements against. Indeed, for many autobiographers, the perceived discrepancy between these contrasting real and ideal images is the primary impetus to autobiographical definition. Speaking of this ideal self, Roger Rosenblatt observes that 'falling short of it is perhaps what inspires the autobiography in the first place; but if we are to understand the lives detailed before us we must know this ideal as fully as we know the "realities" given us.'[18] For O'Casey, writing the autobiography would be an opportunity to justify both himself and his work; by providing relevant background information on each, he could explain who he was, why and how he had evolved that way; and he could show that such factors were shaping influences on his writing. Viewing the autobiography from this perspective may explain why his conception of the work changed. If, indeed, his only desires were literary experimentation and an opportunity to make some money, he could have published the biographical sketches as a collection of stories. In fact, in 1934 he did publish three stories, along with some early poems and two one-act plays, in a collection called *Windfalls*. (It is noteworthy that in the preface to this collection he says, 'the three short stories were an effort to get rid of some of the bitterness that swept into me when the Abbey Theatre rejected *The Silver Tassie*.') He obviously recognized that the sketches would not be published as a collection of stories *per se* but would, instead, be an examination of the shaping forces that had made him who he was. This understanding of the work would explain the change from first-person to third-person narration. First-person narration would have lent a private authority to the material; third-person narration, on the other hand, provides the opportunity to give seemingly objective validation to the subjective view. As a response to the forces which challenged his self-image as man and writer, the work would, following the Wordsworthian paradigm, circle back to his origins and explore 'the things that made me,' so that the crisis years of the recent past could be assessed in the broader context of his whole life. Obviously, as remarked in Chapter I, in the process of writing subsequent volumes, of examining the details of his personal history, the scope of his materials would grow to reflect the contours of his life's journey, affecting both the size and form of the work. But his perception of his primary purpose — a showing forth to the world of the circumstances which moulded his character — was now defined. And the contents of the autobiography confirm that his intentions in the work were crystallized significantly by the ten-year pattern of rejection and frustration ushered in by the Abbey's refusal of the *Tassie*.

If the relationship between materials and O'Casey's desire for self-knowledge and self-definition is recognized, then we have a better understanding of the function of many seemingly redundant or irrelevant passages. In recounting the protagonist's crucial experiences, explaining his relationships with specific people, and describing his involvement in public events, such sequences clarify the evolution of his unique personality and identify the factors controlling his individual destiny. They also contribute to the gradual shifts in emphasis and changes in tone which increasingly characterize the work.

Because the adjustment in both emphasis and tone is most clearly evident in the materials of *Rose* and *Sunset*, these two books have evoked much adverse criticism. In comparing them with the first four, several critics see a marked discrepancy in quality: a decline in intensity, fewer deep-felt scenes, and too many passages of personal opinions. The view that the nature of the work has somehow undergone a radical transformation in these volumes is best summarized by Roy Pascal:

> . . . the character of the autobiography involuntarily begins to change, the story loses in concrete substantiality; convictions which had the massiveness of experience now thin out into opinions and opinion-ativeness; and when O'Casey leaves Dublin, inconsequent reminiscences, tender or hilarious, take the place of autobiography. . . . His arguments with critics and producers, his continued feud with the catholic hierarchy, his ideas, lack direction, and have none of the compulsive reality of the childhood and earlier life.[19]

Pascal's statement must not be taken lightly, but before dealing with the crucial issues it raises, one may observe that O'Casey's ability to create such lyrical and evocative passages as are a pronouned feature of earlier volumes is also evident in the last two books. Some examples are Sean's reconcilatory meeting with the feeble Yeats; the sense of wonder and excitement in the chapters dealing with his trip to the United States; the disillusionment captured in the account of his visit to Cambridge; and the memorable picture of Eileen O'Casey at the bedside of the dying George Bernard Shaw. Indeed, some of O'Casey's most lyrical prose is to be found in the last chapter of *Sunset*. Here, for example, is Sean's serene yet wistful farewell to life:

He was writing now in the Fall of the Year, while the leave of the trees were taking a last flutter through the air, whispering a goodbye to life as they fell. Sere and yellow, they were useless now to the tree; they had done their work, and the newer buds beneath were busy pushing them off; pushing them away from life, never to return again. Sere and yellow leaf, fall fluttering, and fade from all you knew, carrying to earth with you some tender fragment of the summer's dream. So are many now, so was he — waiting for that gentle but insistent push that would detach his clinging desire, and send him, like the tumbling autumn leaf, sinking from life's busy tree to the dull flavour of death in the kingly dust where all men mingle in a sleep unending. (VI, 234–235)

While O'Casey could still create such highly charged auto-biographical images, it is true that fewer evocative passages are to be found in the later volumes which, instead, are charactrerized by more frequent expressions of O'Casey's opinions and beliefs. These changing features of the work raise important questions, especially since, as Ronald Ayling has observed, 'the lack of a balanced critical analysis of this apparent change of emphasis in the narrative sequence and its artistic consequences is one of the big gaps in O'Casey criticism.'[20]

The new characteristics are attributable partly to the nature of the autobiographical genre itself, partly to the unique character of O'Casey's self-portraiture. In all autobiographies, the principles which determine choice of materials are affected both by the changes in the protagonist himself and by the fact that he develops in an environment which is itself being modified, sometimes dramatically, usually imperceptibly. Accordingly, in O'Casey's autobiography the contents chosen to suggest the experiences of the young boy in the streets of Dublin in the 1890s will be different from those which depict the thirty-year-old man's involvement with the social and political affairs of Ireland in 1910. In turn, the latter episodes will be different from those which show the fifty-year-old man battling for financial security and artistic integrity in the London of 1930. Because the biographical story-line of *Rose* and *Sunset* covers the hero's age from forty-six until he becomes the seventy-three-year-old author, the materials and narrative procedures of these volumes are, once more, quite distinct from those of the books dealing with his childhood and formative years. Unlike the sickly child, the curious-minded young man or the unemployed labourer portrayed earlier, the protagonist of these volumes has discovered his metier and is the internationally acclaimed and exiled playwright, Sean O'Casey.

Another inherent feature of the autobiographical process is that, as the protagonist grows into the autobiographer, more and more attention is drawn to the common ground between them, to their increasingly similar vision of the world. This is in contrast to the depiction of the protagonist in earlier volumes, where O'Casey often underlines the discrepancy between innocent hero and mature author, where he focuses on those moments when the earlier self is still in a state of evolutionary maturation. Consequently, the protagonist in the early books is presented as a fully-rounded and distinct historical character, an appreciation of whose emotional and intellectual development is necessary for a full awareness of the contemporary autobiographer. By contrast, the later protagonist tends to be shown more as an earlier version of the autobiographer, than as a figure spatially and temporally distant on the evolutionary journey to the present.

Both of these characteristics of the autobiographical genre help account for the changes in the contents and tone of O'Casey's self-portrait. As we have seen, when he began the process of autobiographical exploration, he had a general sense of the work's size and form. The first book would be a series of 'glances' at the forces that moulded the boy's character until the age of about eleven. The second volume, in its general outlines and its manner of presenting materials, follows a conception of the work similar to the first, and brings the story of the youth's development up to the age of twenty-four. The materials of both books consist predominantly of vignettes, pictures, fantasies, and dramatised scenes that attempt to give a vivid picture of Johnny's world and capture its impressionable influence on his development. The primary tone is lyrical and evocative; in general, the mode can be said to be descriptive.

The presentation of the hero's world and his advancement in it continues in the succeeding two volumes. However, precisely because there are changes both in the growing youth and his environment, the criteria for selecting and presenting materials also change. While lyrical and evocative passages of description can still be found in the third and fourth volumes, there are, increasingly, expositional sections which explain the historical, political, cultural, and social forces shaping the subject's intellectual and emotional development. Highlights of his progression are still described in powerful and intense passages but, for that evolution to stand forth in the clearest possible relief, explanatory passages of background information are often required. In these volumes the predominant mode has changed from descriptive to expository.

A further modification in the choice and treatment of contents is evident in the last two volumes. Now the pace of change both in the subject and in his world becomes more gradual as they move closer to the completed man in his contemporary environment. Clearly, there can still be important forces of change and development at work but, in its fundamental features, the character of the protagonist is more completely defined. Whereas the earlier volumes describe and explain the circumstances in which he develops, the tendency in the later volumes is to confirm, to fill in nuances of a personality whose outlines have already been revealed. And, as with most autobiographies, O'Casey's usually does so in a less highly charged manner. Without the nostalgic distance to help fuel the fires of imagination, an autobiographer tends to present events and people of the immediate past in a more realistic fashion. This phenomenon is dramatically evident in O'Casey's presentation of his wife, Eileen. In *Rose*, he warmly recounts their first meeting and his instant liking for this 'very lovely lass.' In the chapter, 'Feathering His Nest,' he suggests the joy and excitement of their early years which, despite financial insecurity, were marked by love and laughter. In *Sunset*, however, the Eileen O'Casey being described exists on almost the same temporal plane as the author; insufficiently distanced for the transforming power of imagination to come into play, she is presented in a somewhat set and perfunctory manner. It is therefore not surprising that her image in the overall work is less fully realized than that of his mother or Lady Gregory, both of whom belong irrevocably to the past and must be recreated by imaginative memory. Eileen O'Casey remains too much an abiding figure of love and sustenance in the present to emerge as a fully created character in the work.

It is also relevant that when O'Casey was writing the earlier volumes, the self being presented not only was more distanced in time but also was unknown to the world; consequently, he could approach his experiences in a freer and more creative manner. In the last two volumes, where the self is closer to the man writing the autobiography and is the world-famous dramatist, O'Casey has to adopt a different attitude to the events of his past. Since readers are likely to bring to these books some knowledge of O'Casey the playwright, O'Casey the autobiographer feels an added imperative to explain and justify. He begins to shape his protagonist through his writings and in the image of the author; the life-story is aligned with the man behind the literary *oeuvre*.

The fact that these two volumes cover the period of his ongoing struggle to have his increasingly experimental plays staged is also a crucial factor influencing the selection of, and the emphasis given to, their various materials. Because *Rose* deals with the period of the *Tassie* controversy and its aftermath, O'Casey's account of that phase of his life is marked by particularly strenuous defences of his work, repeated justification of his actions, and detailed responses to his critics. Similarly, because the years covered by *Sunset* saw O'Casey still being denied a forum for his dramatic writing, the volume is characterized by his continuing insistence on the right to artistic freedom and to the expression of his religious, social, and political views. Just as the earlier books describe Johnny Casside striving against a myriad of obstacles until he finally emerges as Sean O'Casey the playwright, so now the struggle depicted is that of a man trying to earn a living while maintaining artistic integrity. The experiences of these years may be less dramatic, and therefore presented more directly than those in earlier volumes, but, because they touch upon the nerve-center of his identity, and because they have important implications for the man and the artist, they have as much autobiographical validity as earlier events. O'Casey's denunciation of the Abbey directorate, his attacks on the clergy for their incessant criticism of his books, his observations on the English class-system, his idealistic conception of Russian communism, all accurately reveal the man of these years. It may be easier to sympathize with the subject of the earlier books striving against a host of adverse circumstances, than with the artistic struggle of the later O'Casey. Indeed, we may be ill at ease or, at times, even embarrassed by the personality of the man who emerges, but we should be careful that our response to the protagonist does not distort the evaluation of the work's process of depicting him. There is little to be gained, then, in assuming that the contents of the later volumes will be chosen on similar premises and treated in the same fashion as in the preceding volumes. In both *Rose* and *Sunset*, O'Casey is portraying a different subject in a new reality and, consequently, they must be judged on the basis of how well they capture these changing phenomena.[21] Almost continually embattled and frustrated in the years being described, O'Casey becomes more assertive and defensive in these books; the mode is no longer predominantly descriptive or expository, but rhetorical.

Although these dividing points are arbitrary, and lyrical passages can as readily be found in later volumes as rhetorical passages in earlier ones, O'Casey himself suggests some such division in his life. At the end of *Inishfallen,* referring to the Victorian world of Castle Balls, Lord Lieutenants, and regal trappings into which Sean had been born, he writes, 'All outward trace of the distant grandeur Sean's youth had known, from afar off, had gone into the mothering dust. Yesterday was as if it had never been.' (IV, 274) These changes had begun to take place after the end of the second volume. In the opening pages of the third volume the shift in persona from Johnny to Sean foreshadows the forces of nationalism about to brush away the Tennysonian world of his youth. This second period of his life, in turn, is completed at the end of the fourth volume; 'As of the first, so of the second phase of Sean's life — it had almost all gone. The singing lark in the clear air had left the sky, and the cawing crow was there now.' (IV, 275) To suggest that one phase of his life was indeed over and that another was beginning, O'Casey gives the title, 'London Apprentice,' to the first chapter of the fifth volume. He is sensitive to the fact that, once his autobiographical hero crossed the Irish Sea and joined his creator in England, the work would be quite different, not only in the obvious matter of contents but also in narrative stategy. As we saw in Chapter I of this study, he readily acknowledged that in dealing with his years in England, the self-portrait would be 'more thoughtful' and 'less exciting.' Indeed, his hesitancy in continuing with the story after the protagonist leaves Ireland suggests an awareness that the narrative mode would necessarily move away from a dramatic account of personal development and would, instead, seek to capture the views and actions of an individual who had achieved a clearer sense of self-identity. In this, O'Casey's autobiography evinces a central characteristic of the genre; as a self-portrait moves to a close, the frequency of pivotal, shaping experiences is reduced, and the protagonist, older and more and more resembling the autobiographer, is depicted responding to life with a clearly defined identity, a man very different from the searching and growing individual of formative years. James Olney had noted this phenomenon in several autobiographies: Charles Darwin writes, 'I am not conscious of any change in my mind during the last thirty years'; John Stuart Mill says, 'From this time . . . I have no further mental changes to tell of'; and Newman states that, 'From the time I became a Catholic, of course, I have no further history of my religious opinions to narrate.'[22] Once the salient features of each of these journeys of self-discovery have been traced, time is foreshortened, experiences tend to be summarized not recreated, and statements are more likely to reinforce rather than alter previous images of the self.

Past the mid-point of *Inishfallen*, O'Casey presents the moment at which Sean's political philosophy of international socialism crystallizes and he formulates the principles henceforth governing his perception of himself both as an individual and a dramatist. The crucial autobiographical implications of this newly defined world-view will be explored in more detail in a later chapter of this study but, of importance to our discussion here is that, from that point onwards, events lead to modifications in the protagonist's character rather than the kind of dramatic new orientations in identity which have hitherto marked his persistent search for self-knowledge. Following this pivotal moment of awareness, his reactions to experience are presented in language more direct and explicit, in a tone more assertive and dogmatic, and in a voice more and more like the author's. Significant in this regard is that the eighteen years covered by *Sunset* form the largest time-frame of all six volumes, a confirmation that, as the protagonist becomes increasingly synonymous with his creator, his experiences — now selected much more stringently — are likely to be summarized rather than detailed.[23] They also tend to be presented in a more sequential fashion. It is revealing that the contents of *Rose* and, in particular, *Sunset* most faithfully retain a sense of chronological progression; with less actual room for temporal juggling, and with its narrative destination in increasingly clear view, the story tends to move uninterrupted to the present.

Once O'Casey's protagonist has articulated the defining tenets of his world view, the narrative is characterized by the growing presence of authorial intrusions. For instance, in 'Silence,' the long chapter in *Inishfallen* which details the self-seeking nature of the Irish Catholic hierarchy in its response to Walter McDonald's efforts at rapprochement between Catholics and Protestants, O'Casey writes: 'As it was then, so it is now: there is no more chance of harmony now than there was then.' (IV, 257) Remembering his earlier reaction to the events which engulfed and eventually destroyed McDonald, O'Casey, in the late 1940s, can reinforce his previous assessment of experience by citing supporting examples from his present. Such confirmations of the validity of his protagonist's responses to experiences have the effect of collapsing the temporal gulf separating them from each other. Again, in his discussion of the continuing adverse response of Irish critics to the *Tassie*, O'Casey attempts to lend credence and additional authority to the earlier assessment of the hero by writing, 'This very month of October, nineteen hundred and fifty-one, a revival of the play in the Queen's Theatre by the Abbey brought on more thunderclaps of resentment.' (V, 53) To show that the play had had generally good critical response elsewhere, he continues, 'and only the other day the drama critic of *The Times Literary Supplement* said of this very play, this very act, "If the voluble rapscallions of Dublin tenement life are unforgettable, so, too, is the pre-presentment in universal terms of the horror of war in the expressionist act of *The Silver Tassie*." ' (V, 54) This explicit leapfrogging out of historical context to unite the protagonist with his creator is dramatic evidence of the new impulses affecting the narrative as it moves forward on the continuum to the author's present. Throughout O'Casey's autobiography, then, the changing world of the hero and the phases of his development affect and complement each other; and the dynamic nature of this interdependence creates a complex set of factors influencing the selection and treatment of materials in succeeding volumes.

Even more significant in determining the materials of the concluding two volumes are the unique compositional circumstances of O'Casey's autobiography. Although all autobiographers ideally would like to perceive past experiences from a static moment in the present, they must perforce view them in a dynamic relationship with an ever-changing present. An autobiography composed over a conventional period (a year? two years?) posits a relatively defined vantage-point which minimizes this potentially complicating factor. Since O'Casey's autobiography was written in a period of over twenty years, he was denied even the pretence of one perspective from which the past could be viewed. This circumstance results in overlaps in the narrative, since the years which the first five volumes were written become part of the temporal setting of *Sunset*.

One of the unusual consequences of shifting vantages points on the selection of materials is that the autobiography can respond to its own reception. Like Joyce's reaction to the serialization of the individual sections of *Ulysses* and, even more so, to the publications of extracts of *Finnegans Wake*, O'Casey's decisions on the contents of later volumes could be affected by the public's response to earlier ones. The most dramatic example of this is the presence in *Sunset* of the chapter called 'Rebel Orwell.' In the *Observer* of October 28, 1945, George Orwell had written an *ad hominem* review of *Drums*, bitterly attacking O'Casey and even questioning his right to be allowed to live in England. Never one to shrink from a debate, O'Casey responded to Orwell's charges by writing a letter to the newspaper.[24] Since the letter was refused publication, O'Casey gives a point-by-point rebuttal of the criticism in the autobiography. He follows this by setting an imaginative scene in an English pub in which appear several people including Orwell, O'Casey and Cathleen ni Houlihan. (Her presence is significant because Orwell had singled out for specific criticism the use of her in the earlier volume.) In this dramatic fantasy, O'Casey ridicules Orwell's argument: he points out that England's strength is derived from the diversity of the ancient blood lines flowing in the veins of its present inhabitants; he outlines the restrictive environment for writers in the Ireland of the day; and he suggests that such conditions can exist because of people who, in their own way, are as provincial and narrow-minded as Orwell. In shaping passages such as this, successive vantage-points can enhance O'Casey's primary autobiographical purpose of explaining identity and affirming his vision of the world.

More importantly, however, O'Casey's shifting perspectives play a crucial role in the composition and tone of the concluding volume of the work, where the autobiographical hero becomes the man who earlier had initiated the process of self-portrayal. To understand how the changing vantage points contribute to the unique character of *Sunset* and, in turn, how this volume is central to the overall portrait of the autobiographer, a preliminary discussion is necessary on the relationship of this book to those preceding it.

If 1936 is accepted as the approximate date at which O'Casey's conception of the work crystallized, his intention at that time was to tell the story of his life to that year. However, neither that temporal goal nor a complete, contemporary self-portrait was achieved in the first volume; because Johnny had aged only eleven years, O'Casey had captured but part of his own earlier personality. When he came to write the second volume, the general conception of the work remained the same — self-definition in the present — but he was still unable to provide a comprehensive account of former experiences. This open-endedness continued during the composition of the succeeding three volumes; consequently, because the temporal present that was the destination of each volume continued to recede, nowhere in the first five volumes can the revelation of self that is at the heart of the autobiographical process be said to have been attained. It is only with the conclusion of the sixth volume, at the point when the protagonist and autobiographer are about to merge, that the portrayal of self is at last completed.

Yet, as asserted already, what emerges from the six volumes is not the final portrait that one would expect of an autobiography written from a shorter and more conventional vantage-point. Although a static moment offering an unchanging perspective on the past is never quite accessible to autobiographers, the simulation of such a comprehensive moment is usually attempted. When O'Casey began the autobiography, he was the closest he would be to an ideal position to survey and assess the past from a static point outside it. But the time involved in narrating earlier experiences continued to expand and eventually resulted in the chronological story's engulfing the moment when he had begun it. Succeeding moments from which outside evaluation of the past might have been possible were continually being subsumed into that which was being examined — the contemporary self was inexorably becoming another historical self. (It is the desire to achieve an ideal static moment, from which the totality of life could be examined and a complete self-portrait be made, that would explain O'Casey's need to bring his story up to the present, to unite the objective and subjective selves.) In *Sunset*, particularly, O'Casey had to contend repeatedly with the role of creator being metamorphosed into protagonist, preventing even the pretence of a conventional static moment which would offer a comprehensive view of the past. Consequently, the individual volumes provide but limited access to the identity of the autobiographer; all are partially completed sketches which, to achieve their full effect, must be viewed together. The work is an autobiography, not a series of separate portraits.

Yet, the individual volumes do not contribute equally to the final portrait. The increasing presence of an overlapping resonance makes each successive book a fuller reflection of the autobiographer than were its predecessors. From the second volume onwards, each book — responding to different experiences from personal history, and written from separate temporal perspectives — contributes additional images to the emerging autobiographical portrait. Of all volumes, however, *Sunset* plays the most important role in revealing the character of the autobiographer. While the autobiographical insights provided by the materials of *Sunset* cannot be said to be fully realized, because the whole life has not been viewed from that moment, they do provide a more comprehensive portrait than do the contents of the five preceding ones. In writing the second, third, fourth and fifth volumes, O'Casey was conscious of, and could make adjustments in accordance with, the self-image created in the previous books. At every stage of composition, he was aware that the experiences being recounted would have a resonant tension with both earlier and later materials; the knowledge of what had been written and what would follow results in the kind of assiduous arrangement of materials discussed earlier in this study. For example, the images of Yeats in the work are a dramatic instance of this phenomenon. In *Rose*, O'Casey's response to Yeats's rejection of the *Tassie* is intense, detailed and personal, making the poet the primary adversary (the role of villain is reserved for Lennox Robinson) in the controversy. But, as we have seen, O'Casey later praises and admires Yeats, setting him up as a figure of genius and courage. As further volumes were written, the opportunity to achieve this special quality increased, making each successive book a more legitimate reflection of the autobiographer than its predecessor. Although *Sunset* does not provide a comprehensive assessment of life from one moment in time, it is unique because, while its materials are chosen with an awareness of what has gone before, it is written with the knowledge that upon its completion there will be no more to be told. Even though all six books must still be viewed as partial portraits, this special weighted factor means that *Sunset* offers the widest range of autobiographical insights. Consequently, assessing the six panels simultaneously provides a picture more accurate of O'Casey in the early 1950s than of the man who began the work in the 1930s.

Because of *Sunset's* special position in the overall work, its contents are therefore influenced by several factors; as with the other volumes, they must recount the pertinent biographical experiences of the years under review. But in addition to this essential autobiographical function materials are chosen also to reflect both O'Casey's desire to reinforce images of identity suggested in previous volumes and to provide a sense of completion and finality to the overall work. When the contents of *Sunset* are examined with these considerations in mind, a clearer understanding should emerge not only of the book itself but of its crucial relation to preceding volumes.

In the approximately eighteen years dealt with in *Sunset*, there are few dramatic or startling biographic events to be recounted, certainly none to compare with Sean's heady and exhilarating life in the years of his own and Ireland's awakening consciousness. But if these years were marked by little ostensible public activity, they were, of course, characterized by immense creative effort, particularly for a man of such advanced years. In the solitude of Devon, fortified by the emotional fulfillment provided by his wife and family, he could get on with being what he had spent so many years of his life becoming — a writer. This period, the most prolific in his career, saw the publication of five autobiographical volumes, four full-length plays, several shorter plays, numerous articles and essays, and hundreds of letters to friends and adversaries scattered throughout the world. Because this astonishing creative output constitutes the biographical highlight of this period, and is in fact the central facet of his character in the years under review, the book is punctuated with references to the composition and critical reception of his writing. Given that these were the years in which O'Casey's writing was constantly criticized, his protagonist becomes more overtly assertive in defending his work. In particular, he is bitter that Irish censors seem almost unable to keep pace in banning his work as it is published: 'Bang! went the door against *Purple Dust*, too, against *The Star Turns Red*; sent to go as exiles, along with the outcast *Within the Gates*, *The Silver Tassie*, and *I Knock at the Door*; followed by lesser bangs of library doors shutting to keep the books out in the street.' (VI, 120) In addition to dealing with his literary work, *Sunset* shows Sean the ardent socialist responding to experiences in terms of his political views; thus, he frequently castigates the repressive forces — whether of church, state or institutions — which he perceives as obstacles to social progress.

The materials which echo the contents of previous volumes, particularly *Knock*, also contribute to the unique qualities of *Sunset*. Written at a temporal point furthest removed from the composition of the first volume, *Sunset* offers O'Casey an ideal opportunity to confirm his earliest autobiographical images. For instance, an analysis of the principles governing the selection, ordering and rendering of contents in the opening volume yields O'Casey's contemporary interpretation of the shocking conditions of the Ireland of his youth. His views are most dramatically embodied in the chapter called 'The Tired Cow.' Its biographical core depicts the nine-year-old Johnny, alone at centre stage for the first time in the autobiography, standing guard over a cow on the street. The scene opens with the boy, absent from school because of his sore eyes, standing on his doorstep, watching a heavy rainfall. He allows his mind to pose the question:

How 'ud it be . . . if God opened the windows of heaven, an' let it rain, rain like hell, for forty days an' forty nights, like it did when the earth was filled with violence, an' it repented the Lord that He hath made man, causin' a flood till the waters covered the houses an' the highest tops of the highest mountains in the land? (I, 79–80)

However, Johnny remembers that no second flood was possible, 'for God had promised Noah, a just man and perfect in his generation, there'd never be anything like a flood any more; and as proof positive, set His bow in the cloud as a token of a covenant between Him and the earth.' (I, 80) Despite that promise, the rain continues to fall in Dublin, and Johnny imagines 'the cows that musta given Noah the milk he needed when he was shut off from everything.' (I, 80) This image suddenly reminds him that it is Thursday, the day Irish cattle are 'shipped to England, to feed the big bellies of the English, as Archie said, while the poor Irish got the leavin's.' (I, 81) When he goes to the quays, a driver asks him to watch over one of the exhausted animals. Significantly, Johnny's charge is a cow, for the cow plays a central role in Irish mythology.[25] The great Irish epic, *Tain Bo Cualigne*, centrepiece of the eight-century cycle of heroic tales of Cuchulain, Fergus, Maeve and Deirdre, tells of a giant cattle-raid into Ulster by 'The Men of Eireann.'.(O'Casey gives an imaginative version of the story in *Drums* in the chapter, 'In this Tent, the Repubblicans.') In Ireland's economic relationship with England, the export of cattle has always been a contentious issue, for when the importation was not prohibited by British protectionism, it provided badly needed revenue for Irish tenant farmers to pay their rent, who in turn, however, often had to go without proper food themselves. The cow as a symbol of Ireland's exploited condition has appeared in such literary works as Swift's *A Modest Proposal*, Joyce's *Ulysses* and O'Casey's early play, *Kathleen Listens In*, in which the O'Houlihan cow is an allegorical representation of the country. Indeed, at several other points in the autobiography, O'Casey uses cattle as symbols suggesting the unfortunate predicament of the Irish people.[26]

That the vignette of Johnny with the cow possesses symbolic overtones is confirmed by O'Casey's return to the biblical allusion to the flood. Standing looking at the cow, Johnny sees that,

Beyond an occasional twitch of her tail, she gave no sign of life. Every beast in the forest is God's . . . an' the cattle upon a thousand hills. But a sthray cow lyin' on a rain-wet street is not enough to make God bother His head to give a thought about it. (I, 83)

When Johnny leaves the cow, the rainbow — symbol of God's covenant with Noah not to send another deluge, and which earlier in the day was to be seen, 'leanin' on the top of one of the Dublin Mountains' (I, 80) — has now disappeared. Instead, the boy's last sight is of 'the dark mass of the cow still lyin' on the path where everybody walked, starin' straight in front of her as if she saw nothin', while the rain still kept fallin' on her softly; but the sun had stopped her shinin', and the rain was no longer golden.'(I, 84) As this scene makes clear, O'Casey places much of the blame for the poverty, hardship and debilitating conditions of Ireland at the end of the nineteenth century on British imperialism, a system which fostered class distinction, economic exploitation and national subjugation. Other materials in *Knock* show life in that environment was made even more difficult by a vengeful, puritanical religion and a repressive educational system. The effect of such materials is to reveal the author of *Knock* as an individual who possesses a strong skepticism for the proclaimed values of imperialism, capitalism and Christianity.

In *Sunset*, O'Casey returns to the deluge motif, showing Ireland as a desolate and abandoned place cut off from the covenant made between Noah and God. To suggest that his native country does not yet partake of the pulse of a new life, that it remains socially and politically moribund under the twin oppressors of de Valera and the Catholic church, he refers to it as 'a decaying ark anchored in western waters, windows bolted, doors shut tight, afraid of the falling rain of the world's thought.' (VI, 120–121) As other passages in the volume confirm, O'Casey traces the stagnant society of the Free State to the capitalist and church-influenced forces now in power there. In his view, members of the new governing class not only still look to England for financial support but, in their social and economic policies, remain mere imitators of the colonisers they had expelled. The Irish tricolour may have replaced the Union Jack over Dublin Castle but the essential problems of poverty, inequality and lack of opportunity for personal fulfillment have not been seriously addressed. Thus, the views suggested by the materials of *Sunset* are a confirmation of the attitudes and beliefs inherent in *Knock*; in both, O'Casey reveals himself as an opponent of the forces which subjugate, exploit and limit the individual, be they British or Irish. By responding to disparate and widely separate experiences from his past in the same terms, O'Casey not only points to the consistency in his assessment of personal history but, in doing so, confirms essential elements of his autobiographical identity. Notwithstanding the more than four decades which span the temporal setting of the two books, and the fifteen or so years which separate their authors, succeeding volumes bear the indubitable stamp of the same man.

Finally, the contents of *Sunset* have been influenced also by the sense of completion and finality which O'Casey feels during the work's composition. It is common tendency for an autobiographer, as the culmination of the life-story comes into view, to reflect on earlier years and to measure the temporal and metaphorical distance travelled from his beginnings to the present. Such evocations of previous realities and precursory selves satisfy the desire to see a harmonious shape to one's life, to recognize a pattern of possibility and fulfillment, struggle and victory. As we have seen, in composing *Sunset*, O'Casey was unable to provide an account of his entire past from his 1950s perspective; but he could present the philosophic musings which resulted from surveying the sweep of his life. Sharing an identity practically synonymous with that of the autobiographer (who he is about to become), the protagonist of *Sunset* articulates the opinions and beliefs formulated from the experiences of a lifetime. Consequently, much of the book consists of reflective summaries and final assessments of those issues, whether social, political, religious or literary, which have been the abiding concern of the protagonist over the years. Frequently, then, O'Casey reaches outside the eighteen-year temporal framework of *Sunset* to show that the personae of previous volumes have evolved into the protagonist of this book, who, in turn, finds inevitable completion in the autobiographer. For example, at the beginning of *Sunset*, O'Casey depicts a former self who reminisces on a still more distant self. Sean is shown going for daily walks through the Knightsbridge area of London, so that his pregnant wife can get some exercise in the days before their second son was born. The familiar streets brought 'back to him memories of his first fast days in London'; (VI, 25) in particular, he recalls meeting Lady Gregory at her daughter's flat in Knightsbridge before he 'had set out with her to see T. P. O'Connor,' the former Irish M.P. 'who had helped to hound the noble Parnell to his grave', (VI, 28) and whose support Lady Gregory wished to enlist in her fight for the return to Ireland of the Lane Pictures. Writing in the early 1950s, O'Casey gives a layered quality to the narrative by evoking several distinct temporal planes: 1935 when his son, Niall, was born; the days in the late 1920s spent in London with Lady Gregory; and the 1890s when Parnell's downfall occurred. A few pages later, O'Casey muses on his friendship with Lady Gregory, a relationship which lies outside the temporal scope of this volume: 'Each had travelled his or her own different way, very different ways, yet, in the winter of her life, in the late summer of his, they had suddenly met, each facing toward the same direction.' (VI, 29) Now, the brief convergence in their lives is suggested in the overlapping between the earlier and later selves of the author. This pattern is duplicated a few pages later when O'Casey describes the visitors Sean had in these years:

old comrades from Dublin who had gone with him through the great Lock-Out of nineteen hundred and thirteen, grey now, and wrinkled like himself, but eager to go over again the scenes of battles long ago, filling the room with their own husky laughter, mixing with the slender, silvery laughs of Eileen, when they told Dublin stories of man's ridiculous conceit, or woman's comic frailty. (VI, 41)

Significantly, the autobiographical identity suggested by many of the ruminations in *Sunset* reverberates across the entire length of the autobiography lending a sense of completion to the insights provided in the opening volume. The most obvious instance of this stems from the fact that the temporal framework of *Sunset* embraces the actual moment when *Knock* was begun. As a consequence, an account of the origins of the self-portrait — traditionally found, if at all, at the outset of an autobiography — can logically be included in *Sunset*:

Here, now, in a house in Devon, he was looking over the page-proofs of his first biographical book; for, while writing plays and thinking about the theatre, his mind had become flushed with the idea of setting down some of the things that had happened to himself; the thoughts that had darkened or lightened the roads along which he had travelled; the things that had woven his life into strange patterns; with the words of a song weaving a way through a ragged coat, or a shroud, maybe, that had missed him and covered another. (VI, 70)

The unusual phenomenon of an autobiographer's offering some indication of his purposes in a work which began fifteen years and two thousand pages earlier facilitates a strengthening of the bond between the two books.

This relationship is reinforced further in *Sunset* by an expanded discussion of issues explored indirectly in the first volume. Primary among these is the emphasis given to the education and welfare of children. Michael Casside's dictum on the need for his children to acquire a proper education is an omnipresent concern in the opening autobiographical volume:

My children, he would say, raising himself up stiff and defiant in his chair, will get the best education my means, and the most careful use of those means, will allow . . . and on themselves will then rest the chance of making a good position better, with the knowledge they have gained from a few men and a lot of books. . . . Shield and spear shall they have when the day comes for them to go forward. (I, 64–65)

However, what little schooling Johnny Casside acquired is presented as an inhibiting and often painful experience, in which conformity and submission to authority are more important than individual growth and learning. Chapters in *Knock* such as 'Pain Parades Again,' 'A Child of God,' 'Battle Royal' and 'The Dream School' depict the classroom as a place where children, far from reaching fulfillment and maturity by responding to diverse and challenging aspects of life, are stifled and often punished by authoritarian and doctrinaire teachers. In *Sunset*, as O'Casey reflects on the years in which his own children were growing up and attending school, Johnny Casside's harsh school days are never far from his mind. Indeed, the relationship of Michael Casside to Johnny finds a counterpart in Sean's role of father to his own children; this duplication is underlined by his statement that 'his children would throw a wider chest than his own,' a hope echoing the spirit of Michael Casside's attitude toward learning. Chapters such as 'A Drive of Snobs,' 'Cambridge,' 'Deep in Devon' and 'Childermess' focus in varying degrees on the present-day educational system which Sean sees, for the most part, still possessing many of the life-denying traditions Johnny Casside encountered.

Reiterated throughout much of *Sunset*, this thematic concern is announced on the opening pages when an account is given of neighbours in Sean's London apartment who object to their children's playing with poorer and possibly flea-infested children: 'No one could blame them for dividing their children from the louse and the flea; they were to be blamed, though, for raising no word against the conditions which inflicted these dangers and torture upon the children of others.' (VI, 12) No such accusation can be levelled at O'Casey for, in the following chapter, 'Childermess' (a pun on Childermass, a mass to commemorate Herod's slaughter of the Holy Innocents, as well as on the book of the same title by Wyndham Lewis), as Sean awaits the birth of his second child, he criticizes the fate of children in England, Ireland and even America who, daily, are being mistreated through denial of adequate food, proper education and human love: 'We have begun to realize that children need not only life, but liberty too. For too long the children had been buried alive in church, in school, in the home.' (VI, 32) Later, he makes an impassioned plea that the child, 'the greatest, the loveliest, and the most delicate equipment we have for the development of life's future,' (VI, 68) be freed from oppression and deprivation, and sustained with care and love. He claims that, despite social progress, there are still millions of ageing minds who think that the best way to fit a child for happiness and resolution in life is to stuff his delicate mind with a creed, Christian or Communist. For Christ's sake, let the child laugh, let the child play, let the child sing, let the child learn, let the child alone. (VI, 68)

That the views of the author of *Sunset* on children's education are a more comprehensive response to the issue than those suggested in *Knock* is apparent in the different means of rendering them. In the opening volume, O'Casey's views on repressive educational practices are inherent in the scenes approximating deeply felt events from personal history; in 'The Dream School' for example, no explicit criticism is made of Slogan's harsh and unsuccessful teaching methods, although Johnny's reverie on the features of an ideal school leaves no doubt of the autobiographer's attitude. In *Sunset*, such views are now clearly shown as belonging to the protagonist who, unlike the naive and inarticulate hero of *Knock*, is able to state them in his own legitimate voice. This shift from oblique to direct statement is indicative of the alteration in narrative strategy which occurs as the work procedes, and is, of course, symptomatic of the evolution from the boy's imprecise perception of reality to the verdict of an individual who has worked out a comprehensive set of values in responding to the world.

Another pervasive concern of *Sunset* is the protagonist's assessment of the significant improvements of the conditions of workers over the years. By actively seeking to control their own destiny, they have begun to emerge from oppression and mistreatment to claim their rightful share in the bounty of life. This motif is introduced on the opening pages where O'Casey creates a discussion between Sean and 'an old codger' he meets in his daily visits to a London park. Having observed this retired working-class man speaking to middle-class ladies who also frequent the park, Sean gently suggests to him that 'it isn't good to be always humble. The lower classes are busy casting humbleness aside, and are shedding their respect for those who rob and rot them.' (VI, 19) Too much a product of the class system, the man is horrified by such talk and replies earnestly:

Our class can do better by knowing their place and keeping it. Ruin themselves, they will, if they go on like that, sir; or talk about being as good as their betters. Oh, a bad sign, sir; a very bad sign! God never meant us to be equal. (VI, 19)

Sean's response to this is that 'All will be equal one day . . . but each will differ from the other; but difference is very different from inequality.' (VI, 19–20) This brief opening dialogue begins an orchestration, continued throughout the volume, of Sean's reflections on the changes — many of them already achieved, some still to be won — in the lives of working-class people. In his view, the old man in the park happily represents the passing of a social order:

But workers were getting less and less like him. The old faithful retainer had become but a mummified memory. The bowed head before a master existed no longer, even in a picture. They had become conscious of their power, and as this consciousness grew, they saw less importance in those to whom they had been for so long such a comfort, such a stay. They were breeding importance within themselves. (VI, 20)

The end of an era is confirmed with the final view of the old man making his way out of the park, briefly lingering under two trees:

There he paused, his head below the murmuring foliage, his feet touching fading petals on the ground; an old mind trying to bud old thoughts; an old man standing in the shadow of the trees as if he stood hesitant in the valley of the shadow of death. Here, he paused, turned, and looked towards Sean. Sean waved a hand; the old man took no notice, but turned and went his way, and his old world went with him. (VI, 21)

At the conclusion of the next chapter, the protagonist casts his mind back to his own union activities which he believes contributed to the improvement of conditions for children and workers alike:

Yes, we have all done something to change the childermess to a Childermass of security, health, and a bonnie-looking life. You, Promethean Jim Larkin, with the voice born of the bugle and the drum, Barney Conway and Paddy Walsh of the docks, Paddy Mooney of the horses, Shawn Shelly of the workshop, O'Casey of the pick and shovel. (VI, 43)

Having suggested Sean's contribution to the struggles of the working class, O'Casey then evokes the names of Yeats, Lady Gregory, Shaw and Joyce, identifying with them also: 'We all ate of the great sacrament of life together.' His reflections culminate in a song from his childhood:

Yes, we had some bread and wine,
We were the Rovers;
Yes, we had some bread and wine,
For we were the gallant Soldiers.

What car'd we for the red-coat men?
We were the Rovers;

> What car'd we for the blue-coat men?
> For we were the gallant Soldiers.
>> Nothing, comrades. (VI, 43)

That song was originally used in *Knock* when the Protestant Johnny joyously played on the street with a group of Catholic boys:

> We are ready for to fight,
> We are the rovers;
> We are all brave Parnell's men,
> We are his gallant soldiers! (I, 86)

Although at the time he had ambiguous feelings about the nationalist sentiments of the song, Johnny Casside grew up to become the socialist and writer who, side by side with Catholics and Protestants alike, played his part in the political and cultural developments in the Ireland of his time. The presence of the song, as do the other examples from *Sunset* outlined above, reinforces the special bond between the materials of the opening and closing volumes and provides a pattern of unity and completion to the narrative.

O'Casey's efforts to unify his story are a response to a basic predicament which confronts all autobiographers. By definition, an autobiography must leave the story of its author's life incomplete; because the logical culmination of a life — death — cannot be presented within its pages, the work necessarily retains an unresolved quality. The autobiographer is torn between the desire to give the work artistic unity, and the recognition that his life will continue beyond the closing episodes of the book. In presenting past experiences, autobiographers may, as O'Casey does, have their protagonists reflect on their own death, obviously a moment envisioned taking place outside the pages of the work. (As we saw in Chapter I of this study, this issue was at the heart of O'Casey's difficulties in choosing a suitable title for his concluding volume.) At the end of *Sunset*, while O'Casey's protagonist is willing to bid farewell to his world, he also asks that the twilight 'stay with us another hour and keep the last and loving light of day from fading,' (VI, 205) an obvious plea for life beyond the work's completion. The dilemma facing all autobiographers as the narrative moves towards the present is, then, to achieve aesthetic unity in the account of his life — his artistic material — but also to suggest the extension of the life — his biographical material. Sometimes, in an effort to circumvent this predicament and foreshadow their own end, autobiographers will suggest the cyclical nature of life by focusing on death at the outset of their stories. This strategy aesthetically satisfies the desire for harmony and completion in a work which is arbitrarily concluded when the narrative reaches the present. Yeats, for example, concludes the first book of his autobiography with accounts of the deaths of two of his grandparents. O'Casey accomplishes a more dramatic instance of this phenomenon by opening his autobiography with the deaths of two brothers, whose identification with the hero is underlined by all three having been given the same name. But the special relationship which he establishes between *Sunlet* and *Knock* is a more successful means of dealing with the predicament. While, on the one hand, the protagonist is shown looking beyond the conclusion of the work, his story within its covers is given the cohesiveness and unity of an artistic creation. Thus, the tension which O'Casey creates between the opening and closing volumes allows both the sense of an ending and the irresolution inherent in the genre to coexist in tenuous harmony.

The foregoing discussion of the factors governing the selection of contents in both *Rose* and *Sunset* should suggest that these volumes, rather than being a mere coda or a series of 'inconsequent reminiscences' as Pascal suggests, are crucial in establishing O'Casey's full autobiographical identity. In recounting the important experiences of the years under review, the two books do not create a reality similar to that of 'the childhood and earlier life' but do accurately reflect the attitudes and opinions of the later protagonist. They are, therefore, integral both to the significance of earlier experiences and the meaning of the six-volume work. In particular, the unusual circumstances surrounding the composition of the work emphasize the central contribution which the concluding volume makes to the overall portrait. Indeed, examining the rationale and function of materials in this book points to the changing principles of selection that have been operative throughout all six volumes. As well as the ongoing autobiographical purpose of presenting the story of the hero's development, other factors determining content not only account for continual shifts and adjustments in narrative focus but, of more significance, provide keys to the autobiographical relevance of many passages that may initially seem unwarranted or gratuitous. In taking advantage of the freedom offered by the genre, O'Casey has been able to create multiple self-images which vitally enhance his autobiographical identity.

4. PRINCIPLES OF ARRANGEMENT

One of the most striking features of O'Casey's autobiography is that within the general forward thrust of the story there is often a flouting of chronological sequence in the presentation of the protagonist's development. While personal experiences and their historical contexts do establish an approximate chronological framework, most events and incidents are not identified with specific points in time. References to the clock and calendar — those essential structuring devices for many autobiographies — rarely appear in O'Casey's narrative.

He may have considered a tight, logical ordering of his materials as too artificial, too distortive or, simply, too restrictive. But his methods may strike us as too random, too arbitrary, even too indulgent to serve his autobiographical purposes effectively; disgressions and other rapid shifts in the continuity of the narrative might readily be considered distractions in the presentation of explicit stages in the hero's growth. While such disregard for conventional narrative structure is far from common in autobiography, is not unique to O'Casey; among others, both George Moore and Yeats, obviously wary of continuous narrative, chose impressionistic clusters of memory as a more accurate mode of setting forth their intellectual and emotional development. Neither writer was primarily interested in providing strict chronological sequence: Moore shaped and rearranged memories to clarify his thematic subject and cast it into distinct relief, while Yeats moulded his personal history into patterns that would be symbolic of his imaginative growth.

Despite the seemingly random fashion in which O'Casey's materials appear, he too, having rejected chronological sequence, carefully devised principles of organization for the work. As Ronald Ayling has pointed out, 'His notebooks made clear that he was, above all else, a literary craftsman in his working habits. Throughout his long writing career he searched assiduously for the right words in the right order and for the most effective organizing

of his materials.'[1] An example of his preoccupation with finding the
right order and sequence is apparent in Volume IX of the holograph
notebooks, which shows that there were originally twenty chapter
titles for *Knock*. Of these, some were actually placed as late as the
third volume, while others were never used at all.[2] Moreover,
when Daniel Macmillan read the manuscript of *Pictures* and wrote
advising that it might be compressed, O'Casey replied: 'I have been
surprised that the stuff I sent in was so full of words. I have since
looked over and looked over the list of chapters, and find it
undesirable to evict any of them from their holding.'[3] Volume VI
of the notebooks contains ten chapter titles for *Inishfallen*, the
arrangement of which bears little resemblance to the eighteen in the
published version.[4] Or again, in Volume XIII of the notebooks,
O'Casey made six different sequences before deciding that the
chapter entitled, 'Inishfallen, Fare Thee Well', should indeed be the
final chapter of the fourth volume. Obviously, O'Casey, in striving
for artistic unity and wholeness, took painstaking care in the
ordering of the contents of a particular volume.

The materials of O'Casey's autobiography do, as we have seen,
establish a sequence of events which, beginning with the hero's
birth and having touched upon his numerous stages of
development, finally merges with the narrator on the closing page.
However, an autobiographer can, in the act of exploring his past,
of recollecting experiences long submerged in the unconscious, of
imaginatively assisting the faultiness of memory, and of making
new discoveries about the nature of the self, be presented with
other structural options. These factors may modify or alter an
autobiographer's sense of purpose, and the consequent changing
relation between intention and content can, in turn, effect the
emerging shape of the work. Since there is a dynamic reciprocal
dependency between evolving intention and structural principles, a
preconceived form is not to be sought in autobiographical
literature; instead, readers of the genre should seek an organic
form, one sufficiently flexible to accommodate options presenting
themselves during the author's encounters with past selves. In
O'Casey's autobiography, organizational patterns are sometimes
readily apparent — particularly in a chapter or group of chapters
— and at other times are rather less obvious. A dramatic instance
of structuring materials is the brief chapter called 'Comrades' in
Inishfallen. It describes an incident during the Irish Civil War in
which three soldiers track down and shoot a former comrade-in-
arms. The imaginative reconstruction of this cold-blooded murder
is interspersed with an account of Sean watching two ducks mating

in Stephen's Green. The typescript of this chapter makes it clear that each narrative was written separately and then arranged in this alternating fashion. O'Casey has juxtaposed his materials in this way to heighten the contrast between the natural behaviour of the ducks who were fulfilling *'God's commandment to multiply and replenish the earth,'* and the life-denying actions of the murdering soldiers. (IV, 109) Their callous behaviour is presented as having its origins in the excessive patriotism from which Sean has become dissociated.

A different example of obvious structural unity within a chapter is to be found in 'The Cap in the Counting-House,' where Johnny's allegiance is sought by three separate organizations. During this period, he works by day in a newspaper and magazine warehouse and, in the evenings, he has begun to attend meetings of the Gaelic League. As he busies himself at work, a leaflet announcing a Gospel meeting appears on the counter before him, encouraging him to 'Come And Be Born Again!' A few minutes later, a second leaflet appears before him inviting him to attend a 'Gigantic Rally of the Socialist Republican Party of Ireland' to be held in Foster Place. At this point in his life, Johnny has no knowledge of socialism — 'What was that?' — so he disregards this message, as he had the previous one. The third leaflet to appear announces a ' '98 Great Commemoration Concert" of Irish music, songs and recitations in the Rotunda Hall. From a strictly factual view, the likelihood of the three leaflets appearing in succession, if indeed at all, is quite remote. If the three incidents did occur at separate times, then the inherent historical truth of each event is substantially modifed here by being associated with the truth of the others. However, the patently false arrangement contains capillary truths that are autobiographically relevant in their own right. By juxtaposing the appeals — 'for God, for Man, and for Country' — O'Casey manages to clarify, in a way that historical authenticity might fail to do, Johnny's options at this juncture of his life.

Of equal importance, the anonymous and surreptitious way the notices are supposedly placed before him emphasizes his unease with his fellow workers and his dislike of the atmosphere in the warehouse: 'The call to freedom from sin, freedom from employers, freedom from national oppression, had each been delivered stealthily, in the murky darkness. . . . He didn't like it; didn't like to be even distantly connected with this fear of being caught in the pleasuance of an idle moment.' (II, 179) The incident has made him realize 'He was down among the dead men here' and so he decides to leave this job. Wishing to show his defiance of the demeaning, humbling attitude of employees to their bosses, he provokes a scene with his boss by refusing to take off his cap as he picks up his wages. Although he is immediately dismissed from the job, and he is acutely aware of the financial consequences of his actions, he finds consolation at the thought of no longer working at Jason's because 'Now I can find a little time to read the books I love.' (II, 183) Thus, the appeal from the three associations is shown to have led to Johnny's assessment of his position at Jason's: he recognizes what he is being denied by working there, and what he could accomplish if he had more time for study. In the previous chapter, 'Work While It Is Not Yet Day,' he was shown working long hours as a vanboy, out in the cold dark mornings, with no time to himself for education or reflection. At the beginning of the chapter subsequent to 'The Cap in the Counting-House,' he is depicted discovering a sense of patriotic fervor. Thus, O'Casey's contrived arrangement of the three covert appeals lends focus and unity to the overall chapter, while simultaneously showing its relationship with those which precede and follow it.

At other times, a chapter might have internal unity but be related to those around it only in a general way. This can be seen, for example, in the chapter, 'His Da, His Poor Da,' from *Knock*, which gives an account of the failing health and approaching death of Michael Casside. Strict chronological order has already been abandoned, for the previous chapter, 'Hill of Healing,' in which Johny is shown attending St Mark's Ophthalmic Hospital for his ulcerous eyes, has established that his father has died. 'His Da, His Poor Da' opens with the statement that Michael Casside, for many months, 'was lying in a big horsehair-covered armchair, shrinking from something that everybody thought of, but nobody ever mentioned.' (I, 33) So frightening does the father's appearance become that Johnny is forbidden to go near the room where the wasted figure constantly sits motionless by the fire. One day, however, curiosity leads the young boy to look through the doorway at the spectral shape; when his father becomes aware of Johnny he shouts weakly for him to go away for 'this is no place for little boys.' Terrified by both the appearance and sound of his father, 'Johnny had closed the door quick, had run for his life through the hall out into the street, full of the fear of something strange, leaving his da, his poor da, shrinking from something that everyone thought of, but nobody ever mentioned.' (I, 37) This repetition of the opening sentence has the effect of bracketing the chapter, allowing it to be inserted here as a self-contained unit, despite the chronological interruption. The three subsequent chapters focus on Michael Casside's death, his funeral and his family's response, thereby carrying forward the plot line of the narrative to the same temporal plane as 'The Hill of Healing,' four chapters earlier.

Many such instances of specific, relatively local patterns of arrangement can be found throughout O'Casey's autobiography. Such obvious narrative patterns, whether in a chapter or a group of chapters, clarify our understanding of O'Casey's evaluation of the meaning and significance of past experiences. For example, when his father died, the boy was too young to respond emotionally to his loss or to understand its economic consequences for him and his family. Now as autobiographer, by arranging information around the isolated memory of seeing his father through the door, O'Casey can suggest that, retrospectively, that experience is associated not only with the prolonged period of Michael Casside's illness but the time when his own future was being determined.

In addition to positioning materials for such immediate effects, other, broader principles of arrangement are operative in the autobiography. One of the most comprehensive of these is made clear in *Inishfallen*, when O'Casey, having described the new building that housed the headquarters of the Labour Movement, writes:

Strange influence buildings had on the memory and the heart! Thousands of buildings were passed, maybe entered, in a lifetime, but only a few were remembered in the soul and mind. Of all the buildings in Dublin, but four of them remained forever and vividly in the heart and mind of Sean: his home, the Church of St Burnupus, the Abbey Theatre, and Liberty Hall; and, indeed, they were four symbols of his life. Each was woven deftly and deep into flesh and spirit. (IV, 76)

These symbols suggest four facets of his personality each of which are, intermittently, given prominence in the autobiography: O'Casey's ordering of his materials encompasses the story of Sean the family man, the religious man, the theatrical man, and the political man. Although these four strands of the life-story do, of course, develop simultaneously and interchangeably, they emerge as useful guiding principles in the organization of materials. As a playwright rather than a novelist, O'Casey is perhaps more concerned with the impact achieved through a dramatic arrangement of scenes and episodes than with the kind of fictional logic of construction one might expect in a conventional novelist.

In any event, this pattern of arrangment is one of the important factors determining balance and proportion in the work.

This fourfold principle is especially prevalent in the third and fourth volumes where active changes are occurring in several areas of the protagonist's life. For an understanding of how these structural methods accentuate the autobiographical relevance of the events recorded, it is useful to examine in some detail how they function throughout *Drums*. The plot of this volume traces the life of the protagonist from his early twenties into his mid-thirties, a period marked by family tragedies and involvement in many patriotic clubs and political organizations. In approaching the experiences of these formative and varied years, O'Casey employs this fourfold principle of arrangement in several ways. It is manifested, for example, in the cluster of four chapters, 'Home of the Living,' 'Drums Under the Window,' 'Song of a Shift,' and 'Lost Leader'. The first of these focuses primarily on the encroachment on the domestic life of the protagonist by his sister Ella and her five children, after her husband, Bugler Benson, has been committed to the asylum. For a time, they come to live with Sean and his mother, who not only must tolerate the invasion and crowding of their small home, but must also share their already meagre food resources with six hungry mouths. It is upon Sean that the responsibility falls of finding another home for them; in the process, he has to endure the pain and embarrassment of waiting for the eviction of the previous tenant (an old, lamentable woman who has nowhere to go but the poorhouse), as well as involve himself in the task of moving Ella's pathetic few possessions into her new home. Finally, when Ella dies, the proud Sean has to undergo the shame of accepting money for her funeral from the rector and even more excruciating the humiliation of the cab driver's refusal to follow directly behind Ella's cheap coffin. These are the events dominating Sean's family life in the years under review.

This chapter is followed by an account of the various movements and exciting developments marking the highpoints of the Irish cultural revival, the period when 'Ireland's life of the golden, scarlet, and sable past came creeping out into the sun from many hidden corners.' (III, 101) 'Drums Under the Windows' presents the different manifestations of the national revival — its societies, leaders, parades, banners and songs — and captures the early euphoric days of the Irish awakening when, 'Everywhere the drums beat again their lusty rolls, making the bright stars in the sky quiver, and bands blew Ireland's past into every ear, and called forth her history of the future.' (III, 114) While the chapter deals with the multifaceted phenomenon that constituted Ireland's rediscovery of its history and culture, showing it turning optimistically to the future, it also serves the autobiographical purpose of depicting the protagonist, under the influence of these forces, learning the Irish language, playing hurling, organizing a pipe band and acquainting himself with all aspects of Ireland's past. Thus, his many patriotic activities are an indication of his newly-awakened political consciousness.

'Song of a Shift' deals with the riots at the Abbey Theatre over Synge's *The Playboy of the Western World*. O'Casey describes the irrational hysteria whipped up in various elements of the Dublin public by the use of the word 'shift' in the play. The chapter opens, 'Ireland had become again the Woeman of the Piercing Wail. Every wall in Dublin was a wall of weeping.' (III, 115) The bitter tone, here and throughout the chapter, contrasts vividly with the high optimism expressed in the preceding chapter. Sean's initial confusion at the reception of Synge's play sharpens the contrast between the goals and ideals of the national revival and the actual treatment given to Synge, its greatest playwright. When Sean attempts to discuss the play at his branch of the Gaelic League, he discovers the prejudice and narrow Catholic pietism of his fellow members. He learns how quickly and savagely Cathleen Ni Houlihan can turn on her literary sons if their vision threatens her. Since this chapter was, of course, writen after O'Casey's own experiences with similar hostile, Irish-Catholic audiences, it serves both to foreshadow and confirm the frustrations expressed in the next volume over the treatment of the *Plough*. For the moment, however, the primary autobiographical significance of 'Song Of a Shift' is that Sean's education in the realities of literary Ireland has begun.

'Lost Leader' gives many details of the conflict between Dr Michael O'Hickey and the upper echelons of the Irish Catholic hierarchy and the Roman Rota over the question of Irish being taught at the New National University. Having described the meagre support given to O'Hickey, O'Casey outlines the cause of the professor's defeat and describes his unhappy isolation and death. In this chapter the protagonist discovers the hypocritical and often devious means by which the bishops can deal with their opponents. The O'Hickey case becomes for him the first blatant instance of the Church hierarchy acting in a fashion that was contrary to the best interests of the Irish people. In addition, he learns with surprise that few of the nationalists had the will or courage to stand up to the clergy. The seeds of Sean's later conviction that institutional religion was a major obstacle on man's road to enlightenment are now sown.

Although the fourfold principle of arrangement operating in these chapters shows the four facets of the hero's personality being carried to new and significant stages of development, it is subsumed by different organizational criteria in other parts of the volume where the balanced patterning of these chapters is not to be found. For example, the three chapters immediately following this foursome take little account of other aspects of Sean's persona and are almost exclusively concerned with his political involvements. Family, literary and religious references are kept to a minimum while information is provided on figures such as Connolly, Griffith, de Valera and Pearse, and details are given about the Labour movement and its relationship with the Irish Republican Brotherhood. Indeed, even in the above foursome, while the main focus is on those facets of his personality just outlined, other issues also surface in the individual chapters. O'Casey achieves this by modulating his narrative from one concern to another, weaving his story to form a tapestry out of the experiences of his past. Such threading together of contents captures more realistically the natural interaction between the domestic, political, religious and literary strands of his hero's character, showing the whole man evolving in several arenas simultaneously. Having rejected the limitations of tight chronological sequence, and using his fourfold framework in a flexible, non-restrictive manner, O'Casey lays claim to all the freedom and potential variation to be derived from his tapestry-like approach.

Such multiplicity of design is in evidence, for example, in 'Home of the Living' which serves other functions beyond the depiction of how Ella's straitened circumstances influence Sean's domestic situation. Indeed, in terms of strict autobiographical relevance, it may seem that Ella, as a secondary character in the plot, receives undue prominence; her actual role, however, is that of a catalyst precipating in the protagonist a series of significant discoveries. For example, Ella's degradation is presented as a contributing factor in challenging his belief in a beneficent God. Having described the appalling poverty of Ella and her family when they move in with Sean and his mother, O'Casey continues: 'And now this added heap of misery was sleeping heavily under his feet, while by a light from a shaded, guttering candle, he tried to read, and reading, remember all the startling things in Darwin's *Descent of Man*.' (III,

83) Under Darwin's influence, his religious commitments are undermined, while the predicament of Ella and her family is a vindication from the reality of his own world of that shaken faith.

Ella is also used as a coalescing force in his political maturation; and, simultaneously, this new stage of political education is shown to be an additional cause of losing his religious beliefs. O'Casey shows Sean reading Prescott's *Conquest of Peru* and there discovering the brutality with which the Spanish, in the name of Christianity, treated the Incas. His reading is interrupted by the news of Ella's death. When he goes to her house to begin the funeral arrangements, the frustration and anger aroused in him by Prescott's book finds an outlet in his reaction to the poverty permeating what he sees:

Jasus! It was terrible! A hell's penticost to all the genteel thieves who batten on the poor! May a flame on every head eat into every brain of them, to be a soft and simple baptism of the fuller flaming life to come! (III, 95)

When he realizes that he has no money to pay for her funeral, he asks:

Where in the name of Christ was he going to get the money to bury her, even in the slinking way destitution buries its out-of-benefit dead? And to only think that she had paid enough in premiums to bury herself and her family a dozen times over! Oh, these thieving, rascally, money-conjuring insurance societies! Asps on the breasts of the poor! (III, 95)

The oppressive conditions of his family, accentuated and highlighted by Ella's death, are, it is implied, an important motivating factor in his wholehearted support of the rights of workers and his involvement with Larkin's union, both of which take place towards the end of this volume.

Finally, O'Casey uses the narrative dealing with Ella to reveal new stages in Sean's literary development. Because of his obligation to contribute to the upkeep of Ella's family, he recognizes that he will be unable to buy all the books he had planned. In addition, the strain and frustration Ella and her children cause to his domestic life are presented as a further hindrance to his literary education. For example, on hearing about Frazer's *The Golden Bough* from a friend, Sean tries, unsuccessfully, to have the library order it. He describes it to the head librarian, whose response is, 'If it's anything like what you make it out to be, it's neither a safe nor a proper book to have knocking about here! But now Sean had something else to think of besides *The Golden Bough*.' (III, 85) With that, the narrative returns to the description of Ella's further engulfment by poverty and degradation. Despite these obstacles, however, he continually strives to pursue his exploration of the world of literature and, in a passing reference during the description of the imposition by Ella and her family, he reflects:

Anyhow, he had a right to think of himself. How could he read right, study things, and write, the way things were? How was he to write articles for the Gaelic League manuscript journal in the midst of this ragged, hunger-agitated commotion? (III, 82)

As the first indication that he had begun to write regularly, this announcement heralds an important development in the literary man.

A chapter that ostensibly deals with the family man can, therefore, suggest the progression in other areas of his life, showing all such developments enhancing and complementing each other: although his home environment is not conducive to study, Sean continues with his private reading; his self-education allows him to write for the Gaelic League, while it also leads to his loss of religious faith; his rejection of religion is, in turn, accompanied by a clearer perception of the exploitation of the poor, an increasing involvement in union activities, and a growing commitment to socialist principles. The unifying device which helps to render the evolution of these inter-twining threads of identity is the account of the events surrounding Ella's death. To explain and qualify the details of Sean's religious, political or literary changes, O'Casey may introduce disparate and wide ranging materials; but the narrative uses Ella's story as the linking device that provides focus and unity to the chapter. In this fashion, O'Casey can suggest the confluence of contrapuntal aspects of the hero's character at this particular phase of his development.

A different instance of O'Casey's structuring of materials is dramatically evident in 'Dark Kaleidoscope,' a multi-faceted chapter in which several aspects of the protagonist's personality are examined together. Opening with a domestic scene, the chapter shows Sean, at home, sick and bed-ridden, with the conditions in his family reaching a new level of poverty as he and his mother try to live on her insignificant old-age pension. In the process of describing these straitened circumstances, O'Casey gradually adjusts the focus of his lens until his hero is shown in a political context. This subtle transition is achieved by first describing Sean's impatience with staying in bed, vaguely hoping his health will improve. He finally decides that he is of a different generation to his tolerant and stoical mother:

Ah, t'hell with it! he thought, he wouldn't stay here to dry up and die! She'd have to stick it, but he wouldn't. Her life was nearly over. She belonged to a different world, the world of submission, patience, resignation; he to that of discontent, resentment, resistance. (III, 210)

He gets up and goes to Liberty Hall and, with that refocusing of the narrative, the political Sean is now seen busily helping out with the relief efforts for the wives and children of the strikers during the 1913 lockout. With yet another adjustment in focus the materials change once more to reveal the religious dimensions of Sean's personality at this period. After Ella's death, the Protestant Orphan Society had made him guardian of her youngest son and, in exchange for the small allowance it provided for his upkeep, the Society demanded that the child be sent regularly to Sunday School. In a discussion with a representative of the Society Sean reveals that his attitude towards religion is now such that he will not force the boy to attend religious classes.

At this juncture in the chapter O'Casey provides the rationale behind his continual readjustment in the narrative focus. He writes that, at this time, Ireland was 'A magic shadow-show, played in a box whose candle is the sun, round which we phantom figures come and go. But Ireland was rather more of a kaleidoscope than a shadow-show: always re-shaping itself into a different pattern.' (III, 219) So far, the chapter has provided information relating to Sean's family, his politics and his religion. Accordingly, when toward the end of the chapter, O'Casey wishes to change the focus yet again so that he can introduce information related to his hero's literary interests, he writes: 'Sean gave the cap of the kaleidoscope a twist, and there he was between two comrades who were carrying a round wreath to one of their Union who had been battered to death by many police batons.' (III, 221) Reacting to the sight of his battered dead comrade, and sensing his own desire for creative expression, Sean vows to avoid confrontations with the police.

Within the broad outline of this fourfold approach other more specific instances of structure are also in evidence. For example, in the group of chapters 'Home of the Living,' 'Drums Under the Windows,' 'Song of a Sift,' and 'Lost Leader,' it is clear that O'Casey is not concerned with chronological progression, even in the most general terms, since the riots over Synge's play took place in 1907 while the death of Sean's sister Ella occurred in 1918, a sequence which is reversed here. To account for such blatant disregard for chronology it is necessary to look to another criterion used in arranging experiences. When an autobiographer begins the process of reviewing his life, of attempting to describe his journey from the past, one of the benefits of seeing everything from his present vantage point is that he can perceive the seeds of later developments in earlier experiences. His new perspective on events can reveal an understanding and appreciation of them usually not accessible as they occurred. Consequently, in the composition of the autobiography, he will highlight and accentuate certain incidents whose role in his evolution has only later become fully apparent. One of the conventional devices of compression and clarification used to render these stages of growth is the structural metaphor of the turning-point. It allows for a careful orchestration of, and preparation for, new levels of maturation and growth: incidents in life can be manipulated so that the contexts in which they occurred will stand in greater relief; experiences can be shaped so that their respective importance can be shown to be a principle operative from the beginning. In autobiography, life's long arcs often become sharply drawn changes in direction.

In *Drums*, O'Casey has organized his contents to highlight the major turning-point in Sean's growth during what is, arguably, the most formative decade of his life. While the volume deals with his loss of religious faith, periodically touches upon his continual exploration of the world of literature, and outlines the difficult conditions of his home life, its primary focus is on contextual material which explains the forces that gradually erode his intense support for Irish nationalism and arouse his sympathy for, and identification with, his fellow workers. Consequently, passages describing various personalities of the national revival, recounting squabbles and infighting among different patriotic factions, or presenting imaginary discussions about Ireland between St Partrick, St Laurence O'Toole and Nelson are autobiographically pertinent because they provide the contexts and indicate the nuances of his earlier changes in political affiliation. That this ideological shift is the paramount experience of this third volume is confirmed by the arrangment of its eighteen chapters. The first eight chapters deal with the influences eventually leading to Sean's decision to move away from active support of nationalism. The turning-point is reached in the two middle chapters of the book: the ninth chapter is an open and explicit expression of Sean's doubts, while the tenth contains a direct statement of his commitment to the workers. After this new political orientation has been announced, the final eight chapters show the con-solidation of his involvement with union-related matters. Thus, the book builds up to his doubts by revealing the inadequacies of nationalist policies; once he has made his decision it then confirms this new commitment.

The introductory chapter, 'At the Sign of the Pick and Shovel,' plays a special role in relation to the rest of the volume. It is a carefully constructed overture foreshadowing both the primary focus and the structural shape of the whole book. References to domestic, literary, religious and political affairs in Sean's life indicate that the materials will be approached from the fourfold principle of organization operative elsewhere in the autobiography. Most important, however, the chapter foreshadows the specific changes about to take place in his political allegiances. It opens with Sean getting a job as a labourer with the Great Northern Railway and returns full circle to this topic at the end. Within this framework, O'Casey provides a brief indication of Sean's disillusionment with the objectives of Irish nationalism by stressing the essential differences between the leaders of the movement and people like himself. Imagining what the response of the executive of the Gaelic League would be if he, an ordinary labourer, applied for financial assistance to go to an Irish district to learn the language, Sean responds:

. . . what would happen? The tidy-minded, uninspirable Secretary, Paddy O'Daly, would come over, grip his arm, lead him to the door, and say, Now, now, we're engaged in very important business. The like of them would hurry by Whitman spitting out of him as he leaned by a corner of the Bowery. And doing so, they'll die, for whoever walks a furlong without sympathy walks to his own funeral dressed in his shroud. Ah, to hell with them! (III, 25)

The break between Sean the worker and the nationalists is clearly foreshadowed here, and it is no accident that, at the actual moment when this decision is made in Chapter X, O'Casey echoes these same words.

The primary concern of the four chapters following the introduction — 'Poor Tom's Acold,' 'House of the Dead,' 'Behold, My Family is Poor,' and 'Home of the Living' — is, as we have seen, to show the harsh reality of Sean's family life. It is a world where poverty is the norm, where suffering is seen as an essential part of life, and where death is often welcomed for the release it provides from misery and anguish. The four chapters are placed here because they depict the bleak and extreme conditions of life in the back streets of Dublin, a social environment which fosters physical debilitation and pervasive despair, and which is crying out for immediate and radical solutions.

In sharp contrast to this pessimistic picture, the subsequent chapter, 'Drums Under the Windows,' captures the excited hopes and aspirations that the rising tide of patriotic fervour arouses in Sean. By positioning this chapter immediately following those that painted such a depressing picture of Dublin's poor, O'Casey's inference is that, with the revival of Ireland's language, with the blossoming again of her culture, with the attainment of her freedom, such poverty and suffering will be eradicated. The vision of the nationalists was that Ireland free would be Ireland released from the shackles of destitution. Because this infectious patriotic enthusiasm captivates Sean's imagination, detailed accounts of his political activities and cultural interests are presented.

But, just as the idealism of this chapter is in sharp contrast to the grim reality presented in those that precede it, so now is Sean's optimism deflated by the events described in the three ensuing chapters. In the first of these, 'Song of a Shift,' he becomes somewhat more knowledgeable about the world of Irish letters: he hears of Synge and learns about his controversial play, and he gets his first glimpse of Yeats. But his introduction to Ireland's literary renaissance is also an initiation into the realities of Ireland's treatment of her literary sons. The chapter is structured around a series of conversations: between the Viceroy and his police sergeant, between Sean and various protestors (over the play), between Sean and fellow-members of his branch of the Gaelic League, and between Sean and his friend Donal O'Murachadha. The tone of these conversations varies from the wide-eyed fear of the Viceroy to the hysteria of the people on the street, from the prejudice of the Gaelic Leaguers to the rational interpretation of events that Donal O'Murachadha offers. Sean himself, still under the influence of patriotic fervour and therefore sensitive to any possible slur on Ireland's name, expresses some doubts about Yeats's loyalties. However, as a result of his discussion with Donal, he changes his mind and at the end of the chapter expresses the wish to see the plays of both Yeats and Synge. In this chapter, then, not only is he shown becoming familiar with some of the plays of Ireland's literary revival but, equally important, he learns how the Irish public can mistreat its writers. In listening to the suspicious and prejudiced comments on Synge's *Playboy*, and in witnessing the irrational reaction to Yeats, Sean senses that his zealous and unquestioning support of Irish-Ireland has begun to be undermined. It is to achieve this effect of disillusionment that O'Casey has placed this chapter on Synge's play two chapters after the account of Ella's death, although the *Playboy* riots occurred eleven years before Ella died. The Irish cultural and political revival is presented as a potential antidote to the circumstances which caused her death; the controversy over Synge's play is given as a concrete example of the betrayal of those expectations.

In the next chapter, Sean's disillusionment increases with his discovery of the discrepancy between Catholic-Ireland and his own conception of Irish-Ireland. 'Lost Leader' provides a detailed account of the stages of the O'Hickey controversy over the issue of teaching Irish at the New National University, from the support Sean expected the different Irish clubs to give to the professor, to O'Hickey's defeat at Rome and his neglect upon returning to Ireland. O'Casey compares the indifference shown to O'Hickey, even in death, to the grandiose public approval given a Father O'Growney who, it is maintained, had not done half as much for Irish culture:

What a loneliness there was in the silent burial of Dr O'Hickey on that cold, damp day in Carrick Beg! A few faithful friends were there to honour a death that had a sting, and a grave that won a victory. How lonely compared to the stir and vivacity around the burial of a Father O'Growney a few short years before. What a flutter there was when *his* body was brought all the way from California to be buried in Maynooth College. (III, 140)

That funeral, particularly the fawning behaviour towards the bishops of Douglas Hyde, founder of the Gaelic League, increases Sean's perception of the narrow and church-dominated views that permeated such movements. He has learned his second lesson in the precise nature of Irish nationalism.

These reservations are crystallized in the next chapter, 'Gaelstroem,' which begins, appropriately: 'Sean stood on the borders of doubt again. He was a bit bewildered about the essences in the freedom they were struggling to gain.' (III, 143) What then follows is an enumeration of some of the questionable incidents in recent Irish affairs that show the true face of Irish nationalism, suggesting to Sean the kind of society that would exist were Ireland to achieve independence. These include the treatment of Parnell, the defeat of W. P. O'Ryan and his Boyne Valley Enterprise, the bishops' criticism of the Fenians and the I.R.B., and the refusal of the Dean of St Patrick's Cathedral to allow the church to be used for a religious service in Irish during St Patrick's festival. The domination of Irish life by an excessively pietistic and reactionary Catholic clergy, together with the lack of courage among the leaders of the various movements, are all personified for Sean by Douglas Hyde. In a dramatised conversation with Donal O'Murachadha, O'Casey presents the sectarian biases that Hyde displays in the Gaelic League, a supposedly non-religious organization. He concludes: 'The passion to be all things to all men is too strong in him to allow a leadership bringing the people into the promised land.' (III, 154) Sean's hopes of finding such a political leader in the ranks of the nationalists are now fading rapidly.

For Sean, the *Playboy* riots, the treatment of O'Hickey, and the behaviour of Hyde are symptomatic of a larger set of attitudes that causes him to question his support of republican goals. His reservations are made clear in the tenth chapter, 'Hora Novissima,' which begins: 'Sean was growing tired. He saw how few had gathered around Eire.' (III, 160) Looking to the Gaelic League, the Irish Republican Brotherhood, and the Irish Socialist Republican Party, he asks:

Who would be the first to make an army out of these active and diligent dry bones? Who the first to breathe into them a breath from the flame of endeavour and strife and defiance? Whose lips would first be touched by a red coal from God's altar? Who would be daring enough to snatch a flame from the burning bush and light the land with it? (III, 160)

Having assessed the available leaders who might show the way to the future he envisioned, Sean decides that his aims are at odds with all their aspirations. Accordingly, he has reached the turning-point of rejection which has been prepared for since the beginning of the volume:

Well, to hell with them then! . . . Few of the Republicans were of his kinship. Here, in these houses in the purple of poverty and decay, dwelt his genuine brethren. Why shouldn't he fight for them against the frauds that kept them prisoners there? (III, 165)

Sean's education in the reality of the nationalist movement has been completed and his commitment to the workers sealed. The significance of the earlier chapters outlining the appalling conditions in the slums of Sean's world is now fully apparent. He recognizes that the objectives of the republicans have very little to do with the realities of deprivation and death that are so much a part of his family situation. He sees the discrepancies between them and himself over both the analysis of Ireland's problems and the perception of Ireland's future; because their vision is restricted by what he sees as a lack of true courage, by a religious conservatism, and by an ignorance of the working-class people, his faith in nationalism is irredeemably shaken.

Just as the first eight chapters of the volume prepare the context and outline the causes of this turning-point, the last eight chapters confirm his change. The events and experiences presented in them consolidate the new directions in Sean's life and demonstrate the continuing divergence between him and the republicans.

The first of these, 'Green Fire on the Hearth,' is used to corroborate his assessment that the intense vision of the nationalists ignores the plight of the Irish worker. Just as O'Casey used Yeats and Synge as instruments to reveal the intolerance of the Irish public, so now he uses Shaw as a means of crystallizing Sean's decision to dissociate himself from republican ideals. A friend advises him to read *John Bull's Other Island*, and it is revealing that the account of his actual buying and reading of the play stresses that, to do so, he must miss attending his weekly meeting of the Gaelic League. Shaw's play bears out Sean's sense of a different Ireland, more destitute and woebegone than the romanticized one of republican imagination. His continued reading helps remove the distorting veils of nationalism from the face of Cathleen ni Houlihan, revealing a stark and sombre picture of a country needing a strong and dynamic leader, one possessing the insight and perception to recognize its problems and the imagination and courage to offer appropriate solutions.

The following chapter, 'Prometheus Hibernica,' shows Sean's discovery that the leader he has been looking for is not to be found in the ranks of the republicans. Two chapters previously, he had concluded that 'The people still waited for a Prometheus to bring down a brand of the divine fire, and set the leaden hearts of the poor aflame from one end of Ireland to the other.' (III, 162) He now decides that Jim Larkin is such a man: 'Following afar off for a while, Sean had come at last to hear Larkin speak, to stand under a red flag rather than the green banner.' (III, 187) His commitment to mutual support among workers is soon shown when he quits a temporary job as a labourer rather than sign a document which would pledge him to have nothing to do with the union. If anything, his support of the union is strengthened by the loss of his job. In addition to writing regular articles for the Irish Worker, he devotes much of his time to Larkin who soon leads the workers in their most crucial hour — the Dublin Transport Strike of 1913 which results in a general lockout. 'Dark Kaleidoscope' recounts how Sean is made 'Secretary to a Committee formed to collect funds to provide clothes and boots for women and children of locked-out workers.' (III, 210) The growing divergence between Sean's affiliations and Irish society is reinforced dramatically for him when, at the instigation of the Archbishop of Dublin, there is a public outcry over Larkin's suggestion of sending these children to be housed and fed by families of trade unionists in England, until the lockout is over.

In 'Under the Plough and the Stars,' Sean is shown becoming more deeply involved with the cause of the workers when he is asked to help in the organization of the Irish Citizen Army. When his attempts to forge a bond between the Army and the Irish Volunteers (the army of the Republicans) are rebuked, another wedge is driven between him and the republican movement. In the following chapter, the final link is broken when he officially resigns from the I.R.B. rather than cease to criticize some of its policies.

While Sean's reading increases his awareness of the conditions of workers and the efforts of socialists in other countries, the last three chapters of *Drums* indicate that the immediate consequence of his newly clarified political views is his further estrangement from Irish life. During a period of illness, he leaves the hospital prematurely when one of the nurses — a nun — accuses him of godlessness and berates him for his involvement in the transport strike. The subsequent chapter depicts him discovering further evidence of the hostility of republicans to the workers when the Irish Volunteers do everything in their power to avoid sharing a shipload of guns with the Irish Citizen Army. In the final chapter, with Larkin gone to America, and James Connolly the new leader of the Army, Sean is unhappy with what he sees as the betrayal of the workers' cause by Connolly whose 'fine eyes saw red no longer, but stared into the sky for a green dawn.' (III, 266) For Sean, the outbreak of the Easter Rising, described in the final chapter of the volume, did not hold out much prospect that the workers' rights would be recognized. The account of that shift in allegiance is the major structural element in *Drums*; by arranging the experiences of this period around the pivotal moments of patriotic disillusionment and commitment to proletarian goals, O'Casey highlights the meaning of those years in the context of his contemporary views.

On other occasions, O'Casey uses the device in a less-rigid manner, in which it provides an underpinning to the general sweep of the narrative rather than a principle of order evident on every page. An arrangement of this kind is evident in *Inishfallen* in the account of Sean's decision to leave Dublin for London. As we have seen, when O'Casey went to England in 1926 he had no clear intention of leaving

Ireland permanently. Yet, when this proved to be the case, and he came to deal with this event in the autobiography, he presented it as a decision that had been in the making for many months, even years, in advance. O'Casey, obviously very conscious of the claim, particularly among Irish critics of his work, that he lost much of his inspiration when he removed himself from his roots in Dublin, is careful to build up a detailed account of the restrictive forces in Ireland that would have greatly hampered his development as an artist. Thus, to his retrospective eyes, his departure from Ireland was the major event of these years, if not of his life, but it was so for reasons quite different from those commonly held. The plot of the book traces the highlights in the decade beginning when Sean, at the age of thirty-seven, is an unemployed labourer, and ending when the forty-six-year-old man has achieved success at the Abbey and sets sail for England. However, throughout the volume, all the influential experiences of this ten-year period are shaped and orchestrated to accentuate their role as contributing factors leading to his exile.

The first direct expression of Sean's intentions is to be found, significantly, as the mid-point of the volume in the chapter, 'A Terrible Beauty is Borneo,' which describes his response to the establishment of the Irish Free State: 'Turn your back on the green and the gold, on the old hag that once had the walk of a queen! What's ni Houlihan to you, or you to ni Houlihan? Nothing now.' (IV, 148) In addition, not only is he no longer closely involved with the destiny of Ireland but he senses that his own future as a developing individual and a maturing writer will be hampered by remaining there, because he 'felt that Dublin had told him all she knew.' (IV, 150) While this decision is presented as primarily a consequence of immediate events in Irish public life, he has, in fact, been shown as alienated from the forces controlling contemporary Irish society since the outset of the volume. In the opening chapter, after assessing de Valera's political manoeuvring and William O'Brien's assuming control of the union, Sean concludes that there would now be a

tripartite government of all Irish life, the one to be supreme in politics, the other in labour, with a churchman to see that all went well with the faith, so that a new trinity, one and indivisible, should live in peace, unity, joy, and quadragesimal jubilation under the siestal shadow of the mighty mitre of Armagh. (IV, 13)

Prior to the mid-point statement of Sean's intention to leave Ireland, other aspects of his life are also shown as having been severed from their past. Most notable is the death of Mrs Casside

whose attention, care and love were constants through so many of
the vicissitudes of his early years. That her death marked a clear
division between a defined past and an uncertain future is stressed in
Sean's reaction to her passing: 'He knew that this hurly-burly of
thought and confused vision would gradually resolve itself into a
newly-ordered life; a life broken sharply from the more immediate
past; and that his new life would go on striding ever further away
from the geranium, the fuchsia, and the musk.' (IV, 34) Similarly,
before the explicit announcement of his plan to leave, Sean is shown
becoming frustrated with his career as a playwright. He had
originally turned to writing because of his disillusionment with the
religious and political atmosphere in the new Ireland. Upon
achieving his goal as a successful dramatist, however, he becomes
increasingly uneasy with his new status and disappointed with
Ireland's literary milieu. These attitudes are given reinforcement in
the three chapters which follow the announcement of leaving
Ireland, each of which gives further instances of his disillusionment.
In 'The Temple Entered,' the Dublin audience's violent response to
the *Plough* opens his eyes to a new side of Irish society, a perception
increased by his sense of personal mistreatment at the Abbey.
Having expressed the desire 'to move somewhere else to a place in
which he would find fairer comfort, greater space, and a steady
quietness,' (IV, 172) he decides, at the end of the chapter, to 'hoist his
sail and go to England.' (IV, 184)

   In 'Dublin's Gods and Half-Gods,' he is amazed to discover that
the great Irish literary figures he has admired from afar prove, on
closer acquaintance, to have clay feet. He is surprised when he learns
that Yeats read Zane Grey and Dorothy Sayers for relaxation; he is
similarly taken aback when he finds Lady Gregory with a copy of *Peg
O' My Heart*. The awe in which he held these people is replaced by
the realization that 'The lordly ones weren't always quite so lordly
with literature as they generally posed to be.' (IV, 195) In 'Dublin's
Glittering Guy,' his initial uneasiness with Dublin's literary world,
the shallowness and artificiality of which is epitomized by George
Russell and his coterie of supporters, is followed by his outright
rejection of it: 'This man is not for me; none of these here are for me;
you must go, Sean, go from them, for their people are not your
people, neither is their god your god.' (IV, 207)

   The subsequent chapter, 'The Girl He Left Behind Him,' shows him
discovering that, much as he likes his girlfriend Nora Creena, she
lacks the qualities necessary for their happiness together. Although
'she was good to look at, gentle in manner, wistfully patient in listening to his talk,' (IV, 219) she is also 'scantily equipped with the

courage to defy, or resist, the bitter respectability' of her family. (IV, 218) Together, they would read the poems of Milton and Keats, and discuss Shaw's writings on socialism, leading Sean to believe that they shared a special sympathy and mutual vision of the world. But eventually he realizes that he is deluding himself, for the Catholic Nora 'hadn't it in her to stand out safely against opposition. She wilted under the family's resentment and the priest's advice.' (IV, 221) At the end of the chapter, having concluded that 'Nora wasn't for him', (IV, 230) he faces the future on his own, but knowing 'that he could never be alone, however lonely he might be.' (IV, 232)

To verify that there was little redeemable about contemporary Irish life, that Sean could not, in fact, identify with this society, O'Casey places 'Silence' as the penultimate chapter of the book. Focusing on the controversies of the Reverend Walter McDonald's life, the chapter gives a detailed account of the hypocritical and often patently immoral practices of the Catholic hierarchy in the new Ireland: 'There are the Irish bishops for you, men and women of Eireann! What a gang they were! In his heart, Sean had known it all along, and he had always hated their hypocrisy, made more splendidly odious by the Tyrian dye of their purple magna cappas.' (IV, 249)

The presentation of the circumstances that made leaving Ireland inevitable for Sean is now complete: accordingly, the final chapter expresses what has been established as an inevitable and logical decision. The chapter begins:

It was time for Sean to go. He had had enough of it. He would be no more of an exile in another land than he was in his own. He was a voluntary and settled exile from every creed, from every Party, and from every literary clique, fanning themselves into silence with unmitigated praise of each other in the most select corners of the city's highways and byebye-ways. He would stay no longer to view life through a stained-glass window, a Sinn Fein spy-glass, from a *prie-dieu*, or through the thigh-bone of a hare. He would go beyond these, and view life through his own eyes. (IV, 267–268)

Several times throughout the chapter, O'Casey repeats the phrase, 'It was time for Sean to go,' until, in the final line, Sean does what has been prepared for throughout the volume — he bids goodbye to Ireland: 'Sweet Inishfallen, fare thee well! For ever!' (IV, 286) By expressing the idea of exile at the halfway point of *Inishfallen*, O'Casey organizes the events of his past around a turning-point that provides order for the contents of the whole volume. The experiences described in the second half of the book do not merely give additional reasons for that decision but confirm its retrospectively-perceived wisdom.

A more concentrated example of O'Casey's use of a turning-point as a structural device is to be found in the three opening chapters of *Rose*. In them, the ostensible subject matter is Sean's arrival and initial experiences in London; the actual focus, however, is on theatre matters, particularly the circumstances leading to the submission and rejection of the *Tassie*. Because the *Tassie* had, as we have seen, such a pivotal influence on his career as a dramatist, the background to its composition, along with its reception and its history down to the present become an important focus in the account of this period. In 'London Apprentice,' the play itself is not mentioned; instead, the chapter deals with Sean's initial response to London, his many visits to the theatre, his interviews with drama critics, and his introduction to some of England's social and artistic elite. His impression of English theatre is that its drama is superficial and trite, lacking passion and vitality. He believes these characteristics stem from the fact that much of English life — London life, at least — seems to have lost its strong, rural folk tradition. He poses the question:

Why is the English Theatre so low in mind, so scanty in fancy and imagination, and the play-acting so fond of fasting from manly action and a lusty voice? Let him who spoke thirty years ago, speak again. Go on, Mr Yeats — we're all listening. (V, 21)

With that, O'Casey quotes Yeats's statements about the vulgarization of the modern imagination, particularly in the theatre which he saw as growing

more elaborate, developing the player at the expense of the poet, developing the scenery at the expense of the player, . . . until at last life turns to other things, content to leave specialized energy to weaklings and triflers, to those in whose body there is the least quantity of herself. (V, 21)

O'Casey continues to discuss the present state of the theatre leading to the point where he cites Yeats's opinion that

The arts have always lost something of their sap when they have been cut off from the people as a whole. The old culture came to a man at his work; it was not at the expense of life, but an exaltation of life itself. . . . It is possible to speak the universal truths of human nature whether the speakers be peasants or wealthy men. (V, 27–28)

Sean enthusiastically concurs with Yeats's beliefs — 'You never spoke a truer word, Yeats' — because he believes that the poet understood the hearts and minds of the common people.

The implication of O'Casey's assessment of the barren condition of English drama, and his use of Yeats in support of his contention that art can achieve passion and vigour only if it never strays too far from its folk roots, is only understood fully by its juxtaposition with the contents of the following chapter. There, he recounts how he got the title of the *Tassie* from a folk song, and he explains that his intention was to examine the effects of war on the ordinary soldier, 'those who, not understanding the bloodied melody of war, went forth to fight, to die, or to return again with tarnished bodies and complaining minds.' (V, 31) Unlike the idealized pictures of war in plays such as Sherriff's *Journey's End*, his play would strip away the glory and honour falsely associated with military enterprises, revealing the toll it exacts in simple human terms: 'The ruin, the squeal of the mangled, the softening moan of the badly rended are horrible, be the battle just or unjust; be the fighters striving for the good or manifesting faith in evil.' (V, 31) Believing that the *Tassie* brought human passion, emotion and suffering to the stage, thereby coincidently fulfilling Yeats's dictum that great art must deal honestly with these fundamental verities, O'Casey can show his incomprehension at Yeats's rejection of the play. The emphasis on the moribund English theatre and the exalted praise of Yeats's views on art, given in the previous chapter, underscore the incongruity of the poet's decision.

To stress that his original views on the *Tassie* were substantially correct and his actions justified, O'Casey, in 'The Friggin Frogs' chapter of *Rose*, traces the fate of the play down to his own present in 1952. In doing this, he can indicate that Yeats and the other Abbey directors must have had a change of heart about the play's merit, since it was produced at the Abbey in 1935. By giving a summary of the *Tassie*'s history, O'Casey can also demonstrate the changes in Sean's feelings toward Yeats, from his open and bitter hostility in 1928 to the friendly reconciliation with him in Dublin in 1935. Even more important, by citing productions and reviews, he can show clearly that, aside from its continual mistreatment at the hands of Irish critics, 'Everywhere else, the play has been accepted as a fine and courageous experiment in modern drama.' (V, 53–54) Evaluating the *Tassie* controversy more than twenty years after the fact, O'Casey, only too aware of its consequences on his life, and if anything more fully convinced of the validity of his initial estimate of the play's worth, can marshall relevant material from intervening years to substantiate his argument. Not restricted by a tight chronological recounting of his hero's life, O'Casey suspends the presentation of other experiences while he deals with this major watershed in his career as a playwright. For example, in anticipating how much royalties the Abbey's staging of the *Tassie* would likely earn, Sean casually estimates that they 'would about cover the expenses of the birth of his child.' (V, 32) Prior to this, there has been no mention of Sean either meeting or marrying Eileen Carey. Not until the fourth chapter, 'Feathering His Nest,' does the focus return to 1926 and the narrative picks up the story of his relationship with Eileen Carey.

Turning-points such as these allow O'Casey to make sense of former experiences, to view them in the larger context of his life, and to structure them in a manner that indicates his contemporary perspective on them. Thus, disregard for precise chronological sequences, far from being an unfaithful reflection of the past, can suggest its long-term implications and more enduring truths.

Another influence on the shape of the work, particularly so in those volumes depicting intense periods of transformation and growth, is the presence of figures of mediation. In an autobiography, a mediator is usually presented as a symbolic embodiment and articulation of the aspirations of the protagonist which so far have been only latent facets of his personality. More immediately and demonstrably influential in the hero's growth than models (whose role was discussed in the previous chapter of this study), mediators arouse and crystallize stages of progression in the intellectual and emotional development of the protagonist. They accomplish this by bringing to the level of consciousness orientations of identity which, hitherto, have been only vague and diffuse aspects of character. As W. David Shaw has observed, the mediator is one 'who helps make accessible to the speaker the truths or values he is trying to reach.'[5] Some mediation figures may play a general role, serving as relatively impersonal agents who happen to be instrumental in determining a specific aspect of the protagonist's education. For example, in *Pictures*, O'Casey recounts how Johnny, who 'had always loved sketching,' is introduced to the world of paintings through prints of Fra Angelico and Constable:

So, through these two men, beauty of colour and form above and beside him came closer; came to his hand; and he began to build a house of vision with them, a house not made with hands, eternal in his imagination, so that the street he lived in was peopled with the sparkling saints and angels of Angelico, and jewelled with the serene loveliness Constable created out of the radiance of uncommon clay. (II, 226)

Other mediators play much more sustained roles, particularly during formative periods in the hero's life. Such a figure is the ubiquitous tram-conductor who appears so frequently that he becomes one of the unifying motifs of the first four volumes; he appropriates the role of mediator by fostering in the maturing youth an awareness of, and interest in, Ireland's history and culture. The conductor makes his first appearance when the young Johnny and his mother are delayed on a tram by the crowds making their way to a ball at Dublin Castle. When the conductor begins to sing a Fenian song, Mrs Casside leads Johnny off the tram, warning him that 'Little Protestant boys should never listen to Fenian songs . . . whenever you hear one, you must always murmur God Save the Queen to yourself.' (I, 22) At the end of *Knock*, in an almost identical scene, Johnny and his mother meet the voluble conductor again, this time during the illuminations celebrating Victoria's birthday. In this encounter, he berates his passengers for showing such slavish interest in celebrations for a foreign monarch. As this dramatic scene unfolds, the young boy makes a series of discoveries from his mother: he learns that she now feels the 'conductor's a very sensible man'; he finds out that his father believed the 'Fenians were all honest, outspoken men'; (I, 175) and he is reassured that, despite being a Protestant, he himself is indeed Irish. These facts established, the stage is set for the conductor to have the maximum influence on the impressionable and receptive boy. While the passengers stare at the procession, 'The conductor kept shaking his head scornfully as he went from one outstretched hand to another. Poor Wolfe Tone, poor Wolfe Tone, he kept murmuring, as he mouched along, poor Wolfe Tone.' (I, 177) Hearing the conductor break into a song about Wolfe Tone's tombless grave, the boy is prompted to inquire, 'Who was Wolfe Tone, Ma? whispered Johnny, moved strangely by seeing tears trickling down the cheeks of the conductor as he sang.' (I, 178) Although his mother expressed the loyalist view that Tone was a rebel and a troublemaker, an awareness of Tone's identity is instilled in the boy.

In succeeding volumes, the conductor continues in this role of mediating information about heroes and events from Ireland's past. In *Pictures*, under his encouragement, Johnny begins to learn the Irish language from a book which the conductor 'had given . . . to him during a theatrical night in the stable of Hill Street, saying, I couldn't make anything out of it; but you're young, and everyone should know the language of his country.' (II, 159) Although the guiding tutelage of the conductor has made Johnny an avid student of Ireland's language, history and culture, the youth's sense of identity is far from being clearly defined. He is still emotionally involved with, and committed to his religious beliefs, especially because of the strong influence of the Reverend Harry Fletcher, whose embodiment of Christian ideals as well as his close friendship with the teen-aged Johnny establish him as another mediating figure. At this point in his life Johnny has failed to set priorities in his allegiances to the attractive power of these very different mediators. To highlight the disparate intellectual worlds of these twin influences O'Casey, in an obvious manipulation of content, arranges a visit by both men to Johnny as he studies at home, late into a cold winter's night. When he hears a knock at the door, Johnny expects it to be the rector but, instead, discovers 'his old friend, the tram conductor' who has brought two books, *Speeches From the Dock* and *The Life of Wolfe Tone* and the words of the song, 'The Felons of Our Land.' The enthusiastic conductor even sings part of the song so Johnny can learn the air, although he does so quietly so as not to disturb the sleeping Mrs Casside. Johnny has been reading Ruskin's *Crown of Wild Olives* and now naively attempts to share his liking for the book with the conductor. So intense and blind is the conductor's patriotism, however, that he is incredulous that any true Irishman would read a book by an English writer. His claim that only the Irish 'have th' light' further confuses the surprised Johnny:

> The Catholic Faith, you mean? asked Johnny.
> No, no, no, he said impatiently. That's there, too; but I mean th' light o' freedom we're goin' to win from th' English — th' leprosy o' want desthroy them! (II, 193)

Their discussion is interrupted by the arrival of Harry Fletcher who, because he has been transferred to another parish for being too liberal, including allowing songs to be sung for the dead, has dropped by to bid farewell to Johnny and Mrs Casside. This is an awkward situation for the youth who is embarrassed at the thought of an encounter between these representatives of contradictory elements in his own character. In what could be a farcical scene out of one of his plays, O'Casey has the conductor hide behind a sofa out of the rector's view. In the ensuing conversation, Harry Fletcher explains to Johnny why singing prayers for the dead is not a radical gesture:

> Surely it is good to pray that God may give them eternal rest, and let perpetual light shine upon their suffering souls.
> We say in Irish, said Johnny, of one who is dead, Solus Dé dá anam — Light o' God to his soul!
> Eh? said Mr Harry, puzzled; Irish what?
> Irish, Irish language, you know, murmured Johnny ashamedly.

Oh, yes, yes, quite, murmured Mr Harry so indifferently that Johnny's face was reddened, and he wished he hadn't said it.

A prayer for the departed, went on Mr Harry, is plainly implied in the prayer for Christ's church militant here on earth, too.

Quite, murmured Johnny, trying to get back his ease of manner after the thoughtless slip of mentioning the Irish language. (II, 194)

As he bids goodbye, the rector makes an appeal to Johnny to keep 'the Faith alive and fresh in our hearts.'

The youth must now deal with his single-minded Gaelic friend who, predictably, has difficulty making sense of the conversation he has just overheard. The references to the 'Irish Church' and 'apostolic faith' convince him that these so-called Protestants must, in their hearts, be Catholics. Johnny attempts to explain the nature of his and Harry Fletcher's Protestantism: 'We belong to the one, Catholic, and apostolic church,' to which the conductor responds, 'There's me for you now! I always thought yous were Protestants.' When Johnny claims 'St Patrick founded our church as he founded yours,' the conductor is further mystified: 'That's the first time I ever heard tell St Patrick was a Protestant.' Eventually, the conductor brings the conversation around to the only topic of real interest to him, by asking how the rector feels about Ireland. He is astounded to be told that Ireland 'never enters his head.' His immediate response — 'A gay lot o' foreigners there's in this counthry' — is typical of his one-dimensional view of Ireland. For the moment, however, his limitations as a mediator are quickly forgotten; at the end of the chapter, he is both the real and symbolic agent of Johnny Casside's transformation into Sean O'Cathasaigh: 'I'm goin' to call you Sean from this out, said the conductor, as he held Johnny's hand at parting.' (II, 196) Following so close on the rector's appeal to Johnny's religious beliefs, this figurative baptism into the secular affiliation of patriotism highlights the conflicting interests these mediators arouse in the youth. In the juxtaposition of the rival self-images represented by these relationships lies the true indication of the protagonist's character at this time.

While Johnny's friendship with the conductor continues as they participate in various political demonstrations together, the essential differences between the conductor's narrow patriotism and Sean's open-mindedness surface again during the riots over Synge's play. In this instance, the conductor is quick to take umbrage at the least suggestion of an insult to Ireland's name, although he has no idea what that insult might be. Later, when an Irish government is finally established, the conductor makes his last appearance in the autobiography and is shown to be utterly disillusioned with what he considers the betrayal of his vision of an Irish-Ireland. Earlier in this volume, O'Casey has foreshadowed the conductor's suspicions about an independent Ireland. In the chapter which describes the many different clubs and associations marching under their banners through the streets of Dublin, Sean is shown to be 'a little uneasy' by the presence of prominent figures such as Alderman Jay Jay Farrell, a wealthy businessman who had voted 'for an official welcome to an English King.' Sean T. O'Kelly's presence in the role of High Steward of the parade creates further unease in Sean. O'Casey as autobiographer, aware that O'Kelly was a founding member of de Valera's Fianna Fail party in 1926, and was Minister of Finance in the Irish government at the time of composition of this volume (later still, he would be elected for two terms as President of Ireland, from 1945 to 1959), allows the conductor to voice open suspicion of Ireland's future under men like O'Kelly:

Eh, Sean, whispered the tram conductor, holding Sean by the skirt of his coat, looka that fella doin' the big with the top hat an' frock-coat! Where did he break out from?
    Shush! said Sean. That's Shawn Tee O'Kelly, Chairman of the Gaelic League Dublin Committee and High Steward of today's gathering. It's queer, said the conductor, an' it gives me a pang to see th' like of that on a day like this. I see a glint of a thing here I don't like. It isn't natural. It's a dictum that's dangerous. It doesn't augur well for th' future. (III, 107)

His fears are realized with the emergence of the middle-class, capitalist and conservative social order in Ireland after independence. However, despite his eventual loss of faith in seeing the establishment of a truly Gaelic Ireland, the conductor played an important role in fostering Sean's original enthusiasm for all things Irish. Sean learns what the conductor has to offer but eventually progresses beyond those interests and beliefs, leaving the unchanged conductor stranded on the shores of his outdated rhetoric.

By far the most influential mediator, not only during the period of Sean's intellectual maturation but throughout much of his life, is George Bernard Shaw. No other figure is referred to with such approval or credited with such a pervasive role in Sean's intellectual, literary and even family life. Shaw emerges as the archetypal mediator who again and again unveils intellectual realms and social ideas which, to this point, have been only vaguely sensed by the hero. As we have seen, reading *John Bull's Other Island* helps crystallize Sean's changing views on the contemporary state of Ireland and the remedies needed to secure true freedom:

Shaw showed an Ireland very different from the lady Yeats made her out to be, peasants dancing around her to the sound of tabor and drum, their homespun shirts buttoned up with stars. Shaw's was rather grimy, almost naked, save for the green flag draped round her middle. She was grey with the dustiness of flour mixed with the dung of pigs, and her fair hands were horny with the hard work of turning stony ground into a state of fertility. The look on her fine face was one of unholy resignation, like one once in agony, now at ease in the thick torpor of murphia. (III, 173)

Similarly, it is Shaw who sharpens Sean's knowledge and understanding of the theatre, and Shaw is even cited as a significant factor in Sean's decision to end his relationship with Nora Creena, his Dublin girlfriend. These changes in the political, theatrical and personal areas of his life are, as we have previously seen, credited as important contributing factors in his decision to go into exile.

When Sean moves to England, Shaw's role increases after the two men meet and become friends. Shaw offers advice to him on how to deal with the rights of his plays; it is on Shaw's recommendation that the family moves to Devon so that they can send their eldest son to Dartington Hall School. Again and again, Shaw's name appears, as his opinions and beliefs are quoted on a wide range of topics, from the clergy to the raising of children, from the bible to the music of Beethoven.

Perhaps the most important event in their relationship occurs during Sean's dark hour of frustration and isolation over the Abbey's rejection of the *Tassie*. Shaw's support and encouragement at this time were all-important to the embattled dramatist. Eager to show commendation from so significant a mediative figure in his life, as well as justifying his own interpretation of events, O'Casey, in the text of the autobiography, quotes a letter in which Shaw called the *Tassie* a 'hell of a play' and criticized the Abbey directorate for not staging it.

O'Casey's acknowledgement of Shaw's role in his life reaches its finest expression in 'Shaw's Corner,' the long chapter devoted to the writer at the end of *Sunset*. He gradually builds up his praise of his countryman, who he calls 'the noblest Irishman of all Irishmen,' by presenting a list of some of his outstanding characteristics. At the end of the chapter O'Casey concludes his tribute to Shaw: 'The earth was his home and he loved it. He was at home among the mortals. His epiphany was the showing forth of man to man.' (VI, 190) So pervasive and all-embracing was the influence of Shaw, so profoundly did this mediator affect the development of the protagonist that, in the general sweep of Sean's life, in his perception of human strengths and frailties, and in his vision of man's capabilities, the values of the disciple have become almost synonymous with those of the mediator.

From the preceding discussion, it is clear perhaps that O'Casey, rejecting the limitations of a strictly chronological arrangement of his materials, and exploiting to the full the artistic freedom provided by a genre which implies no formal ordering of content, has devised multiple principles of design in his autobiography. His continual shifts in narrative, his juxtapositions of incongruous materials, and his rearrangement of chronological sequence are all products of alternating and sometimes simultaneous organizing criteria that may emerge briefly or be sustained through one or more volumes. Whatever their duration, these explicit attempts to give structure, shape and emphasis to contents highlight both the protagonist's encounters with his changing world and the author's contemporary perception of their significance. For readers of the work, the transformation of life through such manipulation of autobiographical form offers yet another means of perceiving the multi-dimensional character of the autobiographer.

5. MODES OF REPRESENTATION: NARRATIVE STRATEGIES

Just as the materials and shape of an autobiography are compatible with, and a reflection of, individual predilections, so also are devices of self-portrayal a matter of personal disposition. We have seen that the principles influencing the choice and structuring of contents provide insights which clarify the portrait of O'Casey the autobiographer; in a similar fashion, the means by which he attempts to render previous selves establish legitimate images of the author. Given the vitally exponential role that modes of representation can play in the building up of an author's character, O'Casey's many technical experiments and stylistic variations offer multiple indices of autobiographical identity. His attempt to get at the essence of experience by eschewing a realistic and strictly factual account of it is clarified by comments he made on the occasion of the 1934 New York production of *Within the Gates*:

The closer we approach to actual life the further we move away from the drama. There is a deeper life than the life we see and hear with the open ear and the open eye, and this is the life important and the life everlasting. And this life can be caught from the group rather than from the individual. 'We can know a man only imperfectly,' says George Jean Nathan, in his *Intimate Notebooks*, 'for every man has an emotional, spiritual, philosophical and personal fourth dimension, of which no camera can catch a photograph.' So no dominant character in a play can give a full portrait of a man or a woman. Even Hamlet is not a picture of the whole man. Know a man all your life and you do not know him wholly, and how then can we expect to picture the nature of a man in the space of a couple of hours? True to life on the stage, as far as drama is concerned, really means true to death. So to hell with so-called realism, for it leads nowhere.[1]

Given O'Casey's awareness of the difficulty of catching this 'fourth dimension' through realistic means, it is not surprising that his autobiography explores such a wide range of devices for representing past selves. In examining some of the more obvious of these attempts to render versions of the self, this chapter and the

127

next will approach the work under two broad categories: narrative technique and language. The former will entail an assessment of the function of the rhetorical possibilities stemming from third-person omniscient point of view such as intrusive narrator, reveries, fantasies and staged vignettes, while the latter will involve an analysis of some defining characteristics of prose, such as diction, syntax, dialogue and figurative language. Such an exercise should demonstrate that when O'Casey's writing achieves its full effect, it is a potent instrument for conveying the values and beliefs that constitute his vision of the world; but it will also reveal that even when the sometimes innovative devices do not quite succeed and the language displays weaknesses, they can still be highly suggestive vehicles of autobiographical revelation. Thus, when the various modes of representing the self are examined, an individual emerges whose character is obscure yet accessible, complex yet understandable.

The most striking feature of O'Casey's narrative method, certainly the one which has caused the most controversy, is his decision to refer to himself in the third person. An autobiographical novelist, by being able to go outside the self, establishes the necessary distance between himself as author and the personal history which is transformed in the work. Unless an autobiographer can find some similar method of formal control, his presence, in the unrelenting perspective of the personal pronoun, is persistently felt in the narrative. By creating a series of personae, O'Casey ostensibly dissociates himself from the hero developing in the work. In fact, third-person perspective emphasizes the double focus that every autobiographer, as subject and author, possesses. This inherent duality of the genre has been the concern of almost all critics who have discussed autobiography. For example, Stephen Spender, in the introduction to his own autobiography, clearly identifies the divided consciousness which is necessary for self-portrayal:

An autobiographer is really writing the story of two lives: his life as it appears to himself, from his own position, when he looks at the world from behind his eyes' sockets; and his life as it appears from outside in the minds of others; a view which tends to become in part his own view of himself also, since he is influenced by the opinion of those others. An account of the interior view would be entirely subjective; and of the exterior would hardly be autobiography but biography of oneself as if he were another person. However, the great problem of autobiography remains, which is to create the true tension between these inner and outer, subjective and objective worlds.[2]

O'Casey's third-person narration serves to accentuate this inherent tension; he can present an apparently objective account of his hero but one still pervaded by the subjective awareness which is the sole preserve of the autobiographer. This dual focus presents the protagonist as a more rounded figure, one whose complexities are viewed through as wide a consciousness, and in as complete a context, as possible. Commenting on this duality — in a particularly revealing manner given O'Casey's choice of *Mirror in My House* for the complete edition of the autobiography —, Stephen Shapiro says:

The way others see oneself, the way other becomes self, the way one sees previous selves — these are the themes and processes of the autobiographical mirror phenomenon. But autobiography transfers subject into object without a mirror or rather, through the metaphorical, metaphoric mirror of memory and imagination. At the center of this labyrinthian hall of mirrors, shimmers the dynamic representation of the interaction of self and world, the miraculous process of identity formation.[3]

O'Casey's particular narrative perspective provides additional opportunities for approximating that difficult process.

Yet, certain readers of the work have been uncomfortable with the use of third-person narration. Roy Pascal believes it is based on the pretence of O'Casey having an objective relationship with himself, and therefore is in danger of creating a 'contradiction between the autobiographical form and viewpoint.'[4] Pascal's perception of risk stems from the legitimate concern over the response this narrative posture is likely to elicit from the reader. Both Francis Hart and Norman Holland have explored this issue in ways that are relevant to our discussion. Hart claims that the potential ambiguity arising when an autobiographer employs this narrative angle results from one's different response to fiction and personal history. He believes that 'in understanding fiction one seeks an imaginative grasp of another's meaning; in understanding personal history one seeks an imaginative grasp of another's historic identity.' He goes on to state that when fantasy or fiction is found in autobiography the reader is not free to allow his imagination to be 'liberated to carry on its own "profitable invention."'[5] Instead, Hart points out — I have argued this in Chapter II of this study — that fictional and other rhetorical devices remain subservient to autobiographical purposes; they are in themselves an attempt to get at the truth of identity by every available means. Indeed, the distance between author and protagonist which is a product of third-person narration serves to underscore, if not direct attention to, the fact that his personality, his very selfhood, is accessible to himself only obliquely in the act of writing itself. Seemingly freeing himself from the obsessive concern with self that characterizes first-person narration, O'Casey has shifted focus to the very means by which the self can be known and rendered; the presence of his personae is a formal acknowledgement of the essentially creative effort which an autobiographical self-portrait necessarily entails. Use of Johnny/Sean is, then, a flexible narrative device capable of shaping the reader's response to particular facets of identity being suggested in the ongoing narrative.

In addition to directing the reader's attention to 'identity' rather than 'meaning', third-person narration also affects the sympathy and judgement which will be brought to bear on the work. In his study, *The Dynamics of Literary Response*, Norman Holland makes the following observation:

Usually, one cannot tell from an isolated paragraph whether a work is fiction or non-fiction. Yet our response to the two genres differs sharply. Therefore, it must not be the paragraph alone that shapes our response. Rather . . . it is the expectation we bring to the paragraph that determines the degree to which we test it against our everyday experience. If we think the paragraph speaks truth, we will check it for truth. If we think it speaks fiction, we will not.[6]

In reading fiction, then, we apply a Coleridgean willing suspension of disbelief: judgement of the protagonist is withheld and premises are granted to facilitate the presentation of materials that embody 'meaning'. In autobiography, there is no such ready acquiescence in responding to the depiction of the protagonist. Indeed, the act of self-portrayal implies that not just the author but also the reader takes a detached and scrutinizing attitude. Because an autobiographer is perceived as existing simultaneously within and outside the work, as a created character as well as creator, there hovers over the author's account of experience not only his own awareness but the reader's general knowledge of what he is to become. As a consequence, the reader will be less willing to grant unalloyed sympathy and understanding but will, instead, be tempted to exercise evaluation and judgement; thus, the subject of an autobiography elicits a much more exacting response than does the hero of a fictional work. O'Casey attempts to forestall such a demanding assessment of materials through his use of third-person narration. While the masks of Johnny/Sean serve the pretence of freeing O'Casey from the restrictive angle of the 'I,' they also inhibit the instinctively circumspect response in the reader which the genre traditionally evokes. Consequently, third-person narration affords O'Casey a larger range of rhetorical opportunities to suggest the nature of his autobiographical truth.

Throughout most of the autobiography, O'Casey uses third-person limited omniscience as the most effective method of describing and analysing past selves. At certain times, however, he departs from the norm of this point of view and manages, indirectly, to have the protagonist speak in his own voice. At those moments when O'Casey does not wish to sacrifice the immediacy inherent in first-person narration, he employs stream of consciousness as the most accurate way of registering his hero's reaction to experience. This approach is particularly prevalent in the early volumes where Johnny, unable to give full expression to his thoughts and emotions in dialogue, especially at intense moments of feeling, conveys them in the unstructured narrative of interior monologue. For example, when the young boy attends Sunday School, he valiantly feigns interest in Reverend Hunter's sermon, despite the attempts by his friend Massey to distract him with jokes about the minister:

How would you like to have a swing outa Hunter's whiskers? asked Massey.
Johnny said hush, and giggled, screwed up his face seriously, for he was afraid that he would laugh out loud at the picture rushing into his mind of Hunter yellin' 'n yellin' while he was swingin' outa his whiskers, swing-swong swing-swong, now we're off to London Town, safe 'n sound in Hunter's whiskers, take your seats, take you seats, please, for I wish Massey hadn' come into my pew, 'cause he'll do somethin' to make me laugh, 'n Hunter'll tell me ma about it 'n turn her against me for days, 'n I hate the hard 'n cold look comin' into her eyes when Hunter howls a complaint against me. . . . (I,120)

This subtle transition to unbroken flow of thought and awareness — it goes on for about a page — allows the hero of the autobiography to speak, as it were, in his own voice, thereby neutralizing the distance that is a product of third-person narrative. What O'Casey accomplishes in such passages is to draw on the benefits of both narrative modes. When third-person narrative proves inadequate for rendering the vital thoughts and feelings of the protagonist — who may become merely another character created by that vantage point — O'Casey modulates his narrative back into the awareness of the central character, foregrounding the consciousness of the 'I'.

O'Casey's narrative perspective sometimes switches to third-person omniscient. As such, it offers enormous possibilities for understanding the thoughts and emotions, not only of Johnny/Sean, but also of whatever secondary characters O'Casey chooses to present. An obvious advantage of omniscient point of view is that it permits the inclusion and description of events in which the protagonist is in the background, if not absent altogether. Thus, the central character does not always have to be shown responding to, and interpreting, reality; the reader is able to gain an understanding of circumstances and events — and through these of the protagonist himself — through vehicles other than the protagonist. This ability to adjust the autobiographical lens, to cast in bolder relief the experiences of the hero and the environment in which they occur, manifests itself in a variety of ways. In the account of Michael Casside's wake, for example, the focus shifts from Johnny to the stream of consciousness of the anonymous women neighbours. Their thoughts serve as a Greek-like chorus, giving additional information on the circumstances leading to the father's death, as well as providing added details confirming the precarious future awaiting the widowed Mrs Casside and her youngest son. Enlarging the viewpoint beyond the naive awareness of the protagonist in this manner highlights the dramatic interplay between him and the shaping forces of his world.

At other times, when this relationship is not readily apparent, the protagonist is moved offstage altogether so that sufficient background details of the events in his life can be presented. For example, the 'Pax' chapter from *Inishfallen* gives an imaginary account of the meeting which took place in July 1921 between de Valera and Lloyd George, and a subsequent encounter between de Valera and Michael Collins. Both meetings produced crucial decisions immediately affecting the larger social and political reality of Sean's life. Another of the more memorable consequences of O'Casey's flexible narrative angle is the account of his wife's beside visit to the dying George Bernard Shaw. The sense of immediacy and emotional intensity of this passage — it is as if O'Casey had undergone the experience himself — is derived from the freedom to approach dialogue, characterization and description with all the flexibility of third-person omniscient point-of-view.

On other occasions omniscience allows O'Casey, as intrusive narrator, to comment on the conditions in the protagonist's environment. In *Pictures*, 'The Hawthorn Tree' opens with an account of Johnny's reaction to the extremes of beauty and ugliness of life on his street. The beneficial, exhilarating grandeur of nature is represented by the lone hawthorn tree which in Spring bursts into bloom at the end of the street, revitalizing the inhabitants, giving them 'a new hope, for the praties were dug, the frost was all over, and summer was comin' at last.' (II, 41) The spoilers in this transformed world are the 'dung-dodgers' who arrive 'at stated times to empty out the petties and ashpits in the back yards of the people, filling the whole place with a stench that didn't disappear for a week.' (II, 42) The image of the 'dung-dodgers' carrying their filty, dripping loads through the houses vividly suggests the squalid forces of degradation against which the tenants must constantly struggle. However, even the 'dung-dodgers' manage to escape periodically from their grim occupation: Johnny listens to them discussing which operetta — *The Bohemian Girl* or *The Lily of Killarney* — they should attend. The boy himself temporarily seeks escape from this oppressive and dreary world by sitting under the scented and gloriously beautiful hawthorn tree. Throughout most of the chapter the point of view is limited to the factual-minded and none-too-critical Johnny. However, it is possible to see an implicit social criticism in some of the contrasts O'Casey draws here between ugliness and beauty, reality and imagination: the deflation of the tenants' springtime exuberance, the aspiration of the 'dung-dodgers' for the colour and excitement of the music hall, even the gesture of the boy leaving the 'mounds of mire' to sit under the tree all suggest the competing forces in the characters' lives. Then, as the chapter draws to a close, the perspective makes a subtle transition so that the voice of the intrusive narrator can further accentuate the implications of the debilitating conditions of the tenants. In describing Mrs Casside washing and cleaning up after the 'dung-dodgers' have left, O'Casey writes:

So she toiled as all in the street did on the day of their purification, in the midst of a dense smell, shaken with tremors towards vomiting, hard and fast at it, all together, boys, cleansing the sanctuary of her home, breathing the breath of death into her nostrils, scrubbing the floor, knees bent, worshipping dirt, washing away the venom of poverty, persuaded that this was all in the day's work. (II, 46)

The strong editorial note here is in contrast to the somewhat muted response of Johnny who, although repulsed at the filth of the 'dung-dodgers,' is too young to identify the causes of such conditions.

Another instance of the capability of third-person omniscient narration to clarify the autobiographer's views is the account of Johnny's first day at work as a stockboy for Hymdim, Leadem & Company. It happens to be the day for the monthly selection of the two most diligent employees of the firm, who are then publicly rewarded by being presented with the cast-off clothes of the two owners. Johnny witnesses the scene in which Mr Anthony and

Mr Hewson, with great fanfare and much self-righteousness, make their donations in front of all the gathered employees. Only recently hired, and in any case too young and inexperienced, the fourteen-year-old youth fails to recognize that the employees should be paid sufficient wages without degrading their self-respect and human dignity by being subjected to such servile practices. At any rate, were he to perceive the demeaning significance of these gestures, Johnny would be unable to express his sense of disquietude, although he does feel that something is amiss in this public display of hypocritical kindness: 'Peace and fellowship were everywhere; but Johnny felt uneasy, and saw that it was not good.' (II, 77) It is the mock biblical language in which this event is described — in itself, a subliminal reminder of the religious values being perverted, and one particularly appropriate in this context since the two owners of the firm are Plymouth Brethren — that conveys the anger and outrage which the boy only senses. First-person narrative would have precluded the option of the author explaining that his former self did not fully comprehend what he sees so clearly now; if he were to express such sentiments, he would have diluted the very immediacy that is the hallmark of that vantage point. However inappropriate the biblical phraseology is for the teenaged hero, it is less of an intrusion in the narrative of past events than would an obvious distortion of his former awareness. This more subtle insinuation of the autobiographer's contemporary knowledge allows for a greater impression of cohesion between the dual perspective inherent in the process of self-portrayal.

The flexibility of O'Casey's narrative mode manifests itself in a somewhat different fashion a few pages later. After working for a year and a half in the dark oppressive atmosphere of the firm, Johnny is frustrated and unhappy, without being able to identify, let alone express, the source of his unease:

Yet he wasn't satisfied. There was a sting of discontent in his heart. He had come to hate the shop and hate the men who owned it. Why, he couldn't say, rightly, but though the reasons were dim, the hate was bitter; ay, and he hated all, or almost all, who worked for the two Plymouth Brethren. (II, 79)

In a previous passage, to suggest the stultifying nature of this working environment, O'Casey had relied heavily on imagery in the description of Mr Anthony, 'hurrying up the street, black suit, black bowler hat, black gloves, and black umbrella, like a thin black bat fluttering in a hurry along to get in out of the daylight.'

Mr Anthony opens 'the black wicket-gate' into the 'darkened shop,' and Johnny follows, finding himself standing 'alone in a darkened world, with the hundreds of lamps hanging overhead looking like stars that had died down, had lost their light, and shone in the firmament no longer.' (II, 72) Working in this gloomy and depressing place for so long has given rise to the frustration Johnny feels. Unable to pin down the precise object of his dislike, he can, however, respond to the possibilities of a different life when he encounters them. Because the firm insists that all male employees leave the premises to eat their lunches, Johnny usually sits on the steps of the General Post Office, 'with shoulders bunched up, and the dry bread bitter in his mouth, when the cold winds blew, or the rain fell heavily.' (II, 81) The glimpse of a girl's pretty, stockinged ankle or the sight of the colourful, exotic uniforms of passing soldiers, whether Lancer, Hussar or Dragoon, is capable of becoming a momentary experience of transformation, an indication of the boy's yearning for a more exciting and fulfilling life. Thus, while imagery conveys the sense of oppression which the boy cannot identify, the account of his reactions to the passing street scenes suggests the feelings he cannot articulate.

O'Casey's narrative perspective affords the additional liberty of presenting dream sequences and full-blown fantasies, the presence of which, especially those with surreal or supernatural events, places the autobiography squarely in an Irish literary tradition.[7] Indeed, to appreciate fully many of the unusual features of O'Casey's modes of representation, we must look to the long and extraordinary tradition of highly inventive, sometimes outrageous and always impassioned writing in Ireland, in both Gaelic and English. Most illuminating in this regard is Vivian Mercier's *The Irish Comic Tradition* which surveys the characteristics and analyses many forms of humorous writing in Ireland.[8] When O'Casey's autobiography is examined against this rich and unique literary background, it is provided with a context which can both clarify and enhance its achievement as autobiographical revelation. That is not to claim that an awareness of this tradition is vital for an appreciation of O'Casey's methods and purposes, but it is to point out that what many critics perceive as the more outrageous and self-indulgent aspects of the writing are not uncommon in Irish literature. For example, Mercier, after his comprehensive assessment of the continuing presence of fantasy in both literary traditions, writes, 'Inductively, I have reached the conclusion that Irish humour shows two direct emphases — one on fantasy, the other on the grotesque and macabre.' (11) He traces the origins of

this tradition to Celtic religion and mythology, emphasizing that
the term 'religion' should probably not be used, since Celtic beliefs
and practices were steeped in magic, its priests more aptly
described as 'wizards or magi.' In Mercier's view,

This ancient belief in magic, which notoriously has never died out in
Ireland, pervades every form of Early Irish Literature, corrupting the
realism of the sagas, and completely overwhelming the saints' lives. Not
a single Irish saint, from St Patrick onwards and downwards, has escaped
the flood of magical folklore which obliterates all but the most immoveable
landmarks of a saint's actual life on earth. (12)

He sees the influence of magic or the marvellous as 'but one stage
in the development of many an Irish tale; in a later version, the
same story may appear as parody or burlesque or humorous
fantasy.' Having traced this propensity for the fantastical through
representative Gaelic tales and stories, Mercier points to its
continuity and further diversity in Anglo-Irish writing, particularly
in Swift, who reveals himself in *Gulliver's Travels* as 'a master of
fantasy'. (188) In twentieth-century Irish writing in English, he sees
the fantasy tradition reaching further levels of accomplishment in
Yeats's *Land of Heart's Desire* and *The Cat and the Moon*, Synge's
The Well of the Saints and O'Casey's *Cock-a-Doodle Dandy*.
Other contributors to the tradition, in Mercier's view, are Lady
Gregory, George Fitzmaurice, Austin Clarke, Eimar O'Duffy,
James Stephens and Flann O'Brien whose *At Swim-Two-Birds* he
calls 'the most fantastic novel written by an Irishman in the
twentieth century — with the doubtful exception of *Finnegans
Wake*.' (38)

Although the flights of imaginative fantasies in O'Casey's
autobiography are sometimes repetitious or over-extended, when
successful, they can be effective instruments of social criticism and
deflation of individuals, clarifying the protagonist's reaction to
experiences, and establishing the author's assessment of the
significance of events and people in the overall sweep of his life. It
is a telling characteristic of the autobiography that reveries and
fantasies are a predominant feature in the earlier volumes,
particularly the first two, where the innocent and naive boy cannot
be fully cognizant of the forces shaping his life or aware of all the
implications of experience; certainly, he is incapable of articulating
a response to them or assigning them a position in a broader
pattern of events as can the more mature protagonist of subsequent
volumes. Imaginative reveries are also especially appropriate in
these early volumes since they can enhance the suggestion of the

imprecise and unfocused manner in which the boy, with his poor eyesight and frequently-bandaged eyes, registers the visible world. One of the most dramatic fantasies occurs in *Knock*, in a chapter which has as one of its ostensible concerns Mrs Casside's worry that her five-year-old son might go blind because of the disease in his eyes. As autobiographer, O'Casey shows his awareness that the pain and suffering his eye affliction brought him throughout his life were caused by malnutrition and the unhygienic conditions so prevalent in Dublin at the end of the nineteenth century, circumstances which were exacerbated in a society where proper medical attention was only available to those who could afford to pay for it. The glaring discrepancy between the sordid living standards of so many Dubliners and the wealth and ostentation of the Anglo-Irish aristocracy, with the Vice-Regal at its symbolic head, is viewed by O'Casey as the root cause of many of Dublin's social ills. When Mrs Casside, Johnny, Archie and Ella are blocked on the street by the parade of carriages journeying to Dublin Castle for the Vice-Regal Ball, the five-year-old boy cannot recognize the bitter irony of his mother worrying over the sixpence the eye clinic will cost while such a display of wealth and extravagance parades before them. O'Casey's indignation and outrage at this blatant injustice finds expression in a fanciful account — part prose-poem, part stream of consciousness narrative punctuated with snippets of songs — of the gala event inside the Castle. He conjures up the obsequious and fawning behaviour 'of earls, barons, bishops, ambassadors, judges, privy councillors, right honourables, most honourables, honourables, archdeacons, spiritual pastors, and masters and mistresses,' (I, 23) as they make their way to be welcomed by the Vice-Regal, 'a man made by God in a hurry and tired and eager to get the thing over and done with.' (I, 24) In describing the sycophants who pay obeisance to this representative of foreign control and exploitation, O'Casey leaves no doubt of his anger and bitter resentment at the presence of this glittering display of wealth side by side with appalling deprivation and suffering. Appropriately, after providing the imaginative picture of the aristocracy at leisure, the narrative focus returns, in the concluding paragraph, to the suffering Johnny as he waits for his appointment at the eye clinic. The boy passes two more nights of misery, 'squirming his body and grinding his teeth' with pain, while his mother provides care, sympathy and whatever consolation can be derived from humming a hymn, the words of which only add to the irony:

There's a Friend for little children above the bright blue sky, a Friend who never changes, whose love will never die; our earthly friends may fail us, and change with changing years, this Friend is always worthy of that dear name he bears; and the two of them slumbered together. (I, 27)

The juxtaposition of 'The Castle Ball' with this scene of domestic hardship conveys O'Casey's view that, in their indifference to the plight of the poor, the political forces in British-controlled Ireland, as well as established religion, are morally reprehensible.

Fantasies involving St Patrick, who is O'Casey's personification of much that was wrong with Catholic Ireland, are a recurring feature in those volumes dealing with the protagonist's Irish years. It is significant that Mercier, after a survey of its most representative works, concludes that 'Gaelic literature revels in exposing to ridicule its greatest heroes: not merely the pagans Finn and Cuchulain but the blessed Saint Patrick himself.' (246) Throughout the autobiography, O'Casey never flinches from both open criticism and outrageous satire of even the most hallowed figures in Irish life and history. And the frequent technique of accomplishing this in fanciful conversation, is also reminscent of the Gaelic tradition of the 'colloquy', a verbal contest between poets in which wit, erudition and traditional lore are spun out in the form of riddles, kennings and epigrammatic statements. Robin Flower, in his discussion of the Irish bardic heritage, explains that from the eighth century onwards oral tales and poems about the *fiana*, the wandering warriors whose most famous group was that led by Fionn Mac Cumaill, had circulated all over Ireland. These were collected in the thirteenth century in a work known as *Agallamh na Senórach*, the *Colloquy of the Ancient Men*. The central device employed in this collection, one also found in earlier tales of historic cycles, is an imagined conversation between St Patrick and a spokesman of the *fiana*, usually Caoilte or Oisin. In later transformations of these stories, the conversation with St Patrick is dropped in the prose accounts but persists in the lays, which, with Oisin as now the sole interlocutor with the saint, became known as Ossianic lays. Initially, Flower says,

the relation between the saint and the heroes is one of perfect courtesy. They defer to him and he is tender to their pagan memories. But in later lays the opposition of pagan and Christian sentiment is more sharply conceived. The hero and the saint rail upon one another in good set terms.[9]

In O'Casey's third volume of autobiography, Ireland's national saint emerges as the leading figure in the church's opposition to Jim Larkin's efforts on behalf of the Dublin workers. In a highly amusing scene, O'Casey describes the continual embarrassment of

St Patrick — in front of other saints, especially English ones — at the repeated clamour and commotion of his unruly Irish flock. Larkin's organization of the workers to demand basic wages and working rights is the latest dilemma facing St Patrick, particularly since 'Bishop Eblananus,' the bishop of Dublin, has failed to deal with this issue expeditiously. In a scene reminiscent of the dialogue between Don Juan, the devil and the statue in Shaw's *Man and Superman*, the saint meets the bishop at the top of Dublin's Nelson's Pillar during one of the demonstrations by Larkin's men, and, with riots breaking out on the street below, he castigates the clergymen for failing to curb the materialistic expectations of his people. The high point of St Patrick's reprimand is when he accusingly asks the bishop:

Don't they know the law — that, in its blessed equality, it forbids the rich as well as the poor to resist authority coming from God, to steal bread, to sleep in the open, or to beg in the streets? Have you been teaching them anything at all, man? (III, 204)

Many of the protagonist's emerging views about his reality — his perception of the church as an oppressive force in Irish life, his belief in the rights of workers to have access to the fundamental necessities of life, and his sense of injustice at the disparity between rich and poor — which have been presented more explicitly elsewhere in the narrative, are reinforced and given added intensity by the power of this satire. In fact, the pattern of realistically describing a significant stage in the hero's maturation and then supplementing it with a scene of fantasy accentuating this development is a recurrent technique in the autobiography.

O'Casey's most obvious use of such juxtaposition is found in *Inishfallen*, as he recounts Sean's participation in the preparation and serving of hot meals to undernourished Dublin schoolchildren. Having observed the discrepancy between the comfortable, well-fed appearance of those who organized this 'dismal charity' and the pathetic, hungry-looking children, he continues:

There they were: of the one fold, the well-kept servers and the ill-kept kids, of the one hope, the one faith, the one baptism; the few amply supplied with corn and wine, the many gulping down as best they could the husks shaken from the finer corn. (IV, 81)

Sean feels that this scene of deprivation 'would make as good a circle as any seen by Dante in the inferno of his imagination,' and to counter it with a product of his own imagination,

Sean closed his eyes, and saw a better sight: the convents of the teaching sisters of Loretto and Ursula; the Catholic colleges, and the higher schools of the better-off followers of episcopus and presbyter. Green grass, gravelled paths, flowers in the centre and at the sides; playgrounds made for play; clean food, and wholesome on the whole, served decently over white cloths; snowy sheets and healthy beds in rooms where the air flows freely, (IV, 82)

In passages such as this, it is as if O'Casey, uncertain that both the full historical and contemporary implications of an incident may not be appreciated in all its nuances, turns to fantasy to ensure that all such perspectives are registered. By juxtaposing fanciful passages with more realistic accounts of experience, the intensity of the protagonist's indignation and frustration with many facets of Irish life can be captured, while confirmation that such reactions are shared by the author is simultaneously achieved.

One of the most successful instances of fantasy reinforcing straightforward narration is found in *Drums*, in a chapter called 'Green Fire on the Hearth,' where the hero's attitudes toward both religion and patriotism are shown to be tempered significantly by the influence of Shaw, Darwin, Frazer and Anatole France. Until about the mid-point of the chapter, the focus is on the changes in Sean's outlook as a consequence of this new reading: 'Not a week passed but he was found hobnobbing with Shaw, Darwin, Frazer and France, and the volubility and loudness of their positive talk were having a dangerous effect upon him.' (III, 175) That statement marks the end of expository narrative, as O'Casey switches to unrealistic material to clarify the nuances of influence these writers have exerted. The fantasy that follows — this one echoes Shaw's *Back to Methusaleh* — satirizes the conventional biblical account of Adam and Eve in the Garden of Eden; rather than an idyllic place of delight and ease, it is discovered by Sean, who has quietly crept over the wall, 'to be different and disturbed' and 'shaking with the roaaoaring, yelelling, squeeealing, and growowling of fierce, huge, and unnatural beasts.' (III, 179) Paradise turns out to be 'a vast expanse of slime and swamp', inhabited by 'long-baked, snaky-necked, leather-winged pterodactyls,' and over further 'near to the mouth of a big, deep, dark dugout, squatted a hairy man and a hairy woman, and Sean knew at once that they must be Adam and Eve, for they had their arms round each other.' (III, 180) In a further flight of fancy, O'Casey depicts them being interviewed by the strange threesome of Chesterton's Father Brown (Daabruin), Chesterton himself, and a journalist; in the ensuing questions and answers, O'Casey exposes what he sees as the incongruities in the biblical account of creation. Reversing the biblical contention that it was the woman who led Adam astray, and in keeping with the

O'Casey view of women as stonger and more courageous figures than men, Eve is depicted as the heroine of the day, leading Adam out of the hideously ugly atmosphere of Paradise, where the dinosaurs and other pre-historic monsters fight terrible battles to the death. In the O'Casey version, man's exit from Eden, rather than a fall, is a triumph of the human spirit in which individuals courageously face the challenges of their environment, with only their own strength and resources to draw upon. Initially, the timid Adam is shocked by Eve's suggestion that they leave Paradise to seek a new life of their own elsewhere:

Go from here! echoed Adam. Are you mad, woman? Go from the softness and security here to where things may be worse?

To where things my be better, responded Eve quietly. I've a child coming, and he won't be born here. There will be others too; and in higher ground and purer air they can start to build a Paradise of their own, safer, firmer, and more lovely than anything even a God can give. So on we go, too human to be unafraid, but too human to let fear put an end to us! . . .

And the crowds of lumbering dinnaseer and dipladoci gathered to watch them go, their huge bodies drooping and their scaly eyes dim, and as the mobled mother of man and her mate went by, they raised their heads and called out submissively, Farewell, brave beginners of the human kind, hail and farewell: those who are about to die, salute you!

Under the darkened sky, in the midst of a flash of lightning, Sean saw that the low brow, the timid eye, the shivering step of Adam had changed to the alert walk, the gleaming eye, the lofty brow, and the reddish thrust-out beard of Bernard Shaw. And Sean, bending low under the Golden Bough, followed close behind him. (III, 185–186)

In this powerful scene, the full ramifications of Sean's reading are made explicit: his sympathies are now squarely behind man's struggle against the obstacles inherent in the human condition, and, in that ongoing effort, he will seek no temporary support of false comfort from the teachings of any religion but, instead, will look to man's own talents, his ingenuity and intelligence for the continual improvement of life on this earth. In the presentation of successful fantasies such as this, O'Casey achieves a bold new level in the narrative technique of rendering the stages of his protagonist's development. More important, by stretching the possibilities offered by third-person narration, he can present the narrator's vision of life as far more comprehensive than the immediate and limited understanding available to his protagonist; thus, in their ability to encompass far-ranging materials and explore diverse and often tangential issues, imaginative fantasies contribute to the representative dimensions of the hero's story.

Indeed, O'Casey's narrative perspective facilitates the depiction of the protagonist as a universal figure, one whose personal story (as we will see in the next chapter) is identified with historical and biblical figures. These archetypal resonances might be seen as far too cloying, altogether too self-centred, perhaps even too preposterous without the attenuating virtue of third-person narration.

Reveries and fantasies are particularly useful devices for heightening the discrepancy between the world as it is and as O'Casey believes it might be. Sometimes, this dichotomy is suggested by simple contrast, an effect accomplished, for example, in *Drums* when Sean, on the street, guarding Ella's few tattered possessions, eventually falls asleep and dreams of the grandeur and style of famous eighteenth-century Dubliners, only to have harsh reality impinge on his reverie in the form of two policemen who unceremoniously wake him and tell him to be moving on. While such passages imply a condemnation of the hero's reality, others are more obviously exhortatory and propagandistic, offering antidotes to an imperfect social order by setting forth the standards of O'Casey's social and political vision. Such is the case in 'The Dream School,' a self-contained chapter from *Knock* which derives much of its power from the contrast drawn between the real and the ideal. During one of his periods of recuperation from eye troubles, Johnny is brought to school where he is soon bored by the monotonous recitation of arithmetic figures. With one eye already bandaged, it is not long before the mindless repetition lulls Johnny into a dream-like reverie in which he envisions an ideal school environment; it is a paradisal place which provides everything required so that 'no kid could forget for a moment that he was a member of Christ, a child of God, and an inheritor of the Kingdom of Heaven.' (I, 102) If this desirable place is in sharp contrast to the regimented and frightening atmosphere of the school, it is made doubly so when Johnny is suddenly awakened from his fantasy as his hand is torn by a bitter pain from a slap of the schoolmaster's stick. He is promptly given another stinging strike on the other hand so that the pain in both hands will, as the teacher puts it, 'keep you awake for a couple of seconds.' (I, 103) Other than the criticism implied when an older student says, in a voice overheard by the teacher, 'It was a God-damned shame to hit a half-dead kid like that,' O'Casey does not intervene to make comparisons between the actual school and the ideal school of Johnny's imaginings. Instead, the reverie functions as an implicit condemnation of all that was deficient in traditional methods of education, while simultaneously offering, in principle if not in practical terms, the kind of educational environment in which the growth and development of young children should be nurtured.

O'Casey's presentation of fanciful and surreal scenes is a vivid reminder that the autobiography was written in the years when his plays showed evidence of continual experimentation with dramatic form. Many of the more unusual and daring devices which he employed with increasing frequency from *Tassie* onwards — the rapid shifts in temporal planes, the introduction of fantasies and reveries, the rendering of inner states and feelings — are parallel to techniques which are associated with expressionism. The degree of influence which this artistic movement had on O'Casey's plays is an issue which has been vigorously debated by his critics and one which need not concern us here. What is clear, nonetheless, is that the impetus behind some of the technical innovations which manifest themselves in the autobiography do have affinities with the general aesthetic principles and practices of expressionism, and with expressionist drama in particular.

Expressionist writers believed that violent changes in style and continual disruptions in chronological narration, whether through surreal scenes, introductions of songs and ritualistic action, shifts in spatial and temporal settings, radical movements from realism to fantasy, or approximations of consciousness, could all reflect the horror and at times grotesque nature of modern life. Anti-realistic distortions of form and manner of presentation are especially pronounced, not merely because they better capture the flux and fluidity of life, but because they facilitate the desire to raise the focus from the motivations and aspirations of the individual to that of a whole class of society. In particular, for those writers who possessed radical political views, expressionism was a means of projecting their idealistic views of a new man in a regenerated human community.

Some of the basic similarities between the aesthetic tenets of expressionism, especially as practised by its playwrights, and O'Casey's purposes and techniques in the autobiography are readily in evidence. If the expressionists depict the essential rather than the apparent, the elemental rather than the transient, then O'Casey's efforts to cut through the veneer of individual and historical reality to arrive at the heart of personal identity have similar impulses. As we have seen repeatedly, O'Casey's primary concern is not with the palpable events which might constitute historical truth, but with their impact on the shaping consciousness of the protagonist. Since his goal is not a precise replication of personal history but rather an imaginative exploration of how past experiences shaped present awareness, his use of unusual techniques to render subjective states and feelings is similar to the expressionists' aim of capturing those same sensations. In addition, O'Casey the auto-biographer shares the expressionists' desire to depict the individual as a universal figure, one whose thoughts and feelings are representative of a particular social strata. This motive is manifested throughout the autobiography when O'Casey draws parallels between the struggles, obstacles and achievements of the protagonist and those of his wider community as it experiences a mass awakening of consciousness and begins its march towards social justice and enlightenment. Whether he equates his past activities with the struggle of the 'pippa passas' or, following Whitman, the En-Masse man, O'Casey shares the ideology of those expressionists, such as Ernst Toller, who not only exposed the ills of life but projected a new social vision based on true equality and freedom. In the dual process of demonstrating those evils and offering the political ideology that he believed provided the only antidote to them, O'Casey employs a variety of representational methods associated with expressionist dramatists.

Yet, while the practices of such playwrights can shed light on certain innovations which O'Casey brings to the genre of autobiography, it must be stressed that he very much adapts them for his own ends. Ronald Ayling's cautionary statements about seeing the influence of expressionism in the plays apply with even greater relevance to the autobiography:

O'Casey found in certain expressionist techniques a kind of dramatic shorthand with which to realise certain aspects of contemporary life. Yet one is constantly forced to qualify or modify judgements concerning his use or adaptations of such material, for it rarely appears in his work without having been transformed in the process.[10]

O'Casey's dislike of realistic portrayal of events and experiences can also be traced to his familiarity with the methods found in the plays of Dion Boucicault, Shakespeare and the Elizabethans, all of which employ, in varying degrees, sharp contrasts, unexpected occurrences, interruptions through songs, dance and dramatic vignettes, and even shifts in spatial and temporal settings. And, as his use of fantasies makes evident, some of the more noteworthy aspects of his writing have roots in the two literary traditions in Ireland. All such influences, combined with O'Casey's own instinctive desire for experimentsl narrative procedures, help explain his willingness to use imaginary passages in attempting to render subjective states and ephemeral experiences.

Another of the possibilities facilitated by third-person omniscience is the integration of dramatic scenes, or what Padraic Colum, tracing the influence of Boucicault on O'Casey, calls 'tableau.'[11] The dramatic qualities of much of the autobiographical material have been confirmed by the successful adaptation of several of the volumes for the stage.[12] It is not surprising that O'Casey should draw on his talents as a playwright, his ability to place characters in memorable dramatic contexts, in order to enhance the re-creation of events and incidents from his own past. Yet several readers of the autobiography have lamented what they view as O'Casey's squandering of his abilities as a playwright, wasting material which might otherwise have become plays.[13] Aside from showing an unwillingness to treat such dramatic scenes as an integral part of the autobiography, as an obvious element in O'Casey's desire to write in a genre other than drama, such a critical response overlooks the many instances of duplication in the materials of the plays and the autobiography. Familiarity with O'Casey's drama reveals that several of the dramatic scenes supposedly buried in the autobiography did, in fact, become transformed into plays. For example, some of the material in *Drums* recounting the hero's growing identification with the working class is, along with experiences from *Pictures*, the embryonic material of *Red Roses For Me*. The chapter from *Inishfallen* called 'The Raid' is a dramatic vignette which derives much of its impact from O'Casey's controlled handling of character, action, setting and atmosphere. It has obvious parallels with *The Shadow of a Gunman*, although in the autobiography O'Casey reverses the male and female roles, giving to the seemingly timid and weak man the exceptional courage and stature which belong to Minnie Powell in the play.

Rather than viewing the dramatic scenes as material that might profitably have been reworked as plays, the reader of the autobiography can usefully assess such passages as another facet of autobiographical technique, as an additional method of success-fully creating further images of the historical self. As noted in Chapter II above, strictly descriptive or expository narration may not always be a suitable means of capturing the intangible essence and emotional intensity of a moment. Although direct narration is often an appropriate, indeed sometimes a necessary, device for salvaging from the amorphous past those materials that are a key to contemporary self-understanding, the explanation, justification and defining contexts of a particular moment may periodically require more innovative and spontaneous narrative modes. The ultimate truth of a remembered event is sometimes accessible only indirectly, through the prism of imaginative creation; certain truths may be better comprehended by being re-created rather than described, encompassed rather than stated. Frequently then, O'Casey uses his narrative perspective to create dramatic vignettes which are an attempt to capture the elusive significance of a given moment.

In *Drums*, the chapter 'Behold, My Family is Poor' contains one of the most effective scenes deriving its power and ultimate autobiographical meaning from its dramatic qualities. At the outset of the chapter, as Sean is helping to move Ella's meagre possessions to yet another house, he encounters as well-known street character, Mild Millie, a young and potentially beautiful woman who, degraded by poverty and the adverse circumstances of her life, spends most of her time boisterously drunk on 'red biddy'. Sipping on her bottle, she now chats to Sean in language that becomes increasingly vulgar and aggressive. Earlier in the chapter, he had singled out landlords as the special cause of his sister's plight; now, in Millie's drunken talk, O'Casey traces the real forces that have brought about such sorry conditions in Ireland. Sean's reference to the Act of Union is Millie's cue to recite a litany of abuse at England's treatment of her country. Several leaders in Ireland's long, heroic but futile attempt to throw off the shackles of domination are mentioned: Wolfe Tone, Grattan, Emmet, and Parnell. O'Casey adds a further poignant touch to Millie's sorrowful complaint with the introduction of 'a short-legged, long-headed, oldish man, dolorously playing on a fife, whose brown skin had lost all its dandy gloss.' (III, 76) Appropriate to this dismal scene of squandered opportunity and personal enervation, he plays Thomas Moore's 'The Harp That Once Through Tara's Halls,' a nostalgic song that laments the glorious days of Ireland's past. Seeing the tears 'trickling down his cheeks, slowly too, as if in harmony with the slow sad air,' Sean concludes 'We all feel it . . . feel it in the deep heart's core, however poor and wretched we may be: they feel the hatred due to that which has turned Ireland's glory into a half-forgotten fable.' (III, 77) This eloquent expression of betrayal, loss and hopelessness is indicative of the festering wound at the heart of the Irish psyche, and complements Millie's racier, angrier statement of the same sentiments. After Millie eventually drinks herself into oblivion and collapses in a stupor on the street, Sean expresses his analysis of Ireland's predicament through his commentary on Millie:

She loves Cathleen ni Houlihan, he thought, in her own reckless way. In a way, she is Cathleen ni Houlihan — a Cathleen with the flame out of

her eyes turned downwards. The feet of this Cathleen, the daughter of
Houlihan, are quiet now, but none have bent low and low to kiss them.
   Her courage breaks like an old tree in a black wind, and dies.
   The pure tall candle that may have stood before the Holy Rood, was
sadly huddled now, and melting down into the mire of the street, beneath
the British lion and unicorn. (III, 80)

Like Millie, the Irish nation has been sapped of its vigour and
reduced to this woebegone state; Millie's anguished lament is the
cry of a mistreated and downtrodden country, a situation
confirmed by the debilitating conditions into which Ella's family
has fallen. This scene derives much of its effectiveness from a
variety of staging techniques — the careful depiction of setting, the
revelation of character through exaggerated dialogue and
heightened gesture, the control of atmosphere through lighting,
colour and sound. These theatrical elements contribute to the
cohesion of the scene, the autobiographical function of which is to
pave the way for the maturing Sean, in succeeding chapters, to
involve himself wholeheartedly in the activities of the National
Revival in the hope of finding the instrument of Ireland's salvation.

   O'Casey creates a wide variety of vignettes which rely, in
various degrees, on dramaturgical techniques to achieve their full
impact. For example, Johnny's visit to Kilmainham Jail takes on all
the ominous overtones of a ghostly visitation through Ireland's
recent bloody history. Much of this effect is achieved through
O'Casey's superb balancing of dialogue and silence, light and
darkness — techniques which reduce the palpable presence of the
wardens and Johnny's uncle, while successfully evoking the dead
spirits which still influence Irish political life, thereby confirming
the experience as an essential moment in Johnny's education about
his country's history and its current political status.

   Finally, to gain a more complete understanding of the variety of
possibilities and benefits in third-person narration, it is worth
looking in some detail at 'A Coffin Comes to Ireland,' the opening
chapter of *Pictures*. The biographical thrust of this chapter is
straightforward enough: the eleven year-old Johnny wakes in the
middle of a bitterly cold winter's night to discover that Parnell has
died. The focus of the opening paragraph widens to encompass the
many sleeping inhabitants of Dublin, and emphasizes that the
different classes are all momentarily unified by sleep on this wet,
dreary night. (The image of harmony evoked here might be
suggestive of Parnell's vision of an Ireland where all social elements
might live in accord, a possibility now thwarted by his death.)
When the focus shifts to Johnny, O'Casey reveals him sleeping

fitfully as he attempts to ward off the cold until, eventually, he wakens fully and learns the tragic news from his mother. The announcement is the stimulus for a series of reflections by the boy who tries to assign significance and implication to an event he cannot fully comprehend. For several subsequent paragraphs, O'Casey outlines the political circumstances that have led to Parnell's death, clearly implicating the Catholic forces for 'making an end of him, so that they might keep a tight hold on the people.' (II, 12)

Dressed and drinking tea, Johnny sits reading by the fire until he becomes drowsy and conjures up a reverie in which St Patrick is 'calling over the bannisters of the top storey of heaven' and is castigating Irish Catholics for being interested in improving their material conditions. O'Casey's language becomes charged with indignation as he presents a highly interpretative account of the conspiracy that led to the downfall of Parnell; the passage reaches its climax when the saint urges his flock to forget Parnell and attend to thoughts of the afterlife:

Ye backsliders! seekin' security o' tenure when yous ought to be savin' your souls, followin' Parnell when yous ought to be followin' me, rushin' with money for the plan o' campaign, while your fathers in God sweat in an effort to collect their dues. There's no use in yous shoutin' at me that if yous as much as put a coat of whitewash on your walls th' rent goes up; let it; yous have heaven. I'm not listening. . . . an' sing silent about your livin' an' sleepin' an' dyin' undher one coverin', an' the quarter acre's clause killin' thousands, an' that women are dyin' o' starvation with babies at their dhried-up breasts; for yous should be well used to these things be now, and, mind yous, while yous are watchin' your little homes gettin' levelled by th' crowbar brigade, or lyin' with your childher on the hard frosty road undher a red-berried rowan three, be night or be day, dyin' of hunger or perishin' o' cold, your last breath blessin' God for everything, yous'll all be slowly floatin' up here to me, unbeknown to yourselves, till yous are near enough for me to haul yous in be th' hand, the scruff o' th' neck, or th' sate of your throusers. . . . (II, 15–16)

By presenting this tour-de-force in the accent of a Dublin street character — the kind of colourful idiom found in his early plays —, O'Casey simultaneously reduces the dignity of the national saint and ridicules the nature of Irish Catholicism, whose repressive and detrimental role in Irish history is re-enacted once more in the circumstances surrounding the fall of Parnell. Disregarding the conventional demands of plot, character, even setting, O'Casey can have St Patrick spin out his outrageous monologue in all its elaborate detail and oratorical flourish. And the flexibility of third-person narration resolves the dilemma, facing all autobiographers, of resisting the temptation to have the protagonist express in his own voice attitudes and observations incompatible with past awareness. This narrative strategy reinforces the illusion of preserving the historical integrity of the protagonist, while simultaneously providing opportunities for O'Casey to articulate his current views.

When Johnny is roused from his reverie, O'Casey stages a scene in the Casside kitchen with Archie, Mrs Casside and the boy talking about the dead Parnell. After Archie leaves for work, Johnny returns to bed and dozes off again. In the dreamy thoughts that conclude the chapter, O'Casey shifts both the temporal and spatial focus of the narrative to depict the dramatic arrival of Parnell's coffin in Dublin and its reception by the lamenting and broken-hearted people.

In this chapter, then, within a dozen or so pages, O'Casey's narrative perspective allows him to achieve several distinct ends: he continues the plot; he provides explanatory information obviously not accessible to the boy at this time; he describes the highly emotional scene of the return of Parnell's body to Ireland — an event the boy does not witness; and he expresses both his sympathy for the political aspirations of Parnell and his criticism of the forces that caused the politician's downfall. Because the biographical core of the chapter is scant — an eleven-year-old boy's sleepy reaction to the death of an unknown and essentially abstract figure — a first-person account would offer little opportunity of rendering all the nuances of an event whose significance is appreciated only retrospectively by the protagonist. Taking advantage of the possibilities of his omniscient angle of perception, O'Casey can orchestrate the experience into a fully articulated and mature reflection of his own past, while at the same time transforming it so that it captures a crucial turning-point in his country's history.

O'Casey's use of reveries, fantasies and staged vignettes is dramatic evidence of his unwillingness to be restricted to what may be termed a conventional method of narration, one which would attempt to duplicate events in the manner that they were experienced. However, several instances of his narrative approach, along with certain features of his language, may be readily considered — at least, from the perspective of an objective witness — as blatant disruptions in the essential sequences of biographical events, as fractures in the cause-and-effect relationships that lend a sense of unity to a life. Seen from the viewpoint of the historian or the biographer, O'Casey's technical experiments and highly

individualistic style may be perceived as not only misrepresentations of historical truth but as gratuitous interventions in the
chronological unfolding of events.

To understand how the more unusual aspects of O'Casey's mode
of expression can possess autobiographical significance beyond their
immediate contextual effects, it is salutary to look at Louis Renza's
essay, 'A Theory of Autobiography,'[14] in which he makes the claim
that seemingly incongruous material, such obvious disruptions in
the continuity of the narrative play a central, if not the defining role
in autobiographical revelation. Renza sees the autobiographer's
essential predicament as the need to prevent the textual requirements
of the autobiographical act from inhibiting or distorting the carrying
out of the autobiographical purpose as a whole. He claims that,
'Nothing plays more havoc with the continuity of autobiographical
narrative than this dilemma.' To appreciate the full implications of
Renza's argument, we must recall the observation made in Chapter II
above, that all autobiographers are forced, by the very demands of
objectifying inner consciousness, to create a persona which possesses
but general correspondences to the self. Because an autobiographer
must draw on words and the conventions of writing, must, as Renza
puts it, 'make his language refer to himself allegorically,' he
immediately creates a gulf between himself and his protagonist.
Consequently, even if he employs the artifice of first-person
narration, the autobiographical portrait drawn will still exist at
several removes from the residual consciousness of self. If speech
itself is a transformation of one's thoughts and feelings, the written
word places them at a further distance, since whatever authenticity
intonation, inflection, rhythm and bodily gesture can lend to the
spoken word is sacrificed; the distortive consequences of literary
expression, with its need to place events within the carapace of story,
plot and character development, further separate consciousness
from the object which pretends to embody it. Autobiographical
expression, perforce, remains but an approximation, in that it is
forever seeking to render an elusive and ultimately intangible self.
William Spengemann has observed:

The language of autobiography has been allegorical in this sense from the
beginning — the biographical metaphors of Dante, Bunyan, and Franklin
no less so than the fictive metaphors of De Quincey and Carlyle. None of
these historical autobiographers thought that the truth about his life lay in
its historical events. They simply considered these events an adequate
medium for the apprehension and transmission of a truth beyond the facts,
while De Quincey and Carlyle found fictive metaphors better suited to the
same allegorical purpose.[15]

Regardless, then, of the balance struck between 'biographical' or 'fictive' metaphors, an autobiographer remains separated from the self which his metaphors suggest. Yet, the actual process of writing about that persona, particularly so if it is presented as 'I', creates the illusion for the autobiographer that the distance has been overcome, that the literary work produced by writing about the self is a sufficiently accurate reflection of inner consciousness. The quandary facing him is that, as Renza observes, 'his own narrative activity . . . tempts him to forget his constitutive separation from the "I" of his discursive acts.' Consequently, to offset 'his narrative's totalizing unity,' to write so that he resists the temptation to consider the narrative a replica of the life, an autobiographer, Renza believes, will intervene in the narrative to undermine the sense of unity and cohesion which the writing of the life tends to foster. To achieve that effect, the autobiographer will, as Renza puts it, 'jam' the work by 'overdetermining its parts.' Renza explains the consequences of an autobiographer's refusal to yield his life up to what is finally the distortive process of written composition:

For this reason as much as any other, a given autobiographical work tends to be a composite — an eclecticism of distinct verbal moments. It tends to accrue discrete pockets of verbal irrelevancies such as casual or ironic self-references; compressed or abbreviated narratives within — and redundantly digressing from — the major narrative line; letters substantiating the factuality of the narrative's references, the former which thus 'frame' the narrative so as to place its textual priority into question; journal and/or diary entries that in effect displace the narrative's present by evoking a past-present verbal act; and especially imaginative ramblings, digressions, 'visions,' reveries, unusual or drawn-out depictions of other persons — all 'spots of time,' in other words, that seem complete or sufficient by themselves. Each and all of these allow the autobiographer to evade, at least temporarily, *his* displacement of himself through narrative and thus promote the monological appearance of his writing to himself.

O'Casey's fantasies, imaginative reveries, individualistic prose — all those aspects of his writing which constitute a digression from the forward chronological thrust of the narrative — may thus be seen as attempts, consciously or unconsciously, to withstand the displacement of himself involved in the very act of autobiographical narration. The tendency to salvage the self from the misrepresentations inherent in the act of literary composition is particularly understandable in the light of his decision to use omniscient narration, since the creation of evolving personae increases the impression of having shaped his life into an image too removed from consciousness of the self. The need to counteract that distancing process would account for his insistent search for innovative procedures to be used in rendering consciousness, and would explain his ongoing desire to prevent it from being distortively subsumed by the very act of attempting to give it objective existence. As Renza says of the seemingly redundant material and procedures which characterize most autobiographical portraits,

these eccentric verbal moments act as signs of vigilance, guarding the writer's consciousness of himself, his self-identity, from slipping into whatever norms of self-reference he is aware of, if only subliminally, at the time of writing.

O'Casey's experiments with autobiographical form and narrative methods suggest his mistrust of the genre as a suitable vehicle for conveying identity. (As we saw in Chapter II, his letters show his hesitancy in calling his self-portrait a conventional autobiography; in almost every mention of the work, he insists that his was an unusual and highly unorthodox attempt at self-definition.) His technical innovations and — as we shall see in the next chapter — his insistent variations in prose style, are evidence of his strong resistance to the consequences of literary expression on the rendering of the self. Those features of his writing that are ostensible impediments to the strict continuity of the narrative serve, in fact, to withstand the appeal of permitting the self to be embodied in a set of images which, shaped to suit the conventions of story, plot and character, may be essentially false. All his experiments with technique and language allow him to preserve inviolate, for a little longer, a consciousness of self; they are a means of increasing those moments when it appears that he is 'writing for himself.' Rather than being evidence of O'Casey's digressions from a supposedly legitimate narrative of the life-story, his unique methods of representation can, in the end, be the truest indices of autobiographical identity.

6. MODES OF REPRESENTATION: LANGUAGE

Before proceeding to examine some of the more idiosyncratic features of O'Casey's writing, it is worthwhile to point out the presence of many passages of what may be termed conventional prose. Relying on traditional descriptive and expository techniques, and devoid of those syntactical distortions, periphrastic expressions, idiomatic diction and figurative language found elsewhere, these sequences derive authority and compelling effect from O'Casey's assured sense of balance, restraint and proportion. There is, for instance, the vivid and graceful prose which describes Sean's sea voyage to the United States:

The deck he stood on was forty feet above the sea, and was surrounded by thick glass so that the wind gave no feeling of its strength, the breaking sea not strong enough to smash the glass, so he could face it all, and enjoy it all, with acclamation at the wonder of its fierceness. As far as the eye could reach, wave after wave, in close battalions, came rushing towards the ship, the waves following those about to strike her pushing the ones in front, as if in a desperate hurry to strike the ship themselves. The cleaving prow of the huge vessel cut through the surge of the piled-up mass of agitated waters, which, after a ponderous pause, roared over the deck, everything on it disappearing under the swell of the green-and-white tumble of waters, so that Sean seemed to be standing in a glass-house tossed about in a surging greenery of waves, the tops of them shattering asunder to slash viciously against the thick glass through which Sean looked, often now but a screen of streaming water between him and the tumult outside. (V, 174–175)

O'Casey's eye for telling detail is even more evident in the meticulous, finely drawn portrait of the impoverished Jewish glazier who, carrying a heavy frame filled with glass, attempts to make a living by repairing broken windows in the tenement houses of Dublin's back streets:

The Jew was short and stocky; bushy-headed, and a tiny black beard, tinged with grey, blossomed meagrely on his chin. A pair of deep black eyes stared out from a fat white face. Long locks of jet-black hair straggled

153

down his forehead. The trousers of a shabby black suit were well frayed at the bottoms; his boots were well down at the heels; a new black bowler tightly clasped his head; his neck was rasped with a high and hard and shining white collar, set off by a gallant red, green, and yellow patterned tie. The Jew's arms were held out in front of his body to strengthen the resistance to the heavy weight on his back. His body was so much bent that the back of his head was sunk into the back of his neck to enable him to look to his front and to see any possible need for his services. The sweat was trickling down his cheeks, and glistening patches showed where it had soaked through his clothes near his armpits and the inner parts of his thighs. He walked with short steps because of the heavy pressure of the burden on his back. As he trudged along, he kept twisting his head as well as he could, now to the right, now to the left, ever on the alert for a possible job, chanting tirelessly as he marched along, Vindys to mend, to mend; vindys to mend! He kept his eyes well skinned for any window that might have been broken by a marble, a stone, a ball, or a drunken husband, as he went on chanting his Vindys to mend, to mend; vindys to mend! (I, 135–136)

In painting this portrait, O'Casey takes advantage of his late 1930s compositional perspective, a time when word of German atrocities towards Jews was already in the news. Consequently, the accumulation of evocative details in the description of the old man, bent and physically distorted by his burden, enhances the depiction of him as representative of his exiled and victimized race. O'Casey's highly-charged yet controlled prose lends a universal dimension to the old man's plight, a symbolic value which is heightened when, in this ostensible re-enactment of a childhood experience, O'Casey shows him being cruelly teased, mocked and finally stoned by the insensitive street children.

Equally impressive is O'Casey's ability to portray, in a few deft strokes, well-known characters whose prior image in the reader's mind becomes indelibly refocused. Almost all those figures who played a prominent part in the public life of the Ireland of his time are memorably etched in the work. Here, for example, is one of several sketches of Lady Gregory:

There she was, a sturdy, stout little figure soberly clad in solemn black, made gay with a touch of something white under a long, soft, black silk veil that covered her grey hair and flowed gracefully behind halfway down her back. A simply brooch shyly glistened under her throat, like a bejewelled lady making her first retreat, feeling a little ashamed of it. Her face was a rugged one, hardy as that of a peasant, curiously lit with an odd dignity, and softened with a careless touch of humour in the bright eyes and the curving wrinkles crowding around the corners of the firm little mouth. She looked like an old, elegant nun of a new order, a blend of the

Lord Jesus Christ and of Puck, an order that Ireland had never known before, and wasn't likely to know again for a long time to come. (IV, 122)

O'Casey's language reaches further levels of intensity in the elegiac tributes to loved ones such as his mother, or to a lesser degree, his sister; similarly, his eulogies to admired figures such as McDonald or Shaw, his descriptions of future human achievements, and his tributes to man's potential for greatness frequently acquire impressive dignity, power and eloquence. In such instances, O'Casey's lyric gifts stamp the autobiography with his highly personalized prose style. Here, for example, is a moment of heightened awareness, an epiphany of understanding which the weary Johnny achieves at the end of a long day of delivering newspapers and magazines:

The twilight was getting close to the skirts of day when Johnny swung his chariot on to the quays confining the river like a pair of lusty arms round a pretty lass. Over to the sou'-west the sky was a vivid green mantle, bordered with gold, a crimson gold that flowered grandly against the green, darkening into a gentle magenta higher up and farther away in the sky; and farther away still, the faint glimmer of the first stars was peeping out from a purple glow of purple gloom . . . . He left the crippled handcart by the side of the street, and went over to lean upon the river wall to gaze at Dublin in the grip of God. The old tattered warehouses and shops, bespangled with the dirt of ages, had turned to glory. Children, born into a maze of dirt, their vagrant garments clinging wildly to their spattered bodies, put on new raiment, satinized with the princely rays of the sun, as if she had winced at their ugliness and had thrown her own fair mantle over them all. The great dome of the Four Courts shone like a golden rose in a great bronze cup. The river flowing below was now a purple flood, marbled with gold and crimson ripples. Seagulls flew upward, or went gliding swooning down through thin amber air; white gems palpitating on the river's purple bosom. And far away in the deep blue the stars grew braver, and sat with dignity in their high places, bowing the sun away out of the silken heavens. Johnny bowed his head and closed his eyes, for it was very beautiful, and he felt that his city could catch an hour of loveliness and hold it tightly to her panting breast. (II, 216–217)

With the exception of the somewhat infelicitous 'clinging wildly,' and despite its rich texture and daring images, this passage generally avoids the excesses which can mark the prose elsewhere; here, the focus shifts in measured and even paces, while simile, metaphor and personification — those staples of his writing — are reasonably controlled.

The presence of such conventional passages serves to highlight the wide range of moods and tones O'Casey's prose usually achieves in the autobiography, from sonorous to colloquial, lyrical to strident, comic to banal, sentimental to idiomatic. In particular, his language is characterized by an exuberance and inventiveness which many readers have traced to the influence of James Joyce. But O'Casey's propensity for colourful and skilful manipulation of language can be found in his earliest writings — in the essays, pamphlets, songs, ballads and poems he wrote before he ever read Joyce. Bernard Benstock, in a lively and insightful essay which approaches the autobiography 'as a mock epic in comic prose,' argues that O'Casey was one of the few writers to absorb the impact of Joyce without being overwhelmed in the process.[1] Benstock believes that the playwright could write successfully in the Joycean vein because he was a mature writer before he encountered *Ulysses* and *Finnegans Wake*, and he shared 'a natural affinity for certain Joycean tendencies.' Thus, Benstock argues, it is in O'Casey's own plays, *Juno and the Paycock*, *The Plough and the Stars*, *Within the Gates* and *The Star Turns Red* that the multiplicity of style in the autobiography has its genesis:

The dizzying blends of playfulness and polemic, of caustic commentary and unashamed sentiment, are already established, and the tendencies toward fanciful language, puns and word play, malapropisms and neologisms, are already there.

Because the essay proceeds to examine some of these aspects of style in the autobiography — in particular, O'Casey's catalogue lists, his tampering with names, and what Benstock describes as his gift for 'lilting' — there is little need to dwell on them at any length here. What may be reiterated, however, is that many such features of O'Casey's idiosyncratic language derive, ultimately, from his desire to deflate pretentiousness and direct attention to injustices in his world.

As Benstock notes, the two-page introductory sentence of the opening volume, with its long list of balanced phrases and alliterative compound words, foreshadows O'Casey's unusual approach to prose in the work. But the seemingly gratuitous catalogue of items is a carefully crafted sequence serving, as will be shown in the next chapter of this study, to evoke the social, cultural, political and religious dimensions of late-Victorian life as manifested in Dublin. This long sentence is inherently critical of that world: for, while the language flows with its own apparent momentum, the eye of O'Casey the social commentator remains determinedly fixed on the subjects being described. Although in passages such as this he takes conventional prose and stretches it in a manner that may be reminiscent of Joyce, his purposes, more socially motivated than those of his contemporary Dubliner, are closer to those of Swift (whose deep moral sense and reflexive satiric impulse he shares), and to the long tradition of stylistic virtuosity and social criticism which characterizes both Gaelic and English writing in Ireland.

For example, the alliterative principle operative in the long opening sentence is not only a recurring element in O'Casey's autobiographical prose but is also an especially marked feature of both these literary traditions. Mercier believes that the propensity for alliteration 'originally evolved from the utterance of magic spells — some of which, indeed, survive in this form — though, it was later employed for eulogy, satire, and the preservation of all kinds of legal, genealogical and topographical lore.' (85) Alliteration thus became a staple feature of Gaelic kennings, epigrams and bardic poetry, and found its way into English writing in Ireland as a pronounced characteristic of language. O'Casey uses alliteration for a variety of purposes, although it does not always achieve the evenness of effect found in the opening sentence.

It is overdone, for example, in the passage where St Patrick warns supporters of Parnellism that they will find themselves in hell, 'in a sea o' fire, surgin', singein', scourgin', scorchin', scarifyin', skinnin', waves o' fire gorgin' themselves on every part of your bodies.' (II, 16) Yet, earlier in the same chapter, as O'Casey describes the sleeping inhabitants of Dublin, alliteration successfully hints at his sardonic view of the discrepancy in material possessions between the rich and poor:

Behind heavy silken curtains, in happy-looking beds, slept the nicely nightgowned; behind tattered and tumbled curtains, on muddled mattresses, gowned in paltry calico or faded flannelette, slept the sisters and brothers of the nicely nightgowned. (II, 7)

At other times, alliteration can be the primary vehicle for conveying meaning. For instance, in the brief scene in which Johnny's brother, Archie, mockingly questions a canal bargeman whose travels carry him back and forth on the same few miles of waterway, 'Is it to Yokohama you're settin' your course, or dim an' distant Valparaiso?', he is met with the swift retort: 'Farther than ever you'll wandher, you pinched an' parched an' puckered worm,' (II, 49) a series of staccato adjectives particularly appropriate to the landlocked Archie. Alliteration can also determine the rhythm of passages, as when a Father Malone encourages his followers to join in denouncing Synge's use of the word 'shift' in the *Playboy*.

Beginning with the apt pun of describing how the priest called 'on all the fightful,' O'Casey then depicts Malone exhorting his flock to bestir itself and 'denounce and dismember, disjoint and distender, this sable-faced, lying offender.' (III, 116) Frequently, the effect of alliteration is reinforced in passages which are also characterized by parallel phrasing. In advising his Irish followers to turn their backs on Parnell, St Patrick exhorts them:

So arise today through th' sthrength of th' love o' cherubim, in obedience to angels, an' down Parnell; in th' service of archangels, in th' hope o' resurrection to meet with a good greetin', an' down Parnell; in th' prayers o' pathriachs in predictions of prophets, in preachings of apostles, rise up today, an' down Parnell; in faiths of confessors, in innocence of holy virgins, an' in deeds o' righteous men, rise up today, an' down Parnell! (II, 17)

Balanced construction such as this is a favourite syntactical device used to achieve a disparate range of effects. To indicate that, in the twentieth century, the landed and established classes are having their power wrested from them, O'Casey writes approvingly of the social changes underway as the ordinary man takes his rightful place in the world:

But now these selfish ones are being challenged as never before; by those who have never gone to Lyonesse, but who have magic in their eyes; by a truth far greater than any share of truth they may have had in the beginning; by a dignity no less than theirs; by a kindliness that makes each man and woman, through labour, a golden digit in the sum of man. (V, 168)

Or, to set the tone, mood and atmosphere of Johnny's visit to Kilmainham Jail, O'Casey describes it as a 'city of cells':

A place where silence is a piercing wail; where discipline is an urgent order from heaven; where a word of goodwill is as far away as the right hand of God; where the wildest wind never blows a withered leaf over the wall; where a black sky is as kind as blue sky; where a hand-clasp would be low treason; where a warder's vanished frown creates a carnival; where there's a place for everything, and everything in its improper place; where a haphazard song can never be sung; where the bread of life is always stale; where God is worshipped warily; and where loneliness is a frightened, hunted thing. (II, 31–32)

Parallel phrasing can itself be enhanced by the insistent repetition of key words, a technique which gives added impact, for example, in the description of the roused and enraged Johnny as he hits his teacher on the head after Slogan has unfairly singled him out for punishment in front of the class:

he whipped up the heavy ebony ruler, and with all the hate in all his heart, in all his mind, in all his soul, and in all his strength, and a swift upward swing of his arm, he brought the ebony ruler down on the pink, baldy, hoary oul' head of hoary oul' Slogan. (I, 149)

While effectively suggesting the intensity of the boy's anger which finds explosive release in the actual blow, the parallelism also captures the autobiographer's vividly preserved feelings of outrage at the cruelty and unfairness of that experience of fifty years ago.

O'Casey's penchant for enumeration and lists, another feature of his prose, is particularly prevalent in the third volume where it is a successful means of evoking the multifaceted and changing character of Irish society in its first energetic moments of national awakening at the turn of the century. Recounting Douglas Hyde's influence over Irish life at that time, O'Casey imagines him

... shouting in a strange tongue, Come, and follow me, for behind me marches the only Ireland worth knowing; in me is all that went to make the valour and wisdom and woe of Clan Hugh and Clan Owen, Clan of Conn and of Oscar, of Fergus and Finn, of Dermot and Cormac, of Caoilte and Kevin, and of Brian Boy Magee; the crooning, sad and impudent, of Piper Torlogh MacSweeny; or Sarsfield, Wolfe Tone, Michael Dwyer, O'Donovan Rossa, and the Manchester Martyrs; of Power's whiskey, Limerick lace, Belfast linen, Foxford wool, Dublin tabinet, and Guinness' stout. (III, 102–103)

These representative figures from past generations of Irishmen embody the characteristics of courage and commitment which Hyde's Gaelic League hoped to nurture and develop in its members. Such men of substance and ability are contrasted with the weak and unimaginative public figures of the preceding paragraph — T. P. O'Connor, Tim Healy, William O'Brien, John Dillon and John Redmond — whose ingratiating and compliant policies toward England have, in the years since Parnell's death, increased Ireland's sense of failure and national debilitation. Similarly, the list of worthwhile and internationally renowned Irish products points to the competitive and industrious capabilities of the Irish people, an image in sharp contrast to the patronizing picture evoked by the flags and banners associated with Ireland in the nineteenth-century: the old-fashioned fancy-free ones of green cotton made in Manchester, with yellow shamrocks, wolf dogs, round towers, harps, and sunbursts on their fields' which only served to reinforce the British stereotype of the Stage Irishman, 'in his leather breeches, [emerging] from his cottage with the roses round the door. (III, 101)

In addition to listing specific names for the purpose of commending the new national initiatives to restore Irishmen's pride and dignity in themselves and their past, O'Casey uses catalogues of fabricated names to satirize anomalies in Irish life. St Patrick is depicted encouraging Irish Catholics not to honour foreign saints,

> . . . when we have enough an' to spare of our own, like meself, Columbus, Bridget, Kieran of Kilkenny, Finbarr of Cork, Codalot of Queery Isle, Damawluvus of Sinisagoner, Tatther Jacwelsh, patron of hoboes, Corruckther, patron of dancers, with his sacred companion and martyr, Kayleegoer, Feckimgumoy, patron of seelots, Janethainayrin, patron of factories, Sheemsa, patron of marrymakers, Sullisanlay, patron of slums, Hillolureus and Ardalaunus, brother patrons of free-drinkers, Willogod, patron of workers, Ellesdeea, patron of employers, and money more who are a credit to our native land. (III, 159)

While some of these distorted and punned allusions remain obscured by their historical context, the more obvious ones — for example, Damn-All-of-us as the saint of Sin-is-a-Goner, Ardalaunus (Lord Ardilaun was the brewer, Sir Arthur Guinness) as the saint of free drinkers, Will-of-God as the patron saint of workers, Ellesdeea (pounds, shillings and pence) as the saint of employers — are indicative of O'Casey's criticism of the predicament of the Irish working classes: they are confronted, on the one hand, by an exploitative economic system and, on the other, by a puritanical clergy. Consequently, they are forced to find solace in drinking.

Providing a list of saints, each of which is associated with a specific locality, is another feature of O'Casey's style which has deep roots in the Gaelic bardic tradition of poetry. In *The Irish Tradition*, Robin Flower explains how

> the poets of Ireland cultivated with an unremitting assiduity a study to which they gave the name *dindshenchas*[sic], the lore of the high places, until by the accretion of centuries there came into existence a large body of literature in prose and verse, forming a kind of Dictionary of National Topography, which fitted the famous sites of the country each with its appropriate legend.[2]

Because Old Irish society was structured, as Flower goes on to explain, on an artistocratic basis, it placed great significance on those places associated with past achievement, the memory and recollection of which reinforced the pride and sense of accomplishment of the dominant social class. O'Casey exploits this tradition of place-name lore so that the autobiography contains a topographical guide to both ancient and contemporary Ireland. But as well as placing events in a wider national context, O'Casey, like Joyce, draws on the *dinnshenchas* tradition of Gaelic literature for purposes of irony and deflation. St Patrick's list of real and facetiously-imagined Irish saints is in itself a discreet reminder of the patriotic ideals being perverted by contemporary Irish society.

The saint's catalogue also directs attention to O'Casey's fondness for verbal virtuosity which, in its many manifestations, is never far removed from the pun. In this, O'Casey is again echoing a long tradition of both Gaelic and Anglo-Irish literature, a predominant characteristic of which is word play and a spontaneous, creative response to language. Mercier shows how

the archaic, tradition-bound nature of Gaelic literature and culture preserved into modern times something of the ancient, playful attitude to language, thus creating in English-speaking Ireland a climate favourable to the growth of the great Anglo-Irish wits and ultimately of Joyce. (80)

In the course of tracing the influence of riddles, kennings and other forms of Gaelic word play on Anglo-Irish writing, Mercier discusses the linguistic fascination that marked the relationship of Swift with a Dr Thomas Sheridan, both of whom he sees as 'the most ingenious Irish exponents of word play between the Early Irish period and *Finnegans Wake.*' (95) Sheridan was the author of a treatise on punning which gave thirty-four rules, with examples from Greek, Latin and French, on how to achieve puns. 'The Golden Rule' of the list, for example, ' "allows you to change one Syllable for another; by this you may either Lop off, Insert, or Add to a word." '[3]

O'Casey particularly delighted in this form of verbal dismantling and restructuring, as he shows in another list of patron saints for Ireland's industries:

All Ireland's temporal activities had been placed under saintly protection — Textiles under St Clotherius, Building under Saints Bricin and Cementino, Brewing and Distilling under St Scinful, Agriculture under St Spudadoremus, Metal Work under St Ironicomus, Pottery under St Teepotolo, Fishing under St Codoleus, Book-making under St Banaway, the whole of them presided over by the Prayerman, St Preservius, a most holy man of great spiritual preprotensity, who was a young man in the reign of Brian Boru, and who passed to his rest through a purelytic seizure the day he tried to read the first few lines of Joyce's damnable *Ulysses*. (VI, 206)

The reference to Joyce might be seen as an implicit acknowledgement of the continuity of the tradition of verbal playfulness in the twentieth century.

O'Casey, as did Joyce, also shows a marked propensity for Sheridan's 'Rule of Concatenation' which involves ' "making a

String of Puns . . . 'till you have exhausted the Subject." ' (97) Here is O'Casey's list of Irish religious groups participating in a nationalist parade:

> . . . the renowned Orders of Laurestinians, Holy Hards of Eireann, Vigilantians of the Clean Mind, Sacred Sodality of Ruddy Roverians, Standardarians, Universalists, Catholic Timerians, Bellopatricians, Crossoconglians, Monasterboiceans, Holsomlititurians, the Most Primitive Order of Ancient Hibeernians, led by Weejodavlin; Catholic Heralangelists, Greenflaggregorians, Knights and Squires of Honestogodians, the 1872 Company of Griffithians, Cullenites, Macabians, Breenboruvians, Tirnalogians, Banabanians; The Black and White Assembly of Censorians, Sleevenamonites, the Knights of Columnbannus with their blazon, on a field sable, a dove with a money order in its beak, all proper. . . . (III, 152–153)

In addition to such distorted and stretched punning, by means of which he satirizes contemporary Irish life, O'Casey shows a fondness for the more conventional pun which has instant comic impact. Some examples: a fellow worker of Johnny's, discovered with his hand under the skirt of a co-worker is described as being caught 'rude-handed'; the devout and priestly Edward Martyn, who had a life-long passion for liturgical choir music, is impishly re-named Edward Myrrthyn; and, when Sean brings the ex-soldier, Benson, to the asylum because he is suffering from General Paralysis of the Insane, O'Casey, hinting that his condition is a legacy of his sexual promiscuity, has the whimsical doctor who admits him ask: ' "what's this novice's *tour-de-force*?" ' Sean answers: ' "Bad case of GPI, Doctor" ' to which the doctor replies: ' "Aha! Whores-de-Combat, what?" ' (III, 56)

At other times O'Casey's word play can be strained to the point of losing its humorous effect, as it does in the mock account of Mr Harmsworth (a name requiring no pun) being called to his vocation as a supplier of comics, puzzles and self-help magazines to popular audiences in England: '. . . in Dublin shall one be born before whom all hads shall bow, and infonts and succkerlings shall give thee willcome, and the great ones there shall be akneeled and anulled for ever.' (II, 214) Because they do not work with spontaneous and instantly recognizable double implications, these puns are not funny; 'hads' is somewhat successful but even it is too forced to be sharply effective; 'akneeled', 'anulled', 'infonts' and 'succkerlings' fail to embody a confluence of two disparate ideas in an appropriate and humorous manner. The weakness of such puns is that, as Robert Hogan has pointed out, 'O'Casey's wordplay tends to be a half-pun. It lacks sufficient under-punning; it has one exact meaning and one shadow of meaning or, even worse, one pointless meaning.'[4] Hogan cites as example O'Casey's manipulation of the Yeatsian line in 'A Terrible Beauty is Borneo' which is used as the title for the chapter in which Sean gives his assessment of the failure of newly independent Ireland to realize the aspirations of the martyrs of 1916. The parody of the line is carried further in a pseudo-ballad debunking the conservative minded and religiously motivated middle-class that has moved to centre stage in Irish political life:

> *A terrible beauty is borneo,*
> *Republicans once so forlorneo,*
> *Subjected to all kinds of scorneo,*
> *Top-hatted, frock-coated, with manifest skill,*
> *Are well away now on St Patrick's steep hill,*
> *Directing the labour of Jack and of Jill,*
> *In the dawn of a wonderful morneo.*   (IV, 157)

Hogan correctly remarks that 'The traditional ballad ending tacked on to the word "born" entails a kind of flip criticism, but the intrusion of the place, Borneo, is neither funny nor relevant.' Yet, if the additional rhyming ending given all four words is neither obviously relevant nor inherently funny, it does place them on the same level as the silly, nonsense words which mark the diction at other places in the work. This attraction to words themselves, regardless of their denotative values, is yet another characteristic of the Irish tradition of verbal dexterity. Mercier, after his comprehensive study of both literatures in Ireland, concludes that it is this fascination for words as objective entities that is the dominant feature of both traditions: 'I am convinced that the Irish reputation for wit, in so far as it is deserved, is in the last analysis a reputation for playing wth words rather than with ideas.' (79) O'Casey's perception of words as being capable of use isolated from a syntactical structure is evident throughout the autobiography. There is, for example, the passage which depicts the children in Sunday School being led in prayer by the Reverend Mr Hunter: 'There was a hurried sound of many moving as all knelt down on the floor to listen to the wary hairy airy fairy dairy prayery of the bearded shepherd the leopard the rix stix steppard.' (I, 116) All the rhyming words in the first group have but minimal contextual meaning: 'airy fairy' may suggest the emptiness and lack of substance in the prayers; 'hairy' has but strained associations with 'bearded' without adding further meaning; and both 'wary' and 'dairy' have neither denotative nor connotative relevance to the passage. Although carrying dubious literal significance, the seemingly gratuitous repetition of these words suggests the empty

and mechanical recitation of the prayers of Hunter. That they
operate on this level is confirmed by the closing sequence of words
in the sentence — 'leopard the rix stix steppard' — none of which
provides further literal clarification to the meaning, nor are any
meant to do so. 'Leopard' has been chosen because of the com-
patibility of its rhythm and rhyme with 'shepherd.' Except for the
definite article, which is necessary for purposes of beat and
spacing, the others are nonsense words, the kind of diction
belonging to the silly expressions of children's play.[5] They are part
of the elemental and usually mocking sing-song voice of children
too young to give clear expression to feelings. As such, they are
appropriate here to suggest the anger and frustration of the boy
who cannot articulate his sense of loathing at the self-righteous,
smug and pretentious minister. Johnny, with holes in his shoes and
ill-fitting clothes, has walked to Sunday School in the rain; once
there, he is condescended to by the other students, all of whom are
from well-to-do Protestant families. His feelings of humiliation
along with his sense of impatience with the minister's sermon are
conveyed in similar elemental diction:

. . . there's Hunter goin' to preach, settlin' his glasses on his nose 'n
coughin' a little before startin' on his sermon, sayin' somethin' about
becoming followers of the Lord having heard the word in much affliction
he rambled on an' rumbled on an' gambled on an' ambled on an' scrambled
on an' mummy-mummy-mumbled on an' yambled on an' yumbled on an'
scrambled on an' scumbled on an' humbled on an' grumbled on an'
stummy-stummy-stumbled on an' tumbled on an' fumbled on an' jumbled
on an' drumbled on an' numbled on an' bummy-bummy-bumbled on,
while here 'm I sittin' in the pew shiverin' cold as cold can be with me wet
clothes clingin' to me back 'n stickin' to me legs. (I, 121)

This combination of pun and nonsense words realistically evokes the
monotony of the sermon, while it simultaneously captures the sense
of the boy venting his irritation and discomfort. In passages where
nonsense words predominate, O'Casey's meaning is carried primarily
through rhythm, rhyme, stress and repetition, all of which build to a
cumulative effect of emotional climax that usually, as in this instance,
finds but partial expression in subsequent conventional words. In
O'Casey's newly coined words, then, sense is suggested through the
sound patterns immanent in the words themselves. Thus, in the earlier
example, while borneo does not operate at the level of pun, it is
successful in conjuring up the critical and dismissive quality associated
with a mocking street ballad. The sing-song rhyme of meaningless
words is another method through which O'Casey can express scorn for
certain facets of post-treaty Irish society.

Closely allied to puns and nonsense words are O'Casey's distortions of Latin words and phrases. These manipulations appear in several forms and for a variety of purposes. Recounting how the Spanish Conquistadors, in the name of Christianity, brought death and destruction to the Incas, O'Casey writes: 'Had the Incas been able to moisten the air with cries of Domino woebescums, had they been able to darken the sky with clouds of query eleisons, it would have profiteth them nothing, for the Christians were out on the make.' (III, 89) Later in the work, in a passage dotted with re-shaped Latin phrases, O'Casey denounces the control the clergy has over Irish life, thirty years after independence: 'Where's the Catholic Herald? He's on the rumparts of infidelium proclaiming a dies irae erin on all shinners.' (VI, 178) The word 'shinners,' itself a phonetic approximation of a heavily accented Irish pronounciation of 'sinners', was the name used to describe diehard supporters of Sinn Fein who, long after Ireland had won a limited form of freedom, still clung to the ideal of a republic embracing all Ireland. After de Valera had outlawed his former comrades, members of Sinn Fein were forced underground and were subjected to the additional threat of excommunication from the Catholic Church. Thus, a loose translation of O'Casey's expression here — Ireland's day of wrath on all sinners — is particularly appropriate.[6]

Frequently, this tendency to pun on obscure Latin phrases can produce expressions which remain incomprehensible without the aid of a lexicon. For example, the deflationary impact of 'Quiz seberrabbit' is lost if it is not recognized as a pun on the motto of the knights of Saint Patrick, 'Quis Separabit?' (Who Shall Separate?), and on the fictional character, Brer Rabbit. Further obscurity results when the Latin pun relies for its effect on a Gaelic expression, as for example, 'Mea na meala culpas,' which is a pun on 'mea culpa' and 'Mi na meala' which means honeymoon, and is also the title of an Irish song by Thomas Davis. At other times, Latin expressions can have immediate impact, even without precise knowledge of their denotative meaning. For example, in describing how the Catholic hierarchy treated O'Hickey for openly advocating teaching Irish at the New National University, O'Casey tells how O'Hickey was dismissed from his teaching post as Professor in Maynooth College and ostracized by his fellow-clergymen:

banished from the good cheer, sacred associations, from chapel, refectory, infirmarium, lecture room, and Chair of the College, and from all paths therefrom and thereto, garden, playing-fields, cloisters, theological continuities, in complaince with, and in consequence of a *nullo tremulato antea profundi craniumalis omnibusiboss episcopalitis.* (III, 132–133)

Although a translation of these Latin approximations — do not tremble before the deep, evil minds of the big boss bishops — is contextually applicable, these pseudo-Latin words also suggest the official bureaucratic jargon behind which the clergy hid, and on the basis of which it justified its treatment of O'Hickey.

The use of metaphors is also an important characteristic of O'Casey's prose. Although sometimes too insistent or hackneyed, these recurring motifs may offer new levels of autobiographical insight. The metaphor of the dance, for example, appears at various times until it accrues significance beyond its traditional connotations of an exuberant and creative response to life. O'Casey invariably associates the dance with feelings of defiance, scorn, and triumph — positive assertions of the individual over weaknesses and challenges. As such, it is an indicator of the author's approbation, instantly clarifying his attitudes to the characters and events under discussion. For example, in *Inishfallen*, O'Casey gives his assessment of Arthur Griffith and Michael Collins who together had signed the Treaty with England, thereby causing the rift with de Valera which led to the Civil War:

One could never conceive of Griffith dancing a reel, even in the privacy of his own home; but one could easily imagine Collins doing a wild dance in the courtyard of the Castle, or of him singing a song out loud in the porch of Parliament House. (IV, 96)

The dance is most dramatically associated with the pulse of life, with a spontaneous expression of vitality and energy; it bespeaks an affirmation over the forces of oppression and negation. Appropriately, it is employed at several key moments on the hero's journey to full awareness of self and world. One of the most significant of these occurs when the twenty-one-year-old Johnny is depicted working, uneasily, at Jason and Son, while continuing to educate himself privately through his reading. Having already concluded that, at work, 'things would never be the same again . . . and that the money for the rent, the liver, and the spuds was in danger,' (II, 212) Johnny expresses his new-found belief in republicanism to his shocked and uncomprehending boss. Disregarding what might happen to his job, he decides to pursue his ideals, to realize as much of life's potential as possible: 'He resolved to be strong; to stand out among many; to quit himself like a man.' (II, 218) After he has made this commitment to strive for all that life had to offer, he continues on his delivery route, and soon encounters a hurdy-gurdy player who begins to play a dance tune. The music entices a young woman to tap her feet and wave her hands until, eventually, she begins a slow rhythmic dance:

Johnny watched her. She laughingly beckoned to him with a golden hand. He flung off his coat, took a great red handkerchief from a pocket and bound it round his waist like a sash. He hurried over, caught in the golden glamour of the dancer's face, beat time for a moment to the tune, got the swing of it, and then jumped into the hilarious dance of the young woman . . . [who] caught Johnny's hand in her own, and the two of them whirled round in the bonny madness of a sun-dance, separating then so that she whirled into a violet shadow, while he danced into a golden pool, dancing there for a little, then changing places, he to be garbed in the hue of a purple shadow, and she to be robed in a golden light. (II, 219)

Because of the intensity of Johnny's religious feelings at this period of his life, the golden moment with the girl is experienced with something akin to spiritual ecstasy; it is proof sufficient to the youth that a divine presence presides over existence. After he has left the girl,

He shoved his handcart along again under the motley dome of the sky, tired, but joyous, praising God for His brightness and the will towards joy in the breasts of men, the swiftness of leg and foot in the heart of a dance, for the gift of song and laughter, for the sense of victory, and the dream that God's right hand held firm. (II, 220)

Like a voice raised in song, the dance is synonymous with the pulse of life; it is a means of expressing and celebrating all that is worthwhile and beautiful about man's condition.[7]

Descriptions of the physical attributes of secondary characters constitute another ready stylistic index to autobiographical perspective. Those who are admired and belong to O'Casey's canon of worthwhile people are usually shown possessing refined and graceful bodily features which, invariably, are made synonymous with integrity and honour. Here, for instance, is a portrait of Jim Larkin:

His was a handsome tense face, the forehead swept by deep black hair, the upper lip of the generous, mobile mouth hardened into fierceness by a thick moustache, the voice deep, dark, and husky, carrying to the extreme corners of the square, and reaching, Sean thought, to the uttermost ends of the earth. (III, 188)

On the other hand, those who, for whatever reasons, have aroused Sean's ire, are frequently portrayed with weak and ugly physical characteristics. One of the employers at Jason and Son that Johnny particularly dislikes is described as

. . . short and stout, with a head as big as the globe of the world in a first-class school, and as beautifully bald, set on a neck that was no neck at all; he had tiny eyes that glittered like smoky sparks, and were half hidden by beetling brows, as if over each a portcullis was about to drop and close both of them up for ever; but most remarkable of all were the thick legs curving out from the hips in such a bandy way that, when his two clumsy feet met below, his legs formed a perfect circle, as good as any correct compass could draw. (II, 163)

In descriptive passages such as this there is no mistaking the author's evaluative stance.

Yet another striking feature of O'Casey's prose is the presence, on almost every page of the autobiography, of allusions to songs, poems, and popular sayings, as well as to a whole body of Irish history, literature, myth and folklore. Robert Lowery's *Annotated Index* to the autobiography, a mammoth work of dedication and research, is in itself testament to the integral role that allusions play in O'Casey's autobiographical style.[8] Lowery's painstaking efforts have resulted in the identification of over four thousand references to a wide range of characters and events — contemporary and historical, factual and legendary, literary and mythological — as well as a host of items from the popular culture of the day. In particular, the *Annotated Index* demonstrates that, on one level, the autobiography constitutes a veritable encyclopaedic guide to most of the social, cultural and political events in Irish life from the end of the nineteenth century down to recent times, confirming the extra-personal and epic dimension of the work.

The allusive quality of O'Casey's writing in the autobiography is, of course, prefigured in his three Dublin plays, characterized as they are by multiple references to Irish life. In this, his writing is typical of much modern Irish literature: most of Joyce's work (the 'Circe' section of *Ulysses*, for example) presumes a quite detailed knowledge of mythological, historical and contemporary Ireland; Denis Johnston's play, *The Old Lady Says No* [itself a reference to Lady Gregory's supposed rejection of the play, leading O'Casey to use the expression 'The old lady had said Yes,' (V, 53) when recounting Lady Gregory's changed opinion that the Abbey should have staged the *Tassie*] is full of quotations and snippets from patriotic Irish songs, poems and political speeches. O'Casey's allusions, like those of his fellow-Irish writers, place special demands on his readers, particularly those unfamiliar with a wide spectrum of information on Irish affairs. If recognized, however, they are capable of accomplishing a variety of effects.

The immediate impact of allusions may be readily apparent: they can clarify character or incident, place action in an identifiable social or historical milieu, or adjust the atmosphere in a given scene, changing its emotional or intellectual register for purposes of satire, humorous contrast or ironic implication. More often than not, allusions can serve several of these functions simultaneously, providing unity and additional interpretative possibilities to the narrative. If O'Casey's autobiography is sometimes characterized by direct expressions of his feelings and beliefs — too much so, as some critics would have it — his tendency is often to leave unstated the full implication of experiences and events. In such instances, allusions are often an attempt to indicate an autobiographical perspective on the incidents being recounted.

For example, when O'Casey wishes to show Sean's impatience and artistic frustration at the pietistic objections some Abbey players had to certain passages in *Plough*, he employs a well-known Irish ballad to register his feelings of anger:

'I refuse to say the word Snotty', said F. J. McCormick, while someone, in the background, murmured For righteous men must make our land a nation once again; 'and I', said Miss Eileen Crowe — having first asked her priest about it — 'refuse to say the words "Ne'er a one o' Jennie Gogan's kids was born outside of th' bordhers of the ten commandments"', a chorus in the background chanting,

> *Oh, sure you're right allanna, for decent people know*
> *That every girl in Ireland, as things at present go,*
> *Is the soul of truth and of melting ruth,*
> *With a smile like a summer at dawn;*
> *Like the colleens that trip up and the colleens that trip down*
> *The sweet valley of Slieve na Man, amen.* (IV, 280)

Being parodied here is the popular ballad 'Slievenamon,' composed by Charles J. Kickham, a nineteenth-century Fenian who, in the time-honoured manner, identifies his feeling for his beloved with his hopes for Ireland's freedom. The song concludes with the verse,

> My love, oh, my love, shall I ne'er see you more?
> And, my land, will you never uprise?
> By night and by day, I ever, ever pray,
> While lonely my life flows on,
> To see our flag unrolled, and true love to enfold,
> In the valley near Slievenamon.

In O'Casey's view, Kickham's vision of a liberated Ireland is sullied, if not betrayed, by the society that has emerged under the new flag; now that Ireland has become a nation once again (the title of a patriotic song by Thomas Davis), its people hypocritically insist on seeing themselves in idealized and excessively self-righteous terms, exemplified by the smugly-virtuous Abbey actors. As a rationalist who has outgrown his own Protestant background, and, more revealing, as a playwright who believes in artistic freedom, Sean cannot tolerate the impingement of the puritanical Irish environment on his writing.

When the protagonist actually leaves Dublin for London, O'Casey once again uses a song to place that decision in the context of the larger national perspective:

Any minute now the jaunting-car would come to take him to the station where he was to take the train for the boat. He went to the window, and looked out — a cold, windy, harsh March morning. Early on a wild March morning. An old song strayed into his mind:

> *And as I stood upon the quay, a tear fell from my eye,*
> *For divil a blessed soul was there to say, old friend, goodbye;*
> *They were glad to see me sail, far away from Inisfail,*
> *Early on that wild March morning!* (IV, 283)

Speaking of this account of Sean's departure from the quays of Dublin, Gabriel Fallon his pointed out that, far from being alone, the playwright was accompanied by Fallon himself.[9] For the autobiographer, however, the song is appropriate in conjuring up an image that captures the essential truth of the matter: Sean is an isolated figure, one in a long line of individuals driven into exile by a society unable to tolerate criticism. Because of the irony that, historically, it was the British forces in Ireland which caused the exile of a succession of political heroes, O'Casey can give added poignancy to the departure of someone who had exerted himself so energetically and with such dedication for the liberation of his country from those forces. By depicting Sean as another of the patriotic Irishmen driven to foreign shores by repressive forces at home, O'Casey is castigating the newly-emergent Irish state as a travesty of the aspirations of those previous generations of Irishmen who chose exile rather than compromise their patriotic vision.

Snatches of several exile songs are used inversely in the account of the withdrawal of British forces from Ireland after the Treaty was signed. O'Casey pretends to give the thoughts of Earl Fitzalan, the English Viceroy who handed over Dublin Castle, the seat of British power, to the Irish authorities:

Here's the key of the Throne Room, and this one's the key of St Patrick's Hall, my good man. A long, long trail from Fitzhenry to Fitzalan, Alpha and Omega. Goodbye, all. Farewell, but whenever I welcome the hour of the flight of the Earl, I feel kind of sad. The last glimpse of Erin with sorrow I see, regretting the time I've lost in wooing; 'tis gone, and for ever the time when first I met thee, warm and young, a bright May moon was shining, love; but the dream of those days when first I sung thee is o'er; 'tis gone, and for ever, the light we saw breaking, and no longer can you come to rest in this bosom, my own stricken dear; so, farewell, and go where the glory waits thee, where the harp that once can function again, and the ministrel boy will be your well-known warrior. (IV, 91–92)

Composed of titles and lines from several of Thomas Moore's songs, this densely allusive passage mocks the supposedly kind-hearted and somewhat confused departing British, whose professed altruism has been misunderstood by the unappreciative Irish.[10] Several of the songs conjure up spirited images of Ireland: 'The Harp That Once Through Tara's Halls' evokes the faraway grandeur of ancient Ireland; 'The Ministrel Boy' glorifies the individual who has fought and died for his country; and 'The Last Glimpse of Erin With Sorrow I See' deals with the forced exile of an individual fleeing the oppressors of his native land. These echoes of Ireland's exalted past create a unique lexicon which gives yet another level of irony to the replacement of the British by a reactionary Irish government; it is an irony which is double-edged, since the attitude toward Ireland which Moore revealed in his songs and ballads has frequently been viewed by Irish nationalists as condescending and pandering to a negative stereotype of both the country and its people. O'Casey's ironic perspective is further confirmed when, in the passage immediately following this, he mockingly lists the new forces of oppression in Ireland:

From henceforth you will have your own disorders, surrendering the Order of Macha's Brooch for that of Armagh's Red Hat; Order of the Black Peeler and the Green Goat; Order of the Old Turf Fire; Order of Knights Hospitallers of the Clean Sweep; Order of the Little Greyhound in the West; the Sublime Order of Excommunication for Catholics i Collegio Trinitatis; Order of the Banned Books; and many such, and many more. There's nothing to stop ye now! (IV, 92)

A more complex and obscure instance of song functioning as an oblique commentary occurs in 'His Da, His Poor Da,' the chapter which presents a brief biography of Johnny's father, as well as several vignettes of the sickly Michael Casside as he nears death. O'Casey explains that Michael Casside was the youngest child in a large family in which the father was Catholic and the mother Protestant. All the other children had been brought up as Catholics but, upon the death of the father, the mother decided to rear her youngest child in her own faith. When religious differences later led to quarrels with his Catholic siblings, Michael Casside 'set his face towards Dublin, and turned his back on the city of Limerick for ever and ever, amen.' (I, 33) Immediately following this statement, O'Casey quotes two verses from Thomas Davis's song 'The Battle of Limerick,' which details the defeat of the Protestant William of Orange by the Irish Catholic forces under Patrick Sarsfield. If Michael Casside's analogous confrontation with his Catholic family and his subsequent retreat from Limerick are fairly obvious here, not so readily evident perhaps is the implication that Michael Casside's abandonment of Limerick was, like King William's, only a temporary setback before he would go on, as William's forces had done, to consolidate himself in Dublin.

While extracts and snatches of songs constitute the most apparent category of allusions, references to writers and quotations from their works are also a significant feature of O'Casey's autobiographical prose.[11] Foremost among the many literary figures whose names appear and whose works are cited are Yeats, Shakespeare, Milton, Wordsworth, Shelley, Tennyson, Ruskin, and Whitman. Whereas the many allusions to patriotic songs help to suggest the larger, national scope of O'Casey's autobiography, allowing it to encompass the epic convolutions in Irish society in its modern, formative period, the references to writers and their work serve in a contrapuntal fashion as a reminder that the personal story of Sean O'Casey is an account of the growing awareness, initiation, and development of the literary artist. On this essential level, the autobiography traces how the hero emerges from the back streets of Dublin, and overcomes financial deprivation, insignificant formal education, sporadic ill-health, political disillusionment and initial rejection to become, in his mid-forties, a writer of international stature. Names of writers and extracts from their works are used to chart the progress of his literary sensibilities and to attest — proudly and sometimes arrogantly — to the dedication and thoroughness with which he approached the goal of self-fulfilment. Such references also establish books and learning as instruments of personal salvation for the otherwise precariously situated Johnny Casside; the efficacy of the written word is presented as the means of escape from the social and economic conditions which engulfed his siblings. The critic, John Jordan, sees O'Casey's generous sprinkling of his autobiographical narrative with literary references as a projection of himself as 'Everyman redeeming himself from the depths by the power of the Book, of *litera scripta*.'[12] Certainly, the direction of Sean's intellectual and artistic maturation is acknowledged to have been influenced by his familiarity with literary figures: 'The light of other days would light the days to come. Shakespeare in his way, Marlowe, Goldsmith, and Ruskin in theirs, were lights showing him where to plant his feet safely; kindly lights guiding him to a fuller light in the future.' (II, 185)

In recounting Sean's reconcilatory meeting with Yeats, O'Casey uses references to Thoor Ballylee, Yeats's tower, to indicate the ageing poet's extraordinary energy and curiosity, despite his continual physical decline.

Sean noticed how stiffly Yeats slid into the comfortable chair by the cosy fire. He was bright, though, and aimed at gaiety; had he nestled sooner here and longer, letting restlessness ooze out of him, he'd have had a chance of a longer life. He couldn't, for there was in Yeats an irresistible leaven of childlike desire for glitter in imagination and masqued activity. He loved to *pace upon the battlements and stare at the foundations of a house*. The battlements, the battlements of a tower; the winding stair to the same battlements, with Sato's gift, a changeless sword on a table, forged before Chaucer saw the light o' day; and the poet's crook o' th' knee to an old and gallant ancestry. (V, 44–45)

But O'Casey's high estimation of the poet did not blind him to the essential differences in the views of the conservative, aristocratic Yeats and his own proletarian sympathies, distinctions which are clarified by again drawing on extracts from Yeats's poetry. Having quoted the lines in which Yeats declares the tower as his symbol, O'Casey continues:

Signs and symbols! Seeking substance from shadows, shining or shrieking. The poet had played with his toys too long. Aristocratic toys, self-fashioned; a few coloured with a wild philosophy, all tinged with beauty, some even with a gracious grandeur; but he had played with them all too long. More than half of life had passed him by while he was unsheathing and sheathing Sato's sword, staring over decaying battlements, or restamping out a dim impression of a long-forgotten ancestral crest. Young mortality. Ancestry had long since lost its handfast hold of man's mind. (V, 45)

Familiarity with more obscure corners of Irish literature is also required for a comprehensive response to O'Casey's allusive style. When O'Hickey is dismissed from Maynooth, Sean asks many of the leading figures in the various cultural and political societies to help him appeal this decision. Having described Sean's failure to find support from the Gaelic Leaguers, O'Casey continues: 'so he ran round again, asking questions of Cunnin Mwail, Mickey Free,

Harry Lorrequer, Louis J. Walsh of Killebook, the Vicar of Bray,
Charles O'Malley, Luke Delmege and his new curate, a lad of the
O'Friels, and found them a centre of silence.' (III, 133) This list
of names — real, literary and punned — conjures up the representative types of the Irish character who were unsuccessfully
canvassed to support the cause of O'Hickey. Significant, in
instances such as this, is that O'Casey provides sufficient allusions
so that his general inferences may be understood, even by those
who might not recognize all the references. At other points,
however, knowledge about a specific reference is necessary for
comprehension. Recounting Sean's meeting with Baldwin, the
newly-elected Conservative Prime Minister of England, O'Casey
relates how the conversation turned to de Valera and Ireland, with
Baldwin attempting to show that he has some understanding of,
and sympathy for, Irish affairs:

The Selt is well outside of the world of men. That's why your heroes are
so universally renowned. You do well to remember your heroes — Daniel
O'Connell, T. P. O'Connor, and Timothy Healy.
    Ay, and Mister McGilligan, the famous father of Dublin's wonderful
Mary Anne, added Sean.
    Him, too, added Baldwin; all good Irishmen. You do well to remember
them.
    Never fear, said Sean. They shall be remembered for ever. (V, 81)

Elsewhere in the autobiography, O'Casey has made clear what he
thinks of T. P. O'Connor and Timothy Healy; Baldwin's
encomium indicates his suspect knowledge of these figures. And the
reference to Mick McGilligan — the uncouth, ignorant caricature
in Louis Tierney's ballad — exposes the Prime Minister's shallow
awareness of Irish life, as well as invalidating his assessment of
O'Connell, O'Connor and Healy.

    O'Casey's language is also marked by internal allusions,
recurring motifs which accumulate implication and meaning as the
narrative unfolds. In their initial use, they function with immediate
textual significance but with each successive appearance they are
invested with increasing evocative and connotative meaning.
Sometimes appearing on widely separated pages of the work and
spanning many years in the hero's life, internal references can serve
to reinforce a consistent pattern of response to experience or,
inversely, chart the process of development. As with his many
esoteric and obscure Irish allusions, O'Casey assumes that the
reader, increasingly familiar with the details of the protagonist's
personal history can both recall and recognize the significance of
such motifs. Perhaps the most vivid example of internal allusions

unifying widely separated experiences occurs in the third, fourth and fifth volumes of the work. In *Drums*, Sean, just released from St Vincent's hospital, is seen sitting on a grassy bank gazing at a plant with beautiful red berries:

He had read that this plant was close to the tomato plant whose fruit, it was said, was very good to eat. He had often seen them, red and luscious, lying in shallow wooden boxes, fringed with purple-and-yellow tissue paper, among green cabbages in the green-grocer's shop. He wondered if he'd like them, for up to now he had never tasted one. Come to that, he had never tasted a lot of things. What now? Well, peaches, pineapple, figs, apricots, or those funny-looking things called bananas. It was some years now since he had tasted an apple, a plum, or a strawberry, or any fruit, be God, now that he thought of it! If he were an knight-errant, with an escutcheon, he'd bear as a motto, Poverty Must Go — *Declenda est pauperium*, or whatever the hell the Latin was. (III, 259–260)

The obvious autobiographical relevance here is that Sean has reached the age of thirty-four without tasting these fruits, a situation which O'Casey directly traces to the economic disparities between rich and poor. But after Sean has tried to imagine the taste of apricots, he concludes: 'Well, such as he had but little to do with the kindly fruits of the earth. How often had he prayed to God that He might give and preserve to his use the kindly fruits of the earth, so as in due time he might enjoy them! The time wasn't due yet — that must be it.' Enjoying such fruits is no longer presented as merely an experience denied to Sean but, instead, has become symbolic of a future where such inequities will be eradicated. O'Casey's criticism of the present social order, an indictment expressed directly and passionately in the previous quotation, is reinforced in this passage by the ironic tone.

The reference to exotic and inaccessible fruits appears again at the outset of *Inishfallen*, where Sean is shown involved in the task of 'campaigning for Meals for Necessitous Schoolchildren.' After organizing a very successful concert at the Olympia Theatre, Sean is able to see to it that 'Sister Helena, of the St Laurence O'Toole Sisters of Charity, received a goodly sum to furnish out penny dinners for the poor.' (IV, 14) However, he goes on to make the observation that 'no one needed a penny dinner more than his mother and himself; but pride kept the two of them miles away from one. Oh, pride, oh, foolish pride.' (IV, 15) With that, in a passage where the bitter tone is heightened by the parody of biblical language, O'Casey launches into a facetious prayer of gratitude to the Lord,

for the fruits of the earth which Thou hast not bestowed upon us, though Thy intention was good; though Thou hast failed to fill our hearts with

food and gladness, we praise Thee, at least, for the fine display of all Thy
good gifts in the wide shop windows . . . We rejoice in our foiled dreams
of the luscious plums, pears, and peaches of Europe, the delicious citrus
fruits of Africa, the dates and figs of Barbary, making our poor mouths
water, and our hearts widen out in freewill acknowledgement of Thy
goodness and fair play. (IV, 15)

Exotic fruits are not mentioned again until a chapter at the end
of *Rose* that describes a weekend Sean spent in Pennsylvania at the
home of George Buschar Markell, the producer of the New York
production of *Within the Gates*. After supper Sean goes out to 'a
garden of tremendous growing tomatoes' where he is shocked to
discover

tens of thousands of them, ripe, luscious, and full of goodness; thousands
dying, too, within a tangled mass of leaf, blossom, and fruit . . . slinking
into a pulpy decay to hide from man's refusal to make a kindly use of
them. So hard to come by at home; as plentiful here as blackberries on a
bramble-covered English common. Here they were, lost, their richness
trickling sulkily away into the indifferent ground. (V, 209)

Given the deprivation of his earlier years, Sean's amazed reaction
to this abundance and waste is hardly surprising. That O'Casey
wishes this experience to resonate with the earlier scene on the
grassy bank is suggested when, a few pages later, he evokes images
of Dublin in 1913. On the second day of Sean's visit, he is indoors,
responding nostalgically to a heavy downpour of rain:

So Sean stood, so many years ago, within the doorway of Liberty Hall
between two friends, Larkin and Conway, watching a Dublin storm, just
as he stood now with two new friends, within the portals of a house in
the Pennsylvanian hills, watching the fall of the pelting, blinding
Pennsylvanian rain, bringing to his mind a night-long vigil, in the throes
of a great lock-out, through a storm of lightning and of rain, standing
between two great comrades in the doorway of Liberty Hall: life staring
back at him again, reminding him of old and happy, far-off things, and
battles long ago: far away and long ago. (V, 212)

The juxtaposition of Sean's reaction to the rotting tomatoes and his
recollection of his struggles with Larkin against poverty and the
unequal distribution of worldly wealth reinforces the consistency
of vision to which his life has been witness.

In the presentation of these related experiences, O'Casey takes
advantage of the different temporal planes available to the autobiographer. The scene on the grassy bank in Dublin occurred
around 1914, while the Pennsylvanian visit took place in 1934.
Significantly, seven years after the American trip, in a 1941 letter

to George Jean Nathan, written during the dark days of the war when food was scarce and rationed, O'Casey mentions that he is 'digging in the back garden to furnish us with an odd spud — God be wi' the days when I trampled on thousands of crimson tomatoes growing wild in [George] Buschar [Markle]'s garden on the mountains of Pennsylvania!'[13] When he came to the composition of *Drums* (written after 1942) all three experiences — in Dublin, Pennsylvania and his own garden — could be assessed simultaneously from his present vantage-point. His shock at the waste in Markell's garden, made acute by his earlier deprivation, is given added intensity by his awareness of war-time conditions in England. The unified perspective on all three incidents allows O'Casey to include the reference to tomatoes and other exotic fruits in *Drums*; later, when writing *Rose*, he can pick up the reference again, orchestrating it into a symbol of the unequal distribution of the earth's wealth. The inordinate length of O'Casey's autobiography places much strain on a reader's remembrance of such isolated incidents but, if James Joyce envisioned an insomniac as the ideal reader of *Finnegans Wake*, then O'Casey's ideal reader should have the gift of perfect recollection. As was pointed out at the outset of this study, the autobiographical act may be viewed as essentially a paradoxical one, whereby the author attempts to render into existence his consciousness of the self, a task made all the more difficult because of his reliance on the meagre resources of the written word. Since any one individual can never hope to understand, at least not with any degree of accuracy, the complexity of thoughts, feelings, and memory associations of another, all attempts at autobiographical definition remain, of necessity, but vague approximations of what it feels like to view the world through another's eyes. Yet, one of the means by which that ultimately incomprehensible sense can be made a little more accurate, a little more authentic, is when the reader's remembrance of the author's past moves closer to the autobiographer's own. Thus, an autobiographer's success in evoking his past world will be measured, to a degree, by his ability to have his reader perceive his past — or, at least, those experiences he has chosen to deal with — with the kind of similar overview he himself possesses. At one level, then, O'Casey's autobiography can only fully achieve its purpose when its reader views the wealth of past incidents with as close a comprehensiveness as O'Casey's own. The ideal reader of this long work would be able to move, step by step, with the same kind of associative responses O'Casey brings to the multiplicity of experiences, as he momentarily salvages them from the recesses of memory, analyses and relates them to other events, before allowing them to slip from the narrative once again. The primary function of all of O'Casey's references, both to external and internal entities alike, is to reinforce the sense of comprehensiveness which would promote the reader's alignment with the autobiographer's own view of reality.

In addition to the motif of exotic fruits, there are many diverse experiences from O'Casey's past which are introduced, enlarged upon and shown in a variety of manifestations. Beginning with the opening scene of the autobiography, the narrative of his years spent in Ireland is puncturated with accounts of deaths and funeral processions, which create a sense of sadness and change on a personal level while often invoking a feeling of national infirmity and loss. On the other hand, countering this sense of national disillusionment and malaise is the impression of energetic patriotic renewal created by the many parades and street demonstrations. Or, to cite another motif appearing at disparate moments in the work, there are the repeated references to the threesome of Kelly, Burke and Shea who make appearances in all but the initial volume. While perhaps originally a reference to actual acquaintances of the hero, the names are sometimes reversed, sometimes pluralised as O'Casey attempts to depict them as interchangeable types — Irish versions of Tom, Dick and Harry — who represent much that he sees as narrow-minded and regressive in the Irish character.[14]

One of the surest means by which autobiographical prose facilitates access to that range of values, beliefs and attitudes forming the core of an author's identity is the nature of the imagery appearing in the narrative. In O'Casey's autobiography, fluctuating patterns of imagery are employed to direct attention to what is perceived as ultimately of significance in disparate and often widely separated moments. Such motifs may be used to outline the progression of, or underline the consistency in, the protagonist's response to experience. Whatever their explicit function, patterns of imagery are ongoing stylistic manifestations of the autobiographer's presence behind his materials.

By far the most frequently used images are those associated with light, whether it be the sword of light, the flame of fire, or the simple ability to perceive the light of day. As an indelible feature of O'Casey's prose, images pertaining to some aspect of light are especially prevalent at key stages in the hero's gradual journey through his world. On the opening pages of the autobiography, as O'Casey presents the anguish of Mrs Casside's futile struggle to save her dying child from croup, he describes her eyes as seeming 'to hide in their deeps an intense glow of many dreams, veiled by the nearer vision of things that were husband and children and home'. (I, 11) Throughout the autobiography, Mrs Casside continues to be shown as being so overwhelmed and worn down by the never-ending effort to supply the practical necessities of life that she has little inclination to imagine or aspire towards a better world. Initially, it seems that straitened circumstances will also deprive her son of the energy required for such noble endeavours, as well as increasing the likelihood of his going blind. The torment from his afflicted eyes causes the boy 'to dread the light; to keep his eyes closed; to sit and moan restlessly in the darkest places he could find'. (I, 18) It is only his mother who 'raised the banner of fear for him in the face of everyone she met, and pried everywhere for assistance to save him from the evil of perpetual darkness'. (I, 20) The threat of blindness is presented by O'Casey as not just a physical handicap but as an obstacle to learning, to the intellectual development and growth that comes from reading.

Somewhat later in this volume, O'Casey uses light imagery in its more traditional role as a metaphor for God's manifest presence in the world. The Reverend Hunter is depicted leading his congregation in prayers which ask the Lord 'that all our eyes open to see wonderful things coming out of God's law', a particularly ironic statement given the tattered condition of Johnny's shoes and clothing. When the ill clad boy gets flu as a result of going home from the sermon in a downpour, Hunter's assistant, Miss Valentine, pays Johnny a visit. As a parting gift, she leaves him a religious postcard which the half-blind child peers at for a long time before making out a picture of daffodils, and an accompanying biblical verse which he cannot decipher: 'Spelling the words out slowly, he could not make them out, but they were these: And the light shineth in darkness; and the darkness comprehended it not.' (I, 125) Thus, before the boy can recognize that the principles of established religion are not synonymous with social equality and justice, his experiences are rendered in imagery which clarifies O'Casey's views.

Light imagery accrues wider significance in *Pictures* where the curious and questing youth is shown reaching out to many facets of Ireland's burgeoning cultural and political life. O'Casey could conveniently draw on the association of Ireland's patriotic aspirations with this imagery: *An Claidheamh Soluis* (The Sword of Light) was the name given to the weekly publication of the Gaelic League, which, edited by such nationalists as Eoin MacNeil

and Patrick Pearse, had espoused the cause of Ireland's language
and cultural heritage; in addition, the symbol of the sword of light
had associations in ancient Irish lore with knowledge, enlightenment and social progress, and came to be associated with both the
Easter Rising and the literary renaissance.[15] In the chapter from
Pictures to which O'Casey gives this symbolic and highly evocative
title, the youth is depicted as eagerly seeking both a focus and a
context for his inspirational goals: 'Johnny wished that he had more
light; more light to see by; and light in his eye to see with, for the
light of the body is the eye.' (II, 183) Although he acknowledges
that 'The old and the new testaments had a lot about light in them;
and Christ Himself talked quite a lot about it, even saying that He
was the light of the world,' Johnny now has decided that
Christianity cannot be the means through which he could express
his desire for a new social order. Indeed, in assessing his Irish
environment, he finds little manifest evidence of true spiritual light:

Hardly a house that he had been in that wasn't dark in daylight. The sun,
they said, shone on all; yet, really, if you looked round, many saw very
little of it. He knew street after street in which there was no sun. Where
was it in Hymdim & Leadems? Or in Jasons? . . . The old sun was doing
his best, but many blinds were pulled down to warn him away; or hide him
from those who needed him most. Like the sunburst of Ireland forever
hidden behind the King of England's crown. A great shower of jewelled
hands were veiling the sun's face, and hiding his light from many men. (II,
183–184)

Given the paralysis and life-denying atmosphere of this world,
Johnny seeks enlightenment first from books, then from nationalist
policies and, finally, from socialism. The founding of Larkin's Irish
Transport and General Workers' Union is, for Sean, 'a tiny speck
of flame now, but soon to become a pillar of fire.' (III, 190) Later,
when Sean's socialist views have taken on an international
dimension, Moscow is described as 'a flame to light the way of all
men towards the people's ownership of the world; where
revolution stands in man's holy fire, as in the rich mosaic of a red
wall.' (V, 75) O'Casey again draws on this imagery to clarify a
point Sean makes in a political discussion with Yeats:

Communism's no new *lux mundi*, he said. Its bud-ray shone when first a
class that had all, or most, of what was going, became opposed by a class
that had little or nothing. It has grown in power and intensity till today
it floods half of the world's skies. We give it the symbol of a red star.
Earlier it was called the sword of light; Prometheus; Lugh of the Long
Hand. (V, 114)

No matter which term is used, each suggests Sean's perception of the fundamental desire in man for equality and justice; and by using the terms interchangeably here, O'Casey confirms that Sean's previous expressions of approval for, and his pursuit of, such aspirations have now coalesced in the goals of communism. Henceforth in the autobiography, light imagery is primarily associated with the political principles which he views as the means of clearing away the debris of a corrupt social order and replacing it with a more equitable and compassionate system.

O'Casey's style derives additional power from the many passages of dialogue appearing in the work, particularly in those staged scenes where he draws on his ability to define people through idiomatic speech. When Lady Gregory encouraged the fledgling Abbey playwright by telling him that his strong point was characterization, she did not need to observe that his chief means of giving depth and life to his characters was through their colourful and exuberant dialogue. Perhaps O'Casey's lifelong eyesight problems sharpened his sensitivity to the spoken word so that he could recognize specific people through their individuating diction and speech rhythms.[16] Whatever its source, his unerring instinct for appropriate phrases and colloquial speech patterns allows language to define character instantly, often precluding the necessity of providing conventional descriptions or analytical assessment of an individual. Christopher Murray's observation that in the plays O'Casey 'has the knack of making language *precede* character'[17] is equally true in the autobiography, which contains a host of people whose idiomatic speech immediately brings them to life.

A classic instance of the power of dialogue to delineate character is found in the account of the meeting between Johnny, his boss Mr Anthony, and Biddy, a street hawker who buys damaged crockery and, precariously carrying it through the back streets on a donkey, sells it to the poor of Dublin. The predictable retorts between them — the scene is re-enacted every week — achieve a somewhat ritualistic quality as the insensitive and mean-spirited Mr Anthony confronts the shrewd and enterprising Biddy. Her deprecating observations on the sorry condition of the merchandise is pitted against his self-righteous, condescending tone of false charity:

Now, Biddy, Biddy, don't exaggerate. The cracks go barely halfway down the saucepans. With a little care in handling, they'll serve the poor people excellently, excellently. It looks the best, it is the best lot yet you've had before you. Come, now, be reasonable: say ten shillings, then? Look

over them while you're carrying them out, and you'll see ten shillings is
a reasonable, a most reasonable figure. . . .

Oh, then, it's not deaf I'm gettin', but only listenin' to a gentleman eager
to make his joke to frighten a poor innocent woman. A gentleman who
knows th' poor woman 'ud never redeem herself from lifelong poverty if
she gave him what he's askin. Ten shillin's! If th' moon was made o' gold,
an' I had it on th' mantelshelf, I might be willin', if I was in a given' mood,
to part with th' half-sovereign. For goodness' sake, thry to think of th' job
I'll have thrying to mesmerize th' shy buyers into imaginin' th' goods'll hold
water, an' won't vanish into glassy dew if they hold them too tight. (II,
94–95)

Acutely aware of all the manoeuvres of good bargaining, Biddy
goes through a series of postures: she criticizes the goods, appeals
to fairness, casts herself in the role of the weak-willed and innocent
old woman, exaggerates the difficulties she will have in finding
buyers, and finally appeals to Anthony's reason. But in addition to
such conventional tactics, she sustains her essential position
through outrageous simile, hyperbole and elaborate metaphor, for
she is cunning enough to realize that the contest of wills will be won
by the ability of her words to overwhelm rather than convince.
When the deal has been struck and Anthony has gone inside, the
spirited Biddy reveals her true perception of his callous and miserly
nature in an outpouring of impassioned speech overheard by the
amazed and impressionable Johnny:

. . . th' next time I'm here, Mr. Anthony'll find a woman awake to what
is due to her, an' can put a flush of shame on his white sly kisser ever alert
for the main chance, ever on th' make, ever head bent over th' thrack of
a lost coin, thryin' to make his Sunday-curtained gob look like a twinklin'
star, an' it's oh, wouldn't I like to hammer me fist in it, an' muck it about
a bit, an' dim its shinin'; but praise be to the Almighty God, it's little leisure
he'll have to jingle his coins an' count his gains snibbed from an oul'
innocent creature, when his shrinkin', shudderin' body goes woefully
down the icy slope o' death, thin an' tottherin', naked as the day he was
born on, with the cowld snow fallin' on th' oul' schemer's head, and the
nippin frost askin' him how's he feelin'. (II, 96–97)

Biddy's lively and figurative outbursts, with their alliterative
rhythms, colourful diction and unstructured syntax build to several
of these climaxes, each time leaving the flabbergasted Johnny
speechless. Ironically, when he finally musters up a few words of
salutation to the departing Biddy — 'Farewell, Sweet Lady
O'Shalott' — she thinks that he has said something indecent, and
so unleashes a further sound of invective directed at him. In
addition to its function of characterization, Biddy's outrageous

language deflates the pomposity and hypocrisy of Anthony, and, as such, is a reflection of the sentiments which Johnny, restricted by his position of employee and, in any case, lacking the capacity for such a diatribe, cannot express in his voice. Thus, Biddy serves as a surrogate figure who conveys the intensity of the author's remembered feelings of loathing for his miserable and parsimonious former boss.

One of the keys to the power and impact of the language of characters such as Biddy is their ability to overlook the strictures of syntax, to allow words to flow with but scant attention to considerations of grammatical structure. Concepts and phrases are repeated, re-echoed and tagged on; using all the devices of heightened speech such passages build to a climactic pitch of intensity. This effect is achieved in a memorable fashion in the long monologues of individuals such as Biddy and Mild Mille, but it is also evident in short outbursts of other characters, In *Knock*, while his classmates play cards during lunch break, Johnny is designated the lookout, so that the teacher will not discover the forbidden activity of the boys. With one eye bandaged, he fails to notice the arrival of the teacher who promptly confiscates all the cards and money. Middleton, a leader of the group, and up to now a friend of Johnny's, is enraged that the boy has failed in his assignment:

Middleton turned and struck Johnny sharply across the mouth with the back of his hand, making the boy's lip bleed, as he shouted, You half-blind, sappy-lidded, dead-in-the-head dummy, you couldn't keep your eyes skinned for a minute to two an' save the few bob we were bettin' from buyin' Bibles for the heathen buggers of Bengal!
Caught us all, like a lot of shaggy sheep, muttered Massey. . . .
Away, for Christ's sake outa me sight, you hand-gropin' pig's-eye-in-a-bottle, you! (I, 142)

Here, the compound words, extended alliteration and repetition of ideas combine to convey the intensity of Middleton's rage which can neither find adequate release in hitting the sickly Johnny nor, of course, in confronting the teacher.

O'Casey's use of exaggerated and exuberant dialogue can be seen as giving a particularly Irish quality to his writing, placing the autobiography in a stylistic tradition which has its roots in Gaelic literature and has found such rich expression in twentieth-century Irish literature. Writers from Wilde to Shaw, Yeats to Joyce, Synge to O'Casey himself, have seized the English language and revitalized it with distinctive rhythms, syntax, diction and speech patterns. The Irishman's obsession with language, his regarding it as possessing almost palpable, even talismanic qualities, can be traced to several historical and sociological factors, one of the most obvious of which is the rich idiom of the Gaelic language, itself long nurtured by traditions of story telling and bardic verse. In a rural and largely illiterate society, the spoken word was not only the means of everyday communication but the vehicle which preserved the myths and tales of an heroic past. Exalted to its highest level, language could transform the mundane and provide imaginative access to mythical and spiritual reality. As well, as generations of people whose sensibilities suffered from unrelenting oppression and economic deprivation, words were one of the few outlets for creative energy. More pertinent, for a population long deprived of many essential rights, language — whether figurative, convoluted or evasive — became an effective weapon against one's oppressors, achieving connotative and exponential characteristics akin to a tribal code. It is not surprising, then, that the scathing comment, witty remark, deflationary aside, double entendre, extravagant metaphor — all the elements of repartee — became an essential part of both oral and written traditions in Ireland.

Language certainly takes on these implications for the characters in O'Casey's plays and autobiography, living as they do in extraordinary conditions of poverty and degradation. For them, words become more than gestures of defiance, self-effacement and ironic statement; vitally charged language and excessive and colourful speech are an essential means of preserving individual identity in the face of a debilitating environment. To be carried away on the flow of lively, figurative speech is to be transformed into momentary forgetfulness of their bleak and oppressive world. David Krause stresses this point in his discussion of O'Casey's slum characters in *Plough*: 'His tenement characters are excessive with words because their lives are exposed to excesses of deprivation; and an uninhibited imagination is a natural response to the frustrating experience of unrelieved deprivation.'[18] And Roger McHugh believs that Dublin's tradition 'of racy idiomatic speech, often alliterative and rhythmically phrased' is more typical 'among poorer people where there is more gregariousness, less social pretense, and more fondness for "Says she-in and says I-in," or gossiping.'[19]

If James Joyce was correct in claiming that a destroyed Dublin could be faithfully reconstructed from the topography of his writings, the resurrected city might very well be populated by the Dubliners who move through O'Casey's autobiographical world. His epic canvas includes most of the public figures, from Yeats to

Larkin, Archbishop Logue to Countess Markievicz, who were prominent in Irish life in the several decades which marked its cultural revival and political awakening. Of the several hundred characters who appear briefly in the autobiography, many achieve the level of individual delineation — Mr Anthony, the tram conductor, the Jewish glazier, to name but a few — while a host of other figures never emerge as distinct personalities. Speaking in the highly figurative and idiomatic language of the Dublin streets, these typical figures emerge briefly on stage, and then, their anonymity preserved, disappear from view. Thus for example, the cab-drivers who irreverently discuss their drinking exploits of the previous night while waiting for Michael Casside's coffin are interchangeable with, say, the dung-dodgers, or many other minor characters. However, the recurring accent of the Dubln streets — a voice in the same register as Fluther Good, Maise Madigan, or Captain Boyle — is a reverberating echo evoking the lively and colourful society which produced and nurtured the hero of the work. Of equal significance, the contrapuntal chord of idiomatic language reaffirms the projection of the protagonist as a representative of a particular social milieu, enlarging the personal story until it becomes an archetypal reflection of collective identity.

As a prose stylist, O'Casey is reminiscent of Swift and Joyce in that his writing shows an almost reflexive tendency to parody, a technique which is one of his primary means of deflating specific individuals as well as society as a whole. Like Joyce's parodies of evolving English prose styles in the hospital scene in 'Oxen of the Sun,' O'Casey's parody usually relies on the characteristic style of a text rather than a direct equivalent of all its verbal and syntactical features. His reworking of the line from Yeats's 'Easter 1916' discussed earlier is not parody in the strictest sense since, with the exception of the first line, none of the other lines has counterparts in the original. However, as the expression of a new subject matter in a borrowed form or style, it does evince the essential impulse of parody.

By far the most significant provenance influencing passages of parody are the Old and New Testaments, snatches and echoes of which appear with insistent regularity throughout the autobiography. In a work which, as I have pointed out in the previous chapter, derives major elements of its structural unity by organizing contents around the hero's loss of religious faith, it is initially somewhat surprising to find such pervasive biblical echoes. In old age, O'Casey recounted to David Krause that his reading of the bible was one of the most enduring influences of his formative years:

The Bible was the important book in our house, and full of fine stories and mysterious words for a curious kid to imitate. I liked the sounds of the words long before I knew what they meant, and it gave me a feeling of power to spout them in the house and in front of the other kids.[20]

The abiding influence of the bible, as a book of captivating stories written in rich, sonorous prose, is everywhere evident in his autobiographical language: allusions, whether direct quotations, modifications of scriptural words and phrases, or variations on biblical syntax and rhythms, are used to achieve a variety of functions.

For example, Ella's sleepy, early-morning reverie on the day she is to marry the handsome bugler, Nicholas Benson, is a six-page tour-de-force (possessing much of the power, humour and humanity of Molly Bloom's middle-of-the-night reflections), which opens with direct use of phrases from the Song of Solomon:

Ella found it hard to even doze during the night before the smiling morn that was to see her married to her man. The hilarious ecstasy in store for her tomorrow night was too much in her mind to let her close her eyes for long, for her beloved is white and ruddy, the chiefest among ten thousand. His locks are bushy, and black as a raven. His mouth is most sweet: yea, he is altogether lovely. (I, 70)

The biblical overtones which continue to resonate throughout this passage accentuate Ella's naive, romantic and idealized perception of her beloved, heightening the later tragedy of their miserable lives and degrading, untimely deaths. As well as capturing Ella's sensual feelings towards her bridegroom, the mock biblical language conveys O'Casey's enduring, bitter perception of Nicholas Benson as a prime instrument in his sister's ignoble end. Increasing this sense of blame and reproach are O'Casey's warm feelings of affection for the young, vibrant and educated Ella who, prior to her marrige, had shown such sensitivity as a teacher and such talent as a musician.

In his account of the General Strike in Britain, O'Casey uses biblical language to castigate the behaviour of Ramsay MacDonald, Philip Snowdon and J. H. Thomas for capitulating to the pressures of the financial establishment:

And they hurried to where the bankers were gathered at the gates of the cities, in the churches, in the major manors of Mayfair, in the sanctuary, and in the courts of the lords. And they held up their hands, saying, Is it peace? And the bankers held up theirs, saying, It is peace, provided ye do what is just and lawful, following the commandments of the governors given by God to the Bank of England, true liegemen in financial verity and honour to the Rose and Crown. Honour their commandments, keep their ways, and they shall promote thee, that ye shall possess the land for ever. And the three suppliants bowed down, saying, We're only too anxious to do those things that are righteous in your eyes, to the greater glory of the Crown and the Rose. (V, 96)

Frequently, the echoes of the King James Bible can be less overt, becoming mere suggestive overtones which ridicule some aspect of the hero's world. Scriptural phrases are incorporated, for instance, into the account of the moment when the Protestant minister comes to the Casside household to reprimand Johnny for hitting the teacher, and insisting that the boy return to school to apologize and receive a public beating. In this scene, O'Casey depicts the minister as a vengeful blackmailer, capable of withholding Protestant charity funds from Mrs Casside if she refuses to comply with his demands. While the minister climbs up the darkened stairway to the Casside home, the mother sits,

unaware of the enemy at the gates about to enter where light is as darkness; seeking to set sorrow where joy should stand up, stand up for Jesus shall reign where'er the sun doth his successive journeys run, His kingdom stretch from shore to shore, till moons shall wax and wane no more, cursed be he that perverteth the judgement of the stranger, the fatherless, and widow. (I, 152)

The biblical echoes are particularly appropriate in this case, since they serve as an obvious reminder of the Christian virtues which are openly being perverted by the minister.

Most outrageous are those parodies which draw on Christian hymns and liturgical literature. In this, O'Casey is again sharing in a time-honoured Irish literary exercise, stretching from Joyce back to *The Vision of Mac Conglinne*, a tale which Mercier, among others, believes to be the oldest as well as the most memorable work of parody in Gaelic. This twelfth-century story is a scathing satire against the church, especially its religious orders. Robin Flower explains how the *Vision* is a parody of the literary methods of clerical scholars as well as the form of 'the theological, the historical, and the grammatical literature.' Flower then continues:

And it is not only the literary tricks of the monks that are held up to mockery. The writer makes sport of the most sacred things, not sparing even the Sacraments and Christ's crucifixion. He jests at relics, at tithes, at ascetic practices, at amulets, at the sermons and private devotions of the monks; the flying shafts of his wit spare nothing and nobody.[21]

Mercier, having discussed this seminal work at some length, goes on to show that parody of the sacred texts of Catholic liturgy is an unbroken tradition in Irish writing, one which can readily be traced to the pervasive role of religion in Irish life. In the autobiography, O'Casey shows his familiarity with the *Vision* when, discussing the lifeless qualities of Latin satires, he writes: 'None or few of the translations, read by Sean, seemed to come up to those made from the Gaelic. Even the satirical poem or two in Miss Waddell's collection can't compare with the satires of Mac Conglinne.' (VI, 203)[22] Especially appealing must have been MacConglinne's scathing ridicule of the clergy and his parodies of sacred texts, which display a virulent intensity of the kind O'Casey duplicates in those criticisms which he has couched in pervertions of sacred and liturgical literature. Since such documents retained their religious validity in Irish life, O'Casey's use of them for sardonic purposes is particularly courageous. Indeed, his open and forceful disapprobation of powerful forces such as the clergy and the government establishes him, as Padraic Colum observed, as 'the MacConglinne of our day.'[23]

If, in Catholic Ireland, O'Casey's parodies of sacred texts and ridicule of the Church hierarchy inevitably drew sharp reaction, no less defamatory was his mockery of secular, patriotic documents that were sacrosanct in the Irish imagination. For instance, he conveys his feelings of disillusionment with Irish society after independence — its petty formalities, political squabbling and conservative policies — in a parody of the Proclamation of the Irish Republic Patrick Pearse had read outside the General Post Office when he launched the 1916 Rising. Beginning with the stirring and emotional lines of the actual Proclamation, in which Ireland summons her children to her flag in support of her bid for freedom, O'Casey then continues,

She strikes in the full confidence of victory for —
     The white tie and the tailed coat.
     The right to wear a top-hat, grey or black, according to circumstance or taste, when the occasion demands it.
     The banning of all books mentioning the word Love, except when the word is used in a purely, highly spiritually, insignificant way.
     The banning of any mention whatsoever of the name of James Joyce. . . .
     The right to excommunicate a Catholic student who enters Trinity College. . . .
     The right to give the Catholic clergy the first word, the last word, and all the words in between, whatsoever they may be, on any and every question, whatsoever, without any reservation whatsoever either. (IV, 157–58)

The tendency towards parody, along with the energetic use of language and the often heated tone, confirm that the depiction of the protagonist and his world is rooted to a significant degree in O'Casey's social vision. On this level, the autobiography exists as a work of satire characterized by vehement condemnation of the inequitable social order in which the hero lives, and by insistent reproaches at the moral and intellectual shortcomings of those whose power and authority shape and sustain that system. As is true of all works of self-portrayal, O'Casey's autobiography presents a highly jaundiced view of reality; the self-centred nature of the genre necessarily entails a sharp demarcation between those who support and those who deny the personal vision. This element of self-aggrandizement in the autobiographical genre can often produce a work which remains mere moralizing. At times, O'Casey's autobiography does not transcend this level of personal defense and explanation, where the individual vision has not been sufficiently transformed in the projection of hero and world; nor, at such moments, is the direct statement of personal beliefs relieved by humour, wit or even sarcasm. However, for the most part, O'Casey's views are cloaked by the distinct garb of satire and ironic statement, placing the autobiography in a long line of Irish satiric works, stretching from Gaelic literature, through Swift, to modern Irish writing.

Following the lead of Fred Norris Robinson's landmark essay, 'Satirists and Enchanters in Early Irish Literature,' Vivian Mercier discusses the magical origin of Irish satire, whereby the poet's satiric abilities — which included lampoon, personal attack, even curses — were seen to have derived from the magical powers of the wizard-like druids. Mercier points out that 'Early Irish satire is usually aimed at an individual or a clearly specified group of individuals' and has very few examples that 'ridicule vice or folly in general,' (113) But as Gaelic satire evolved it became more generalized, so that the power of the *fili* was feared alike by the two segments of society most susceptible to the poet's caustic criticism — the nobility and the clergy. Mercier devotes much attention to the evolving tradition of religious satire, as for example in the classical or bardic period (which ends in the first half of the seventeenth century) when it

includes the most diverse treatments of a variety of themes: denunciations of apostasy, theological dissections of heresy, outcries against clerical materialism, and humorously Voltairian criticism of clerical celibacy and other even more fundamental tenets of Roman Catholicism. (129)

In the later period (ending with the Great Famine of 1846–7), religious satire consists of new themes: 'ridicule of Protestantism;

of the Catholic clergy; of fundamental concepts like prayer and penitence, heaven and hell, the sacrament of marriage and the authority of the Bible.' (181)

The twin presence of the Gaelic satiric tradition and the satiric masterpieces of Swift formed the fountainhead which produced the strongly satiric temper of much Irish literature in the twentieth century. Indeed, Mercier sees this characteristic of Irish writing as its most distinguishing feature:

Perhaps the most striking single fact about Irish literature in either Gaelic or English is the high proportion of satire which it contains. Even the most superficial observer can hardly fail to notice the vein of harsh ridicule running through twentieth-century Irish writing: Yeats, Joyce, Synge, George Moore all have their bitter moods, while O'Casey rarely condescends to sweeten his; Lennox Robinson, Liam O'Flaherty, Frank O'Conor, Denis Johnston, Sean O'Faolain, Austin Clarke, and many others show a similar tendency. . . . (105)

O'Casey's satire in the autobiography is given added vigour by the reinforced sense of self and clarified perception of life which the genre automatically promotes. It is significant that Mercier, after a brief discussion of satire in such Irish autobiographies as Moore's *Hail and Farewell*, Gogarty's *As I Was Going Down Sackville Street* and O'Casey's, declines further analysis of them on the grounds that they are 'a spurious form of satire in that their ultimate aim is to inflate their authors rather than deflate the foolish and the evil.' (184) We have seen that all autobiographies involve special pleading and, if not self-glorification, certainly self-defence and self-enhancement. However, whereas Moore and Gogarty may be seen to have confined their efforts to such obviously self-interested purposes, O'Casey's autobiography transcends this strictly personal focus. As well as being a work which explains, defends and promotes the self, his self-portrait is an unmistakable critique of the imperfection of men and an indictment of the ills of society. While, on the one hand, this tendency may lead to blatant moralizing unrelieved by creative ingenuity or felicity of expression, on the other, the unrestrained and often unwarranted satire of individuals or institutions establishes common ground with the more extravagant and extreme qualities of earlier literature. In this regard, Mercier's discussion of Swift's impassioned arrogance and scorn of moderation, particularly in his two most bitterly satiric works, *A Modest Proposal* and Book Four of *Gulliver's Travels*, could have been written of O'Casey the autobiographer: 'It is rather the immoderate fury of his personal satire, the utter disproportion of cause and effect, which reminds us of the Gaelic satirists.' (192) The Irish dramatist, Thomas Kilroy, has described this aspect of O'Casey's writing as 'the elementary value of speaking one's mind, of baring one's feelings at all costs, even at the cost of misjudgement and linguistic extravagance.'[24] In the autobiography this quality becomes a reflection of O'Casey's character, as well as an indication of the lessons he has learned from life. As with Dickens, seering and unforgettable childhood experiences bred a sense of moral revulsion at inequality and mistreatment, and contributed to the unequivocal condemnation of social ills. His division of the world into fools and heroes is reflected in the humorous and impassioned satire of institutions and individuals, often to the point of creating caricatures rather than realistic portraits. As O'Casey examines the reality of his past life, he is struck not merely by the disparities between the rich and the poor, the wealthy and the dispossessed, but by the series of blatant discrepancies between action and feeling that exist in people and society. A recurring function of the autobiography is to convey his reaction to the contradictions he perceived between the professed aim of individuals and their actual behaviour, between the goals of social, religious and political institutions, and the consequences of their policies. Sometimes, confronted by the obvious paradoxes in the actions of individuals and institutions, O'Casey, like Swift did not know when to sheath his sword of criticism. Both men were easily carried away by an impassioned sense of self-righteousness, and could legitimately be accused of impropriety and unfairness. O'Casey's criticisms and denunciations are particularly scathing and acute since, unlike either Swift or Dickens, they go hand in hand with a proscription for a new social order. As the autobiography makes so dramatically evident, the standards by which society and people are measured and found wanting, and the values posited as being worth striving for, are shown to be a product of a long and difficult journey through life.

O'Casey's failure to strike an appropriate tone, his unwillingness to lend a sense of proportion to his criticism of people or institutions, and his inability to recognize that the expenditure of such energy was often not warranted reveal him, at times, as vindictive and mean-spirited, at others, as overly-sensitive and idealistic. Throughout all six volumes he clearly establishes that by nature he was strong-willed and stubborn; he prides himself on inheriting some of his father's proclivity for forthright talk with little consideration of consequences. To these were added both the insecurity and assertiveness often found in people deprived of a formal education. The blunt and direct quality that Kilroy identifies is partially a result of O'Casey' self-education, pursued, as it was, in accordance with personal predispositions and individual tastes. Those writers he read — Shelley, Whitman, Darwin, Ruskin and Shaw — tended to confirm what he had already sensed in his childhood and youth; his interpretation of their ideas was reinforced further by his experiences as a worker and union organizer. In addition, books and learning are repeatedly presented as the means allowing him to transcend the limitations of his inhibiting background; writing is viewed as an essentially redemptive and self-justifying act, and writers are expected to possess almost a sacred obligation to pursue knowledge, expose hypocrisy and present truth, regardless of cost to themselves. His shock is as genuine as his naivete is revealing when he discovers that others do not share that exclusive perception of literature and that exalted role of the writer. Thus, his disappointment that Yeats read detective fiction or that Lady Gregory liked popular novels unwittingly reveals the inverse snobbishness of the self-educated individual who arrogantly believes that such activities are somehow a betrayal of both personal and literary integrity. It is the misplaced scorn of the autodidact who believes that his reading has provided access to a more authentic mode of life than others. Sean, for example, is portrayed as being openly disdainful of the ignorance of his fellow workers at both Jasons and Hymdim & Leadem. Consequently, while his failures to achieve a sense of balance in his criticisms, to strike a more reasonable tone, or to perceive the resultant artistic weaknesses in the writing all provide an authentic indication of O'Casey's impassioned commitment to the validity of his ideas and opinions, they also suggest an intolerance, a self-righteousness and an unwillingness to compromise which are a measure of the man.

However, if passages where the language is overblown, self-indulgent or strident are immediately suggestive of flaws in O'Casey both as man and writer, they are more than counterbalanced by the numerous instances where his writing is extremely effective. It is in the wide range of his powerful and memorable prose — the evocative and highly charged descriptions of Johnny Casside's anguished childhood, the lyrical accounts of the growing youth responding with wonder and excitement to people and events around him, the many humorous, farcical and melodramatic scenes of life on Dublin's streets, the boldly satiric fantasies and reveries, the open and often bitter castigations of the ills of society, the impassioned pleas of man to reach out for a different vision of life, and the calm, reflective musings of the ageing protagonist — that many of O'Casey's positive qualities are readily apparent. Such scenes are permeated with a sense of compassion and equality, a commitment to justice and morality, and an abiding awareness of the humour and beauty that can always be found in life.

The unalloyed presentation of O'Casey's views, particularly in the concluding volumes, is perceived as a weakness by readers such as Pascal because they consider it as an interjection of current opinions into the supposed inviolate reality of historical identity. As has been observed in a previous chapter of this study, the changes in the protagonist as the life story unfolds do, among other factors, noticeably affect both the materials of the work and O'Casey's approach to them. Thus, as the protagonist develops and arrives at a coherent response to life, highly exponential stylistic procedures which determine our response to him are needed less as he can be legitimately shown expressing in his own voice those beliefs which he shares with his creator. If, in the terms outlined by Louis Renza which were discussed in the previous chapter, the particularly colourful prose and idiosyncratic technical devices so predominant in the initial volumes are perceived as an individualizing process, a means for O'Casey not merely to shape and control his contents but through which he reveals his contemporary attitudes and opinions, so also are the more direct and rhetorical styles of later passages. Throughout all six volumes, the narrative is characterized by repeated, albeit different, interventions in those experiences which constitute his past world. His satiric fantasies criticising St Patrick or the Archbishop of Dublin, for example, are just as much an intrusion in the reality of the protagonist, as are the disparaging remarks in the concluding volumes on the Catholic Church or the educational system in England. Indeed, these expressions of the autobiographer's beliefs are, arguably, a more accurate reflection of the character of the later protagonist than the fantasies or staged scenes are of him in his earlier roles. While one narrative mode may be judged more palatable than another, most of O'Casey's means of recreating former experiences are attempts to prevent the displacement of the self by the very means of portraying it; as a direct indication of his unwillingness to yield the self up to the distortions attendant on literary self-portrayal, they provide valid and illuminating indices of autobiographical identity. To a degree found in few other autobiographical portraits, his autobiography, both in its unique narrative strategies and range of prose styles, establishes multiple and diverse images of the self. More than any other single aspect of the work, the modes of representation contribute to the comprehensive and indelible portrait of O'Casey.

7. LITERARY IMAGES AND AUTOBIOGRAPHICAL IDENTITY

O'Casey's choice of materials, his structuring of them, and his methods of presenting them can provide an indication of his purposes and accomplishments at any given instance in the work. Nevertheless, it is the larger, wider effect that possesses true autobiographical significance. Notwithstanding the variety of revelations which may emerge from responding to disparate passages, it is the overall identity suggested by an assessment of the work as a coherent and comprehensive view of life that constitutes the authentic character of the individual. A coordinated response to the composite portrait depicted in the work is therefore necessary for an understanding of that William Howarth calls the theme of autobiography, 'those ideas and beliefs that give an autobiography its meaning, or at least make it a replica of its writer.'[1] The identity being sought goes beyond the obvious level of personal history; it encompasses the more deep-rooted elements of consciousness — all the conglomeration of thoughts, emotions, impulses and feelings that comprise individual character. The essential self an autobiographer reveals is akin to the 'fourth dimension' O'Casey sought to approximate in certain of his plays.[2] A grasp of that identity is to be derived from a reading of the various images of earlier selves which O'Casey has created throughout the autobiography. Products of the aesthetic principles of selection, arrangement and representation which have been examined in the previous chapters of this study, these images provide the ultimate means of access to the identity of the man behind the pen. O'Casey's images of the self initially appear incongruous, even paradoxical, but they are all indicative of his perspective on his past, his acknowledgement of the direction his development took, his recognition of the pattern inherent in his story. It must be reiterated, however, that the facets of identity the reader is seeking do not consist of the same kind of information which interests the biographer or historian. But if the auto-biography cannot be used as a reliable factual source, it can profitably be read as both a conscious and subconscious revelation of O'Casey's perception of himself, his understanding of how the experiences of personal history have shaped his character.

Perhaps the most striking discovery that results from a careful analysis of O'Casey's self-portrait is that it follows a tradition of confessional autobiography. The key to many of his images of the self lies in their similarity to motifs used in delineating the contours of lives in a particular tradition of autobiographical writing. The experiences of O'Casey's autobiographical protagonist often duplicate patterns of behaviour and are presented in figurative language which appear in many confessional autobiographies, particularly those works structured around a crisis of identity or religious doubt. It is not germane whether O'Casey was conscious of that tradition or not but, of importance, is that the correlation of his literary self-portrait with that sub-genre of autobiography provides a very useful point of departure in responding to, and understanding, his character.

In his recent study of autobiography, Avrom Fleishman outlines the basic characteristics or essential 'rubrics' of this sub-genre.[3] Its defining feature is that the life is presented as a cyclical journey which is synonymous with a search for intellectual truth or spiritual knowledge. The initial period is that of natural childhood, followed by a fall from this Edenic state into exile. Expulsion is invariably characterized by a period of wandering or pilgrimage before eventually leading to a crisis of faith or identity. In this phase, the hero goes through a series of experiences, states of mind, and feelings of affiliation, building to the moment when he comes to doubt the merits of past actions and his previous suppositions about himself and his world. An epiphany or dramatic conversion signals the end of uncertainty and waywardness, clearing the way for renewal and symbolic return. Once the crisis of identity is understood the hero thereafter assesses and responds to life from a plateau of assured self-knowledge. That new awareness of self is synonymous with the perspective the autobiographer possesses as he views and records his life journey.

Writers of confessional autobiography, from at least Augustine onwards, have manifested this form by employing analogies with stories and figures from the Old and New Testaments (those of Adam, Moses, Christ and Paul recur most frequently) and echoing the biblical language of exile and return. These sources provide the traditional metaphors for confessional autobiographers in the ordering and rendering of their lives. Fleishman, in pointing out the 'innumerable biblical references and verbal plays on the language of expulsion, exodus, prodigal wanderings and other journeys of life, which thoroughly orchestrate Augustine's peregrinations,' goes on to acknowledge that this reading of Augustine's *Confessions* is far from novel:

It has been observed that the story of the *Confessions* is told as a series of movements — in geographical space as well as in intellectual and spiritual position — and that this dual journey has its analogies in self-writing from Socrate's *Apology* (as in Plato's transcription) to Newman's *Apologia* and beyond.

While acknowledging that the defining features of the Augustinian form do not necessarily 'prescribe a paradigm for autobiography,' Fleishman points out that their 'analytic utility' can enhance our reading of other self-portraits. Indeed, in tracing elements of this figurative pattern in the language of self-writing in Victorian and Modern English, his study explores the degree to which most autobiographical texts of the period 'focus on one or more of these phases.'[4]

O'Casey's autobiography duplicates several key facets of this autobiographical form. In addition to the many biblical allusions and prose rhythms which echo throughout the work (usually, as was shown in the previous chapter, for ironic and satiric purposes), he employs scriptural imagery, biblical phrases and — megalomania notwithstanding — even analogies with Christ to highlight his protagonist's journey through life.[5] His quest is marked by false starts and apparent self-knowledge, only to be followed by disillusion, further isolation and continued searching until true orientations of identity are discovered. Indeed, while O'Casey's protagonist travels on the circuitous route which is a necessary preliminary to genuine understanding of the self and its vision of life, the autobiography is also characterized by seemingly paradoxical images of the hero. At times, his actions and beliefs show him identifying with, indeed often embodying specific values of his world, so that he appears as an individual who is at one with the shaping forces of his social and intellectual milieu. Yet, at other instances, he is presented as an alienated outsider, a figure of opposition and controversy whose views are shared by few others. As we shall see, however, the paradox is merely superficial: the integrated man and the alienated man are actually a reflection of the desire for personal liberation and fulfilment which O'Casey sees as a constant throughout his life.

Alienated images of the protagonist are readily apparent in the account of Johnny Caside's beginnings. His birth itself, as

Fleishman and others have noted, is presented as an archetypal event, a reenactment of the Fall;[6] the figurative language O'Casey uses suggests that the experience is a movement downward — 'a man-child dropped from her womb down into the world; down into a world that was filled up with the needs, ambitions, desires, and ignorances of others' — into a place characterized by pain, hardship and deprivation. Although the chapter begins, as is common in autobiography, with the birth of the protagonist, almost immediately, the presentation of personal or even genealogical material is suspended as the focus shifts to some of the defining characteristics of the reality into which the child is born. In the long, two-page first sentence O'Casey attempts to suggest some of the social, artistic and religious facets of late Victorian life. It is a world predicated on social distinctions, where the upper classes live comfortable and genteel lives isolated from the suffering of the poor and indifferent to the forces of change. Members of this social elite are content with the artificial, precious prose of Ruskin and the stilted, uninspired paintings of Poynter, President of the Royal Academy. Outrightly rejecting Darwin, they are content with the vision of life offered by traditional religious views. In Ireland, these British Empire values are embodied in the landed, mercantile, bureaucratic and military classes; the protection of this minority is evident in the incongruous spectacle of marionettte-like soldiers, gaily dressed in British uniforms, performing mock battles in the Phoenix Park to honour the birthday of a foreign queen. Victorian Dublin is, then, a place of social inequality, moribund art, antiquated religious dogma and foreign domination.

The long opening sentence, structured around a series of clauses beginning with 'where,' is balanced in the next chapter by several sentences each with variations of the phrase, 'It was a time when,' the combined effect of which is to establish the child's world in spatial and temporal dimensions that are synonymous with man's fallen condition. His reality inculcates feelings of displacement and motivates him throughout his life to strive for a world order more compatible with his innate aspirations. That is not to say that O'Casey based his criticism of late-Victorian society on Platonic or Christian principles, by which the newborn child, echoing Wordsworth, arrives into a blemished world 'trailing clouds of glory'; it is to claim, however, that O'Casey's response to the very solidity of that distorted reality, with its structural inequities and institutionalized injustices, was predicated on the strong conviction that man could create an alternate society, one built on a set of values that would do away with economic oppression and deprivation. The prior place from which the child's birth is a symbolic fall remains unstated, unlike the more explicit versions of the Augustinian form, with their periodic allusions to a previous heavenly condition. The absence of this antecedent state in the autobiography stems from the fact that, in O'Casey's secular version of the archetype, the traditional spiritual home, whether it is a return to a prior state of grace or union with God, has been displaced; instead of positing the return in spiritual terms, he holds out the promise of a more equitable social order that awaits the child in an earthly future.

The implication that this newborn child is an archetypal figure struggling to survive in a hostile environment is reinforced by the additional information given in the opening chapter. The specific facts reveal that the child is John, born to the woman Susan, who has had seven previous children, four of whom survived. Two boys, both named John, had died of croup. It is revelatory that a chapter which logically should focus on the hero's beginnings, deals primarily with the death of a previous child. The mother is reluctant to name her third son John, feeling it 'to be a challenge to God to do that,' (I, 12) but, on the death of the last John, the father had insisted, 'if we should have another child, and that other child should be a boy, we shall call his name John.' (I, 17) The implications are that the birth of the hero is closely intertwined with the deaths of his two brothers: since the father wanted a son named John, those namesakes died that he might be born; his life would be a proxy justification of their deaths. Consequently, the onus on this child to survive — made difficult enough in a world pervaded by disease and social injustice — is greatly increased by the presence of these two ghosts in his life. That this chapter functions as an overture to much that appears later in the work is confirmed by its title, 'A Child is Born,' which, in echoing the birth of Christ — another infant born in poverty whose birth was preceded by a precursor named John — establishes the protagonist as an alienated figure who will be misunderstood and victimized throughout his life. In the opening chapter, then, the predicament of the boy born into an unjustly structured world instantly establishes him as having to overcome the exclusion from the privileges available to those 'carrying godwarrants of superiority because they had dropped down into the world a couple of hours earlier.' (I, 11) And yet, despite his hostile environment, the boy survives, asserting himself sufficiently so that he 'kicked against the ambitions, needs, and desires of the others, cleared a patch of room for itself from the trampling feet and snapping hands around

it.' (I, 11) Under his mother's 'ever-verdant care' he develops the
fortitude and resilience to withstand the forces that had claimed the
lives of his two brothers, and, 'Delicately and physically
undecided, he crept along.' (I, 18) For a few years his life does
become an image of joy and happiness as 'he ran about and laughed
like other children.' (I, 18) But, at the age of five, because 'God had
not forgotten, and the trial was sent at last,' (I, 18) he develops the
ulcerous sores in his eyes which would remain a chronic affliction
throughout his life. Thus, is begun a further long cycle of suffering,
deprivation and exclusion.

In the second chapter of *Knock*, O'Casey stages a mock baptismal
scene in which the boy discovers the harshness of his environment. If
traditional baptism is an act which symbolically affirms an eternal
reality and establishes an individual's claim to salvation in it,
O'Casey reverses this implication by having Johnny's secular
baptism dramatically introduce him to the suffering of his fallen
world. The scene occurs after a friend of the family had suggested
that the pain in the boy's eyes could be alleviated if, several times a
day, his head were plunged into a bucket of cold water:

Johnny was seized and, screaming protests, his head was pushed down into
a bucket of dead cold water till the eyes were underneath; and he was
vehemently called upon to open his eyes, open his eyes, damn it, couldn't
he open his eyes, and let the water get at them. When he struggled, cold
and frightened, they pushed him farther down till the water flowing
through his nostrils gurgled down his throat, almost choking him, leaving
him panting for breath, shivering and wet, in the centre of reproaches and
abuse because he had kept his eyes fiercely closed underneath the water.
(I, 19–20)

This initiation scene leaves little doubt that the child's world is a
place of seldom relieved hardship, where his frequently bandaged
eyes not only keep him from the normal socialization involved in
schooling but force on him the role of non-participant, the sickly
child who must remain on the sidelines of children's play: 'He felt
only a curious resentment that he wasn't as others of his age were,
and as he himself had been, able to run, shout, to rejoice when the
sun shone.' (I, 18) Johnny is confirmed in the role of outsider by
the actual circumstances of living surrounded by poor Catholics,
cut off from the privileges associated with his Protestant brethren.
This economic exclusion from his own minority group exposes him
to the sectarian taunts of his Catholic neighbours and leads to
doubts about his national identity.

To reinforce the portrayal of the boy as an alienated figure,
O'Casey periodically associates Johnny with the martyred Christ,

the saviour who is misunderstood and rejected by the very people
he wishes to redeem. At a later point in *Knock*, for instance, the
boy is depicted as a Christ-like sufferer whose afflictions are
exacerbated by inequitable social conditions, symbolized in this
case by the wealth of Queen Victoria. The scene is Mrs Casside's
response to a new flare-up of the boy's eye ulcers which she fears
will lead to blindness. However, she believes that if she had money
she could readily discover his precise ailment, and thus take the
first step in effecting a cure:

She looked at the picture of Queen Victoria, with the little crown on her
gray head and the white veil falling over her neck and down her bare
shoulders. Enough jewels in her little crown to keep them all for the rest
of their lives, with a little left over for the poor. Crown o'jewels, crown
o'thorns, an' her own boy with a crown of soakin' wet rags to deaden the
pain in his temples. (I, 105)

This discreet evocation of Christ allows O'Casey to cast his hero
as set apart and different from others, a ready victim of mistreatment and isolation.

    The parallel between Johnny and Christ is made more explicit
at several other points in the autobiography, an identification
facilitated by the hero's fortuitous initials. For example, when
Johnny has an argument at his first job with his boss, Mr Anthony,
he shows up for work the following morning expecting to be
dismissed for his impudence. Apprehensive, he arrives at the
premises just as Mr Anthony does, so that he enters,

with the cold eyes watching him behind, and the soft steps following his,
follow, follow, I will follow Jesus; anywhere, everywhere, I will follow on;
follow, follow, I will follow Jesus, everywhere He leads me, I will follow
on, but the followed J.C. this time's Johnny Casside, for when he signed
his name in the time-book, the cold eyes were staring down at the moving
hand that wrote. (II, 103)

    Forming opposite images of the hero are those few occasions that
approximate the paradisal conditions traditionally associated with
the phase of natural childhood. The chapter, 'The Street Sings,'
opens with an account of such elusive experiences:

Golden and joyous were the days for Johnny when he was free from pain;
when he could lift the bandage from his eye, and find the light that hurt
him hurt no longer; that the shining sun was as good today as it was when
the Lord first made it; glorifying the dusty streets, and putting a new robe,
like the wedding garment of the redeemed, on the dingy-fronted houses.
Now he could jump into the sunlight, laugh, sing, shout, dance, and make
merry in his heart, with no eye to see what he was doing, save only the

eye of God, far away behind the blue sky in the daytime, and farther away still behind the golden stars of the night-time. (I, 84)

Here, the suggestion of escape from the suffering of the fallen world, the evocation of the first days of creation, and the presence of a benign divinity create feelings of unity and harmony between self and world that are usually denied to the boy. Such joyful and transcendent moments are all the more precious because they are so fleeting.

As a substitution for such actual occasions of Edenic bliss, however, O'Casey presents imaginative reveries in which Johnny conjures up ideal images which serve as antidotes to his harsh reality. It is through the transforming power of such scenes that Johnny has access to the joy that characterizes the phase of natural childhood. Thus, for instance, in 'The Dream Review,' Johnny, unable to attend a military parade in the Phoenix Park in honour of Victoria's birthday, escapes from the dreariness of being confined, on a wet, dark day, in his flea-ridden bed, by dreaming about colourful and heroic soldiers engaged in glorious and exciting battles. Similarly, in 'The Dream School,' the Edenic images of gardens, flowers, fruits and butterflies suggest the kind of pre-lapsarian innocence and joy associated with idealized childhood, and are in sharp contrast to the monotonous and oppressive atmosphere of Slogan's classroom:

The sky above was a far deeper blue than the blue on the wing of the blue-dotted butterfly, while through the deep blue of the sky sailed white clouds so low down that some of them shone with the reflected gold from the blossoms of the daffodils. Many beautiful trees lined the road that Johnny walked on, and from some came the smell of thyme and from others the smell of cinnamon. Some of the trees bent down with the weight of blossoms, and numbers were heavy with plums as big as apples, and cherries bigger than the biggest of plums that hung in hundreds on their branches, so that he ate his fill as he walked along the white road. (I, 100)

Avrom Fleishman rightly reads this passage as a distinct echo of the natural childhood phase of the traditional autobiographical paradigm:

That this is not merely a private fantasy but a cultural endowment is borne out by the rhythms of the prose and the choice of spices; we are in the presence of a biblical paradise, and the mature author joins the hungry boy in his submission to the master figures of the autobiographical tradition.[7]

It is clear that, for Johnny Casside, this period of idealized existence is primarily associated with a world above or beyond his present state and accessible only through imagination.

In subsequent years, as the growing youth finds himself set apart and distinct from others, he is shown making strenuous attempts to overcome the forces alienating him. His effort to counter the segregating consequences of both his Protestant background and his continuing ill-health are evident in his dogged determination to achieve personal liberation and individual fulfilment through self-education. But the consequences of such endeavours cause further ostracization; the maturing process which results from his reading, combined with his readiness to behave as the flaunting, proud autodidact, lead to distrust and resentment from his fellow-workers. Similarly, during his period of zealous religious commitment, his support of one of the feuding factions in his local church brings on the wrathful criticism of the majority group and leads to his break with parish officials. Indeed, throughout the autobiography, the essential traits of his character — his passionate convictions, his stubborn refusal to compromise his integrity, and his outspoken and vehement expression of his views — often conspire to estrange him from those around him whenever the circumstances of his life have not already done so.

By far the most sustained images of alienation are those associated with the protagonist's involvement in some of the historic events in the Ireland of his time. Initially, discovery of patriotic ideals presents him with an opportunity for personal definition and integration with his reality; if Ireland was originally presented as a place where the newborn child feld displaced, it now becomes the object of the protagonist's ardent desire for fulfilment. In fact, this search becomes so intense at times that it takes on larger dimensions; the hero's personal quest becomes synonymous with the aspirations of the nation so that he emerges as a representative figure whose actions transcend personal implications. At such moments, O'Casey creates an image of his former self as not merely that of an individual man among many, but as representing — almost symbolizing — the predicament and hopes of others in his community and even his country. Thus, for a time, the protagonist is cast in the role of soldier for Ireland, a champion who will make sacrifices and do battle for his lady-love, Cathleen ni Houlihan. This aspect of O'Casey's self-portrait suggests a particularly Irish characteristic of the work, since the pattern of the protagonist identifying with lofty national goals which eventually lead to disillusionment is also a marked feature of George Moore's *Hail and Farewell* and W. B. Yeats's *Autobiographies*. The presence of this paradigm in the three great Irish autobiographies of the time underlies the degree to which Irish writers equated self and world. Indeed, this close identification between personal and national aspirations may be the single most defining feature of Irish autobiography in the twentieth century.

For example, George Moore gives as the reason for autobiographical portrayal his perception of himself as a crusader for art in Ireland which, he felt, was being inhibited if not smothered by Catholicism. So closely does Moore tie his own destiny to that of country that he sees himself as the required messiah who would bring art and culture to Ireland. Initially, he is unsure whether his mission is to be accomplished by being involved with the Irish Literary Theatre, helping to revive the Irish language, or writing a novel or collection of stories. Having returned to Ireland, settled in Dublin, and begun the investigation of these possibilities, Moore depicts his former self as gradually becoming disillusioned with the possibility of fostering art in a country so overwhelmingly religious. Yet, Moore finally recognizes that the story of that very discovery, the account of his failed crusade for art in a hostile environment, could itself be transformed into an artistic creation. He discovers that his ten-year effort to awaken Ireland to its artistic potential could be presented as a quest, the narrative of which is its own fulfilment. Thus, *Hail and Farewell* partakes of an autobiographical pattern of self-exploration and portrayal which might be termed Wordsworthian, for the author of *The Prelude* turns to his past to trace the origin and development of his poetic powers. The very process of doing so itself becomes the confirmation Wordsworth seeks: *The Prelude* is a poem which is the object of its own quest. *Hail and Farewell* is pervaded by a similar circular awareness; the moment of insight given towards the end of the book is the perspective from which the work was begun; as such, it is the primary factor influencing the choice of materials, structural devices and representational techniques. Although the biographical story of Moore's ten-year sojourn in Ireland is ultimately one of disappointment and frustration, the artistic transformation of that failed mission produces a highly-wrought and innovative example of the autobiographical genre.

Yeats's autobiography does not evince such an obvious and focused purpose as Moore's, but one of the intentions which periodically surfaces partakes of the same pattern of individual aspirations being closely associated with national destiny. Yeats's changing perception of that evolving relationship is presented as one of the crucial influences on his poetic development. For example, he orchestrates the factual details of his earlier years so that the self that emerges is a figure of exile and alienation searching for unity and integration. The pattern of possession and loss is enhanced by the events of his childhood years spent, as they were, between Sligo and London. The memories of Sligo — its natural beauty, legends and people, and its associations with the stern but romantic figure of his grandfather and his stories of seafaring and foreign lands — accentuate his sense of alienation from London life. In later sections of the autobiography, Yeats presents his relationship with Ireland as a series of high expectations inevitably succeeded by disenchantment. Thus, his early efforts to foster what he saw as Unity of Culture, based on enlightened patriotism and a knowledge of Celtic mythological traditions, are a story of failure, a narrative of petty animosities and continual discord. This pattern is reenacted once again when, together with Lady Gregory, he establishes an Irish Theatre, only to witness the rejection of Synge's dramatic genius. The essential conflict between the Ireland of Yeats's imagination and the hostile reality continually impinging on that image is, as with Moore and O'Casey, a central structural principle in the work. While his effort on Ireland's behalf is a story of false starts and unfulfilled hopes, the narrative of his optimistic perception of his role as Irish poet giving way to a final recognition of his country's failure to achieve Unity of Culture becomes an important shaping principle unifying the work. In the lives of all three writers, Cathleen ni Houlihan was a figure of failure, even of betrayal, but as a key presence in their autobiographical imaginations she gives an epic dimension to each of their self-portraits.

Johnny Casside's most passionate moments of identification with Ireland are conveyed through O'Casey's highly figurative and symbolic language. His role of heroic figure willing to expend his energies for his country is most clearly established in the 'Sword of Light' chapter from *Pictures*. He begins by asking himself which cause might best serve as an outlet for his enthusiasms and be the embodiment of his ideals: 'The Sword of Light! An Claidheamh Solis; the Christian Faith; the sword of the spirit; the freedom of Ireland; the good of the common people; the flaming sword which turned every way, to keep the way of the tree of life — which was it? where would he find it?' (II, 197) These questions have arisen in his mind as a result of a visit from his friend, the fiercely patriotic tram-conductor, who has just baptised Johnny into the religion of patriotic values by declaring that he will call him 'Sean' in future. With the conductor's departure, Johnny, in a semi-mystical moment, discovers his vocation as a priest-like devotee of nationalism:

He went back into the darkened room, sat down, leaned his elbows on the table and his head in his hands. He glanced at the little smoky lamp and fancied that it had changed to a candle — a tall, white, holy candle, its flame taking the shape of a sword; and, in its flaming point, the lovely face of Cathleen, the daughter of Houlihan. (II, 197)

In the subsequent chapter, appropriately called 'I Strike a Blow For You, Dear Land,' Johnny is shown as the patriotic soldier in his first encounter with the enemy. After he knocks a policeman off a horse during a street demonstration, he and the conductor escape to a nearby pub, along with a girl who has admired Johnny's actions. Later, the young woman invites him to her home to minister to his superficial wound, and rewards his brave conduct with her sexual favours. This red-haired girl is wearing 'a gay dark-green dress suit, the skirt barely reaching to her ankles; a black bolero jacket, trimmed with flounced epaulettes which were rimmed with a brighter green than the green of the suit, and flecked with scarlet.' (II, 198–199) Over this, is 'a dark-green shawl.' (II, 207) Here, dressed in the green, black and red colours of popular representation, is Cathleeen ni Houlihan incarnate.

In *Drums*, the account of Sean's development continues to transcend the personal story and to acquire national overtones by being proffered as a product of successive encounters with the social, cultural and political events in contemporary Ireland. Indeed, throughout the volume, the details of family and domestic life are, as we have seen previously, so orchestrated that they become the impetus for many of his patriotic activities: descriptions of Sean and his family being buffeted by economic and social forces become metaphors for the enervated state of his country; and his participation in patriotic organizations such as the Gaelic League and the Irish Republican Brotherhood is made synonymous with national liberation. It is this interplay between self and world, between the individual story and contemporary history, that lends an epic quality to the narrative, making it at times as much a product of historical forces as autobiographical data.

But the identification which he makes for a time between public and private man proves eventually to be misleading. Sean's sense of the incongruity between the various aspects of his personality is suggested by the names associated with the different facets of his life:

Because of his enthusiasm for the Gaelic League and for his never-ending efforts to get all whom he worked with, and all whom he met, to join the

Movement, he was known along the line, from Dublin to Drogheda, as Irish Jack. He had three names: to his mother he was Johnny; his Gaelic friends knew him as Sean; to his workmates he was Jack. (III, 48)

His acknowledgement of his changing personae is a clear indication of the competing elements in his character. Moreover, the image of one who has struck a harmonious relationship between the diverse aspects of his life is soon undermined by his growing recognition that his perception of Ireland's future is quite different from that of other members of patriotic associations. Precisely because the ideals which these organizations worked for were vague, indeed often at odds with each other, individual members could see their own efforts as neatly coinciding with their personal vision of the new country. If Ireland did not yet exist as an independent country, if its future identity was to be based on traditions and aspirations handed down from previous generations, all those actively involved in Ireland's cause could be their own interpreters of their country's past in their imaginative projection of its future. For Sean, it would be a secular, democratic and strongly Gaelic nation, founded on the principles of select Irish heroes such as Wolfe Tone. But, in working closely with republicans, whether in the Gaelic League, the St Laurence O'Toole Pipers' Band, or the Irish Republican Brotherhood, he comes to recognize the irreconcilable differences between his vision of a liberated Ireland and theirs. As his faith in republican ideals wanes, counterparts for personal growth and development are no longer to be found in cultural and political associations; instead his identification with Ireland is now tied to the struggles of the working class:

Now there were two Cathleen ni Houlihans running round Dublin: one, like the traditional, in green dress, shamrocks in her hair, a little Brian Boru harp under her oxster, chanting her share of song, For the rights and liberties common to all Irishmen; they who fight for me shall be rulers in the land; they shall be settled for ever, in good jobs shall they be, for ever, for ever; the other Cathleen coarsely dressed, hair a little tousled, caught roughly together by a pin, barefooted, sometimes with a whiff of whiskey off her breath; brave and brawny; at ease in the smell of sweat and the sound of bad language, vital and asurge with immortality. Those who had any tinge of gentility in them left the Citizen Army for the refeeniated Volunteers. (III, 226)

All of Sean's efforts to act upon his beliefs are thereafter manifested in his work on behalf of this image of Ireland: his part in the organization of the Irish Transport and General Workers' Union, his contributions of articles for Larkin's *Irish Worker* and his duties as Secretary of the Irish Citizen Army.

His most intense and complete commitment to the cause finds expression during the lock-out of Dublin's tramway works in 1913, when, side by side with Larkin, he works tirelessly on behalf of union members and their families. Despite the failure of the workers to win many of their demands, Sean's efforts in the protracted and historic confrontation between management and labour are presented as the one occasion when participation in public events permits a complete identification with a cause reflecting his values. The desire not only to help the union members in practical matters but to articulate their claims for social and political reform, to give voices to the weak, downtrodden and dispossessed, now becomes his motivating priority. And just as his own deprivation is perceived as the deprivation of many, so also is his discovery of the means of salvation offered as theirs.

But the period when personal experiences could be suitably transformed to take on such archetypal dimensions is short-lived, for soon after the lockout he resigns from the Citizen Army in dispute with Countess Markiewicz over the vital issue of whether, as a socialist organization, the Army should support the nationalists. Sean believes the Countess managed to influence James Connolly sufficiently — 'Then she pounced on Connolly, and dazzled his eyes with her flashy enthusiasm' (III, 213) — that he placed national liberation above socialist principles. A few months after his resignation, Sean sees the power base of both the Citizen Army and the Transport Union dissipated when Jim Larkin leaves for the United States. With the outbreak of the First World War, and with the forces of nationalism increasingly on the ascendant, he begins to see that Ireland would fail to achieve the high ideals he had hoped for. Thus, even before Easter 1916, he once again finds himself an outsider, a dissenter who could support neither the association of the Citizen Army with republicans nor the Transport Union under its new leadership. Although in principle he could not fail to applaud Ireland's effort to achieve control over her own destiny, his proleterian sympathies, combined with his knowledge of republicans, make it obvious to him that national liberation would not lead to the kind of social and political changes he envisions for an independent Ireland. His non-participation in the historic events of Easter Week dramatically symbolizes his isolation from the mainstream of Irish political life, confirming, in the most compelling fashion, that his role of soldier for Ireland was over. Henceforth, Ireland is presented as a place of failed opportunity dominated by bourgeois and religious forces, a country where patriotic causes are no longer commensurate with his social and political aspirations.

Up to this point in his life, the protagonist's various activities have been orchestrated as repeated attempts at integration, inevitably leading to further isolation and ostracization from the society around him. This pattern of misplaced affiliation and disillusioned withdrawal constitutes a series of necessary adjustments — what might be termed de-conversions — which must occur before the legitimate conversion, around which the life is structured, can come about. Thus, Sean's loss of religious faith, his dissatisfaction with myopic nationalism, and his disaffection from both the Citizen Army and the Transport Union, are all presented as paving the way for his full commitment to the internationalist ideology that offers him genuine renewal and symbolic return.[8]

O'Casey arranges it so that Sean's conversion — the discovery of the principle of faith which would henceforth orientate his character, and the moment for which his previous and sometime misguided intellectual development has inevitably prepared for — occurs at the midpoint of *Inishfallen*. It is, however, a turning-point which has been foreshadowed at several previous instances in the autobiography. In *Drums*, for example, as O'Casey recounts the obstacles which members of the Irish Volunteers placed in the way of the Irish Citizen Army in its efforts to organize, drill and accumulate arms, he shows Sean deciding that members of the Volunteers have a much too restricted view of the struggle for Irish freedom:

They aren't Internationalists; they aren't even Republicans. They aren't able to see over the head of England out to the world beyond. They would be lost among Desmoulins, Danton, Couthon, St Just, and Robespierre, and Marat would frighten the life out of them. Their eyes can see no further soil than their feet can cover. A frail few would stand at ease under the worker's banner. They would be the heralds of the new power, having time but to sound the reveille, and then sink suddenly down into sleep themselves. (III, 231)

A few pages later, when Sean has already resigned from the Citizen Army, his widening political consciousness is reinforced when he is depicted sitting

on a pediment of a column keeping up the facade of the Post Office, reading, reading the new catechism of the *Communist Manifesto* with all its great commandment of Workers of all lands, unite! And in all the shouting and the tumult and the misery around, he heard the roll of new drums, the blowing of new bugles, and the sound of millions of men marching. (III, 245)

By locating this vignette in the setting where Pearse would later read Ireland's Proclamation of Independence, O'Casey the retrospective autobiographer can simultaneously emphasize the narrowness of republican ideals and the wider focus of Sean's proletarian views. Earlier in *Inishfallen*, O'Casey places the Easter Rising in the context of the cataclysmic events of the Russian Revolution, itself presented as heralding radical social and political transformations that supercede mere national independence:

Two fierce fights were going on for liberty: one on the little green dot in the world's waters, called Ireland; and the other over a wide brown, grey, blue, and scarlet expanse of land, later to overflow into the many-coloured, gigantic bloom of the Soviet Union. The first for a liberty of the soul that was to leave the body and mind still in prison; the other for the liberty of the body that was to send the soul and mind as well out into the seething waters of a troubled world on a new and noble adventure. (IV, 15–16)

Notwithstanding these indications of Sean's prior awareness of internationalism, his expression of support for it is most clearly and comprehensively presented in the 'A Terrible Beauty is Borneo' chapter of *Inishfallen*. Having freed himself from the obligations of strict chronology, O'Casey chooses this particular moment to present Sean's conversion because its impact can be heightened in several ways. Since the chapter ostensibly deals with the setting up of the bourgeois government of the Irish Free State, he can emphasize that the Easter Rising has indeed failed to offer hope to the poor and working classes in Ireland. Moreover, the War of Independence with England and the subsequent tragedy of the Civil War can be offered as further confirmation of Sean's perception of the misplaced priorities of the nationalists. In addition, by the early twenties Sean can be shown possessing personal confirmation of the initial achievements and ambitious plans of the fledgling Soviet state. None of these effects would have been accomplished if O'Casey had presented Sean's internationalist beliefs earlier, either before the Easter Rising or when the Russian Revolution had struck a blow for international socialism. (At that time, Sean was depicted as merely joining 'the few who had formed the little Socialist Party of Ireland' as a gesture of support for the Bolsheviks.[9]) It is therefore appropriate that O'Casey, to achieve the full impact of Sean's disillusionment with the middle-class, capitalist society of the newly established Irish Free State, prepares for the expression of his new political consciousness with a vivid account of his impassioned and bitter reaction to the appalling conditions of Dublin's lower classes — the very circumstances motivating his persistent desire for a radical change in the social order:

Often Sean wandered through the poor streets where these poor poorer [sic] houses were; sometimes going in and out of them, climbing down to see some of the thousands who lived in the basements, the poorest of the poor rooms in the poorer house. No tall-hat, no black tie with jacket, no white tie and black jacket with tails ever went down these stony ways, damp with the green of slimy moss, a decayed carpet honouring the feet of those decaying in the dimmer den below. Nor did anyone, even those happy with the keenest sight, ever see the scarlet or the purple biretta cautiously going down these slime-covered steps. Only when some soul found itself within the dim flicker of a last farewell to life, did some simple, black-coated cleric climb down to give a hasty anointing to the dying soul, indifferently fortifying it against the four last things — heaven, hell, death, and the judgement. (IV, 161)

That these places are a living hell for their inhabitants is suggested by the repetition of 'down' which, as we have seen, has already been associated with the fallen world that is the hero's reality. O'Casey's switch in the next paragraph to physical and organic imagery is in keeping with his perception of these living conditions as little better than the burrows of some subterranean species of animal:

Frequently he wandered, hurt with anger, through these cancerous streets that were incensed into resigned woe by the rotting houses, a desperate and dying humanity, garbage and shit in the roadway; where all the worst diseases were the only nobility present; where the ruddy pictures of the Sacred Heart faded into a dead dullness by the slimy damp of the walls oozing through them; the few little holy images they had, worn, faded, and desperate as the people were themselves; as if the images shared the poverty and the pain of them who did them reverence. Many times, as he wandered there, the tears of rage would flow into his eyes, and thoughts of bitter astonishment made him wonder why the poor worm-eaten souls there couldn't rise in furious activity and tear the guts out of those who kept them as they were. (IV, 161–162)

The heightened personal anger and feelings of impotence stem both from Sean's knowledge of the policies about to be pursued in the new Irish republic, and from his recognition that the workers' union now lacked either the will or moral authority to crusade against such blatant injustices. To highlight Sean's perception of national inertia, O'Casey juxtaposes this crisis of despair (replete with the tears of helplessness that characterize the despondency preceding conversion in the traditional form) and the announcement of his new-found faith: 'But Sean had more than hope now. He had had letters from a Raissa Lomonovska telling him about what was going on in the Soviet Union, enclosing photographs of the people and their new ways.' (IV, 162) Seeing a picture of children from a Caucasian village welcoming the Red Army as it brought the first diesel locomotive to the region, Sean approves of such accomplishments, a shift in orientation made to coincide with his disappointment in post-colonial Irish society:

In the spirit, Sean stood with these children, with these workers, with these Red Army men, pushing away with them the ruin they were rising from, the ruin from which all the people would one day rise, sharing the firmness of their unafraid hearts, adding his cheer to the cheers of the Soviet People.

The terrible beauty had been born there, and not in Ireland. The cause of the Easter Rising had been betrayed by the commonplace bourgeois class, who laid low the concept of the common good and the common task, and were now decorating themselves with the privileges and powers dropped in their flight by those defeated by the dear, dead men. (IV, 162–163)

The acknowledgement that his views are not about to be manifest in Ireland gives way to a full expression of his belief in a world socialist order:

But steady, workers, here and elsewhere; steady, poor of the poorer places; your day is coming. The Red Star shines over the Kremlin, once the citadel of the Czars. Those who tried hard to shake it down have fled homewards, helpless against the might and good courage of a half-starved people. The Red Soldiers with their Red Cavalry are on the frontiers, are on the sea-edges of their vast land. Socialism has found a home, and has created an army to patrol around it. The Red Star is a bright star. No pope, no politician, no cleric, no prince, no Press lord can frighten it down now, or screen its ray from our eyes. It is the evening star, and it is the bright and shining morning star. It is the star shining over the flock in the field, over the mother crooning her little one to rest, over the girl arraying herself for the bridal, over the old couple musing by the fireside, over the youngster playing in the street, over the artist achieving a new vision in colour, over the poet singing his song, over the sculptor carving out a fair thing that he alone can see hidden in a stone, over the hammer building the city, over the sickle cutting the corn, over the sailor sailing the seven seas, over the dreaming scientist discovering better and more magical ways of life, over the lover and his lass in ecstasy on the yellow sands, coming through the rye, or sauntering through the indifferent business of some city street, over the miner bending in the deep tomb where the sun-embalmed coal lies low, over the soldier guarding his country's life, over doctor and nurse, forgetting themselves that they may coax back health into all sick persons and young children. (IV, 163)

The comprehensiveness and intensity of this visionary passage are appropriate to a moment of revelation breaking the pattern of high expectations succeeded by disappointment which has characterized his search up to now; it is a clear annunciation that the crisis of despair and frustration has given way to a recognition of his true emotional and intellectual allegiances.

Not only has O'Casey manipulated the events of his past to give this moment maximum dramatic effect but he has also used his retrospective narrative position — these passages were written in the late 1940s — to draw on his knowledge of the developments in both Ireland and Russia in the three decades since the Easter Rising and the Bolshevik Revolution. He writes with an awareness, on the one hand, of the failure of independent Ireland to eradicate social inequality, economic exploitation and artistic oppression, and, on the other, of the significant strides — despite the devastation caused by the Second World War — made in the economic, social and artistic conditions in the Soviet Union. As do all autobiographers, O'Casey uses the retrospective knowledge derived from the double focus of the genre to confirm and reinforce the perceptions and actions of earlier selves.

Although the culmination of O'Casey's hero's journey to political faith is devoid of the obvious metaphysical dimensions associated with the spiritual quest, it does, nevertheless, evince the same essential transcendent qualities. The inherent similarity in the beliefs of the spiritual hero's discoveries and the international communist principles to which Sean subscribes is dramatically evident in the song of praise concluding this moment of conversion:

> Morning star, hope of the people, shine on us!
> Star of power, may thy rays soon destroy the things that err, things that are foolish, and the power of man to use his brother for profit so as to lay up treasure for himself where moth and rust doth corrupt, and where thieves break through and steal.
> Red Mirror of Wisdom, turning the labour in factory, field, and work shop into the dignity of a fine song;
> Red Health of the sick, Red Refuge of the afflicted, shine on us all.
> Red Cause of our joy, Red Star extending till thy five rays, covering the world, give a great light to those who still sit in the darkness of poverty's persecution.
> Herald of a new life, of true endeavour, of common-sense, of a world's peace, of man's ascent, of things to do bettering all things done;
> The sign of Labour's shield, the symbol on the people's banner;
> Red Star, shine on us all! (IV, 163–164)

O'Casey's orchestration of this central moment in his hero's life finds many counterparts in the tradition of autobiographical literature: Rousseau's *Confessions* highlights the experience on the road to Vincennes; Gibbon's *Autobiography* derives its guiding structure from his moment of perception on the steps of the Capitoline Hill on October 15, 1764; and Newman's *Apologia* presents as it primary event the protagonist's realization, in Rome, that the Catholic Church is the legitimate embodiment of his spiritual aspirations. At such instances of heightened awareness, the individual suddenly sees his life in a different context, possessing previously obscured purpose and direction. Such epiphanic moments shed new light on all past endeavours, endowing them with a transcendent significance which dissolves the original anxiety produced by random behaviour. As Karl Weintraub points out, 'The important matter is that the author subsequently recognizes the significant role of the crisis in his life and that he perceives an order and meaning in that life illuminated by the insights gained at an enlightening moment.'[10] In such self-reflective works, the hero views past wanderings and misguided notions of selfhood from the new consciousness achieved through the recently integrated and compatible relationship between self and world, or, in the spiritual quest, between self and God.

By co-opting the Christian litany of homage to the Virgin Mary, in which she is addressed in a series of roles including that of Star of the Sea, O'Casey clearly establishes the idealism, morality and visionary nature of Sean's socialist beliefs. Despite his overtly secular version of the journey to true knowledge, the vision it provides is that of a reality which bears the same relationship to his hero's quotidian world as the heavenly home does to the traditional figure in the spiritual form. Replacing his previous searches for the 'light', whether through religion or nationalism, the 'Red Star' is recognized as the true beacon guiding the peoples of the world to an equitable social order. As the first communist country, the Soviet Union is perceived as the custodian of the proletarian ideals Sean hopes to see realized one day on an international scale.

After the moment of the protagonist's articulation of his social and political beliefs in *Inishfallen*, the autobiography is characterized by insistent and passionate expressions of them. It need hardly be observed that these views have, from the outset, been at the heart of O'Casey's assessment of his personal history and its contexts. But until the moment of full ideological change is reenacted in the work, this central aspect of the protagonist's character is usually suggested only obliquely; the images O'Casey creates of former selves imply a strong condemnation of the conditions in the protagonist's world and suggest a reality altogether different from that in which he is striving to realize his aspirations. However, once the epiphanic moment of clarification has been presented, O'Casey is free to indicate his views through the protagonist's own expression of his ideology. Without the attenuating distance created by an earlier self's lack of full awareness, the clear presentation of the shared beliefs of the protagonist and creator is a distinct feature of the narrative from the midpoint of *Inishfallen* onwards. It is, incidentally, a characteristic which confirms that the later volumes are integral both to the significance of previous experiences and the autobiographical meaning of the overall portrait. Thereafter in the work, the presentation of the hero responding to, and evaluating, life from his newfound perspective is often indicated through the use of religious terminology. For example, in assessing the virtues of T. S. Eliot and Hugh Mac Diarmuid, O'Casey employs biblical echoes to clarify why Sean's sympathies are with the proletarian sentiments of the Scotsman rather than the elitist, high-Anglicanism of Eliot. Although Eliot is commended because 'he desires the people's redemption as we the commoners do,' it is a qualified praise since he seeks that end 'through the Son of God.' MacDiarmuid's poetry, on the other hand, shows that he sees man's salvation being achieved 'through the sons of men'; like Sean, he believes that 'The right to work is the narrow gate through which alone the workers can enter the kingdom of earth. And who can claim a share in God who does not take the part of man.' (VI, 91)

If, in *Inishfallen*, Sean's socialist views confirm his status as a dissenting and disapproving figure in post-1916 Ireland, he is also shown attempting to seek personal fulfilment through other means. Significantly, it is at this time of social and political isolation that he turns to writing:

He had shifted away from the active Ireland, and was growing contentedly active in himself. Instead of trying to form Ireland's life, he would shape his own. He would splash his thoughts over what he had seen and heard; keep eyes and ears open to see and hear what life did, what life had to say, and how life said it; life drunk or sober; life sickly or sturdy; life sensible or half demented; life well-off or poor; life on its knees in prayer, or shouting up a wild curse to heaven's centre. (IV, 114)

However, because Sean was to discover that there would also be ebbs and flows in his life as a writer, once again the life-story is marked by opposing images of the protagonist. His desire to achieve success and public recognition as a playwright is itself presented as an enormous exercise of will-power to overcome the disadvantages of starting to write plays at the age of forty, without the benefits of a formal education or much practical knowledge of the theatre. That he sees these forces of exclusion as obstacles to be overcome is confirmed by the account of his attempts to have a first play performed at the Abbey, or — to use O'Casey's metaphor — to enter the temple of the Abbey Theatre. The description of the events leading up to the acceptance of his first play makes frequent use of this imagery; he talks of not yet having 'entered within the veil of the temple, and still was allowed to but stand reverent on the doorstep.' (IV, 125) Later, the chapter — appropriately called, 'The Temple Entered' — which goes on to recount his successes at the Abbey, begins: 'The bells were ringing an old year out and a new year in for Sean: he was on his way to the temple of the drama, the Abbey Theatre, where he was an acolyte now, in full canonical costume.' (IV, 164) As he willingly serves his apprenticeship period, Sean's dogged determination to succeed in attaining his quest for personal fulfilment as a dramatist is seen in the account of the submission of his third play to the Abbey directors. Having had two plays rejected, he diligently turns to the writing of *The Crimson in the Tri-Colour*, the only copy of which he sent to the theatre. Presently, he receives word from Lennox Robinson informing him that the manuscript has been lost. Although the thought of so much work gone for nought angers him to the point of physical sickness, Sean, undeterred, turns to the writing of another play:

There was nothing to do but forget, and go on; forget, and go on. He had made up his mind years ago that the Abbey Theatre curtain would go up on a play of his; and up it would go, sooner or later. First decide slowly and deeply whether it is in you to do a thing; if you decide that you can, then do it, even though it kept you busy till the very last hour of life. (IV, 117)

And yet, despite his sense of accomplishment when he finally achieves success at the Abbey, his perception of himself as the acclaimed dramatist is, notwithstanding Yeats's and Lady Gregory's staunch defence of him, undermined by ensuing events: the pettiness and narrow mindedness of nationalists in their reaction to *Plough*, the pietism of certain Abbey players, and his own growing sense of the parochialism of Dublin's literary cliques all confirm his feeelings of alienation.

O'Casey adds to the image of Sean as the misunderstood individual, the writer scorned for criticizing society, by placing his mistreatment in Ireland in the tradition of such other victims as Parnell, Synge and Yeats:

For the first time in his life, Sean felt a surge of hatred for Cathleen ni Houlihan sweeping over him. He saw now that the one who had the walk of a queen could be a bitch at times. She galled the hearts of her children who dared to be above the ordinary, and she often slew her best ones. She had hounded Parnell to death; she had yelled and torn at Yeats, at Synge, and now she was doing the same to him. What an old snarly gob she could be at times; an ignorant one too. (IV, 176)

By being associated with these abused figures in Irish public life, Sean's experiences are equated with those of the lonely and mistreated man of vision, the leader or artist rejected by his own people. As he prepares to set sail for England, he decides that 'There was no making love to Cathleen, daughter of Houlihan, now, untidy termagant, brawling out her prayers.' (IV, 283–284) The image of the rejected lover, whose attempts to woo his beloved through his art have failed, underlines Sean's deep feeling of repugnance for his native country and its misguided leaders.

Yet, upon leaving Ireland, his one consolation is that those whose judgement mattered — selected critics in Dublin and London, and especially Yeats and Lady Gregory — had every confidence in his abilities as a dramatist. When the refusal of the *Tassie* summarily ruptures his relations with the Abbey, not only does he sever an essential bond with Ireland but, of more importance, he deprives himself of the advice and encouragement of some of his earliest supporters. If previously he had little kinship with Irish life, he is now cut off from those few people in Ireland who might have assisted his career. Despite his literary success and acclaim, he once again finds himself an outsider; he is a dramatist effectively isolated not only from the theatre that had nurtured his talents but also, with few exceptions, from the stages of London and New York. Once more he is rejected as an Abbey playwright, excommunicated from the temple by its high priests, Yeats, Robinson and Lady Gregory. Consequently, in the two volumes which cover Sean's years in England, O'Casey need do little to manipulate the events of this period into images of isolation. His predicament of the beleagured writer who, notwithstanding past accomplishments, had to struggle for artistic freedom, as well as economic survival, is sufficient in itself to conjure up the archetypal image of the artist as exile.

To reinforce the portrayal of the neglected writer, to indicate that artistic and financial difficulties continue in England, O'Casey periodically draws parallels between his protagonist and other lonely figures, whether from history, literature or legend. Milton, for example, is one of those with whom he is identified, a parallel facilitated by the poet's blindness and Sean's own failing eyesight. In *Rose*, having summarized the events surrounding the *Tassie* rejection and indicated some of its economic and artistic consequences for Sean, newly burdened with the responsibility of marriage and fatherhood, O'Casey describes him, 'Running from London, fleeing from poverty as aforetime Milton fled from the plague.' (V, 132) His retreat is Chalfont St Giles, a village whose two claims to fame were 'a stump of an oak tree, right in the way of traffic, where, when it was flourishing, Milton was said to have sat himself on sunny days, and the cottage where he fled to when the plague beset London.' (V, 138) In going on to bemoan the neglect of Milton's writings, O'Casey reveals more about his own sense of mistreatment at the hands of literary decision makers than he does about the current state of Milton's reputation:

To all the district around, it was as if Milton had ne'er been born. And no wonder, for to the poets elect of today and to those who garlanded these poets, Milton's name is one to be forgotten by the wisely-cultured moment. Emotion no longer minded him. The voice that sighed or shouted, the voice that sang with music, was not in a state of grace. Milton found no favor now with the Muses, chattering among the cocktails, now in darkness, and with danger compassed round. (V, 139)

The echoes here from *Paradise Lost* reinforce Sean's own sense of a fall from artistic innocence, an exile now being further confirmed by the necessity of his move from London.

In political terms, his isolation in England is no less complete than his neglect as a writer. If, in the dozen or so years before his departure from Ireland, he had found himself socially and politically in disagreement with the direction Irish society was taking, exile in England did not mean he had found his ideological home. Although he could certainly find more sympathizers with his internationalist views than had been been the case in Ireland, in actual terms there were to be few causes that he could support: he identifies with the workers in the General Strike of 1926 and he is periodically encouraged by the policies of the Labour Party. But only very rarely were there concrete events at hand which, serving as objective counterparts for his political aspirations, narrow his sense of disjunction between his reality and his beliefs. The most dramatic occasion when the actual experiences of his daily life could be seen to be practical manifestations of his internationalist socialist vision occurs during the war, when England and Russia are allies against Germany:

The Panzers were racing over Russia! Totnes was busy presenting things, making toys, holding concerts and dances to provide funds for Mrs Churchill's Russian Red Cross Fund. In the window of the Anglo-Soviet Headquarters stood three huge photographs, four feet tall and three feet wide, of Churchill to the right, Stalin to the left, with Franklin D. Roosevelt in the centre. The Soviet Flag was seen for the first time in Totnes, and hundreds wore a little Red Star in the breast of blouses or in the lapels of their coats; for the fight of the Red Army had modified the fear, and had removed the very present danger of invasion. (VI, 142)

Regardless of the fact that the common goal was the defeat of the Nazis rather than a shared vision of international proletarian ideals, the combined struggle stirs the blood of the ageing Sean:

The work for England and for the Soviet Union went forward in the little town of Totnes. The rose and crown looked fine beside the hammer and the sickle. Sean helped as well as he could, addressing envelopes, and delivering circulars, for one thing. (VI, 143)

This seeming confluence of the real and the ideal, this opportunity to participate however marginally in the international struggle of the working class is short-lived; at war's end, bereft of immediate symbols for his beliefs, and still struggling to have his plays produced, he is once again both a political and artistic exile.

The portrayal of the protagonist as an alienated figure continues, then, even after he has worked out a satisfactory philosophic approach to life. However — and this point needs emphasis — Sean's internationalism produces images of alienation quite distinct from those prior to the clarification of his ideology. His commitment to a social order based on communist principles and embracing all countries is indeed the culmination of his long quest for a philosophy that would bridge the gap between the world as it was and as he fervently wished it might be. Internationalism provides him with an intellectual framework and ideological perspective that offers not only a satisfactory analysis of the conditions of his life but a faith in the future. However, as a source of unity between life as he knew it and as he hoped it would become, it offers an antidote — not yet fully realized — to his present reality. If, before he became an internationalist, his search partook of a cyclical pattern of apparent harmony and identification with his world, followed by disillusionment and disaffection on a higher plane, its culmination at the moment of full awareness has distinctive attributes. Although his spiral-like journey has carried Sean to a satisfactory ideological vantage point from which he can glance back at previous stages in his evolution, it is a position offering only philosophic comprehensiveness. In this respect, his arrival at true ideological faith parallels the process found in the spiritual autobiographical model. Although the end of Augustine's or Newman's religious quest is heralded by a discovery of God's grace or belief in the legitimacy of the Catholic Church, it is a journey that can be finally completed only when eventual unification with God has been attained. Despite the hero's achievement of spiritual wisdom and assured self-knowledge signalling the end of uncertainty, his journey retains an open-ended dimension: it remains incomplete not so much because it is dependent on future behaviour — consistency of action is now assumed — but because its fulfilment is predicated on an ideal world existing outside the temporal and physical plane on which his wanderings have taken place. These paradoxical elements coexist in tenuous harmony, since the perspective of grace or selfhood provides a philosophic basis for approaching life, while that very means of apprehending reality awaits vindication of its validity at a point which necessarily exists in a metaphysical realm, be it Christian, Platonic or otherwise. Of autobiographical pertinence, however, is that the tensions marking the years of misguided behaviour and leading to the crisis, along with subsequent self-understanding, become the guiding teleological principles motivating the presentation of the life in the work.

Sean's support of proletarian ideals embraces similar opposing tendencies, and accounts for the ongoing presence of conflicting images in the autobiography. Despite his discovery of political principles that have ended his search, led to authentic self-awareness, and provided a satisfactory perspective for assessing reality, they constitute a philosophy finding no counterpart in his daily life. Russia heralds the promise but not the realization of his vision; the Bolshevik revolution must be consolidated, and its message must then spread to other countries. That Sean's ideology awaits complete manifestation at some future date is confirmed when, at the very moment of expressing his beliefs, he looks to the future:

Time was with the Socialists, and time would push away the anxious queues outside trimly-fashioned convents, waiting for a penny dinner. . . . Time, armed with the power of the people, will push away the slow decay of tuberculosis, the chocking fright of diphtheria, the soiling horridness of

typhoid, the rickets that jellied the fibre in the bones of the growing child.
. . . (IV, 160–161)

In fact, the discovery of a satisfactory political ideology not only
fails to signal the end of the hero's alienation but heightens the
divergence between life as it is and as he envisions it. This
discrepancy is all too apparent in England and further afield in
Spain and elsewhere; it is most obvious, however, in his native
country, languishing under the reactionary politics of de Valera:

One thing alone threatens De Valera — the rising of the people against
poverty; the union of the north and the south, when Labour will become
a hundred times stronger by the natural Republican and Socialist activities
of the Ulster people. When this happens, all those to the left of his Party
will swing into pace with the Movement and De Valera will no longer feel
at home in Leinster House. Then the orange sash and the green sash will
show a red star in the centre of each of them. (IV, 160)

The political conditions he witnesses around him, then, offer
dramatic evidence of the dichotomy between his reality and his
ideology. In particular, his knowledge of the priority accorded
the arts in the Soviet Union, especially the assistance given to
dramatists in the publishing and staging of their plays, heightens
his own sense of artistic repression and increases his admiration for
the advances made in Russia under communism.[11] However, even
though the autobiography continues to be characterized by images
of estrangement stemming from his knowledge, the protagonist,
unlike his earlier selves, now possesses a comprehensive and
satisfactory means of responding to life. Prior to the explicit
expression of his internationalist ideology, the images of exclusion
and alienation are indicative of incomplete knowledge and misplaced allegiance; those appearing subsequent to attaining new
political faith serve to reinforce his sense of the legitimacy of his
perception of self and world.

Having acknowledged that O'Casey's autobiography presents
the protagonist in repeated attempts to find integration with his
reality, the reader of the work can legitimately ask what this
portrayal reveals about the identity of the author. What is the final
meaning of the seemingly conflicting personae presented in the
work: the deprived boy whose religion sets him apart from his
Catholic neighbours, the diligent student who is prevented from
regular attendance at school, the patriot who rejects nationalism,
the playwright who leaves the scene of his successes, the disbeliever
whose philosophy of life has all the fervour and intensity of a

religious faith? The key to the shifting images created in the work lies in O'Casey's perception of himself as the perennial outsider, the exile always struggling to overcome barriers of exclusion and feelings of alienation. Thus, in youth, he is cut off from the mainstream of his society by being Protestant, poor and half-blind, while as a young man his reading separates him from those around him and leads to his loss of religion which reinforces the sense of displacement. His union activities ostracize him from republicans, while the evolution of his socialist views distances him from most Irish workers and the emergent conservative society in Ireland. He is further estranged from Irish public life when his plays are criticised, and from the Abbey when the *Tassie* is rejected. An Irishman in England who continues to encounter artistic difficulties, he must look to a distant future when, he hopes, the kind of society he would approve of might be established. The common denominator of all these images of the self is that in each manifestation the protagonist is shown confronting those obstacles threatening his development and preventing him from expressing his changing responses to life. Thus, the life-story charts an ongoing crusade for freedom and liberation from the restrictions imposed by life-denying forces, whether of poverty, sickness, ignorance, narrow-mindedness, national subjugation, economic exploitation or artistic repression.[12] The diverse images presented in the work are therefore evolutionary rather than contradictory; ultimately, they point to the essential consistency with which O'Casey examines his past. The versions of the self created out of his experiences highlight those aspects of O'Casey's character that have been brought to bear on his assessment of his past: he is a man who passionately believes that no society should tolerate poverty, that proper medical and educational facilities should be available to everyone, that exploitation of one group by another or one country by another is morally reprehensible, and that society should permit the artist the freedom to explore and express his creativity. Only when all individuals are given the opportunity to develop their abilities and nurture their talents can an equitable society exist, one which would contribute to the progress of mankind. The single-minded determination with which O'Casey believes that the exciting possibilities offered by life should be experienced without hindrance is perhaps most convincingly expressed in *Rose*, as Sean muses on his son's freedom 'to find a way for himself' through life: 'The right way to Sean was the desire to see life, to hear life, to feel life, and to use life; to engender in oneself the insistent and unbreakable patience to remove any obstacles life

chanced to place in its own way.' (V, 141) By presenting Sean's life
as a product of that driving motivation, as a repeated struggle for
true liberation — from economic deprivation, physical affliction,
soporific religion, dogmatic nationalism, and artistic repression —,
O'Casey confirms that these values are essential to his own identity.

One of the more revealing aspects of O'Casey's autobiographical
identity is suggested by the rather paradoxical images of Sean who,
on the one hand, is frequently depicted as a harsh critic of
established religion, while on the other, is often shown expressing
his vision of life through religious and scriptural imagery.[13] At
one point, for instance, he states unequivocally, 'Yes, in politics,
he was a Communist; and in religion, a Rationalist,' (IV, 228) while
later he can ask: 'Among all who come and go, who is there fit to
say that in men's anxiety, their bargaining, their lovemaking, their
laughter, there is no sign of the blue of Mary's mantle, the white
of Mary's frock, or the red-like crimson of Jesu's jacket?' (VI, 42)
Agreeing with Shaw that Christ was honoured as long as he
remained a charming picture in a frame, Sean goes on to exclaim:
'The picture is out of the frame now, the figure is off the cross, and
Christ now marches in the surge forward in the masse-men. Blok
saw him march through Leningrad at the head of the Red Guards,
and he has appeared in China amid cheers; today, too, his shadow
falls on Africa: Lo, I am with you always — March! Left, left, left!'
(VI, 176) That O'Casey's vision of life can simultaneously reflect
the essential tenets of Christianity and communism emphasizes its
idealistic qualities: it is a world view imbued with moral passion
and spiritual intensity, and characterized by a keen sense of the
sacred and inviolate rights of the individual. The transcendent
nature of his beliefs is evident in the many passages commending
the accomplishments of the Soviet Union. In this regard, faraway
Russia bears the same relation to his imagination as evidence of
God's grace does for St Augustine or the Catholic Church does for
Newman. For, while his vision of international communism is
located sufficiently in the future to be apprehended as a distinctly
different reality (synonymous in the spiritual quest with the
heavenly state), the concrete achievements of the Soviet Union
(akin to manifestations of God in the world here below) are
evidence that his faith is legitimately grounded in his own world.
The harmony an Augustine or a Newman can perceive between an
acknowledgement of man's sinful condition and a belief in a divine
presence partakes of similar paradoxical elements as Sean's attitude
towards Russia and his ideal of a future world organized on
communist principles. Aware that his political hopes are not about

to be realized in Ireland or England, he views Russia as evidence of the validity of his ideological faith. Endorsing the Soviet experiment with all the fervor of a religious convert, Sean considers its accomplishments a vindication of his former responses to personal circumstances, and views its promised goals as dramatic confirmation of his own desire for social and political change. Notwithstanding Russia's faults, or the mistakes made in its name, he choses to keep his mind firmly fixed on its essential motivating principles; judged from that perspective, it remains for him both a mighty achievement of the Russian people and a highly symbolic initial step on the road to a better life for the ordinary person. Denied counterparts for his political and social vision in Ireland, England and elsewhere, Sean retains faraway Russis as concrete assurance that his aspirations are indeed worthwhile. Its authenticity is as unimpeachable as Augustine's palpable sense of God's grace manifesting itself in the world or the converted Newman's belief that Christ's true custodian on earth was the Roman Catholic Church. That O'Casey's view of social progress is an idealized one is not so important as that these are the goals which O'Casey fervently believes that man, reflecting his noblest aspirations, should pursue with dedication and vigour.[14]

The degree to which the accomplishments of the Soviet Union appeal to the most elemental aspects of O'Casey's character, to which his support of Russia is a measure of his passionate commitment to the ideological premises of communism is dramatically evident in the scene between Sean and the woman who claims that her husband has been taken by the Soviet secret police to one of Stalin's concentration camps. For a man so familiar with personal hardship and suffering, whether in his own life or the lives of those who had grown up around him, Sean shows himself to be stubbornly indifferent to the woman's plight. However, his response is consistent and understandable, even though it cannot be condoned: 'Lady, said Sean, softly, I have been a comrade to the Soviet Union for twenty-three years, and all she stands for in the way of Socialism, and I don't intend to break that bond for a few hasty remarks made by one who obviously hates the very bones of the Soviet people.' (VI, 94) All the events, struggles and experiences of Sean's life have produced an emotional attachment and intellectual commitment too great to be thrown over in an instant — certainly without more evidence than the woman is able to supply. However, subsequent details in the chapter do betray his uneasiness with the woman's claims of repression in the Soviet Union: his *ad hominem* replies, focusing on her behaviour and appearance, are irrelevant to her argument. To the end, he refuses to grant any validity to her story.

Yet the woman's visit evokes a response ripe with implication. After she leaves, Sean involves himself in a long rumination on the nature of truth, concluding with his opinion of the unassailable truths about the Soviet Union:

The great achievements of the Soviet Union; touching material possessions, deprived of all by one war, and most by another, having to start afresh twice with little more than a few flint hammers and a gapped sickle or two. The inexhaustible energy, the irresistible enthusiasm of their Socialistic efforts, were facts to Sean; grand facts, setting the people's feet firmly on the way to the whole truth, calling all men to a more secure destiny in which all heads shall be anointed with oil, and all cups shall be filled. (VI, 98)

Sean prefers to return to first principles, to what remains the essential truth for him: Russia is a country attempting to establish a new social and political order based on an ideology he heartily endorses. For him, such tenets are not merely an acquired intellectual framework derived from abstract or theoretical speculation (as it was for many intellectuals who supported Russia only to become disillusioned) but are deep-felt beliefs forged by the circumstances of personal history. To deny the fundamental premises he sees at the heart of Russian communism would be to renege on a system of values shaped over many years and now forming the very bedrock of identity.

In the recreation of this scene, however, O'Casey the autobiographer reaveals some fundamental elements in his character. Sean's insensitivity, along with his lack of compassion and sympathy are a measure of O'Casey's obduracy and self-righteousness. Yet, in his very failure to recognize that this vignette suggests reprehensible and unworthy aspects of his character, O'Casey indicates the fervor of his views, and the degree of his support for their tentative manifestations in the Societ Union. This is not to say that O'Casey was completely blind to faults and weaknesses in the Russian system; in the autobiography, he chose not to publicise any feelings of dissatisfaction with the Soviet Union because, to do so, would have been incompatible with the images of self he was trying to create and the values he was extolling.[15] Robert Lowery has made the point that O'Casey's 'criticisms of the USSR (and he had many) were rarely for public consumption because he recognized that they would be used by those who were seeking the overthrow of that state. To O'Casey, there was an ongoing war, a class war, between Capitalism and Communism and from his years with Larkin O'Casey always felt a strong sense of loyalty to whichever side he chose.'[16] In the autobiography, supporting Russia against reactionary forces, as well as the matter of loyalty, are considerations subsumed into the more deeply rooted issue of personal identity. It is the language in which glowing praise of the achievements of the Soviet Union is couched, and in which his advocacy of internationalism is expressed that suggests the most vital elements of O'Casey's autobiographical identity. The presentation of his proletarian views in Christian terminolgy confirms that, in their fundamentals, they possess all the optimism, morality and idealism associated with religious faith. Because his socialist beliefs are never sufficiently explained or qualified to make for a specific plan of action, they remain more a reflection of his confidence in man's abilities and his aspirations for the human community than a prescription for concrete policies or detailed programs. Nor must the validity of O'Casey's political vision be gainsaid by pointing to specific flaws in the Soviet system. His political credo can be as revealing of character as are Augustine's sense of God's grace or Newman's spiritual rationalizations. Acceptance of Augustine's re-discovered piety, Newman's Catholicism or O'Casey's communism is not required to recognize that such spiritual, philosophical or ideological affiliations are a significant key to the identity of each individual.

The transcendent nature of O'Casey's vision is ultimately a reflection of his own indomitable spirit, of those elements of character that have allowed him to prevail over all the vicissitudes and challenges of life. The courage, resilience and extraordinary faith in man which have been repeatedly demonstrated in the work emerge as metaphors of the human spirit triumphing over adversity. Notwithstanding all the deprivations, hardships and disappointments recounted in the autobiography, the recurring notes struck are those of joy, humour and optimism. Despite the flaws in his character, the abiding impression of the man is his great humanity: his respect for life in all its forms, his exuberant response to its beauty and his passionate desire that society be characterized by social justice, equality and harmony. Her fervently believes that each individual has an indisputable right to sustenance for both body and mind, to bread on the table and a flower in the window. He is confident that the inherently hostile conditions of this world can be overcome by man's intelligence, by the ability of the human brain to confront, understand and, eventually, defeat the obstacles in life. Man has already unlocked much of the mystery of human existence and has glimpsed at the vast realms that await discovery:

Science has presented life with more life than present life can comprehend or hold. Worlds in bunches away beyond the Milky Way, and worlds alone in space; with new worlds unfolding themselves beneath the microscope and within the atom; new worlds still hidden from the myopic eye of the microscope and the equally myopic eye of the telescope nosing among the stars. New worlds of vitamins, cells, viruses, moulds, chromosomes, isotopes, superseding spermaceti for an inward bruise; new worlds for all, with a new world of democracy thrown in, garlanded with glory and with danger too. Aristotle is becoming a ghost. (VI, 205)

In confronting the difficulties and challenges which the future poses, man need only reflect on past achievements to banish fear and derive strength and encouragement:

When he thought of all the common routine of life that had to be gone through — to eat, to drink, to sleep, to clothe ourselves, to take time for play, lest we perish of care, to suffer and fight common and uncommon ills, then the achievements of man, in spite of all these, are tremendous indeed. Away then with the whine of being miserable sinners, with the whine of we've no abiding city here, with the whine of pray for the wanderer, pray for me! We've important things to do. Fag an bealach! How many tons of coal have we delved from the mines today? How many railway wagons have we loaded? How many yards of textiles have we woven? How many schools, hospitals, houses, cinemas, and theatres have we built? How many railway engines, carriages, and trucks, have we put on the line? How many ships sent to sea? Fag an bealach! Work is the Reveille and the Last Post of life now, providing for man, making leisure safe, enjoyable, and longer, profiting body, soul, and spirit, having a song in itself, even when the sun sets on old age, and the evening star shines a warning of the end. (VI, 224)

In *Sunset*, O'Casey writes that 'Every man must fashion by thought and experience the truth that suits him, the truth he needs.' (VI, 73) His self-portrait is a turning to his own past to trace the forces that have moulded his character and crystallized his vision of the world; the autobiographical 'theme' of the work is the truth he has fashioned in his seventy-year journey through life. That vision is most eloquently expressed as the autobiography comes to a close when, having reflected on the 'courageous virtues' of his fellow-countryman, George Bernard Shaw, he writes:

What time has been wasted during man's destiny in the struggle to decide what man's next world will be like! The keener the effort to find out, the less he knew about the present one he lived in. The one lovely world he knew, lived in, that gave him all he had, was, according to preacher and prelate, the one to be least in his thoughts. He was recommended, ordered, from the day of his birth to bid goodbye to it. Oh, we have had enough of the abuse of this fair earth! It is no sad truth that this should be our home. Were it but to give us simple shelter, simple clothing, simple food, adding the lily and the rose, the apple and the pear, it would be fit home for mortal or immortal men. . . . Man must be his own saviour; man must be his own god. Man must learn, not by prayer, but by experience. Advice from God was within ourselves, and nowhere else. Social sense and social development was the fulfilment of the law and the prophets. A happy people made happy by themselves. There is no other name given among men by which we can be saved, but by the mighty name of Man. (VI, 189–190)

CONCLUSION

This exploration of the essential principles which determined O'Casey's approach to past experiences, followed by an application of the findings to arrive at an understanding of the central elements of his autobiographical identity, should give some measure of his impressive achievements as an autobiographer. As an imaginative response to personal history, which draws on a host of literary devices and narrative techniques, the six-volume autobiography stands as a complex and challenging work of self-portrayal. With its many means of depicting an evolving series of former selves, of presenting the individual developing as a result of successive encounters with the people and events of his historical reality, and with its passionate expression of a deeply held view of live, the work provides a vivid, indelible and comprehensive portrait of its author.

Few autobiographers since Rousseau have explored as many facets of their lives as O'Casey does: the truth he presents about himself is a vital reflection of his emotional, intellectual, social, artistic and even spiritual identities. While the nineteenth century saw autobiographical expression established as a common literary phenomenon, most writers were unwilling to write in the tradition of Rousseau, to strive for an approximation of an all-encompassing portrait of themselves, one which would explore the self in many of its roles and guises. The history of autobiography from the early nineteenth century onwards is that of a genre becoming at once more investigative and more specialized. Increasingly, works of self-exploration and self-definition probed the ways in which specific facets of character and personality responded to, and were determined by, encounters with life. For many individuals the desire for self-understanding arose from the spiritual crisis which marked the age; religious faith was seriously challenged by the skepticism which the Enlightenment, scientific discoveries and the higher criticism produced. Bereft of the authority lent by religious certainty, those moral and spiritual values which had formerly buttressed identity were now seriously eroded. Philosophic and metaphysical issues became pressing concerns when, among others,

228

Darwin and, later, Marx challenged the traditional premises on which were based a moral approach to reality. It is both revealing and symptomatic of this loss of a cohesive view of the world, that the genre of autobiography became such a pronounced form of expression in the nineteenth century; questioning the values and meaning which were embodied in the inherited traditions of social, religious or political institutions, writers turned to personal history and individual consciousness to understand and explain their own relationship with reality. As a genre flexible enough to encompass a wide range of highly intimate autobiographical motives, autobiography was particularly suited to this process of introspection and self-portrayal. But the focused, restrictive quality of much nineteenth-century autobiography speaks profoundly of the unwillingness or inability of the individual to examine personal consciousness in all its complexity or in as wide a context as possible.

The tendency to avoid the delineation of the self as a personality responding to life in all its manifestations, and instead to view its relationship to reality in a schematic fashion, continues in much twentieth-century autobiographical writing. Responding to a world where traditional social and moral imperatives were further challenged if not altogether repudiated, writers and thinkers still turned to autobiography to explore and define their understanding of life and their response to shifting metaphysical propositions. But, in a period when man's sense of dissociation from himself increased, when his feelings of divided consciousness were accentuated, and when his suspicion that no coherent philosophy could embrace all aspects of identity was aroused, the act of autobiographical scrutiny continued to be conducted within narrow boundaries. In the absence of a widely shared system of belief, indeed with the sense of anxiety and the quest for certainty providing the context in which the self might be measured, few twentieth-century autobiographers posited an all-embracing approach to existence. For example, Yeats examines life in terms of the growth of his poetic sensibilities, successfully charting the various aesthetic and artistic forces which determined the nature of his poetic voice. In focusing on such issues as his evolution as a poet, his interest in the occult, and his involvement with the Irish Literary Revival, Yeats's work serves notice that it deals only with specific facets of the self. Consciously glossing over, or omitting a discussion of, many experiences — from the mundane details of his economic survival to crucial events in his life such as the Easter Rising, the Civil War, the War of Independence, and, most

obviously, his long obsession with Maud Gonne — Yeats selected
only those experiences which allowed him to give symbolic shape
and intellectual progression to his development as a poet. His
autobiography derives much of its power and impact from the
success with which he recounts his determined search for the
vehicles in which the self might find full poetic expression. Yet,
several concerns which might have made the autobiography a more
legitimate reflection of the whole man are not included, though
some of them were subsumed, altered and given different form in
his poems.

Later in the century Vladimir Nabokov and Jean-Paul Sartre, for
example, both turned to literary self-definition in an attempt to
resurrect their childhood years and scrutinize them for an
explanation of the sense of loss and alienation that marked their
lives. That both writers were unable to provide fuller accounts of
these years — narrative details which might have produced more
complete images of identity — suggests the difficulties that
individuals attempting self-definition encounter in the modern
world. In fact, the Freudian and Existential inheritance of contemporary reality has called into question the essential premise of
autobiographical definition: the ability of the individual to write of
himself in absolute terms is seen to be so thoroughly compromised
psychologically, philosophically and, more recently, even
linguistically, that the very basis on which a literary self-portrait
might be founded has been severely eroded.

It is in the context of this autobiographical tradition and against
this intellectual framework that O'Casey's autobiography looms
with such impressive proportions; in its scope of conception, its
panoramic canvas and large cast of characters, its exceptional
stylistic and rhetorical procedures, and, most significantly, its
many revelations of its author, the work stands as a unique
achievement in modern autobiographical literature.

One of the most obvious means by which O'Casey gives depth
and authority to his portrait is the degree to which he is able to
evoke the historical context of the personal life, to lend that life a
contrapuntal tension with some of the major events of his time.
Though it contains few dates and lacks many factual details that
would locate the story in concrete spatial settings, the work still
contrives to capture the social and political atmosphere in the
Ireland and England of the period. O'Casey was fortunate to have
lived during a momentous phase in Irish history, so that many of
the dramatic episodes in modern Irish life — the fall of Parnell,
Ireland's awakening cultural and political consciousness, the 1913

lockout, the Easter Rising, the War of Independence, the Civil War, and the establishment of the Free State — could be used to punctuate, highlight and clarify his own development in the years leading to his success as an Abbey playwright. In a less dramatic fashion, events in Ireland from the mid-1920s to the post-war era — its repressive cultural policies, its continuing economic stagnation, its church-dominated social order — could serve as symbolic correspondences which might define and accentuate character. Similarly, the failure of the General Strike in England, the world-wide economic difficulties of the Thirties, the Spanish Civil War and the Second World War could function — sometimes explicitly, sometimes obliquely — as metaphoric extensions of the personal story. O'Casey's extensive canvas supplies, however incidentally, a panorama of historical events and figures, from the Boer War to the Cold War, from Queen Victoria to Hitler. In orchestrating the account of pivotal moments in the public life of his time, O'Casey clarifies the context in which the individual story takes place and, in doing so, lends it a wider, extra-personal dimension.

The sense of the individual moving through the experiences of both public and private history is also attributable to O'Casey's highly unusual approach to autobiographical form and technique. Rejecting a strictly objective and chronological account of the past, he stretches the possibilities inherent in an imaginative rendering of experiences. Freeing himself from the restrictions imposed by a more conventional recounting of life, he devises a whole range of narrative and stylistic means of revealing the self as it was responding to, and being moulded by, diverse and intangible forces. As the creation of a literary artist, the self-portrait draws on many of the devices associated with imaginative literature in order to open up additional avenues to identity, yet does so without carrying the work into a different literary territory. In successfully demonstrating that such compositional tactics can enhance the process of exploring and portraying the self, O'Casey's auto-biography expands the traditional boundaries of the genre and offers exciting rhetorical options to its repertoire of represent-ational techniques.

More important, by virtue of the manner in which it conducts its autobiographical discourse, the self-portrait becomes an integral part of O'Casey's literary canon; it is a vivid testimony to the integrity and scope of his literary imagination, and it provides telling proof of his enormous gifts as a prose stylist. Within the parameters of his autobiographical purposes, he gives full reign to his fondness for lyrical and sonorous prose, his bent for parody and satire, his love of farce and melodrama, his gift for rich, colourful dialogue and outrageous situation, and his ability to create memorable characters. Moreover, the flexibility of the autobiographical form permits O'Casey to pursue further the kinds of experimental techniques — the rapid shifts in the continuity of the narrative and its temporal planes, the incorporation of fanciful and surrealistic passages, the symbolic use of characters and events, and the liberal sprinkling of allusions and snippets of songs and poems — which he was also attempting within the more restrictive confines of his plays. It is, therefore, the success with which the development and growing sensibilities of Sean O'Casey the literary artist are presented, the degree to which form is a reflection of theme, that makes the work such an impressive exemplum of his literary abilities.

And yet, the portrait is not merely the story of the individual who, struggling for forty years to overcome a succession of daunting obstacles, discovers his true vocation as a writer. Because it charts a wide spectrum of his consciousness — the processes and direction of his emotional, intellectual, social, political and artistic development — the autobiography presents a fully rounded and almost palpable character, a man replete with all the complexities and contradictions synonymous with individual identity. Indeed, as we have seen, one of the accomplishments of the work is that, so completely are the details of personal experiences evoked, so thoroughly are the episodes in personal history placed in their temporal and physical environment, that the work periodically transcends the story of one man's growth and evolution to become an epic account of the awakening consciousness of a whole society under the influential forces of nationalism and socialism.

If much of the exceptional authenticity which O'Casey achieves is derived from his artistic courage, from the daring with which he attempts to capture the essence of his various selves, so also are the scope and impact of the work enhanced by the emotional honesty with which he confronts his past. It is a forthrightness most obviously reflected in the ideals and values which the autobiography unashamedly proclaims as worthwhile. O'Casey insists on presenting his story in unqualified terms, often foregoing niceties of discrimination and felicities of expression but, instead, writing with a directness and frankness reminiscent of Rousseau's *Confessions*, a work in which the subject is also depicted as a fully human character whose faults and virtues stand revealed with equal clarity. Having managed to escape the oppressive conditions

of an inequitable social order only after much hardship, deprivation and repeated efforts, O'Casey saw it as a sacred obligation to
remain witness to such evils, to denounce the forces which
sustained them, and to propose an alternate vision of life. The
result is that the man portrayed possesses a sharply dichotomized
view of the world, and he is an individual who expresses his
criticisms and aspirations with equal gusto and fervor. For
example, in *Drums* O'Casey creates one of his more self-revelatory
vignettes when he recounts how Sean refused to compromise his
integrity by not criticizing the Irish Republican Brotherhood when
he recognized its indifference to the plight of Irish workers. After
his friend, Seamus Deakin, a member of the Supreme Council of
the I.R.B., has asked Sean to desist from open criticism of the
movement, Sean replies,

Isn't it because the criticisms are justified that they want them stopped?
. . . Quite a few have got jobs through its influence: have I? Bar ill-health,
pain, and poverty, I have got nothing. Nor do I want anything; but I am
determined to hold on to what is mine own; my way of thinking, and
freedom to give it utterance. Otherwise the little life I have would cease
to be life at all. (III, 232)

Conjuring up as it does the image of a high-principled, passionate
and unyielding individual, this passage could very well be the
caption to the picture of the character presented in the autobiography; the self-portrait is just such an 'utterance,' an exuberant
expression of O'Casey's journey through life.

If the autobiography confirms that his original intention of
glancing 'at the things that made me' is realized, it simultaneously
expands and refines the relationships between many threads of his
life in the act of recounting them; in doing so, the work becomes
an exercise in self-exploration. Only in the attempt to give shape
and assign meaning to amorphous experiences does their role in the
sweep of his life, their contribution to his contemporary sense of
self, emerge clearly. In part, then, self-definition becomes an act of
self-discovery. Furthermore, the autobiography is a response to
the psychological stress which marked the years following the
Tassie controversy, when O'Casey's freedom as a playwright was
being circumscribed and his perception of his essential self
challenged. Turning to his past, he defends his actions and asserts
his rights by proclaiming the beliefs that constitute his views as
man and writer; consequently, the long circuitous journey by
which he arrived at a clear understanding of those values are the
guiding principle in the presentation of his life. In short, writing the

autobiography is also an exercise in self-explanation and self-justification.

Having served these purposes, the autobiography then reaches another level of accomplishment. Although O'Casey's right to artistic freedom continued to be challenged in the period in which the autobiography was composed, and his ideological views still waited for some concrete manifestation in the world around him, they both find full expression in the portrayal of the self in the autobiography. Constantly frustrated in his desire for theatrical experimentation, and denied immediate public counterparts embodying his social and political aspirations, O'Casey makes the work a vehicle for both literary innovation and a full expression of his vision of life. In that, the autobiography readily accommodates O'Casey's sense of his ideal self, himself as he believes he could be if he were untrammelled by the forces of obstruction and denial. The freedom to articulate his views, to demonstrate that they are a product of his life's experiences, and to do so in a manner of his own devising, transcends the purposes of self-clarification and self-justification so that the composition of the autobiography becomes an art of self-liberation.

The combined effect of these achievements is to make O'Casey's autobiography an impressive work of exhortation. So thoroughly and completely does he identify with the values which have contributed to a crystallization of his character that the portrait becomes a profession of the truth he has discovered. O'Casey is not content merely to explain the process of his own journey to truth but also commends the validity of his findings in responding to reality. To accomplish this, he has to impress, not so much by the specific details of his story as by its evocative and connotative dimensions, by the power it could be given through his rhetoric. For O'Casey, then, portraying the self is finally an oratorical act. This impulse, as William Howarth points out (following Northrop Frye's suggestion that the hero of his 'high mimetic' mode defines his superiority through the power of preaching or public oratory), is a recurring pattern in autobiographical literature, stretching from St Augustine and John Bunyan to Edward Gibbon, Henry Adams and Malcolm X. Howarth notes that such writers see their life-story as being essentially 'didactic,' since each seeks 'to represent in a single life an idealized pattern of human behaviour.' The individual story is so transformed that it becomes 'allegorical' and 'often has messianic overtones, replete with suffering and martyrdom, as the orator leads his people to their rightful home. Doctrine alone does not give him this authority; to lead he must master oratory, the art of being heard.'[1] In O'Casey's autobiography, not only is the path to redemption traced through the details of personal suffering — with their periodic overtones of an archetypal figure of martyrdom — but the elements of his newfound faith are explained and extolled. Obviously, the reader does not have to agree with O'Casey's interpretation of experience nor accept the social and political vision proffered; but the work does demand an acknowledgement of the integrity he has displayed in his response to life, and of the legitimacy for him of the ideology he sees as a necessary means of apprehending the world. The reader must grant that the life recreated and the values espoused are the product of a quest, the pursuit of which has been characterized by a sense of integrity and morality, and by an abiding desire for equality and justice. The reader is to be swayed by the power of language and rhetoric, and by the authority of an individual who has developed into full knowledge through the crucible of experience, one whose right to exhort has been determined by personal suffering and discovery. Given the account of his harsh beginnings and the struggles which have moulded his character and forged his values, we are meant to be impressed by the intensity and legitimacy of his artistic and political faith, by a commitment to a vision of life presented in the most sincere and noble terms.

It is O'Casey's success in demonstrating that his social, political and artistic vision is linked to, and derived from, past experiences that makes the work such a comprehensive and compelling portrait of its author and such an impressive achievement as autobiographical literature. The self-portrait commands attention for the manner in which his unique character is irrefutably shown to have been shaped by his past, and for the fact that his world view is the most justifiable, indeed the only rational response to his life experiences. O'Casey's accomplishments are to be measured by the effectiveness with which his childhood deprivation and poor health, his lack of formal education, his frustrations in discovering a social, economic and political system commensurate with his aspirations, and his experiences as the mistreated and shunned playwright are all presented as inexorably leading to his socialist views. The authority with which O'Casey invests his vision, the conviction and passion with which he establishes its legitimacy for him as man and writer, validate the work as a comprehensive and unimpeachable portrait of its author. In charting the long and multifaceted story of the individual who transcends the obstacles which confronted him to become Sean O'Casey the writer, who reacted to the cruelty and injustice of his world by search for an ideology that would transform it, he convincingly shows that he discovered a unique autobiographical form, one superbly suited to convey the truth of life. O'Casey's achievements as autobiographer lie in the degree to which the life portrayed becomes the vision incarnate.

NOTES

I. Constructing the House of Life

1 It is not my intention in this chapter to give a detailed account of the autobiography's beginnings or a history of its evolution. This has already been done by Ronald Ayling in his excellent article, 'The Origin and Evolution of a Dublin Epic,' in *Essays on Sean O'Casey's Autobiographies: Reflections Upon the Mirror*, ed. Robert G. Lowery (Totowa, New Jersey: Barnes & Noble Books, 1981), pp. 1–34. I am indebted in my chapter to Professor Ayling's article, which should be required reading for all commentators on O'Casey's autobiography.

2 Cited in Ayling, 'The Origin and Evolution of a Dublin Epic', p. 4. This letter does not appear, at least not under this date, in the two-volume collection of O'Casey's letters edited by David Krause; see note 5.

3 Reprinted in *The Sean O'Casey Review*, 3 (Spring 1977), 123–124.

4 *New York Times*, 16 September 1956.

5 Unless otherwise indicated, all letters referred to appear in the two-volume collection edited by David Krause: *The Letters of Sean O'Casey 1910–1941* (London: Cassell & Company Ltd., 1975) and *The Letters of Sean O'Casey 1942–1954* (New York: Macmillan Publishing Co., Inc., 1980).

6 This is how he referred to the work in a February 1938 letter to Harold Macmillan. *Letters*, I, 696. In the many letters in which, over the years, he commented on the autobiography, O'Casey tried to avoid the word 'autobiography,' a term which he claimed he disliked, and instead used a wide range of phrases and synonyms. His search for an appropriate substitute expression reflects his awareness of his unusual and innovative approach to the genre. The following is a sampling of some of the references to the work which he used: 'my peculiar biography' (*Letters*, I, 649), ' "curious autobiography" ' (*Letters*, I, 655), 'biographical sketches' (*Letters*, I, 721), ' "reveries" ' (*Letters*, I, 729), 'biographical incidents' (*Letters*, II, 261), and 'biographical commentary' (*Letters*, II, 553).

7 'Sidelighting on Some Pictures', *New York Times*, 16 September 1956. His encouragement at the response to the publication of this vignette is expressed in a significant number of letters composed over a span of many years. See, in particular, his May 1942 letter to Gabriel Fallon, *Letters*, II, 58–59.

8 Letter of 1 July 1941. *Letters*, I, 888.

9 The first letter is to the anonymous Miss Shelia while the second is a 26 November 1946 letter to Jack Daly. *Letters*, II, 259 and 416 respectively.

10 In this regard, O'Casey's proposals for the design of the dust jacket of *Knock* are revealing. In a letter to a member of the editorial staff at Macmillan & Co. Ltd., he describes the various symbols of Ireland which he wishes to be depicted. The principal panelling of the door should have a Celtic Cross, while 'in the corners are 1, the Arms of Dublin; 2, Lion and Unicorn; 3, Nelson's Pillar; 4, a church; and at each side of the cross's circle, a head of Parnell and a head of Queen Victoria.' He then goes on to stress that, in contrast to this main design, 'the figure of the boy should be as small as possible — it is the door of life that he is supposed to be knocking at it [sic]'. *Letters*, I, 773.

11 For the sake of accessibility, all references to the autobiography are to the edition published by Pan Books Ltd., London. Volumes I and II were published in 1971, Volumes III and IV in 1972, and Volumes V and VI in 1973. Quotations will be identifed parenthetically in the text, by referring to the volume number.

12 Letter to Daniel Macmillan, 29 August 1947. *Letters*, II, 475.

13 This letter does not appear in the *Letters*; it is quoted by Ayling in 'The Origin and Evolution of a Dublin Epic,' pp. 28–29.

14 O'Casey was extremely attentive to the details appearing on the design for the dust jacket of all volumes, even providing his own sketches to the publishers to clarify the visual effect he desired. For his comments and contributions to the graphics for the individual volumes, see the following letter entries: *Letters*, I, 773 (*Knock*); I, 889 and 902 (*Pictures*); II, 183 (*Drums*); II, 517 (*Inishfallen*); II, 877 (*Rose*); II, 1044 and 1048 (*Sunset*).

15 The desire to stress the association of the metaphor with the ongoing story of his life may be the explanation for a change in one of the chapter titles in the first published version of *Drums*. 'House of the Living' was the name of Chapter V in both the first British and American editions, but it was changed to 'Home of the Living' in the subsequent Macmillan two-volume edition. The original title was obviously meant to suggest an ironic contrast between a chapter which recounts the events leading to Ella's death and 'House of the Dead,' which evokes the pathetic life, in the lunatic asylum, of Sean's brother-in-law. While on one level 'House of Living' may be seen as an appropriately bitter reflection on Sean's situation at this particular phase of his life, it was ultimately misleading because it connotes a sense of totality. On the other hand, 'House of the Dead' remained a suitable title for suggesting the contrast betwen life itself and the kind of death-in-life existence of the patients in the asylum. Whether or not this is the rationale for O'Casey's alteration of the title, the change itself is evidence of his acute concern for the appropriateness of his titles.

16 Letter to Maroldo. See note 3 above.

II. O'Casey and the Genre of Autobiography

1 Georges Gusdorf, 'Conditions and Limits of Autobiography,' trans. James Olney, in *Autobiography: Essays Theoretical and Critical*, ed. James Olney (Princeton, New Jersey: Princeton University Press, 1980), p. 39.

2 *Letters*, II, 905. Significantly, in 1937, when he had already written several personal sketches, O'Casey reveals, in a letter to Horace Reynolds, 'I have often been asked to write my "reminiscences", but, alas! this I don't seem able to do. I find that anything I want to say about myself must take a colour & a form which seems to hunt all editors away from me.' *Letters*, I, 667.

3 Anthony Trollope, *An Autobiography* (London: Williams and Norgate Ltd., 1946), p. 21.

4 Trollope, p. 77.

5 Trollope, p. 145.

6 Trollope, p. 317.

7 Revealing in this regard is Johnathan Loesberg's estimation of Charles Darwin's *Autobiography*, which he sees as a failed attempt at self-portrayal because Darwin's methods of examining his past could not take into account his innate self. Loesberg writes:

> Darwin's *Autobiography* may be seen as a machine constantly grinding to a halt. It is filled with detail after vivid detail, but the evolution of the mind as a whole never takes form. . . . Darwin so insisted on scientific method that when his method came upon an intuition it broke down; his *Autobiography* remains simply recollections.

'Self-consciousness and Meditation in Victorian Autobiography,' *University of Toronto Quarterly*, 50 (Winter 1980/81), 204.

8 H. G. Wells, *Experiment in Autobiography: Discoveries and Conclusions of a Very Ordinary Brain (Since 1886)* Toronto: Macmillan Company of Canada, 1934), p. 4.

9 Wells, p. 705.

10 In Olney, p. 41.

11 Louis A. Renza, 'The Veto of the Imagination: A Theory of Autobiography,' in *Autobiography: Essays Theoretical and Critical*, ed. James Olney, p. 269.

12 *The Forms of Autobiography: Episodes in the History of a Literary Genre* (New Haven and London: Yale University Press, 1980), p. 120.

13 *An Autobiography* (New York: The Seabury Press, 1954), p. 224. One of the clearest expressions of this creative, transforming power of memory is found in Nicholas Berdyaev's preface to his autobiography:

> The remembrance of my life in its varied manifestations is for me an avowedly active remembrance, that is to say a creative effort of my mind apprehending my past in my present. Between the facts of my life and their record in this book there intervenes a creative cognitive activity, whereby these facts acquire significance; and it is this that interests me above everything else.

Dream and reality: An Essay in Autobiography (London: Geofrey Bles, 1950), Preface, p. X.

14 'Some Versions of Memory/Some Versions of Bios: The Ontology of Autobiography,' in *Autobiography: Essays Theoretical and Critical*, ed. James Olney, p. 241.

15 Quoted by Michael Sprinker, 'Fictions of the Self: The End of Autobiography', in *Autobiography: Essays Theoretical and Critical*, ed. James Olney, p. 329.

16 O'Casey was an admirer of Moore's writing. While the man and his work are mentioned in passing at several points in the autobiography, O'Casey most forcefully expresses his appreciation of Moore's writing in a letter to David Krause on 8 January 1953: 'By the way, George Moore seems to be an under-rated writer. He is held up to scorn in Ireland, yet there isn't one writer there, in my opinion, who could hold a candle to him. His 'Hail and Farewell,' his "The Untilled Field," his "Esther Waters" are fine and large and delightful.' *Letters*, II, 933.

17 *Hail and Farewell*, ed. Richard Cave (Toronto: Macmillan of Canada, 1976), p. 288.

18 *A Portrait of George Moore in a Study of His Work* (London: T. Werner Laurie, Ltd., 1922), p. 3.

19 *Hail and Farewell*, p. 597.

20 *Autobiographies* (London: Macmillan, 1973), p. 3.

21 *The Letters of W. B. Yeats*, ed. Allan Wade (London: Rupert Hart-Davies, 1954), p. 606.

22 Even O'Casey's ability to remember the date of his mother's death — arguably the most emotionally wrenching experience of his life — was unreliable. In a letter of 6 February 1938, to Horace Reynolds he says that she died in November 1919. *Letters*, I, 698.

23 *Lady Gregory's Journals, 1916–1930*, ed. Lennox Robinson (New York: Macmillan Company, 1947), entry for 8 June, 1924.

24 Martin B. Margulies, *The Early Life of Sean O'Casey* (Dublin: The Dolmen Press, 1970), p. 76–77.

25 *Aspects of Biography* (New York: D. Appleton and Company, 1929), p. 176.

26 There is a striking similarity in O'Casey's statement here and Teufelsdroch's comments on factual reliability in Carlyle's *Sartor Resartus*, another problematical autobiographical work which pushed the boundaries of the genre to daring limits. Teufelsdroch asks:

> What are your historical facts; still more your biographical? Wilt thou know a Man above Mankind, by stringing together beadrolls of what thou namest Fact? . . . Facts are engraved Hierograms for which the fewest have the key.

Thomas Carlyle, *Sartor Resartus*, ed. Charles Frederick Harrold (New York: Odyssey Press, 1937), p. 203.

27 Reprinted in *Letters*, II, 274. O'Casey's reply is on p. 276.

28 *A History of Autobiography in Antiquity*, trans. E. W. Dikes, 2 vols. (London: Routledge & Kegan Paul Limited, 1950), p. 11.

29 Jean-Jacques Rousseau, *The Confessions*, trans. and with an introduction by J. M. Cohen (London: Penguin Books, 1954).

30 Rousseau, p. 262. For O'Casey's letter to Macmillan, see *Letters*, II, 779.

31 *Studies in Human Time*, trans. Elliott Coleman (Baltimore: The Johns Hopkins Press, 1956), p. 177–178.

32 G. W. Stonier, who has some words of praise for selected passages of the autobiographical volumes, cannot resist the temptation to demand that they be other than they are. Reviewing *Knock*, he claims that the book would have been better served if O'Casey had given a more realistic presentation of events and people. He believes that 'facts and authentic voices count for a lot in autobiography; in no other kind of writing is it more dangerous for the author to shape in a literary way.' 'Two Autobiographies.' *New Stateman and Nation*, 17 (1939), 396. Stonier finds it difficult to accept that biographical data are obviously not of primary importance for O'Casey, who has approached his material in a literary way.

Gabriel Fallon, a friend of O'Casey during the playwright's years as a struggling writer, complains that the autobiographer does not present the man he knew in Dublin in the early 1920s, and ascribes the changes to psychological causes resulting from O'Casey's reception in London. In his review of *Knock*, Fallon wrote:

I liked the book quite well but it was obvious to me that Sean's mature imagination had gone heavily into the making of it, with the strange result that it seemed to create a distance between the man portrayed and the man I knew, or thought I knew.

As Ronald Ayling has pointed out, Fallon compares the portrait of a boy, from birth to the age of twelve, with that of a forty-year-old man; and begs the question whether O'Casey's immature rather than mature imagination might have been used, and used heavily or lightly. Fallon, as he makes clear his book, *Sean O'Casey: The Man I Knew* (London: Routledge & Kegan Paul, 1965), was too closely involved with the subject of the autobiography to view the work in terms other than comparisons with his own experiences. In reacting to it, he was proceeding from the conventional assumption that he was reading a biography of O'Casey which happened to be written by the playwright himself.

33 'Sean O'Casey Narratives,' review of *Mirror in My House*, reprinted in *Sean O'Casey: Modern Judgements*, ed. Ronald Ayling (Nashville and London: Aurora Publishers Incorporated, 1970), p. 225.

34 The salvoes from each side have been reprinted in 'A Storm in the Fair City,' *Sean O'Casey Review*, 3 (Spring 1977), 127–143. It will be the task of O'Casey's biographer to establish the precise conditions of his childhood years. However, it cannot be denied that most of O'Casey's life in Ireland was characterised by financial shortages and the consequent deprivation of basic material necessities. Alan Simpson, in referring to the Butler-Krause controversy, stresses that 'Poverty is relative, and Sean O'Casey was locked in a recurring cycle of harsh

financial straits, exacerbated by ill-health, pride and an artistic temperament, from which he never could escape until he was in his sixties.' 'O'Casey and the East Wall Area in Dublin,' in *Irish University Review*, 10, No. 1 (1980), 44. Also pertinent in this regard is Padraic Colum's opening remarks in his 1966 review of the autobiography:

Dubliners who come to the republished Autobiographies of Sean O'Casey will feel astonishment, even incredulity as they read the parts dealing with their native city. What will strike him or her as they read chapter after chapter is the penury of the scene. Sixpence represents the difference between gratification and deprivation; men and women sicken and die without the least of the nutriment available today. . . . For a Dubliner who has never seen a barefoot child in the street, for whom a building in memory of labour leaders he finds mentioned is seen as dominating one side of the Liffey, for whom causes are taken care of by ministers of the Republic, the Dublin of Johnny Casside's experience is hardly recognisable.

'Sean O'Casey's Narratives,' p. 220. See note 33 above.

35 Admittedly, lyric poetry is seldom free of autobiographical elements but it rarely becomes sufficiently sustained and comprehensive — as does *The Prelude*, for example — to make a claim to be autobiography.

In his autobiography, Stephen Spender speaks of the autobiographical impulse in poetry, comparing his own poetry to that of some of his contemporaries: 'As for me, I was an autobiographer restlessly searching for forms in which to express stages of my development.' *World Within World* (London: Hamish Hamilton, 1950), p. 119. A few pages later he adds: 'My problem is that which this book must make apparent: what I write are fragments of autobiography: sometimes they are poems, sometimes stories, and the longer passages must take the form of novels.' p. 126. Here, Spender is echoing Goethe's statement that all his writings are 'fragments of a great confession.' *The Autobiography of Johann Wolfgang Von Goethe* (Chicago and London: University of Chicago Press, 1974), p. 305. However, presumably because they were aware of the incomplete nature of such a process of self-revelation, both Goethe and Spender created sustained and unified works when they wrote their autobiographies. Obviously, any attempt at a comprehensive self-definition requires different criteria than do periodic brief efforts at self-reflection and introspection.

36 'Notes for an Anatomy of Modern Autobiography,' *New Literary History*, 1 (1970), 492.

37 In his essay, 'Some Principles of Autobiography,' William L. Howarth, hoping to dispel the notion that autobiography is 'monolithic in form,' and to prove that there is 'more variety among the works and more similarity to established literary genres,' examines several autobiographies, under such headings as 'Autobiography as Oratory.' 'Autobiography as Drama' and 'Autobiography as Poetry.' He sees O'Casey's self-portrait as a 'dramatic autobiography' which displays many of 'the principles of dramaturgy.' While Howarth's

brief discussion provides a sensible assessment of certain features of O'Casey's autobiography, it appears somewhat too prescriptive to accommodate the shifting narrative strategies in the work. The essay appears in *Autobiography: Essays Theoretical and Critical*, ed. James Olney, pp. 84–113. See, in particular, p. 101.

38 James Joyce, 'A Portrait of the Artist' (January 1904), in *The Workshop of Daedalus: James Joyce and the Raw Materials for* A Portrait of the Artist as a Young Man, ed. Robert Scholes and Richard M. Kain (Evanston, Ill.: Northwestern University Press, 1965), p. 60.

39 Joseph Prescott, 'James Joyce's Stephen Hero,' in *Joyce's Portrait: Criticisms and Critiques*, ed. Thomas E. Connolly (New York: Appleton-Century-Crofts, 1962), p. 80, and passim.

40 James Joyce (New York: Oxford University Press, 1965), p. 154.

41 *An Autobiography*, p. 48.

42 'Narrative Time,' *Critical Inquiry*, Autumn 1980, p. 186.

43 *Design and Truth in Autobiography* (London: Routledge & Kegan Paul, 1960), p. 162.

44 Spengemann, p. 120.

45 'Black Autobiography,' in *Autobiography; Essays Theoretical and Critical*, ed. James Olney, p. 176.

III. Principles of Selection

1 'Notes For an Anatomy of Modern Autobiography,' *New Literary History* 1 (1970): 491–492.

2 'The Dark Continent of Literature: Autobiography,' *Comparative Literature Studies*, 5 (1968), 448.

3 'Myth and Terror,' in *The Crane Bag Book of Irish Studies* (Dublin: Blackwater Press, 1982), p. 275.

4 *Last Words: Letters and Statements of the Leaders Executed after the Rising at Easter 1916*. Ed. Piaras F. Mac Lòchlann. (Dublin: Kilmainham Jail Restoration Society, 1971), p. 55. I am grateful to Professor Finn Gallagher for bringing to my attention this version of Mac Donagh's speech.

5 Throughout the autobiography O'Casey's criticism of religion, especially Catholicism, is primarily directed at what he considered the distortion of its basic principles by a haughty clergy. Writing to William J. Maroldo on the treatment of religion in the autobiography, O'Casey urged, 'on my attitude to "Catholicism" be sure to see the difference between the "faith once delivered to the saints" and the bloated blather of Cardinal, Bishop, Monsignor, and Canon.' In another letter to Maroldo, he writes: 'As for the Church, I don't attack or criticise any article, dogma of Faith (I don't believe them myself), but only the practice of that faith — two very different things.' Both letters are reprinted in *The Sean O'Casey Review*, 3 (Spring 1977), 119–121.

6   O'Casey acknowledged that paying tribute to his mother was an important consideration in the composition of the autobiography, particularly the early volumes. He wrote to Ivor Brown, who had reviewed *Knock* in *The Manchester Guardian*: 'I'm glad you found the book a fine tribute to Mrs. Casside. She was, really, a great woman. With her help, I knocked a way out of a hard time.' *Letters*, I, 787.

7   *Letters*, I, 233.

8   *Letters*, I, 40–41.

9   O'Casey was prepared to see Russell's machinations behind Sean O'Faolain's negative review of the *Tassie*. In a letter (April 1939) to Gabriel Fallon, O'Casey wrote of O'Faolain: 'And the only time he criticised a play of mine was when AE got him to criticise 'The Silver Tassie'; & some day, if I live, I'm going to criticise the criticism of the play.' *Letters*, I, 789.

10 Alan Denson, who later edited *Letters From AE* (1961), wrote to O'Casey implying that he had waited until AE's death before criticising him. O'Casey replied to Denson, citing the specific places in which he had expressed the same views of AE while the poet was still alive. See *Letters*, II, 697–699.

11 His evaluation of the play is contained in a letter to Gabriel Fallon, February 27, 1928. His letter to Lady Gregory of 20 April 1928 proclaims the play 'by far the best work I have done.' His letter to Robinson begins, 'Assuming acceptance of "The Silver Tassie," I send above list of those whom I imagine would fill the principal parts of the play.' *Letters*, I, p. 235. Years later, in a letter to the solicitor who had read the galleys of *Rose* for possible libellous material, O'Casey agreed to remove 'the direct and indirect remarks connecting him [Robinson] personally with the rejection of "The Silver Tassie," ' but he adds. 'I remain certain that L. R. was the main cause of the play's first rejection, and Lady Gregory confirms this in her *Journals*.' *Letters*, II, 838.

12 St John Ervine, Ernest Blythe and Shaw wrote to O'Casey commending the play and expressing their conviction that the Abbey should have produced it. In a letter to Gabriel Fallon, O'Casey writes of Blythe's comments: 'Got a letter from Ernie Blythe saying he couldn't understand the rejection of 'The Tassie' by the Abbey, & adding that he thought it a powerful & moving play, which shows that Ernie Blythe knows more about Drama than Yeats, or Robinson, or Starkie, or Lady Gregory.' *Letters*, I, 322. O'Casey proudly forwarded Shaw's letter, in which he hailed O'Casey as a titan, to Macmillan to know if it wished to quote it on the dust jacket of the published version of the play. On the other hand, those who criticized the play on the grounds that the subject matter was alien to O'Casey — Walter Starkie and George Russell — brought the wrath of O'Casey on their heads. In letters to *The Irish Statesman*, he wrote stinging and detailed replies to their criticism. David Krause has reprinted the correspondence related to the controversy. See *Letters*, I, 225–326.

13 'Jean-Paul Sartre on His Autobiography: An Interview with Olivier Todd,' *The Listener*, 6 June 1957, p. 916.

14 *Autobiography, Its Genesis and Phases* (London: Oliver and Boyd, 1935), p. 22.

15 In a letter, 16 September 1937, to George Jean Nathan, O'Casey recounts his suspicions that the Abbey, in negotiating for an American tour with *Juno*, was trying to come between him and his American agent. Giving details of what he perceives as manipulative behaviour, he concludes, 'This is the nth time the Abbey has tried to give me one in the eye.' *Letters*, I, 679.

16 Forefront in the attack on the *Tassey* was a Father M. H. Gaffney who had written to the *Catholic Mind* in September 1930 and who wrote a practically verbatim copy of the same letter to *The Irish Press* and *The Standard* in 1935. Some of his comments:

> Dublin is to have the opportunity of drinking deep from *The Silver Tassie*. But I fancy that Dublin is a little too wise in 1935 to put its lips to a cup that may possibly have been filled from a sewer.
>
> The play has been published in London, and is in our hands for cold inspection. It defies analysis. It is a vigorous medley of lust and hatred and vulgarity. And a Dominican nun, who acts and speaks like a Salvation Army lass, is dragged into the whirl of the movement in order to give point to the chanting *off* of the *Salve Regina* — in a setting that is brutally offensive.
>
> In attempting to analyse this play, I have fallen into despair. I have no hope of conveying any adequate idea of its deliberate indecency and its mean, mocking challenge to the Christian Faith.

> *Letters*, I, 576–577.

17 *Letters*, I, 655.

18 'Black Autobiography,' in *Autobiography: Essays Theoretical and Critical*, ed. James Olney, p. 376.

19 *Design and Truth in Autobiography* (London: Routledge & Kegan Paul, 1960), pp. 151–155.

20 *Sean O'Casey: Modern Judgements* (London and Nashville: Aurora Publishers Inc., 1970), p. 40.

21 In a letter to Brooks Atkinson, O'Casey confirms that the contents of *Sunset* will be quite distinct from earlier volumes since the reality it describes is different: 'As for "Sunset & Evening Star," I don't know that it will be solider — I was aiming at making the end less upright, less vivacious, to trail along with my own physical condition.' *Letters*, II, 909.

22 *Metaphors of Self: The Meaning of Autobiography* (Princeton, New Jersey: Princeton University Press, 1972).

23 At the other extreme, *Rose* covers only eight years in the protagonist's life, which suggest that experiences are explored in a more detailed and concentrated fashion. This is consonant with my claim that the crisis of the *Tassie* controversy and its aftermath are perceived by O'Casey as central to his overall purposes in the autobiography.

24 Orwell's review and O'Casey's letter to the *Observer* can be found in *Letters*, II, 294–298.

25 In his unpublished dissertation, 'O'Casey and Autobiography,' University of Virginia 1965, John M. Firth examines O'Casey's symbolic use of the cow in this chapter against a greater background of mythological and historical references. Although I analyse the cow somewhat differently, I remain indebted to Firth's general idea. The dissertation offers many insights to the autobiography, particular its relationship to Joyce's *Portrait*.

26 In *Pictures*, O'Casey suggests an identification between the poor of Dublin and the slaughtered cattle which they prey on for morsels of food:

There was a heavy reek in the air of filth and decaying blood scattered over the yards, and heaps of offal lay about watched by a restless herd of ragged women and youngsters, taking their chance to dive in and snatch a piece of liver or greenslimed guts to carry home as a feast for the favoured. (II, 92)

This imagery is picked up again in *Drums* when Larkin's followers, with Sean in their midst, are driven through the streets by baton-wielding police, and their frenzied stampede is equated with cattle destined for slaughter:

He could neither get his right arm down nor his left arm up to loosen the collar of his shirt, to get more air, a little more air; he could only sway back and forward as the crowd moved. The breathing of the suffocating crowd sounded like the thick, steamy breathing of a herd of frightened cattle in a cattle-boat tossed about in a storm. (III, 199)

IV. Principles of Organization.

1 Ayling continues:

He was a poet by method as well as by nature, taking infinite trouble over details and writing many drafts, correcting and revising each time. Future detailed analysis will reveal and evaluate the exact nature of his deliberate and painstaking artistry, but even a less-than-thorough examination of the manuscript and typescript material in the Berg Collection affords fascinating insight into the creative processes of a writer whose literary discrimination and self-criticism are plainly apparent in his working methods. ('A Note on Sean O'Casey's Manuscript and His Working Methods,' *Bulletin of the New York Public Library*, 73 (1969), 367.

2 For example, Chapters XIII and XIV, called 'Our House' and 'Their House,' seem to have no direct counterparts in the published version. Chapters XVI, XVII, and XVIII, which all deal with Ella and her husband, are found in *Drums*, while Chapters XIX and XX, relating to Johnny's first job, are found in *Pictures*.

3 *Letters*, I, 888.

4 They are: (1) 'The Old Lady Says Yes'
              (2) 'Mrs. Casside Takes a Holiday'
              (3) 'Girl I left Behind Me'

(4) 'Where Wild Swans Nest'
(5) 'The Raid'
(6) 'Hail and Farewell'
(7) 'High Roads and Low Roads'
(8) 'Pax'
(9) 'Drifting'
(10) 'Into Civil War'

5   *Tennyson's Style* (Ithaca and London: Cornell University Press, 1976), pp. 133–134. Shaw points to the mediating influence of Hallam who 'enables Tennyson to accept a spiritual principle or revelation through withdrawal.' He finds similar patterns in other nineteenth-century works such as Mill's *Autobiography*, Carlyle's *Sartor Resartus* and Newman's *Apologia Pro Vita Sua*. He writes:

> Wordsworth as mediator enables Mill to discover the value of 'states of feeling, and of thought colored by feeling' which were previously inaccessible to him. Mediators like Goethe and Fichte help Carlyle affirm the value of ethical and spiritual truths, and mentors like John Keble and Richard Whately render intelligible intellectual and religious truths for Newman.

V. Modes of Representation: Narrative Strategies

1   'From Within the Gates,' in *Blasts and Benedictions* (London: Macmillan, 1967), ed. Ronald Ayling, pp. 113–114.
2   *World Within World* (London: Hamish Hamilton, 1950), Preface, p. ii.
3   'The Dark Continent of Literature: Autobiography,' in *Comparative Literature Studies*, 5 (1968), 444.
4   *Design and Truth in Autobiography* (London: Routledge and Kegan Paul, 1960), p. 162.
5   'Notes for an Anatomy of Modern Autobiography,' in *New Literary History*, I (1970), 488.
6   *The Dynamics of Literary Response* (New York: Oxford University Press, 1968), p. 68.
7   Such sequences are often offered as neither the mental projections of the protagonist nor indeed any other character; they are further manifestations of the intrusive narrator. Even when the person who imagines such reveries is identified, O'Casey feels no need to present the thoughts and ideas as an accurate reflection of the individual's maturity and knowledge at that time. This freedom confirms that fanciful and surrealistic passages, rather than being read as legitimate creations of the character's imagination or unconscious mind, are in fact another set of indices of autobiographical identity, another means for the author to render former thoughts and feelings in the light of the present.
8   *The Irish Comic Tradition* (London: Oxford University Press, 1969). All subsequent references to Mercier will be indicated parenthetically.

9   *The Irish Tradition* (Oxford: Clarendon Press, 1978), p. 102.

10 Ronald Ayling, *Continuity and Innovation in Sean O'Casey's Drama: A Critical Monograph*, Salzburg Studies in English Literature, No. 23 (Salzburg: Institut fur Englische Sprache und Literatur, 1976), p. 130. For other studies of O'Casey and expressionism see Robert Hogan's *The Experiments of Sean O'Casey* (New York: St Martin's Press, 1960), and also Carol Kleiman's *Sean O'Casey's Bridge of Vision: Four Essays on Structure and Perspective* (Toronto: University of Toronto Press, 1982).

11 'Sean O'Casey's Narratives,' in *Sean O'Casey: Modern Judgements*, ed. Ronald Ayling, p. 223.

12 Paul Shyre adapted *Knock* (1956), *Pictures* (1956) and *Drums* (1960) for the New York stage, while Patrick Funge and David Krause did adaptations of *Pictures* (1965), *Drums* (1968), and *Inishfallen* (1972) for Dublin productions.

13 Most notable among these was Eric Bentley who wrote: 'Though diffuse, and over-full of self-pity and proletarian snobbery, the autobiography may be almost as good as people say it is; even so, it is ersatz: the best passages are scenes from plays that will never be written.' *New Republic*, 12 October 1952.

14 Reprinted in *Autobiography: Essays Theoretical and Critical*, ed. James Olney. In particular, see pp. 286–287.

15 *The Forms of Autobiography* (New Haven and London: Yale University Press, 1980), pp. 120–121.

VI. Modes of Representation: Language

1   'Sean O'Casey as Wordsmith,' in *Essays on Sean O'Casey's Autobiographies*, edited by Robert G. Lowery (Totowa, New Jersey: Barnes & Noble Books, 1981), pp. 232–246.

From the outset, the writing in the autobiographal volumes was seen as being derivative of Joyce, a charge which O'Casey returned to again and again in his letters. Writing to William J. Maroldo on 9 April 1962, he said:

> I wasn't influenced by James Joyce any more than all who read him were. I was too old to be influenced by him (as Joyce is said to have remarked to Yeats). The glimpses of influence given in the biography were more of a desire to show my admiration of this great writer; as a symbol of standing by one who was being attacked on all sides; banned by the nation and publisher, yet unshaken and supreme in his glorious and God-given integrity. . . . Joyce's influence was like a bugle-call, loud and clear first, fading away as it was being heard; or like heavy footsteps passing by an open window, first driving attention to the car [*sic*, ear?], then fading, very soon forgotten. (*The Sean O'Casey Review*, 3 (Spring 1977), 121).

While willing to concede some general influence, O'Casey insisted on the stylistic originality of passages which critics traced directly to specific works by Joyce. In a 17 May, 1942 letter to George Jean Nathan, he wrote: 'Some think that the talk of St. Patrick to the Irish ['A Coffin Comes to Ireland', *Pictures* (1942)] and the Protestant Kid's Idea of the Reformation ['The Protestant Kid Thinks of the Reformation,' *Knock* (1939)] was got from Finnegans Wake; but I have a recollection of writing the latter fourteen years ago, and of being encouraged to go on by a fellow named G. J. Nathan publishing it eight or nine years ago in THE AMERICAN SPECTATOR; and saying it was good.' *Letters*, II, 57. As David Krause observes in the note to this letter, O'Casey is pointing out that he wrote the supposedly 'Joycean' chapter, 'The Protestant Kid Thinks of the Reformation,' in 1928 and had it published in Nathan's the *American Spectator* in July 1934, five years before *Finnegans Wake* appeared.

For a further discussion of this subject, see William J. Maroldo's 'O'Casey's Tributes to Joyce in the First Irish Book,' in *O'Casey Annual No. 1*, ed. Robert G. Lowery (Altantic Highlands, N. J.: Humanities Press, 1982), pp. 17–32.

2   *The Irish Tradition*, p. 1.

3   The book was published under the pseudonym of 'Tom Pun-Sibi' and was entitled *Ars Pun-ica, sive Flos Linguarum: The Art of Punning; or, the Flower of Languages; in Seventy-Nine Rules: for the Farther Improvement of Conversation and Help of Memory*. See Mercier page 96.

4   'O'Casey, Influence and Impact,' *Irish University Review*, 10 (1980), 152.

5   The present author recalls use of 'rix stix' in this capacity as filler words in the childhood songs and sayings of his Irish childhood.

6   The information on 'shinners,' as well as the translation of this and the next three Latinisms are found in Robert Lowery's diligently-researched *Sean O'Casey's Autobiographies: An Annotated Index* (Westport, Connecticut: Greenwood Press, 1983). Of interest in regard to O'Casey's Latinisms is Mercier's account of the puns which Swift and Sheridan achieved by writing phonetic Latin. For example, Swift's letter to Sheridan beginning, 'Am I say vain a Rabble is' which is Amice Venerabilis. Mercier, p. 97.

7   For a fuller discussion of the dance motif see William A. Armstrong's essay, 'Sean O'Casey, W. B. Yeats and the Dance of Life,' in *Sean O'Casey: Modern Judgement*, ed. Ronald Ayling, pp. 131–142.

8   See note 21 above.

9   Fallon made this point in a radio programme that was part of a series on autobiography, called 'The Way They Lived,' broadcast on Radio Telefis Eireann in 1977.

10   The following songs are alluded to or echoed in the passage: 'Farewell, But Whenever I Welcome the Hour,' 'The Last Glimpse of Eireann With Sorrow I See,' 'The Time I've Lost in Wooing,' 'The Dream of Those Days,' ' 'Tis Gone and Forever,' 'Come Rest in This Bosom,' 'Go Where the Glory Waits,' 'The Harp That Once Through Tara's

Halls' and 'The Ministrel Boy'. O'Casey's allusions to songs may sometimes be intentionally quite inaccurate. When the proofs of *Knock* were being prepared by the printers, he wrote to Harold Macmillan:

Some time ago, I wrote to them asking, because of possible alteration in the songs, to hold back the proof of 'The Street Sings.' I have seen the published version of these songs, & find my own is better; so please tell them to carry on with 'The Street Sings.' *Letters*, I, 746

William Maroldo's essay, 'A Darwinian Garden of Eden: A Major Emphasis in Sean O'Casey's Autobiographies,' provides an indication of the extensive background material that is sometimes necessary for a full understanding of O'Casey's allusive passages. Maroldo cites the fantasy in *Drums* in which Sean arrives in Eden and overhears G. K. Chesterton and his character, Father Brown, being interviewed by a reporter:

'I'm Jeecaysee, the fat man said, the mild knight of the little man, the schnapper-up of God's tremendous trifles; past, present, and to come, grand chief arranger of the greybards at play; awethor of the misuses of divorsety; and this, indicating the little man by his side, is Daabruin, suborned into life to make right what's wrong with the world, and to lead the fiat of heretics to the end of the roaman road. (III, 180)

In addition to the puns and portmanteau words here, Maroldo identifies allusions to the following books by Chesteron: *The Wild Knight*, 1900; *The Napoleon of Notting Hill*, 1904; *Tremendous Trifles*, 1909; *Greybeards at Play*, 1900; *The Uses of Diversity*; 1920; *The Superstition of Divorce*, 1920; *What's Wrong With the World?*, 1910; *The Queer Feet*, 1911; *Heretics*, 1905; and *The End of the Roman Road*, 1924. *The Sean O'Casey Review*, 5 (Spring 1979), 172.

12   'The Passionate Autodidact: The Importance of Litera Scripta for O'Casey,' *Irish University Review*, 10 (Spring 1980), 73.

13   *Letters*, I, 905.

14   For a fuller discussion of this threesome, see Bernard Benstock's *Paycocks and Others: Sean O'Casey's World* (Dublin: Gill and Macmillan, 1976), pp. 291–293.

15   In a letter of 15 November 1954 to Carmen Capalbo, who was planning a production of *Purple Dust*, O'Casey provides a list of the unusual expressions used in the play. He gives a particularly detailed description of 'The Sword of Light' in terms practically synonomous with its use in the autobiography. See *Letters*, II, 1112–1113.

16   Significant in this regard is the passage describing the first visit of the half-blind Johnny to the eye clinic, an account in which O'Casey stresses the aural and imaginative elements rather than the visual details. *Knock*, p. 17.

17   Christopher Murray, Introd., *Irish University Review*, Special Issue: Sean O'Casey: Roots & Branches, ed. Christopher Murray, 10 (1980), 17.

18 'Some Truths and Jokes About the Easter Rising,' in *The Sean O'Casey Review*, 3 (Spring 1976), 17.

19 'The Legacy of Sean O'Casey,' in *Sean O'Casey: A Collection of Critical Essays*, ed. Thomas Kilroy (Englewood Cliffs, N.J.: Prentice Hall, Inc., 1975), p. 37.

20 Reported by Krause in his book, *Sean O'Casey: The Man and His Work* (New York: Macmillan Publishing Co., Inc., Enlarged Edition, 1975), p. 296.

21 *The Irish Tradition*, p. 76.

22 O'Casey goes on to mention several other Irish literary pieces: '*The Deer's Cry*, better known or unknown as *St Patrick's Breastplate*; or St. Ita's lovely little lullaby . . . or Crede's lament for Dinertack.' (VI, 203) As an enthusiastic Gaelic Leaguer, he would probably have been familiar with *The Vision of Mac Conglinne* through the 1892 translation by Kuno Meyer.

23 Colum makes this statement in *Irish Writing*, November 1948. In his review article on the autobiography, 'Sean O'Casey's Narratives' (see note 11 above), Colum uses this comparison with Mac Conglinne to place Johnny Casside's fiery character in a context that helps to explain his actions.

24 Thomas Kilroy, 'Introduction,' in *Sean O'Casey: A Collection of Critical Essays*, ed. Thomas Kilroy (Englewood Cliffs, N.J.: Prentice Hall, Inc., 1975), p. 10.

VII Literary Images and Autobiographical identity.

1 *Autobiography: Essay Theoretical and Critical*, edited by James Olney (Princeton: Princeton University Press, 1980), p. 87.

2 See Chapter V, note 1.

3 *Figures of Autobiography: The Language of Self-Writing in Victorian and Modern England* (Berkeley, Los Angeles and London: University of California Press, 1983), pp. 58–69.

4 Fleishman, pp. 56–58.

5 It may initially seem somewhat incongruous to find O'Casey, the ardent critic of the abuses of religious institutions, employing religious references as a means of rendering his life-story but, in this, he was reflecting a common tendency in the writing of other non-believers of his time. As Richard Ellmann has observed, 'Almost to a man, Edwardian writers rejected Christianity, and, having done so, they felt free to *use* it, for while they did not need religion they did need religious metaphors.' Richard Ellmann, 'Two Faces of Edward,' in *Edwardians and Late Victorians: English Institute Essays, 1959*, ed. Richard Ellmann (New York and London, 1960) pp. 191–192.

      Nor was O'Casey unique in his use of Christ and Christian imagery to describe and exalt his communist views. In a detailed and cogent essay, Robert Lowery points out that, in this regard, O'Casey is

following a tradition which shows the use of Christian imagery and
symbols to extol the virtues of communism. 'Sean O'Casey: Art
and Politics,' in *Sean O'Casey: Centenary Essays*, ed David Krause
and Robert G. Lowery (Gerrards Cross: Colin Smythe, 1980), pp.
121–164.

6   Fleishman, p. 357.

7   Fleishman, p. 360.

8   Sean's loss of religious faith is an ironic reversal of the procedure
found in the traditional spiritual journey: in that paradigm it is the
crisis of religious doubt which initiates the period of exile and
wandering, and spiritual renewal becomes the instrument of ultimate
reconciliation with the true self and God.

9   In a further re-shuffling of chronological sequence, O'Casey does not
give Sean's detailed reactions to events surrounding the Bolshevik
Revolution until the account of the irreconcilable differences between
him and Nora Creena:

Never once had he mentioned the Bolshevik Revolution to her, though it was
ever in his mind; never once had he tried by a word to attune her ear to an
echo even of the march of the Red Guards, though he himself had followed,
with quaking heart, the advance of Kolchak from the east, and the advance
of Denikin from the south, till from where they were, Denikin said, they could
see, on a clear night, through the windows of Moscow, the tight-lipped people
getting ready to quit the city. The Press was full of the death and defeat of the
Red madmen; then, suddenly, they fell silent; and Sean knew that the Red Flag
was high in Moscow and Petrograd. O, silver trumpets be ye lifted up, and call
to the great race that is to come! Yeats, Yeats, they are sounding now, though
your ears are cocked in another direction. Sounding loud and brave, not for
all ears yet; but for the many to hear; and Sean's were the first of the Irish ones
to hear them. Christ the King was becoming a Communist! (IV, 230–231)

For a better understanding of O'Casey's contacts with the Soviet Union
in the mid-1920s, see Richard Davies' and W. J. McCormack's 'Sean
O'Casey's Unpublished Correspondence with Raisa Lomonosova,
1925–1926,' in *Irish Slavonic Studies: Irish Russian Contacts* (A Special
Issue) V, (Belfast, 1984), pp. 181–191.

10 'Autobiography and Historical Consciousness,' in *Critical Inquiry*, 1,
No. 4 (June 1975), pp. 824–825.

11 O'Casey's vivid feelings of his own prolonged mistreatment as a writer
in Ireland and England are patently clear from a 1947 letter to his
friend, Brooks Atkinson, drama critic of the *New York Times*:

And you twit me with the Soviet Union! My dear friend, you may be right,
but I have endured so much repression here that, no matter what you may say,
I feel there is just as much (and more) repression here than there is in the USSR.
You just read the Preface to Joyce's N.Y. Edition of 'Ulysses,' & see what he
went through before 'Dubliners' would be published. The present Court
Censor here, Lord Clarendon, banned my 'Star Turns Red,' because 'he didn't
like the theme.' As if I cared a damn whether he did or no; or as if, when I
sat down to try to write a play, I asked myself the question — 'Now what kind
of a play would Lord Clarendon write?' You yourself must remember what the

Jesuits (father O'Connell) & the religious said about 'Within the Gates'; and
how the Abbey Theatre treated 'Silver Tassie.' . . .

Only the other day, a Cahircrvien [*sic*] Drama Co. selected 'The Plough'
as a play for a Drama Festival in Cork. After months of rehearsal, the
Committee of the Festival banned the play. I tried to get the names of this
Committee, but all to whom I wrote, remained silent. They were afraid to
write to me. I don't blame them, for their very livelihood was in question.
Look at what James Agate said about 'Purple Dust'! I could give you many
more instances of oppression. *Letters*, II, 445–446.

12 That the autobiography presents the life-story as a series of fights for
liberty on a variety of levels is readily apparent in the many references
to freedom in the text. For instance, in *Drums* O'Casey enhances the
presentation of Jim Larkin as the Prometheus of Dublin by quoting
from another poem by Shelley, 'The Masque of Anarchy':

> What is freedom? Ye can tell that which slavery is too well,
> For its very name has grown to an echo of your own.
> Rise like lions after slumber . . .
> Shake your chains to earth like dew . . . Ye are many — they are few.
>
> (III, 197)

Another literary allusion is used when Sean is portrayed refusing a
foreman's admonition to sign a paper agreeing to have nothing to do with
Larkin's union, even though the foreman suggests that the agreement is a
formality which can be reneged on later:

> Look, Bill, said Sean, a great poet once wrote,
>
> A knight there was, and that a worthy man,
> That from the time that he first bigan
> To ryden out, he loved chivalrye,
> Truth and honour, freedom and curteisye;

And were I to sign this thing, all these things would turn aside and walk no
more with me. (III, 192)

Or again, in *Sunset*, O'Casey returns to the theme of freedom in his
discussion of children: 'We have begun to realize that children need
not only life, but liberty too.' (VI, 32)

13 O'Casey's perception of communism as an ideology founded on
principles which, in essence, are similar to the basic tenets of Christ's
teachings is a recurring theme in sources other than the
autobiography. When David Krause asked him when he had lost his
faith in the church, the immediate response was:

> 'I never lost my faith, I found it. I found it when Jim Larkin came to Dublin
> a few years later and organized the unskilled laborers. I found it in Jim's great
> socialist motto: "An injury to one is the concern of all".'
> 'Socialist and Christian?'
> 'Socialist and Christian. They've both the one thing — communism — if
> only the people knew it. Jim knew it as well as he knew his penny-catechism,
> but the clergy condemned him for it during the 1913 strike, saying hell wasn't

hot enough nor eternity long enough for the likes of him. Yet he was the saviour of Dublin. He put his faith in the people and their need to live a better and fuller life. And that's where I put my faith.'

David Krause, *Sean O'Casey: The Man and His Work*, Enlarged Edition (New York, Macmillan Publishing Co., Inc., 1975), p. 298.

That analogies between communism and religion, particularly Christianity, were reflexive for O'Casey is obvious from even a superficial glance at his letters. In a 1942 letter to Rev. Canon William Dudley Fletcher, he says: 'My faith for many, many years has been that of Communism, and my hope for 25 years has been, and is, now, in the might of the Red Army. . . .' *Letters*, II, 8.

In a response to an Irishwoman who had written that, although she liked *Inishfallen*, she was uneasy with the exalted references to communism, O'Casey wrote:

As for the 'bright Red Star' — this is the symbol of Communism — not only in the USSR — but for all the peoples of the world. I was a Communist years and years before I even heard the name of Lenin; and, indeed, what is called 'Marxism' owes a lot of its philosophy and practices to — you'd never guess — Thompson, a Cork farmer, a big farmer, who formed his estate into a Community before Lenin was heard of. And, then, there's Fintan Lalor of 1848; and many another Irishman — O'Donovan Rossa, for instance, who kept strong sympathies for the Communist cause. And the greatest living Irishman today, Bernard Shaw, is a Communist too. So there's more than one villain in the woodpile. *Letters*, II, 669.

Again, in 1954, writing to Peter Newmark, he blends Christian terms to explain his understanding of communism:

There are many good Communists who never read a line of Marx. A man who sets out to be a doctor, & becomes a good one, becomes a Communist; a man who sets out to be a teacher, & becomes a good one, becomes a Communist; doing good to his neighbours, & bringing the world onwards. 'Whatsoever thy hand findeth to do, do it with all thy might' — good Communist doctrine, though it was said by St. Paul. *Letters*, II, 1120.

14 He confirms this point in a 1954 letter to Oriana Atkinson:

I was angry just a few minutes ago: slipping on Radio Eireann, I heard a priest appealing on behalf of a Charitable Institution: the voice said — 'The world will never be a Utopia' (right, sir; no one wants it to be a utopia. Even Morris's world, in his 'News from Nowhere,' wants a utopia), 'We will' went on the voice, 'always have the poor and destitute with us.' Christ's words weren't good enough for him — he had to add the one of 'destitute.' God, how they love destitution in Ireland! No, no utopia; but we can have sense, decency, and grace in the world, & we shall fight till they come to us, with laughter as they come, & laughter still when they are entered in as members of the family. *Letters*, II, 1098.

15 In a letter to David Krause of 2 November 1954, O'Casey readily acknowledges that

There is, of course, Nyadnanavery [the Irish village in *Cock-a-Doodle Dandy* which is a symbol of repression] in the USSR. It takes a long time for public consensus to become a common thing. We are not perfect; & we do not know all things yet; very little in fact; but we're trying to learn, & that's a good hold on God's hand. (*Letters*, II, 1104).

In the autobiography itself, O'Casey raises the issue of there being concentration camps in the Soviet Union, but in such a manner as to ridicule the perception of the country as one big prison. It appears in the chapter in *Sunset* where he takes a final look at Ireland, and sees it as a place that is obsessed with the pagan and anti-religious bias of communism. This inordinate fear of communism is satirized in a scene where two typical Irish characters, Mick and Dan, devise a madcap scheme of supplying jeeps to everyone in Ireland so as to escape the invading Russian army:

A nation like Russia that holds fifteen millions and more in concentration camps, and has eliminated twenty millions more and more be vast and frequent purges, man, wouldn't cast a thought about eliminating thousands of Irishmen, women, and children, the expert said, or wait to think twice about exporting the rest of us. It would be only child's play, he said, to the Russians. (VI, 213)

16 'The Socialist Legacy of Sean O'Casey,' *The Crane Bag*, 7, No. 1 (1983), 128–134. This essay provides a thorough account of O'Casey's growing awareness and increasing approval of the social and political developments in Russia following the Bolshevik Revolution.

Conclusion

1 'Some Principles of Autobiography,' in *Autobiography: Essays Theoretical and Critical*, ed. James Olney (Princeton, New Jersey: Princeton University Press, 1980), p. 89.

SELECTED BIBLIOGRAPHY

I. Primary Sources

I.i. Sean O'Casey's Autobiography

O'Casey, Sean. *I Knock at the Door*. London: Pan Books Ltd., 1971.
——. *Pictures in the Hallway*. London: Pan Books Ltd., 1971.
——. *Drums Under the Windows*. London: Pan Books Ltd., 1972.
——. *Inishfallen, Fare Thee Well*. London: Pan Books Ltd., 1972.
——. *Rose and Crown*. London: Pan Books Ltd., 1973.
——. *Sunset and Evening Star*. London: Pan Books Ltd., 1973.
——. *Mirror in My House*. 2 vols. New York: Macmillan, 1956.

I.ii. Sean O'Casey: Other Primary Sources

O'Casey, Sean. *Blasts and Benedictions: Articles and Stories*. Ed. and Introd. Ronald Ayling. London: Macmillan, 1967.
——. *Collected Plays*. 4 vols. London: Macmillan & Co. Ltd., 1957–59.
——. *Feathers from the Green Crow: Sean O'Casey, 1905–1925, Plays and Prose*. Ed. Robert Hogan. London: Macmillan, 1963.
——. *The Green Crow*. New York: George Braziller Inc., 1956.
——. Holographs and typescripts of *I Knock at the Door*, *Pictures in the Hallway*, *Drums Under the Windows*, *Inishfallen, Fare Thee Well*, *Rose and Crown*, and *Sunset and Evening Star*. Henry W. and Albert A. Berg Collection, the New York Public Library (Astor Lenox and Tilden Foundations), New York.
——. *The Letters of Sean O'Casey 1919–41*. Ed. David Krause. Vol. I. London: Cassell & Company Ltd., 1975.
——. *The Letters of Sean O'Casey 1942–54*. Ed. David Krause. Vol. II. New York: Macmillan Publishing Co. Ltd., 1980.
——. *The Sean O'Casey Reader*. Ed. and Introd. Books Atkinson. New York: St. Martin's Press, 1968.
——. 'Sidelighting on Some Pictures.' *New York Times*, 16 September 1956.
——. *The Sting and the Twinkle: Conversations with Sean O'Casey*. Ed. E. H. Mikhail and John O'Riordan. London: Macmillan, 1974.

——. *Under a Coloured Cap: Articles Merry and Mournful with Comments and a Song.* London: Macmillan; New York: St Martin's Press, 1963.

——. *Windfalls: Stories, Poems and Plays.* London: Macmillan and Co. Ltd., 1934.

I.iii. Primary Sources by Other Authors

Adams, Henry. *The Education of Henry Adams.* Ed. and Introd. Ernest Samuels. Boston: Houghton Mifflin, 1918.

Allingham, William. *William Allingham's Diary*, Introd. Geoffrey Grigson. Fontwell, Sussex: Centaur Press Ltd., 1967.

Barrington, Jonah. *Personal Sketches of His Own Times.* 3 vols. London, 1827–32.

Berdyaev, Nicolas. *Dream and Reality: An Essay In Autobiography.* Trans. Katharine Lampert. London: Geofrey Bles, 1950.

Byrne, John Francis. *Silent Years: An Autobiography With Memoirs of James Joyce and Our Ireland.* New York: Farrar, Strauss and Young, 1953.

Carlyle, Thomas. *Sartor Resartus.* Ed. Charles Frederick Harrold. New York: Odyssey Press, 1937.

Cohen, Chapman. *Almost an Autobiography: The Confessions of A Freethinker.* London: Pioneer Press, 1940.

Coulton, G. G. *Fourscore Years: An Autobiography.* Cambridge: University Press, 1943.

Franklin, Benjamin. *The Autobiography of Benjamin Franklin.* Introd. Lewis Leary. New York: Collier Books; London: Collier-Macmillan Ltd., 1962.

Gibbon, Edward. *Autobiography.* Ed. Lord Sheffield. Introd. J. B. Bury. London: Oxford University Press, 1959.

——. *Memoirs of My Life.* Ed. Georges A. Bonnard. London; Nelson, 1966.

Goethe, Johann Wolfgang von. *The Autobiography of Johann Wolfgang Von Goethe.* Trans. John Oxenford. Introd. Karl J. Weintraub. 2 Vols. Chicago and London: The University of Chicago Press, 1974.

Gogarty, Oliver St. John. *As I was Going Down Sackville Street.* London: Sphere Books, 1968.

——. *Tumbling in the Hay.* London: Sphere Books, 1982.

Gosse, Edmund. *Father and Son: Biographical Recollections.* New York: Charles Scribner's Sons, 1907.

Greene, Graham, *A Sort of Life.* New York: Simon and Schuster, 1971.

Gregory, Isabella Augusta, Lady. *Lady Gregory's Journals, 1916–1930.* Ed. Lennox Robinson. New York: Macmillan Company, 1947.

Hellman, Lillian. *Pentimento.* New York: New American Library, 1974.

Joyce, James. 'A Portrait of the Artist' (January 1904). In *The Workshop of Daedalus: James Joyce and the Raw Materials for* A Portrait of the

Artist as a Young Man. Ed. Robert Scholes and Richard M. Kain. Evanston, Ill.: Northwestern University Press, 1965.

——. *A Portrait of the Artist as a Young Man*. New York: The Viking Press, 1969.

——. *Stephen Hero*. London: Jonathan Cape, 1969.

Kavanagh, Patrick. *The Green Fool*. London: Michael Joseph, 1938.

McDonald, Walter. *Reminiscences of a Maynooth Professor*. Edited with a memoir by Denis Gwynn. Cork: The Mercier Press, 1967.

Mill, John Stuart. *Autobiography*. Ed. and Introd. Jack Stillinger. Boston: Houghton Mifflin Company, 1969.

Moore. George. *Confessions of a Young Man*. Ed. Susan Dick. Montreal: McGill-Queen's University Press, 1972.

——. *Hail and Farewell*. Ed. Richard Cave. Toronto: The Macmillan Company of Canada Limited, 1976.

Muir, Edwin, *An Autobiography*. New York: The Seabury Press, 1954.

Nabokov, Vladimir, *Speak, Memory: An Autobiography Revisted*. New York: G. P. Putnam's Sons, 1966.

Newman, John Henry. *Apologia Pro Vita Sua*. Intro. Basil Wiley. London: Oxford University Press, 1964.

O'Connor, Frank. (Michael O'Donovan). *An Only Child*. London: Pan Books Ltd., 1972.

——. *My Father's Son*. London: Macmillan, 1968.

O'Crohan, Thomas, *The Islandman*. Trans. and Introd. Robin Flower. London: Chatto and Windus, 1934.

O'Faolain, Sean. *Vive Moi!* London: Hart-Davis, 1965.

O'Flaherty, Liam. *Shame the Devil*. London: Grayson & Grayson, 1934.

——. *Two Years*. New York: Harcourt, Brace and Company, 1930.

O'Leary, Peter. *My Story*. Trans. Cyril T. Ceirin. Cork: The Mercier Press, 1970.

O'Sullivan, Maurice. *Twenty Years A-Growing*. Trans. Moya Llewellyn Davies and George Thomson. Introd. E. M. Forster. London: Chatto & Windus, 1933.

Pattison, Mark. *Memoirs*. London: Macmillan, 1885.

Rousseau, Jean-Jacques. *The Confessions*. Trans. J. M. Cohen. London: Penguin Books, 1954.

Ruskin, John. *Praeterita*. Orpington: G. Allen, 1899.

Saint Augustine. *The Confessions of Saint Augustine*. Trans. Edward B. Pusey. Introd. Fulton J. Sheen. New York: Modern Library. 1949.

Sartre, Jean-Paul. 'Jean-Paul Sartre on His Autobiography.' Interview with Olivier Todd. *The Listener*, 6 June 1957, pp. 915–916.

——. *Words*. Trans. Irene Clephane. Harmondsworth, Middlesex: Penguin Books Ltd., 1972.

Shaw, George Bernard. *Sixteen Self Sketches*. London, 1949.

Spender, Stephen. *World Within World: The Autobiography of Stephen Spender*. London: Hamish Hamilton, 1950.

Stein, Gertrude. *The Autobiography of Alice B. Toklas*. New York: Vintage Books, 1960.

Thoreau, Henry David. *Walden.* Ed. J. Lyndon Shanley. Princeton, New Jersey: Princeton University Press, 1971.

Trollope, Anthony. *An Autobiography.* Introd. Charles Morgan. London: Williams & Norgate Ltd., 1946.

Wells, H. G. *Experiment in Autobiography: Discoveries and Conclusions of a Very Ordinary Brain (since 1866).* Toronto: The Macmillan Company of Canada Limited, 1934.

Wilde, Oscar. *De Profundis.* Introd. Vyvyn Holland. London: Methuen & Co., 1949.

Wordsworth, William. *The Prelude.* Ed. and Introd. Ernest de Selincourt and Helen Darbishire. Oxford: Oxford Univerisy Press, 1959.

Yeats, William Butler. *Autobiographies.* London: Macmillan, 1973.

———. *The Letters of W. B. Yeats.* Ed. Allan Wade. London: Hart Davis, 1954.

II. Secondary Sources

II.i. O'Casey and his Works

Armstrong, William A. *Sean O'Casey.* London: Longmans Green for the British Council, and the National Book League, 1967.

Atkinson, Brooks. 'Insurgent Penman.' Rev. of *I Knock at the Door. New York Times,* 9 April 1939, section 10, p. 1.

———. 'O'Casey Keeps His Life Moving.' Rev. of *Pictures in the Hallway. New York Times,* 5 April 1942, section 8, p. 1.

———. 'O'Casey's Own Story.' Rev. of *Drums Under the Windows. New York Times,* 22 September 1946, section 2, p. 1.

———. Rev. of *Rose and Crown, New York Times,* 14 September 1952, section 2, p. 1.

Ayling, Ronald. 'A Note on Sean O'Casey's Manuscripts and His Working Methods.' *Bulletin of the New York Public Library,* 73, No. 6 (1969), 359–367.

———. *Continuity and Innovation in Sean O'Casey's Drama: A Critical Monograph.* Salzburg Studies in English literature No. 23. Salzburg: Institut fur Englische Sprache und Literatur, Universitat Salzburg, 1976.

———. 'Detailed Catalogue of Sean O'Casey's Papers at the Time of his Death.' *The Sean O'Casey Review,* I, No. 2 (1975), 48–65.

———. ed. *Sean O'Casey: Modern Judgements.* Nashville and London: Aurora Publishers Incorporated, 1970.

Benstock, Bernard. *Paycocks and Others: Sean O'Casey's World.* Dublin: Gill and Macmillan Ltd., 1976.

———. *Sean O'Casey.* Lewisburg: Bucknell University Press, 1970.

Bentley, Eric. 'The Case of O'Casey.' Rev. of *Rose and Crown. New Republic* (New York), 127 (13 October 1952), 17–18.

Bowen, Elizabeth. 'Dubliner.' Rev. of *Pictures in the Hallway. The Spectator* (London) 168 (1 May 1942), 423.

Boyd, Ernest. 'The Protestant Kid.' Rev. of *I Knock at the Door. Saturday Review of Literature*, 20, No. 14 (29 July 1939), 6.

——. 'Still Knocking at the Door.' Rev. of *Pictures in the Hallway. Saturday Review of Literature* (N.Y.), 25 (21 March 1942), p. 5

Brown, Ivor. 'Dublin Son and Mother.' Rev. of *I Knock at the Door. Manchester Guardian*, 7 March 1939, p. 7.

Butler, Anthony, and David Krause, 'A Storm in the Fair City.' Ed. Robert G. Lowery. *The Sean O'Casey Review*, 3, No. 2 (1977), 127–143.

Carroll, Joseph. 'O'Casey, the Emigrant Titan.' Rev. of *Rose and Crown. Theatre Arts* (N.Y.), 36 (8 December 1952), 6–8.

Clarke, Austin. Rev. of *Sunset and Evening Star. Time and Tide* (London), 35 (13 November 1954), 1524.

Clurman, Harold. 'Bard in a Pub.' Rev. of *Sunset and Evening Star. Nation* (N.Y.), 179 (27 November 1954), 468.

Colum, Padraic. 'A Dramatic Autobiography.' Rev. of *I Knock at the Door. Yale Review*, 29, No. 1 (September 1939), 182–185.

——. 'O'Casey: A Third Instalment.' Rev. of *Drums Under the Windows. Yale Review*, 36 (Autumn 1946), 154–6.

——. 'Wallops in Autobiography.' Rev. of *Sunset and Evening Star. New Republic*, 131 (27 December 1954), 19.

Cowasjee, Saros. *Sean O'Casey: The Man Behind the Plays*. New York: St. Martin's Press, 1964.

Davies, Richard and W. J. McCormack. 'Sean O'Casey's Unpublished Correspondence with Raisa Lomonosova, 1925–1926.' *Irish Slavonic Studies*, V (1984), 181–191.

Dessner, Lawrence J. 'Art and Anger in the *Autobiographies* of Sean O'Casey.' *Eire-Ireland*, 10, No. 3 (1975), 46–61.

Fallon, Gabriel. *Sean O'Casey: The Man I Knew*. London: Routledge & Kegan Paul, 1965.

Firth, John Mirkil, 'O'Casey and Autobiography.' Diss. University of Virginia 1965.

Goldstone, Herbert. *In Search of Community: The Achievement of Sean O'Casey*. Cork: The Mercier Press, 1972.

Greaves, C. Desmond. *Sean O'Casey: Politics and Art*. London: Lawrence and Wishart Ltd., 1979.

Greene, David H. 'A Great Dramatist's Approach to Autobiography.' Rev. of *Mirror in My House. Commonweal*, 65 (25 January 1957), 440–443.

Gwynn, Stephen. 'Manifestations of Ireland.' Rev. of *Pictures in the Hallway. Time and Tide* (London), 23 (28 March 1942), 272–273.

Harmon, Maurice., ed. *Irish University Review: A Journal of Irish Studies*. Vol. 10, No. 1 (Spring 1980). Special Issue: Sean O'Casey: Roots & Branches. Ed. Christopher Murray.

Heilman, Robert B. Rev. of *Drums Under the Windows. Quarterly Review of Literature* (Annandale-on-Hudson), 4, No. 1 (1947), 105–113.

Hicks, Granville, 'The More You Shout . . . the Less I Hear.' Rev. of *Mirror in My House*. New Republic, 135 (22 October 1956), 17–18.

Hogan, Robert. *The Experiments of Sean O'Casey*. New York: St. Martin's Press, 1960.

——. 'O'Casey, Influence and Impact.' *Irish University Review*, 10, No. 1 (1980), 146–158.

Jordan, John, 'The Passionate Autodidact: The Importance of *Litera Scripta* for O'Casey.' *Irish University Review*, 10, No. 1 (1980), 59–76.

Kenneally, Michael. 'Autobiographical Revelation in O'Casey's *I Knock at the Door*.' *The Canadian Journal of Irish Studies*, 7, No. 2 (1981), 21–38.

——. 'The Changing Contents of O'Casey's Autobiography.' In *O'Casey Annual No. 1*. Ed. Robert G. Lowery. Atlantic Highlands, N.J.: Humanities Press, 1982, pp. 148–166.

——. 'Design in the Autobiography of Sean O'Casey.' Diss. University of Toronto 1978.

——. 'Joyce, O'Casey and the Genre of Autobiography.' In *O'Casey Annual No. 3*. Ed. Robert G. Lowery. London: The Macmillan Press Ltd., 1984, pp. 124–133.

——. 'Models and Mediators in the Autobiography of Sean O'Casey.' In *O'Casey Annual No. 2*. Ed. Robert G. Lowery. London: The Macmillan Press Ltd., 1983, pp. 74–87.

——. 'Principles of Organization in O'Casey's *Drums Under the Windows*.' *The Canadian Journal of Irish Studies*, 6, No. 2 (1980), 34–57.

Kilroy, Thomas, ed. *Sean O'Casey: A Collection of Critical Essays*. Englewood Cliffs, N.J.: Prentice-Hall, Inc., 1975.

Kleiman, Carol. *Sean O'Casey's Bridge of Vision: Four Essays on Structure and Perspective*. Toronto, Buffalo and London; Univeristy of Toronto Press, 1982.

Koslow, Jules. *Sean O'Casey: The Man and his Plays*. New York: The Citadel Press, 1966.

Krause, David, and Robert G. Lowery, eds. *Sean O'Casey: Centenary Essays*. Irish Literary Studies 7. Gerrards Cross: Colin Smythe Ltd., 1980.

Krause, David. *Sean O'Casey: The Man and His Work*. Enlarged edition. New York: Macmillan Publishing Co., Inc., 1975.

——. 'Some Truths and Jokes About the Easter Rising.' *The Sean O'Casey Review*, 3, No. 1 (1976), 3–23.

Lowery, Robert G., ed. *Essays on Sean O'Casey's Autobiographies: Reflections Upon the Mirror*. Totowa, N.J.: Barnes & Noble Books, 1981.

——, ed. *O'Casey Annual No. 1*. Atlantic Highlands, N.J.: Humanities Press, 1982.

——, ed. *O'Casey Annual No. 2*. London: The Macmillan Press Ltd., 1983.

——, ed. *O'Casey Annual No. 3*. London: The Macmillan Press Ltd., 1984.

——. *Sean O'Casey's Autobiographies: An Annotated Index*. Westport, Conn.: Greenwood Press, 1983.

——. 'The Socialist Legacy of Sean O'Casey.' *The Crane Bag*, 7 (1983), 128–134.

MacCarthy, Desmond. 'An Irish Childhood; *I Knock at the Door.' Sunday Times* (London), 19 March 1939, p. 6.

MacNeice, Louis. 'An Irish Proletarian.' Rev. of *Inishfallen, Fare Thee Well. New Statesman and Nation*, 37 (19 February 1949), 184–185.

Margulies, Martin. *The Early Life of Sean O'Casey*. Dublin: Dolmen Press, 1970.

Maroldo, William John. 'A Darwinian Garden of Eden: A Major Emphasis in Sean O'Casey's Autobiographies.' *Sean O'Casey Review*, 5, No. 2 (Spring 1979), 167–176.

——. 'Lines from Torquay — Letters by and About Sean O'Casey.' *The Sean O'Casey Review*, 3, No. 2 (1977), 117–126.

——. 'O'Casey's Tributes to Joyce in the First Irish Book.' In *O'Casey Annual No. 1*. Ed. Robert G. Lowery. Atlantic Highlands, N.J.: Humanities Press, 1982, pp. 17–32.

——. 'Sean O'Casey and the Art of Autobiography: Form and Content in the Irish Books.' Diss. Columbia University 1964.

McCann, Sean, ed. *The World Of Sean O'Casey*. London: The New English Library, 1966.

Mercier, Vivian. 'Decline of a Playwright: The Riddle of Sean O'Casey.' *Commonweal*, 69, No. 15 (1956), 366–368.

Moya, Carmela. 'The Mirror and the Plough.' *The Sean O'Casey Review*, 2, No. 2 (1976), 141–153.

O'Casey, Eileen. *Eileen*. Ed. and Introd. J. C. Trewin. New York: St. Martin's Press, 1976.

——. *Sean*. Ed. and Introd. J. C. Trewin. London: Macmillan, 1971.

O'Faoláin, Sean. 'Sean O'Casey Wallops at the Door.' Rev. of *I Knock at the Door. London Mercury*, 39, No. 233 (March 1939), 561–562.

O hAodha, Micheál, ed. *The O'Casey Enigma*. The Thomas Davis Lecture Series. Dublin and Cork: The Mercier Press, 1980.

O'Hearn, Walter. 'Sean O'Casey, Fare Thee Well.' Rev. of *Inishfallen, Fare Thee Well. America*, 81 (11 June 1949), 342–343.

Orwell, George. Rev. of *Drums Under the Windows. Observer* (London), 28 October 1945, p. 3.

O'Shaughnessy, John. 'O'Casey: Forever Fare Thee Well.' Rev. of *Mirror in My House. The Nation* (N.Y.), 184 (16 March 1957), 237–239.

Pritchett, V. S. 'Within the Gates.' Rev. of *Sunset and Evening Star. New Yorker*, 31 (16 April 1955), 147–156.

Reynolds, Horace. 'Irish Puritanism.' Rev. of *Inishfallen, Fare Thee Well. Yale Review*, 39, No. 1 (Autumn 1949), 169–170.

——. 'O'Casey in Erin, 1917–26.' Rev. of *Inishfallen, Fare Thee Well. The Saturday Review of Literature* (N.Y.), 32 (5 March 1949), 18–19.

——. Rev. of *Pictures in the Hallway. New York Times Book Review*, 22 March 1942, p. 5.

——. Rev. of *Rose and Crown. New York Times Book Review*, 2 November 1952, p. 5.

——. Rev. of *Sunset and Evening Star. Christian Science Monitor*, 24 November 1954, p. 9.

——. 'Sean O'Casey, Up to 12.' Rev. of *I Knock at the Door. New York Times Book Review*, 23 July 1939, pp. 4, 16.

Rollins, Ronald. *Sean O'Casey's Drama: Versimilitude and Vision.* University, Alabama: University of Alabama Press, 1979.

Scrimgeour, James R. 'O'Casey's Street People: Characterization in the Autobiographies.' *The Sean O'Casey Review*, 4, No. 1 (1977), 57–65.

——. *Sean O'Casey.* Twayne's English Authors Series. Boston: Twayne Publishers, 1978.

Simmons, James. 'Sean O'Casey: The Autobiographies.' *Threshold*, No.33 (1983), pp. 36–42.

Simpson, Alan. 'O'Casey and the East Wall Area in Dublin.' *Irish University Review*, 10, No. 1 (1980), 41–51.

Smith, Bobby L. *O'Casey's Satiric Vision.* Kent, Ohio: The Kent State University Press, 1978.

Spring, Howard. 'Autobiography of an Irish Exile.' Rev. of *Sunset and Evening Star. Country Life*, 116 (18 November 1954), 1787–1789.

Stonier, G. W. 'Mr. O'Casey's Autobiography.' Rev. of *Drums Under the Windows. The New Statesman and Nation*, 30 (27 October 1945), p. 284.

——. 'Sean O'Casey.' Rev. of *Pictures in the Hallway. New Statesman and Nation*, 23 (28 February 1942), 147.

——. 'Two Autobiographies.' Rev. of *I Knock at the Door. New Statesman and Nation* (London), 17 (11 March 1939), 396.

Wain, John. 'The Heart of O'Casey.' Rev. of *Mirror in My House. The Observer Weekend Review* (London), 11 August 1963, p. 16.

Watts, Richard Jr. 'The Unsmiling Irishman.' Rev. of *Drums Under the Windows, New Republic*, 114 (10 June 1946), 839–840.

West, E. J. Rev. of *Sunset and Evening Star. Educational Theatre Journal* (Ann Arbor, Michigan), 7 (December 1955), 354–356.

White, Marie A. Updike. Rev. of *Rose and Crown. The South Atlantic Quarterly*, 53 (1952), 156–157.

White, Marie A. Updike. Rev. of *Sunset and Evening Star. The South Atlantic Quarterly*, 55 (1954), 242–243.

Worsley, T. C. 'Backgrounds and Foregrounds.' Rev. of *Sunset and Evening Star. New Statesman and Nation*, 48 (30 October 1954), 544.

II.ii. Other Secondary Sources

Abrams, M. H. *Natural Supernaturalism: Tradition and Revolution in Romantic Literature*, New York: W. W. Norton and Company, Inc., 1971.

Altick, Richard D. *Lives and Letters: A History of Literary Biography in England and America.* New York: Alfred A. Knopf, 1965.

Bates, E. Stuart. *Inside Out: An Introduction to Autobiography.* New York: Sheridan House, 1937.

Berthoff, Warner, 'Witness and Testament.' In *Aspects of Narrative:*

Selected Papers from the English Institute. Ed. J. Hillis Miller. New York and London: Columbia University Press, 1971.

Booth, Wayne C. *The Rhetoric of Fiction.* Chicago and London: The University of Chicago Press, 1961.

Bottrall, Margaret, *Every Man A Phoenix: Studies in Seventeenth-Century Autobiography.* London: John Murray, 1958.

Brombert, Victor. *Stendhal: Fiction and the Themes of Freedom.* New York: Random House, 1968.

Bruss, Elizabeth W. *Autobiographical Acts: The Changing Situation of a Literary Genre.* Baltimore and London: The Johns Hopkins University Press, 1976.

Burr, Anna Robeson. *The Autobiography: A Critical and Comparative Study.* Boston and New York: Houghton Mifflin Company, 1909.

Cassirer, Ernst. *An Essay on Man: An Introduction to the Philosophy of Human Culture.* New Haven: Yale University Press, 1944.

Clark, Arthur Melville. *Autobiography, Its Genesis and Phases.* Edinburgh: Oliver and Boyd, 1935.

Cooley, Thomas. *Educated Lives: The Rise of Modern Autobiography in America.* Columbus: Ohio State University Press, 1976.

Cox, James M. 'Autobiography and America.' In *Aspects of Narrative: Selected Papers from the English Insitute.* Ed. J. Hillis Miller. New York and London: Columbia University Press, 1971.

Delany, Paul. *British Autobiography in the Seventeenth Century.* London: Routledge & Kegan Paul, 1969.

Dobree, Bonamy, 'Some Literary Autobiographies of the Present Age.' *The Sewanee Review,* 64 (1956), 689–706.

Ellmann, Richard. *James Joyce.* New York, London and Toronto: Oxford University Press, 1965.

——. 'Two Faces of Edward.' In *Edwardians and Late Victorians: English Institute Essays, 1959.* Ed. Richard Ellmann. New York and London: Columbia University Press, 1960.

Fallis, Richard. *The Irish Renaissance,* Syracuse, N.Y.: Syracuse University Press, 1977.

Fleishman, Avrom. *Figures of Autobiography: The Language of Self-Writing in Victorian and Modern England.* Berkeley, Los Angeles and London: University of California Press, 1983.

Flower, Robin. *The Irish Tradition.* Oxford: Clarendon Press, 1978.

Forguson, Lynd. 'Autobiography as History.' *Univeristy of Toronto Quarterly,* 49, No. 2 (Winter 1979/80), 139–155.

Freeman, John. *A Portrait of George Moore in a Study of His Work.* London: T. Werner Laurie, Ltd., 1922.

Frye, Northrop. *Anatomy of Criticism: Four Essays.* Princeton, N.J.: Princeton University Press, 1957.

Girard, René. *Deceit, Desire, and the Novel: Self and Other in Literary Structure.* Trans. Yvonne Freccero. Baltimore: The Johns Hopkins Press, 1965.

Hart, Francis R. 'Notes For an Anatomy of Modern Autobiography.' *New Literary History,* 1 (1970), 485–511.

Hederman, M. P., and R. Kearney, eds. *The Crane Bag Book of Irish Studies*. Dublin: Blackwater Press, 1982.

Hogan, Robert. 'The Haunted Inkbottle.' *James Joyce Quarterly*, 8 (1970), 76–95.

Hoggart, Richard. 'A Question of Tone: Problems in Autobiographical Writing.' In *Speaking to Each Other: Essays*: I *About Society*, II *About Literature*. London: Chatto & Windus, 1970, 174–200.

Holland, Norman N. *The Dynamics of Literary Response*. New York: Oxford University Press, 1968.

Howarth, William L. 'Some Principles of Autobiography.' *New Literary History*, 5 (1974), 363–381.

Kazin, Alfred. 'Autobiography as Narrative.' *Michigan Quarterly Review*, 3, No. 4 (1964), 210–216.

Kearney, Richard. 'Myth and Terror.' In *The Crane Bag Book of Irish Studies*. Ed. M. P. Hederman and R. Kearney. Dublin: Blackwater Press, 1982, pp. 273–287.

Lee, Laurie. 'Writing Autobiography.' In *I Can't Stay Long*. London: Penguin Books, 1977.

Lejeune, Philippe, 'Autobiography in the Third Person.' Trans. E. Tomarken and A. Tomarken. *New Literary History*, 9 (1977), 27–50.

Levine, George. *The Boundaries of Fiction: Carlyle, Macaulay, Newman*. Princeton, New Jersey: Princeton University Press, 1968.

Lindenberger, Herbert. *On Wordsworth's Prelude*. Princeton, New Jersey: Princeton University Press, 1963.

Loesberg, Jonathan. 'Self-Consciousness and Meditation in Victorian Autobiogrpahy.' *University of Toronto Quarterly*, 50 (Winter 1980/81), 199–220.

Mandel, Barratt John. 'The Autobiographer's Art.' *Journal of Aesthetic and Art Criticism*, 27 (1968), 215–226.

———. 'Bunyan and the Autobiographer's Artistic Purpose.' *Criticism*, 10, No. 3 (1968), 225–243.

———. 'The Problem of Narration in Edward Gibbon's Autobiography.' *Studies in Philology*, 67, No. 4 (1970), 550–564.

Maurois, André. *Aspects of Biography*. Trans. S. C. Roberts. New York: D. Appleton & Company, 1929.

Mehlman, Jeffrey. *A Structural Study of Autobiography: Proust, Leiris, Sartre, Lévi-Strauss*. Ithaca and London: Cornell University Press, 1974.

Mercier, Vivian. *The Irish Comic Tradition*. London, Oxford and New York: Oxford University Press, 1969.

Misch, George. *A History of Autobiography in Antiquity*. 2 Vols. Trans. E. W. Dikes. London: Routledge & Kegan Paul Limited, 1950.

Morris, John N. *Versions of the Self: Studies in English Autobiography From John Bunyan to John Stuart Mill*. London: Basic Books, Inc., 1966.

Olney, James, ed. *Autobiography: Essays Theoretical and Critical*. Princeton, N.J.: Princeton University Press, 1980.

———. *Metaphors of Self: The Meaning of Autobiography*. Princeton, New Jersey: Princeton University Press, 1972.

Pascal, Roy. 'The Autobiographical Novel and The Autobiography.' *Essays in Criticism*, 9, No. 2 (1959), 134–150.

——. *Design and Truth in Autobiography*. London: Routledge & Kegan Paul, 1960.

Perloff, Marjorie. 'The Autobiographical Mode of Goethe: *Dichtung und Wahrheit* and the Lyric Poems.' *Comparative Literature Studies*, 7, No. 3 (1970), 265–296.

——. ' "The Tradition of Myself" ': The Autobiographical Mode of Yeats.' *Journal of Modern Literature*, 4 (1975), 529–573.

Peyre, Henri. *Literature and Sincerity*. New Haven & London: Yale University Press, 1963.

Pilling, John. *Autobiography and Imagination: Studies in Self-Scrutiny*. London and Boston: Routledge & Kegan Paul, 1981.

Poulet, Georges. *Studies in Human Time*. Trans. Elliott Coleman. Baltimore: The Johns Hopkins Press, 1956.

Prescott, Joseph. 'James Joyce's *Stephen Hero*.' In *Joyce's Portrait*: *Criticisms and Critiques*. Ed. Thomas E. Connolly. New York: Appleton-Century-Crofts, 1962, pp. 77–88.

Renza, Louis A. 'The Veto of the Imagination: A Theory of Autobiography.' *New Literary History*, 9 (1977), 1–26.

Ricoeur, Paul. 'Narrative Time.' *Critical Inquiry* 7 (1980), 169–190

Rinehart, Keith. 'The Victorian Approach to Autobiography.' *Modern Philology*, 51, No. 3 (1954), 177–186.

Ronsley, Joseph. *Yeats's Autobiography: Life as Symbolic Pattern*. Cambridge, Massachusetts: Harvard University Press, 1968.

Rosenblatt, Roger. 'Black Autobiography: Life as the Death Weapon.' *The Yale Review*, 65 (1976), 515–527.

Salaman, Esther P. *The Great Confession: From Aksakov and De Quincey to Tolstoy and Proust*. London: Allen Lane, The Penguin Press, 1973.

Scholes, Robert, and Robert Kellog. *The Nature of Narrative*. London: Oxford University Press, 1966.

Sharpiro, Stephen A. 'The Dark Continent of Literature: Autobiography.' *Comparative Literature Studies*, 5 (1968), 421–454.

Shaw, W. David. '*In Memoriam* and the Rhetoric of Confession.' *English Literary History*, 38 (1971), 80–103.

——. *Tennyson's Style*. Ithaca and London: Cornell University Press, 1976.

Shumaker, Wayne. *English Autobiography: Its Emergence, Materials, and Forms*. Berkeley and Los Angeles: University of California Press, 1954.

Spacks, Patricia Meyer. *Imagining A Self: Autobiography and Novel in Eighteenth-Century England*. Cambridge, Mass.: Harvard University Press, 1976.

Spender, Stephen. 'Confessions and Autobiography.' In *The Making of a Poem*. London: Hamish Hamilton, 1955.

Spengemann, William C. *The Forms of Autobiography: Episodes in the History of a Literary Genre*. New Haven and London: Yale University Press, 1980.

Starobinski, Jean. 'The Style of Autobiography.' In *Literary Style: A Symposium*. Ed. Seymour Chatman. London and New York: Oxford University Press, 1971.

Tobin, Patricia. 'A Portrait of the Artist as Autobiographer: Joyce's *Stephen Hero*.' *Genre*, 6, No. 2 (1973), 189–203.

Tolton, C. D. E. *André Gide and the Art of Autobiography: A Study of Si le grain ne meurt*. Toronto: The Macmillan Company of Canada Limited, 1975.

Weintraub, Karl J. 'Autobiography and Historical Consciousness.' *Critical Inquiry*, I (1975), 821–848.

Wethered, H. N. *The Curious Art of Autobiography: From Benvenuto Cellini to Rudyard Kipling*. New York: Philosophical Library, 1956.